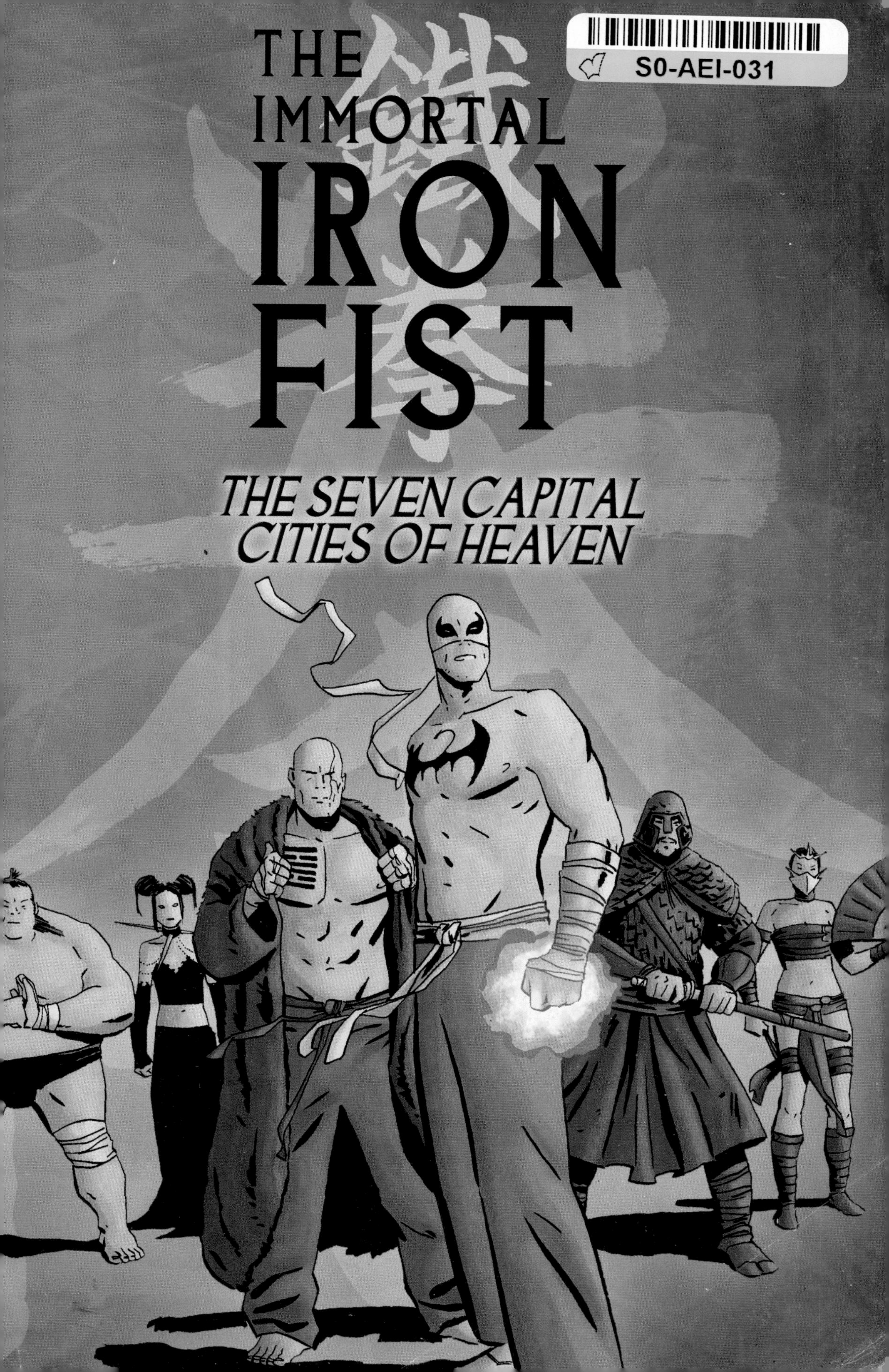
THE IMMORTAL
IRON FIST
THE SEVEN CAPITAL CITIES OF HEAVEN

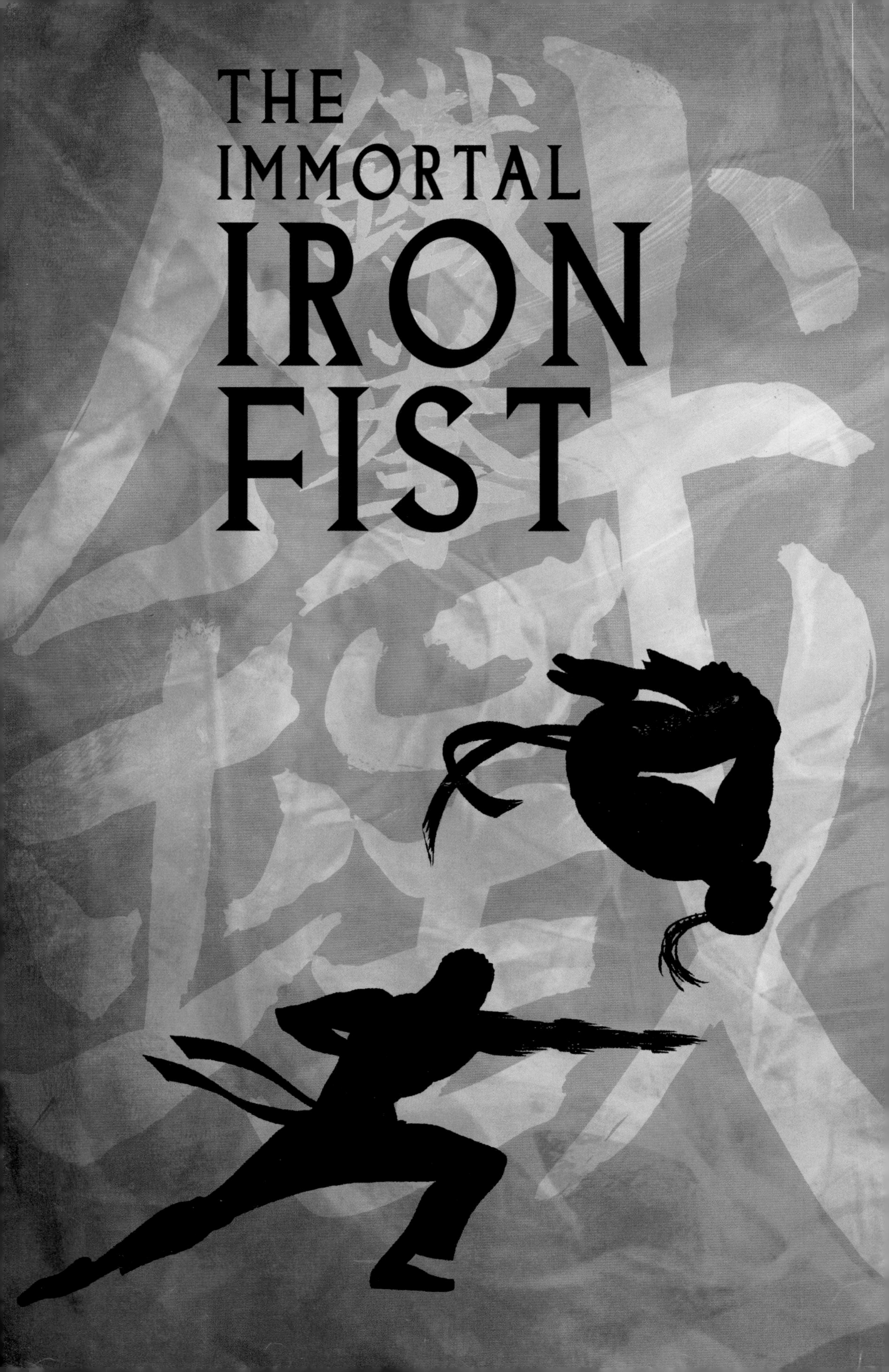
THE
IMMORTAL
IRON
FIST

THE SEVEN CAPITAL CITIES OF HEAVEN

Writers: Matt Fraction & Ed Brubaker
Artists, Issues #8-13: David Aja with
Roy Allan Martinez (Issue #8-9)
Scott Koblish (Issue #9)
Kano (Issues #10-13)
Javier Pulido (Issue #12)
Tonci Zonjic (Issue #13)
Pencilers, Issue #14: Tonci Zonjic with Clay Mann
Inks, Issue #14: Stefano Gaudiano
Additional Art, Issue #14: Kano & Jelena Kevic Djurdjevic
Colorists: Matt Hollingsworth
with June Chung (Issues #8-9), David Aja (Issue #10),
Kano (Issue #10), Javier Rodriguez (Issues #11-14)
& Paul Mounts (Issue #14)

Artists, Annual #1: Howard Chaykin, Dan Brereton
& Jelena Kevic Djurdjevic
Colorists Annual #1: Edgar Delgado & Jelena Kevic Djurdjevic

Letterer: Artmonkeys Studios
Cover Artists: David Aja, Dan Brereton,
Jelena Kevic Djurdjevic, Travel Foreman & Kaare Andrews
Assistant Editor: Alejandro Arbona
Editor: Warren Simons

Collection Editor: Jennifer Grünwald
Assistant Editors: Cory Levine & John Denning
Editor, Special Projects: Mark D. Beazley
Senior Editor, Special Projects: Jeff Youngquist
Senior Vice President of Sales: David Gabriel
Production: Nelson Ribeiro & Jerry Kalinowski

Editor in Chief: Joe Quesada
Publisher: Dan Buckley

IMMORTAL IRON FIST VOL. 2: THE SEVEN CAPITAL CITIES OF HEAVEN. Contains material originally published in magazine form as IMMORTAL IRON FIST #8-14 and ANNUAL #1. First printing 2008. Hardcover ISBN# 978-0-7851-2992-9. Softcover ISBN# 978-0-7851-2535-8. Published by MARVEL PUBLISHING, INC., a subsidiary of MARVEL ENTERTAINMENT, INC. OFFICE OF PUBLICATION: 417 5th Avenue, New York, NY 10016. Copyright © 2007 and 2008 Marvel Characters, Inc. All rights reserved. Hardcover: $24.99 per copy in the U.S. and $26.50 in Canada (GST #R127032852). Softcover: $17.99 per copy in the U.S. and $18.99 in Canada (GST #R127032852). Canadian Agreement #40668537. All characters featured in this issue and the distinctive names and likenesses thereof, and all related indicia are trademarks of Marvel Characters, Inc. No similarity between any of the names, characters, persons, and/or institutions in this magazine with those of any living or dead person or institution is intended, and any such similarity which may exist is purely coincidental. **Printed in the U.S.A.** ALAN FINE, CEO Marvel Toys & Publishing Divisions and CMO Marvel Entertainment, Inc.; DAVID GABRIEL, SVP of Publishing Sales & Circulation; DAVID BOGART, SVP of Business Affairs & Talent Management; MICHAEL PASCIULLO, VP of Merchandising & Communications; JIM O'KEEFE, VP of Operations & Logistics; DAN CARR, Executive Director of Publishing Technology; JUSTIN F. GABRIE, Director of Editorial Operations; SUSAN CRESPI, Editorial Operations Manager; OMAR OTIEKU, Production Manager; STAN LEE, Chairman Emeritus. For information regarding advertising in Marvel Comics or on Marvel.com, please contact Mitch Dane, Advertising Director, at mdane@marvel.com. For Marvel subscription inquiries, please call 800-217-9158.

10 9 8 7 6 5 4 3 2 1

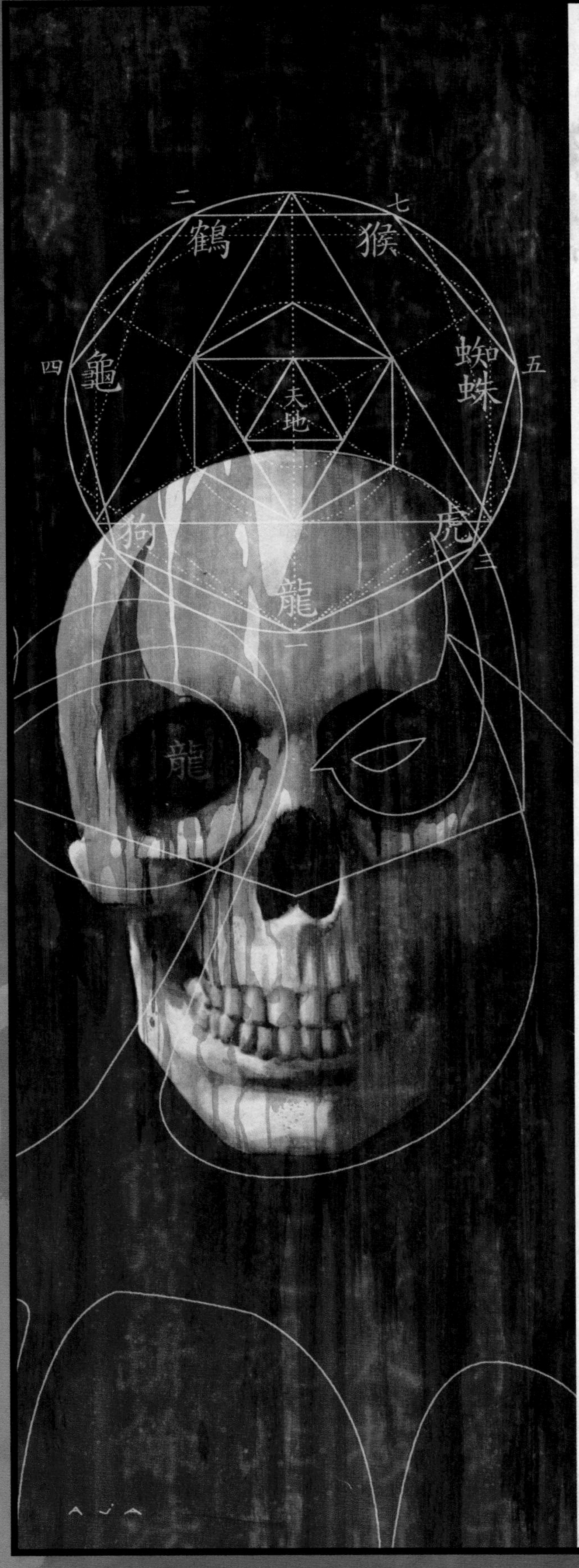
二
七
鶴
猴
四
龜
蜘蛛
五
天地
狗
虎
六
三
龍
一
龍

鐵拳 8

The 7 Capital Cities of Heaven

一

Round 1

K'un-Lun. Many years ago.

You keep climbing.

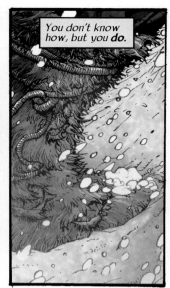

You don't know how, but you **do.**

Every fiber of your being begs to stop, to freeze, to just die and be done with this wretched life once and for all...

You tell it to shut up.

A thousand times a second, you tell it to shut up.

And you keep climbing.

Your name is Wendell Rand...

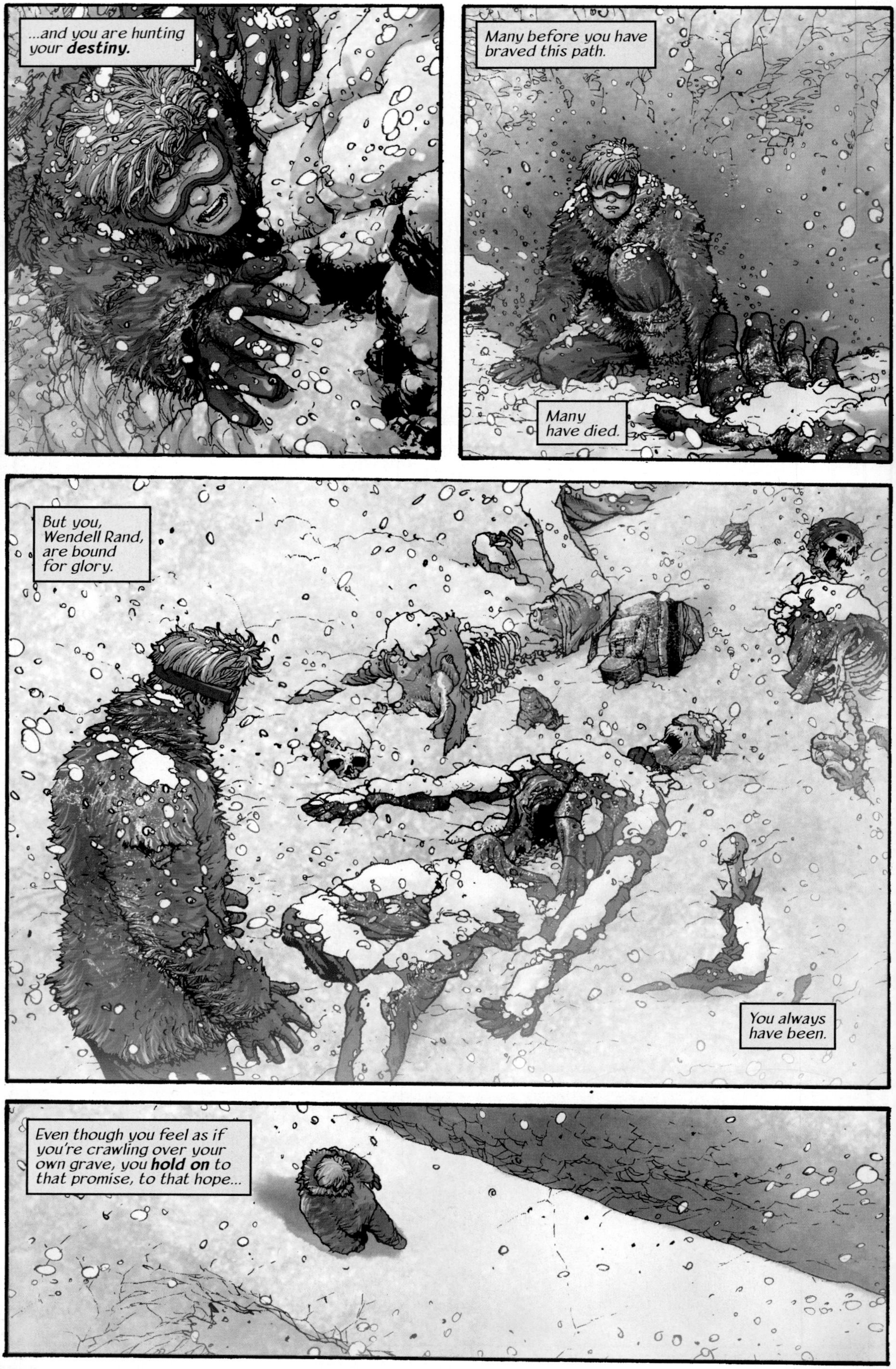
...and you are hunting your **destiny.**
Many before you have braved this path.
Many have died.
But you, Wendell Rand, are bound for glory.
You always have been.
Even though you feel as if you're crawling over your own grave, you **hold on** to that promise, to that hope...

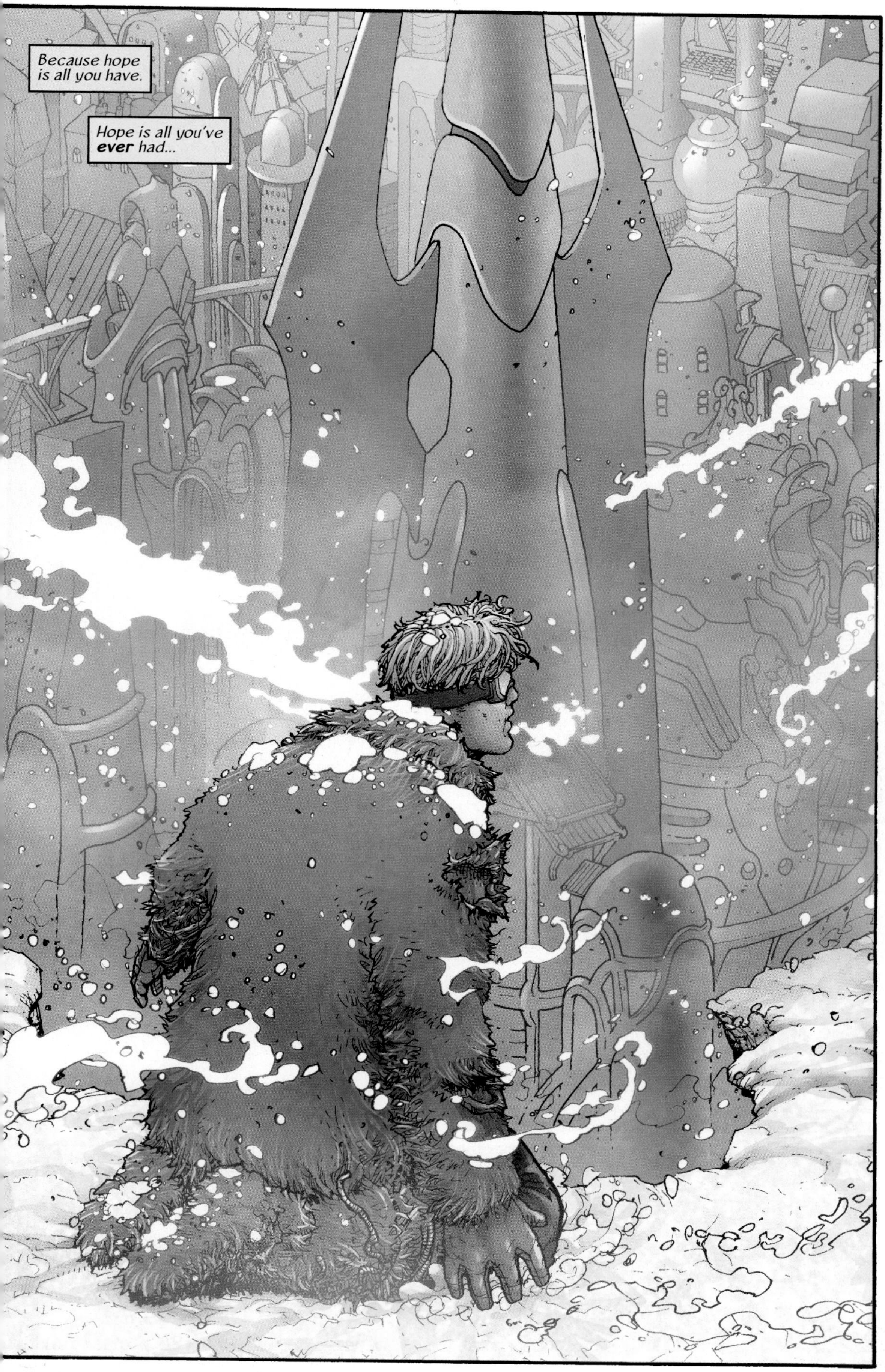
Because hope is all you have.
Hope is all you've **ever** had...

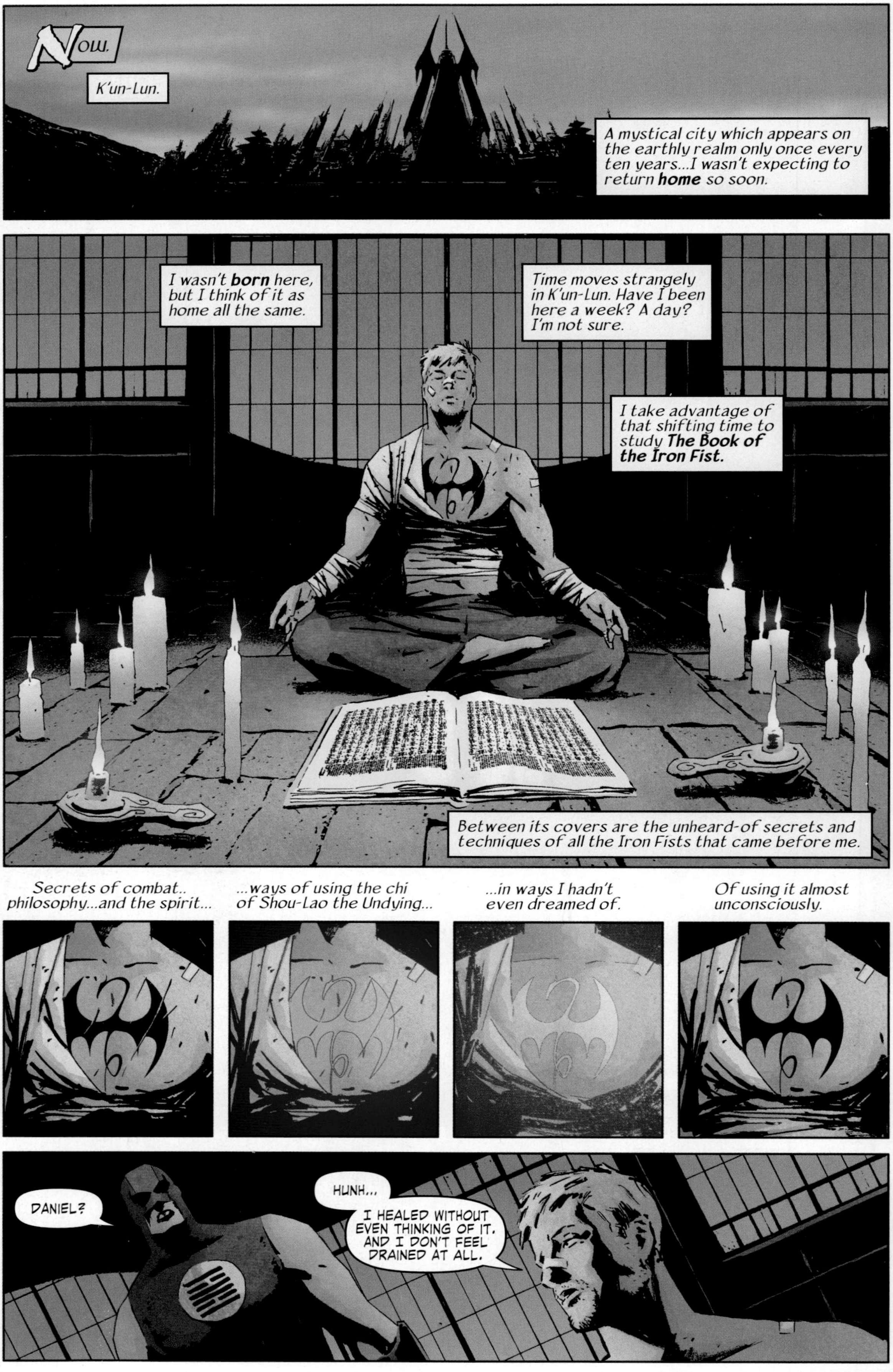
NOW.
K'un-Lun.
A mystical city which appears on the earthly realm only once every ten years...I wasn't expecting to return **home** so soon.
I wasn't **born** here, but I think of it as home all the same.
Time moves strangely in K'un-Lun. Have I been here a week? A day? I'm not sure.
I take advantage of that shifting time to study **The Book of the Iron Fist.**
Between its covers are the unheard-of secrets and techniques of all the Iron Fists that came before me.
Secrets of combat.. philosophy...and the spirit...
...ways of using the chi of Shou-Lao the Undying...
...in ways I hadn't even dreamed of.
Of using it almost unconsciously.
DANIEL?
HUNH...
I HEALED WITHOUT EVEN THINKING OF IT. AND I DON'T FEEL DRAINED AT ALL.

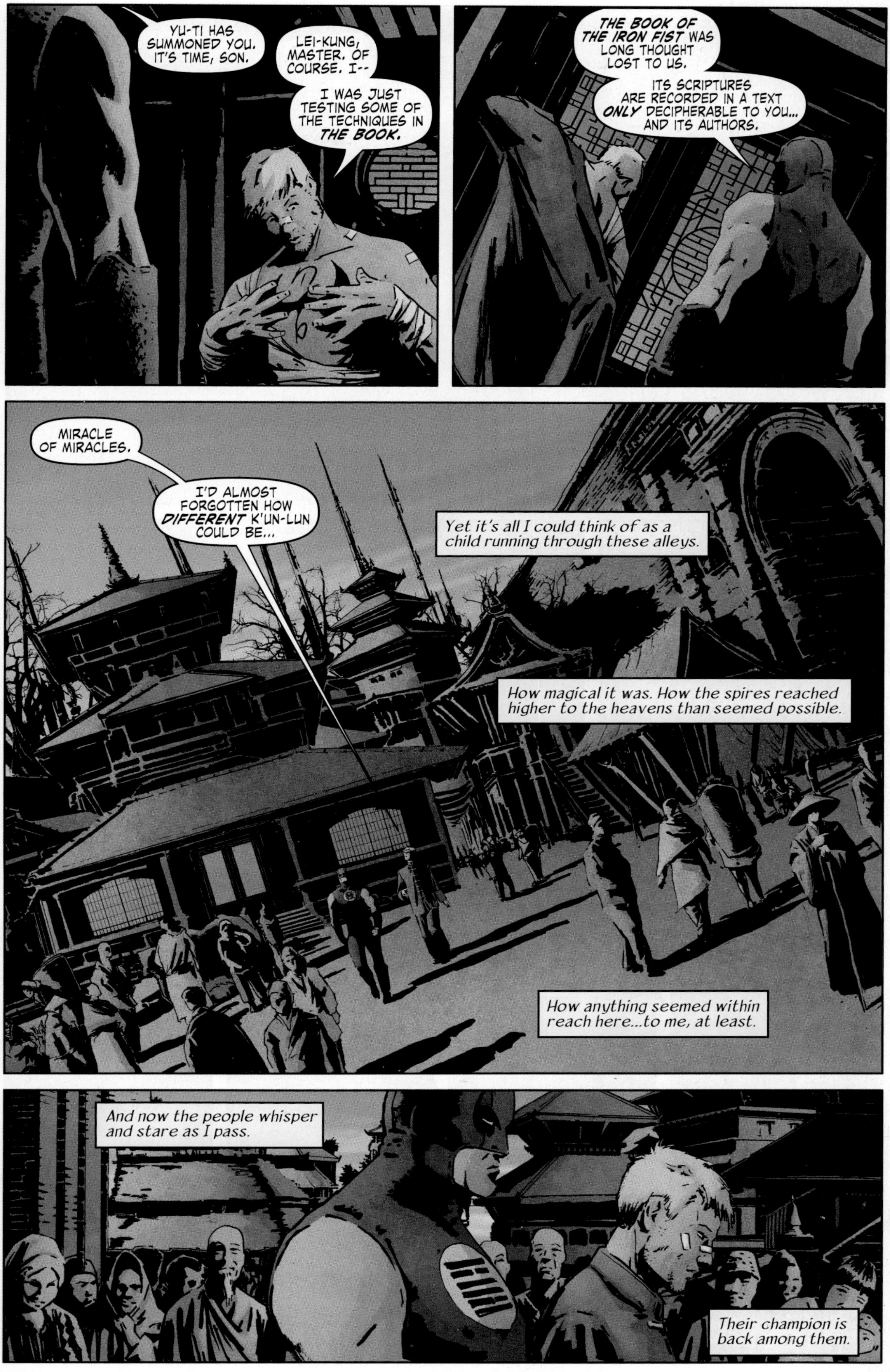
YU-TI HAS SUMMONED YOU. IT'S TIME, SON.
LEI-KUNG, MASTER. OF COURSE. I--
I WAS JUST TESTING SOME OF THE TECHNIQUES IN *THE BOOK.*
THE BOOK OF THE IRON FIST WAS LONG THOUGHT LOST TO US.
ITS SCRIPTURES ARE RECORDED IN A TEXT *ONLY* DECIPHERABLE TO YOU... AND ITS AUTHORS.
MIRACLE OF MIRACLES.
I'D ALMOST FORGOTTEN HOW *DIFFERENT* K'UN-LUN COULD BE...
Yet it's all I could think of as a child running through these alleys.
How magical it was. How the spires reached higher to the heavens than seemed possible.
How anything seemed within reach here...to me, at least.
And now the people whisper and stare as I pass.
Their champion is back among them.

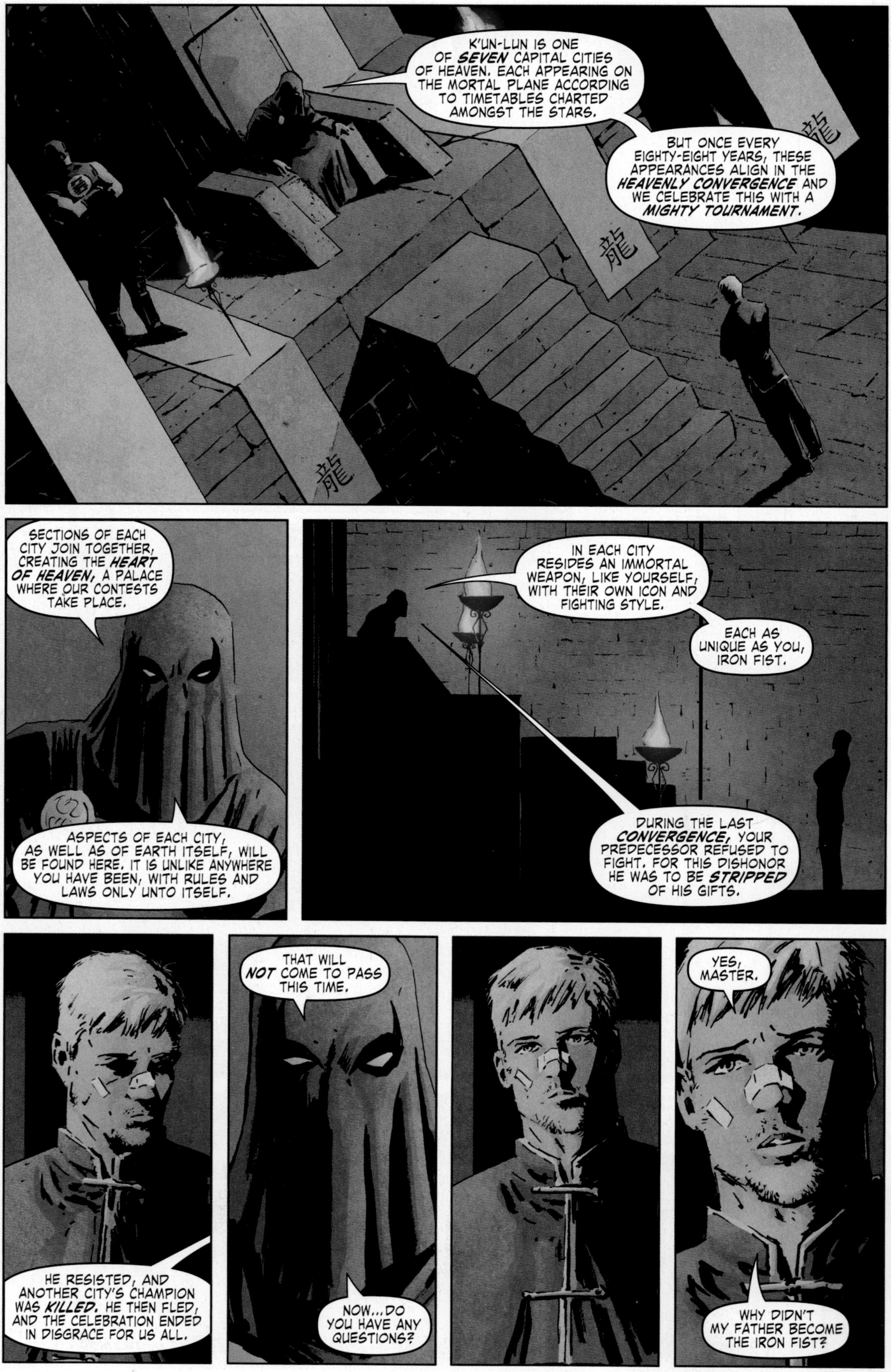
K'UN-LUN IS ONE OF SEVEN CAPITAL CITIES OF HEAVEN. EACH APPEARING ON THE MORTAL PLANE ACCORDING TO TIMETABLES CHARTED AMONGST THE STARS.
BUT ONCE EVERY EIGHTY-EIGHT YEARS, THESE APPEARANCES ALIGN IN THE HEAVENLY CONVERGENCE AND WE CELEBRATE THIS WITH A MIGHTY TOURNAMENT.
龍
龍
龍
SECTIONS OF EACH CITY JOIN TOGETHER, CREATING THE HEART OF HEAVEN, A PALACE WHERE OUR CONTESTS TAKE PLACE.
ASPECTS OF EACH CITY, AS WELL AS OF EARTH ITSELF, WILL BE FOUND HERE. IT IS UNLIKE ANYWHERE YOU HAVE BEEN, WITH RULES AND LAWS ONLY UNTO ITSELF.
IN EACH CITY RESIDES AN IMMORTAL WEAPON, LIKE YOURSELF, WITH THEIR OWN ICON AND FIGHTING STYLE.
EACH AS UNIQUE AS YOU, IRON FIST.
DURING THE LAST CONVERGENCE, YOUR PREDECESSOR REFUSED TO FIGHT. FOR THIS DISHONOR HE WAS TO BE STRIPPED OF HIS GIFTS.
HE RESISTED, AND ANOTHER CITY'S CHAMPION WAS KILLED. HE THEN FLED, AND THE CELEBRATION ENDED IN DISGRACE FOR US ALL.
THAT WILL NOT COME TO PASS THIS TIME.
NOW...DO YOU HAVE ANY QUESTIONS?
YES, MASTER.
WHY DIDN'T MY FATHER BECOME THE IRON FIST?

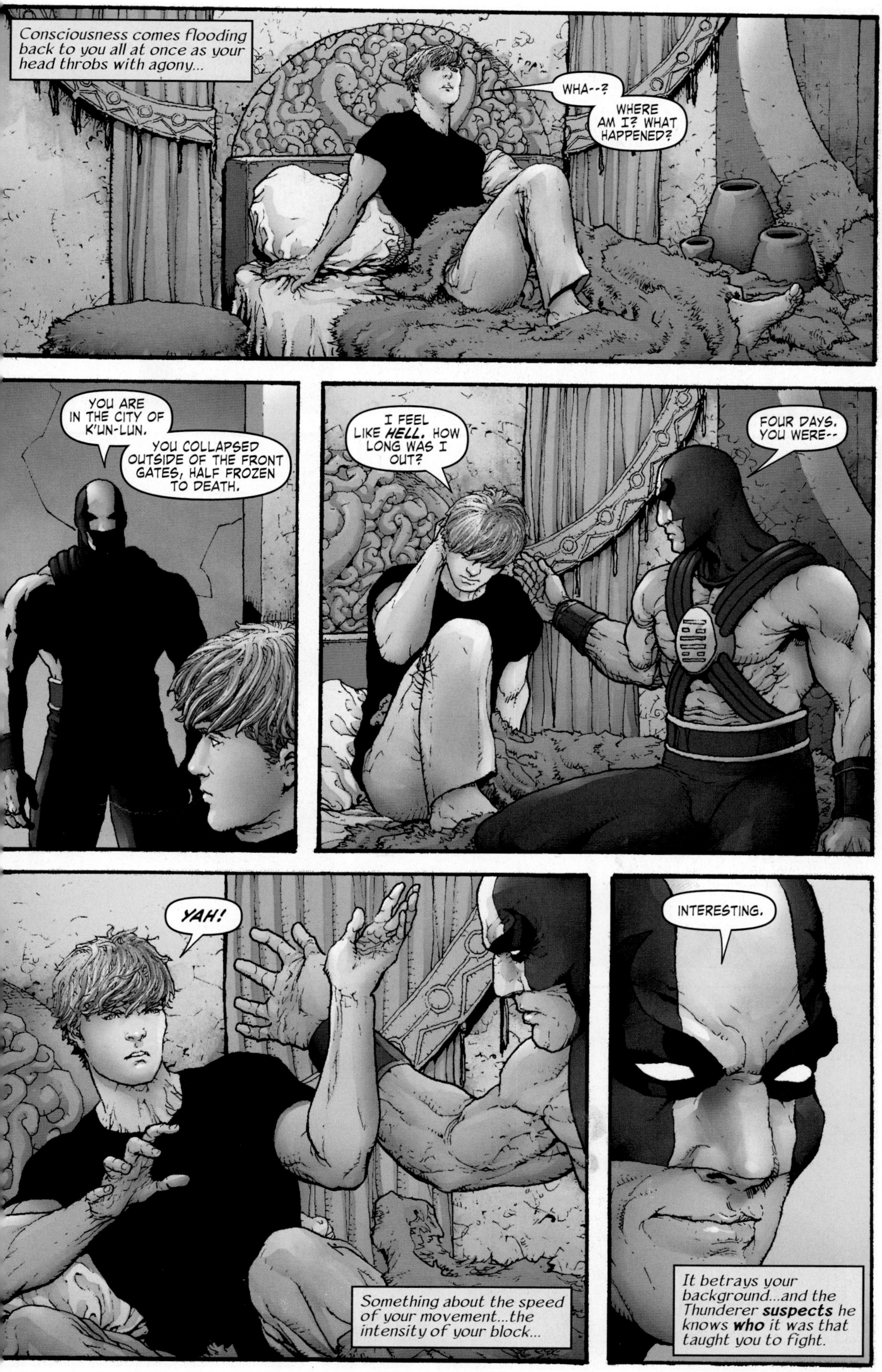

Consciousness comes flooding back to you all at once as your head throbs with agony...
WHA--? WHERE AM I? WHAT HAPPENED?
YOU ARE IN THE CITY OF K'UN-LUN.
YOU COLLAPSED OUTSIDE OF THE FRONT GATES, HALF FROZEN TO DEATH.
I FEEL LIKE HELL. HOW LONG WAS I OUT?
FOUR DAYS. YOU WERE--
YAH!
INTERESTING.
Something about the speed of your movement...the intensity of your block...
It betrays your background...and the Thunderer suspects he knows who it was that taught you to fight.

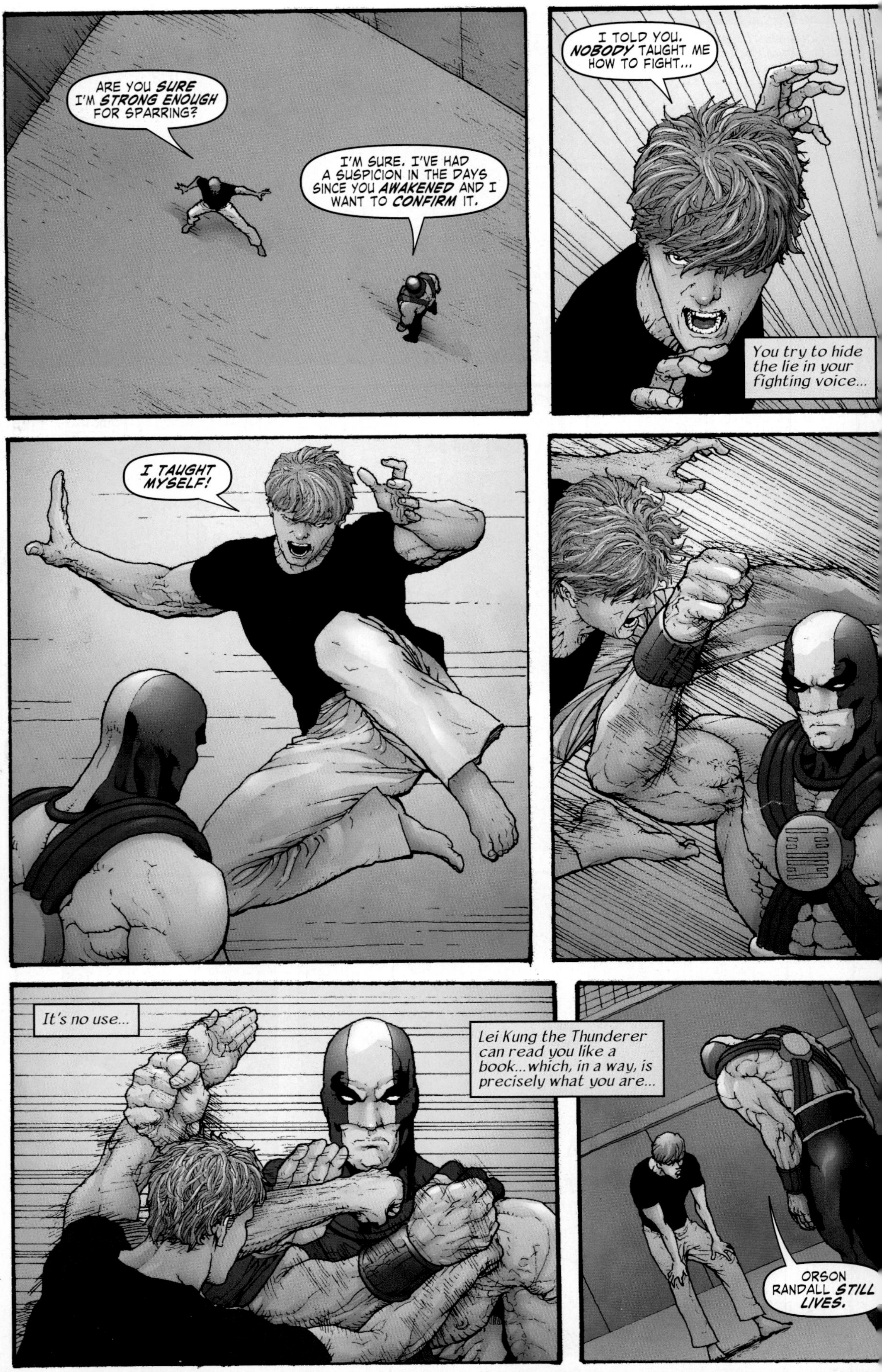
ARE YOU SURE I'M STRONG ENOUGH FOR SPARRING?
I'M SURE. I'VE HAD A SUSPICION IN THE DAYS SINCE YOU AWAKENED AND I WANT TO CONFIRM IT.
I TOLD YOU. NOBODY TAUGHT ME HOW TO FIGHT...
You try to hide the lie in your fighting voice...
I TAUGHT MYSELF!
It's no use...
Lei Kung the Thunderer can read you like a book...which, in a way, is precisely what you are...
ORSON RANDALL STILL LIVES.

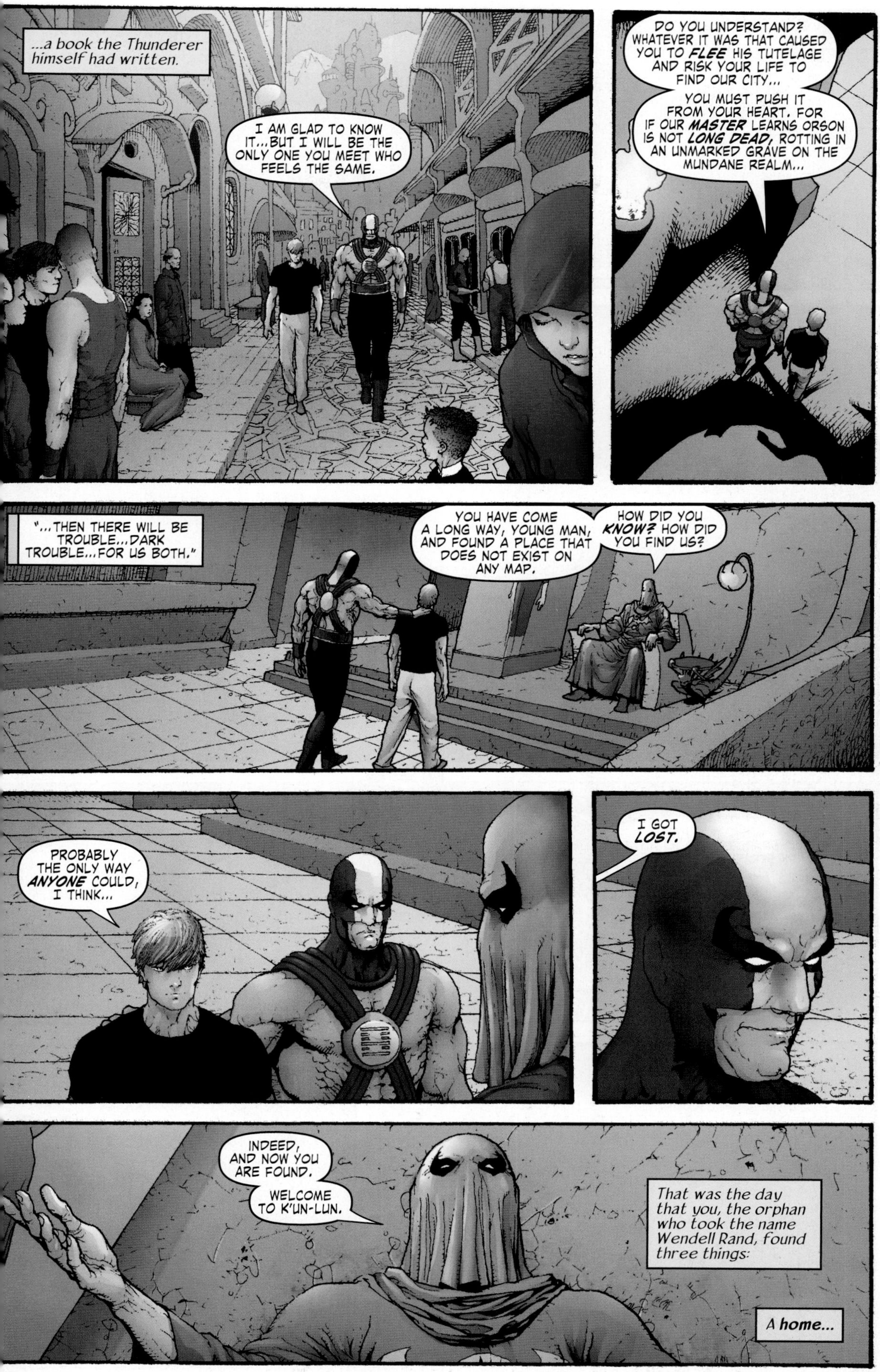
...a book the Thunderer himself had written.
I AM GLAD TO KNOW IT...BUT I WILL BE THE ONLY ONE YOU MEET WHO FEELS THE SAME.
DO YOU UNDERSTAND? WHATEVER IT WAS THAT CAUSED YOU TO FLEE HIS TUTELAGE AND RISK YOUR LIFE TO FIND OUR CITY...
YOU MUST PUSH IT FROM YOUR HEART. FOR IF OUR MASTER LEARNS ORSON IS NOT LONG DEAD, ROTTING IN AN UNMARKED GRAVE ON THE MUNDANE REALM...
"...THEN THERE WILL BE TROUBLE...DARK TROUBLE...FOR US BOTH."
YOU HAVE COME A LONG WAY, YOUNG MAN, AND FOUND A PLACE THAT DOES NOT EXIST ON ANY MAP.
HOW DID YOU KNOW? HOW DID YOU FIND US?
PROBABLY THE ONLY WAY ANYONE COULD, I THINK...
I GOT LOST.
INDEED, AND NOW YOU ARE FOUND.
WELCOME TO K'UN-LUN.
That was the day that you, the orphan who took the name Wendell Rand, found three things:
A home...

...a new *teacher*...

SOME OF YOU ALREADY KNOW A THING OR TWO OF MARTIAL ARTS. SOME OF YOU CALL YOURSELVES *FIGHTERS.*

FORGET IT. ALL OF IT. YOU KNOW...NOTHING. THIS IS NOT FIGHTING.

KARATE IS A THING OF THE *SPIRIT.*

KUNG FU, TAE KWON DO, JUJITSU, JUDO...THESE ARE NOT PHYSICAL PRACTICES, BUT SPIRITUAL PURSUITS.

THIS IS NOT A SCHOOL.

IT IS A TEMPLE.

NEVER FORGET THAT. SPLIT INTO PAIRS AND SPAR. I WANT TO WITNESS FIRSTHAND THE DEPTHS OF YOUR IGNORANCE...

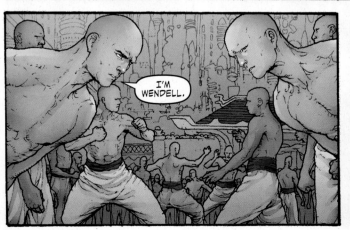

I'M WENDELL.

DAVOS.

...and a new *friend.*

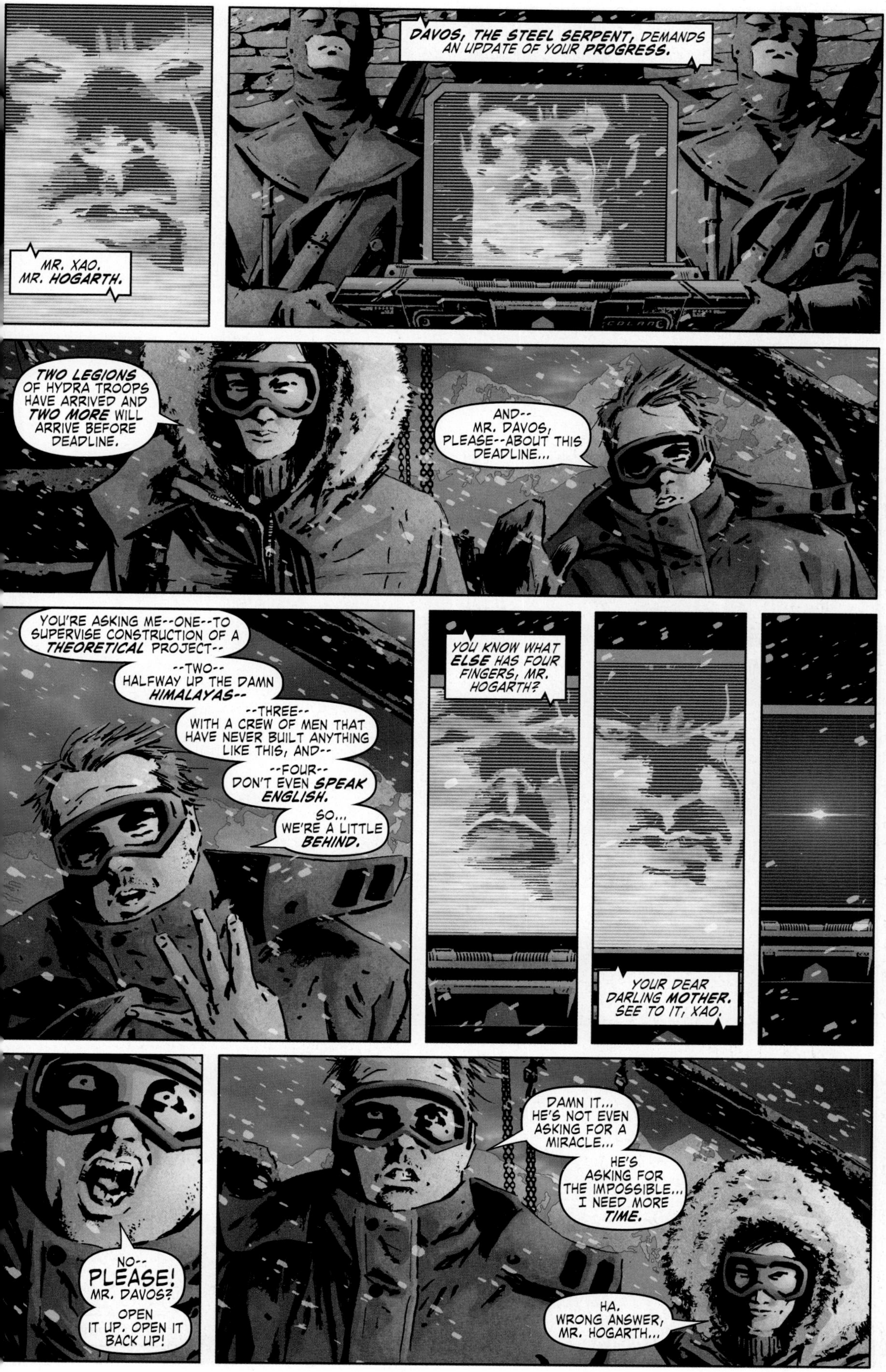
MR. XAO. MR. HOGARTH.
DAVOS, THE STEEL SERPENT, DEMANDS AN UPDATE OF YOUR PROGRESS.
TWO LEGIONS OF HYDRA TROOPS HAVE ARRIVED AND TWO MORE WILL ARRIVE BEFORE DEADLINE.
AND-- MR. DAVOS, PLEASE--ABOUT THIS DEADLINE...
YOU'RE ASKING ME--ONE--TO SUPERVISE CONSTRUCTION OF A THEORETICAL PROJECT--
--TWO-- HALFWAY UP THE DAMN HIMALAYAS--
--THREE-- WITH A CREW OF MEN THAT HAVE NEVER BUILT ANYTHING LIKE THIS, AND--
--FOUR-- DON'T EVEN SPEAK ENGLISH.
SO... WE'RE A LITTLE BEHIND.
YOU KNOW WHAT ELSE HAS FOUR FINGERS, MR. HOGARTH?
YOUR DEAR DARLING MOTHER. SEE TO IT, XAO.
NO-- PLEASE! MR. DAVOS?
OPEN IT UP. OPEN IT BACK UP!
DAMN IT... HE'S NOT EVEN ASKING FOR A MIRACLE...
HE'S ASKING FOR THE IMPOSSIBLE... I NEED MORE TIME.
HA. WRONG ANSWER, MR. HOGARTH...

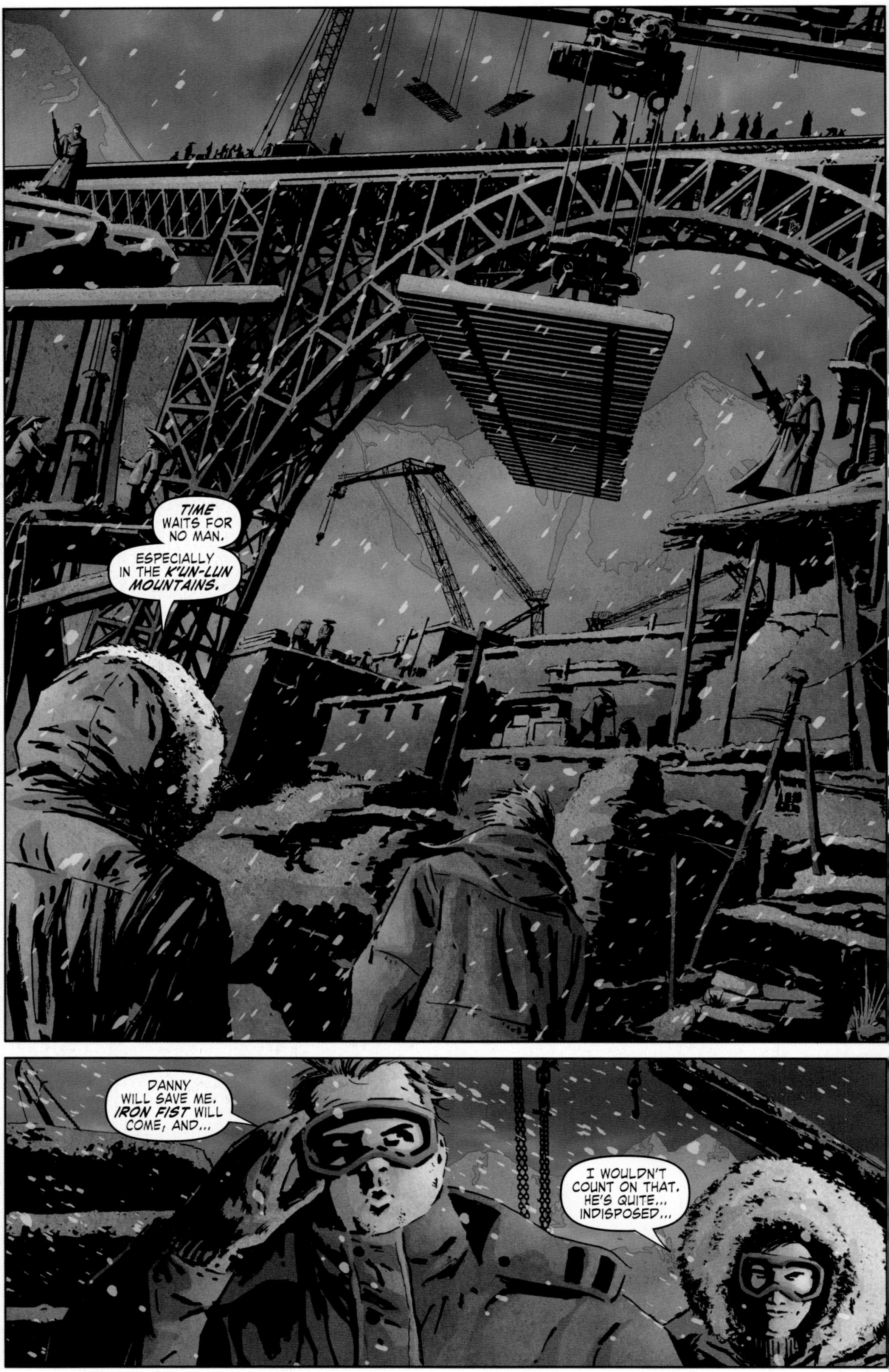
TIME WAITS FOR NO MAN.
ESPECIALLY IN THE K'UN-LUN MOUNTAINS.
DANNY WILL SAVE ME. IRON FIST WILL COME, AND...
I WOULDN'T COUNT ON THAT. HE'S QUITE... INDISPOSED...

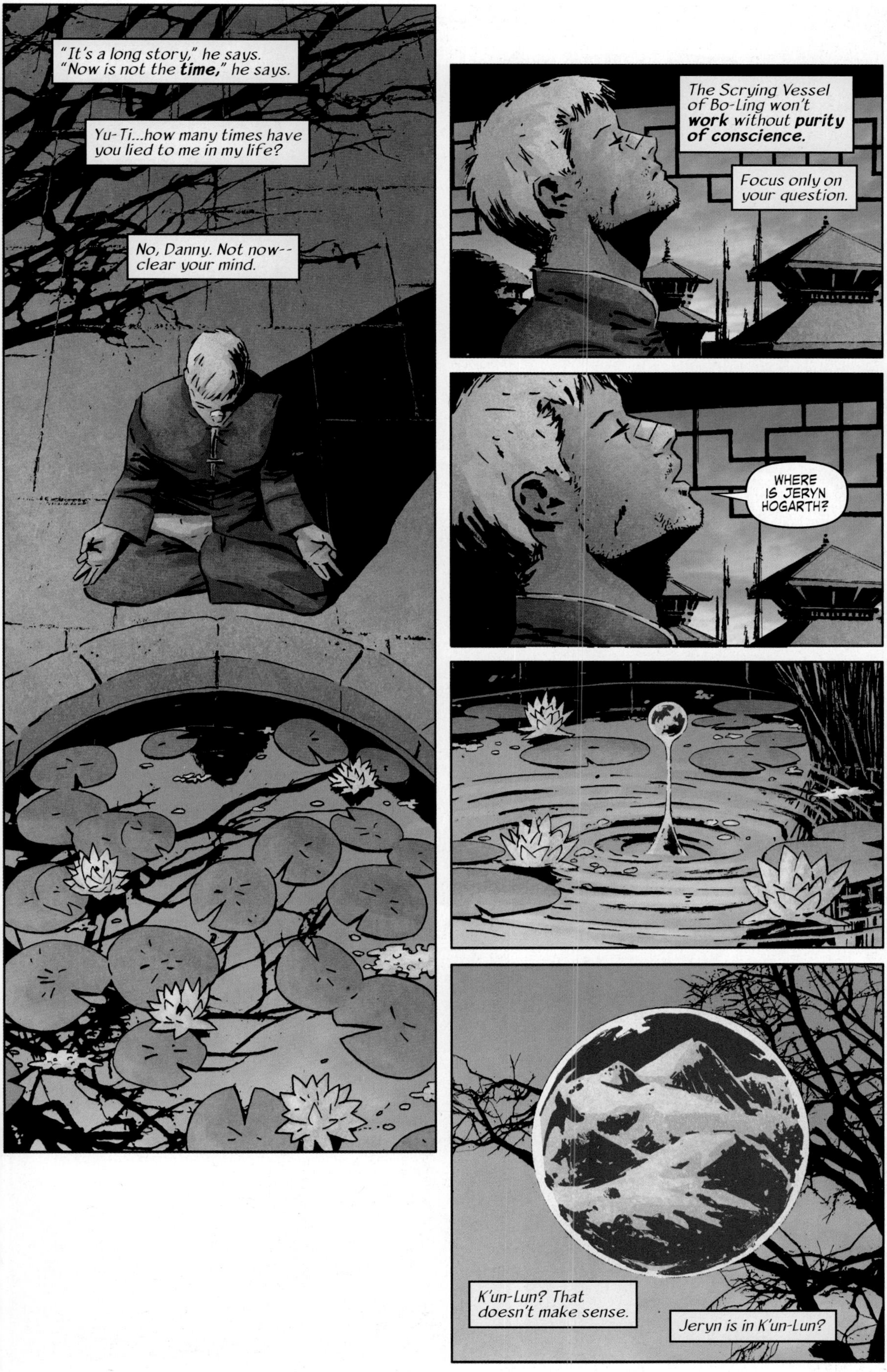
"It's a long story," he says. "Now is not the **time,**" he says.
Yu-Ti...how many times have you lied to me in my life?
No, Danny. Not now--clear your mind.
The Scrying Vessel of Bo-Ling won't **work** without **purity of conscience.**
Focus only on your question.
WHERE IS JERYN HOGARTH?
K'un-Lun? That doesn't make sense.
Jeryn is in K'un-Lun?

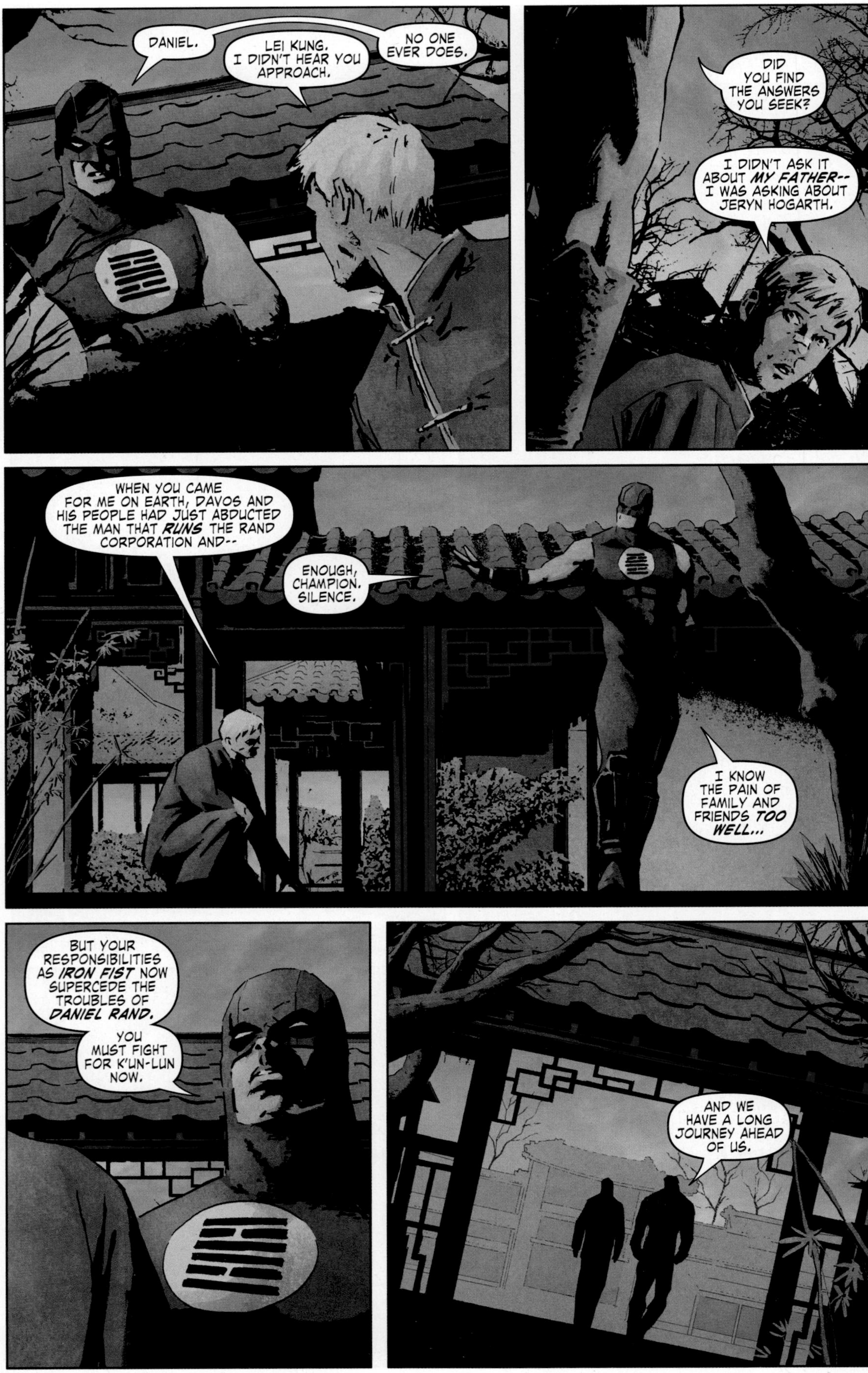
DANIEL.
LEI KUNG. I DIDN'T HEAR YOU APPROACH.
NO ONE EVER DOES.
DID YOU FIND THE ANSWERS YOU SEEK?
I DIDN'T ASK IT ABOUT MY FATHER-- I WAS ASKING ABOUT JERYN HOGARTH.
WHEN YOU CAME FOR ME ON EARTH, DAVOS AND HIS PEOPLE HAD JUST ABDUCTED THE MAN THAT RUNS THE RAND CORPORATION AND--
ENOUGH, CHAMPION. SILENCE.
I KNOW THE PAIN OF FAMILY AND FRIENDS TOO WELL...
BUT YOUR RESPONSIBILITIES AS IRON FIST NOW SUPERCEDE THE TROUBLES OF DANIEL RAND.
YOU MUST FIGHT FOR K'UN-LUN NOW.
AND WE HAVE A LONG JOURNEY AHEAD OF US.

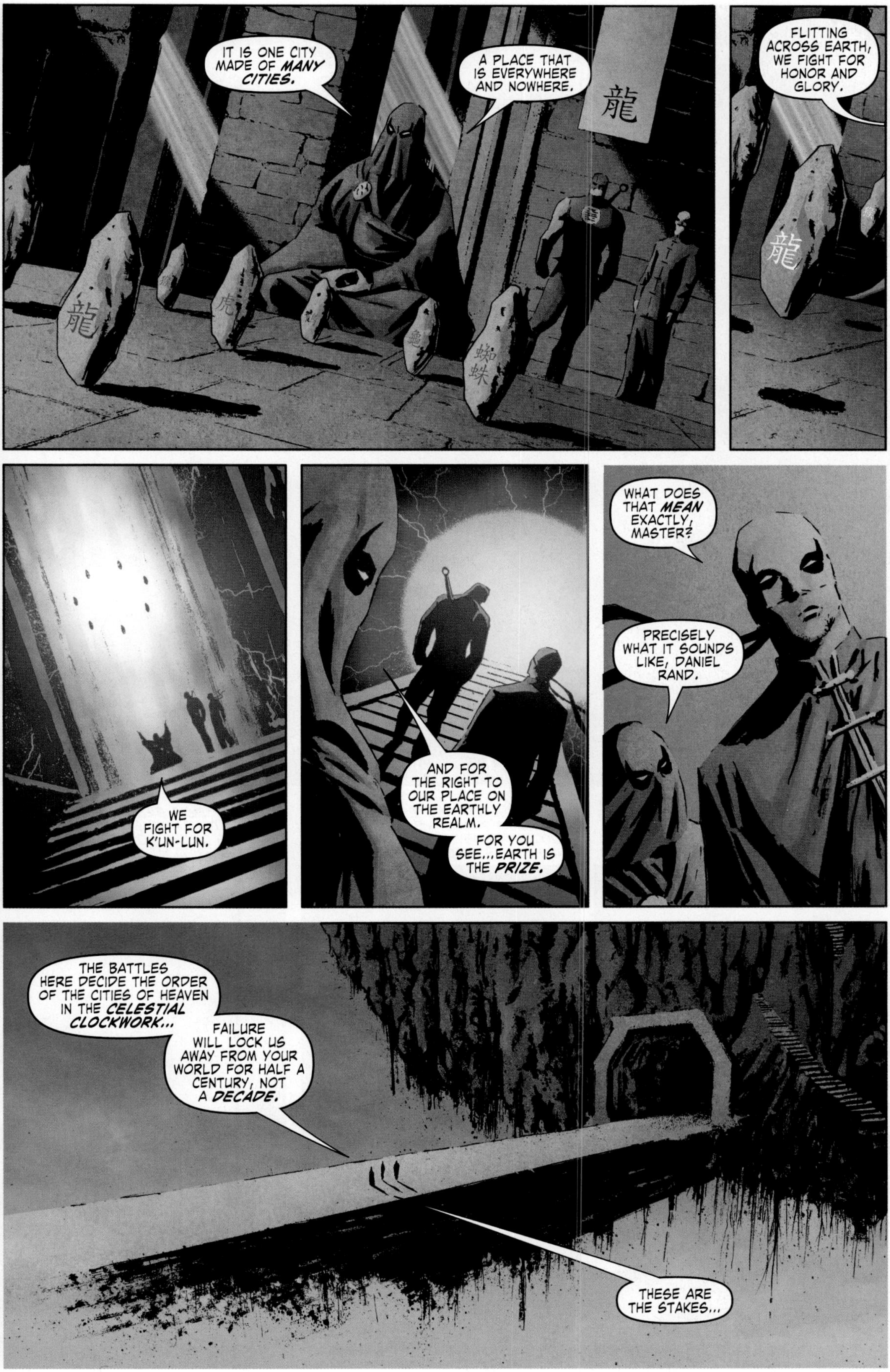
IT IS ONE CITY MADE OF MANY CITIES.
A PLACE THAT IS EVERYWHERE AND NOWHERE.
龍
虎
龜
蜘蛛
龍
FLITTING ACROSS EARTH, WE FIGHT FOR HONOR AND GLORY.
龍
WE FIGHT FOR K'UN-LUN.
AND FOR THE RIGHT TO OUR PLACE ON THE EARTHLY REALM.
FOR YOU SEE...EARTH IS THE PRIZE.
WHAT DOES THAT MEAN EXACTLY, MASTER?
PRECISELY WHAT IT SOUNDS LIKE, DANIEL RAND.
THE BATTLES HERE DECIDE THE ORDER OF THE CITIES OF HEAVEN IN THE CELESTIAL CLOCKWORK...
FAILURE WILL LOCK US AWAY FROM YOUR WORLD FOR HALF A CENTURY, NOT A DECADE.
THESE ARE THE STAKES...

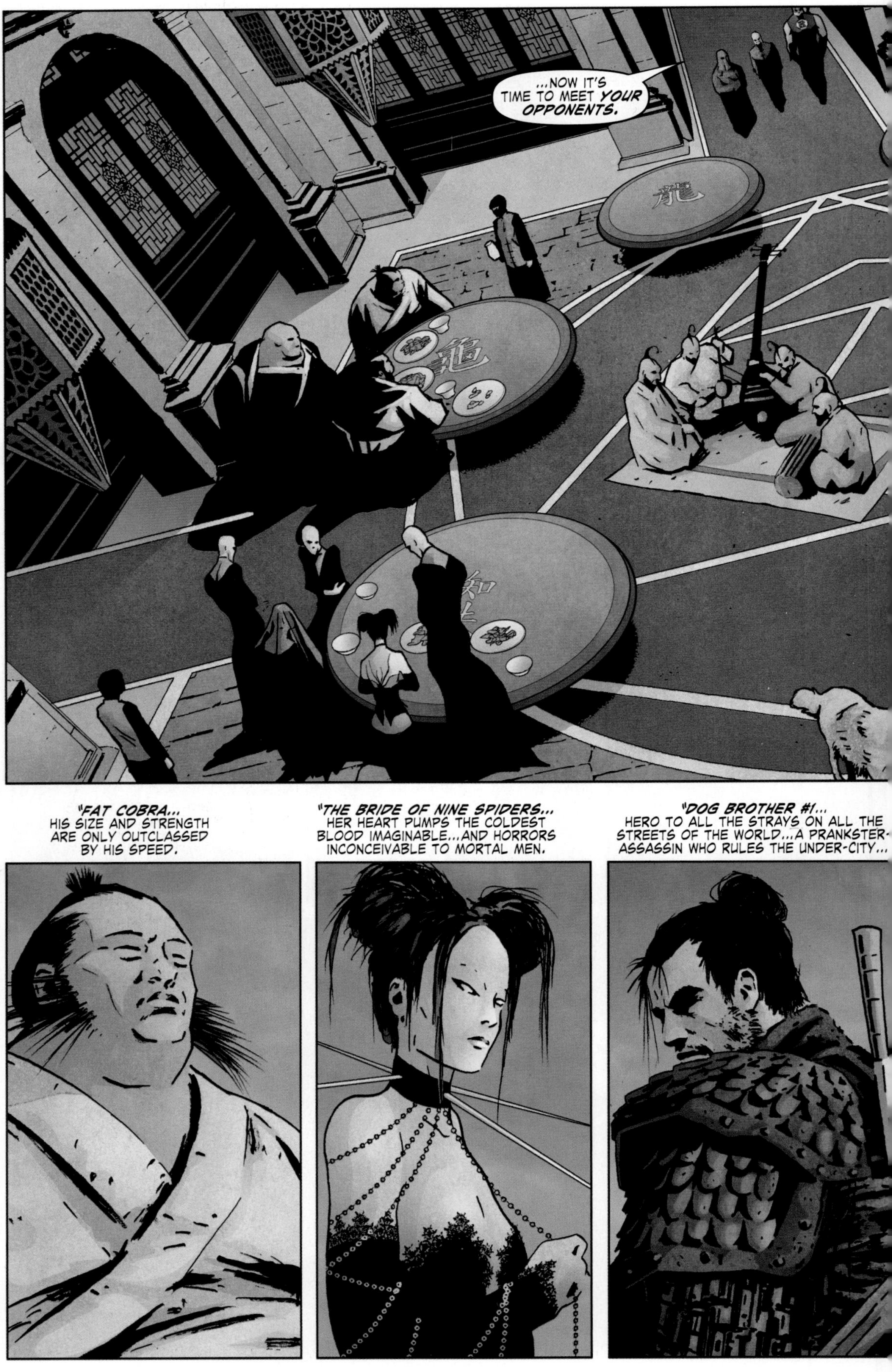
...NOW IT'S TIME TO MEET YOUR OPPONENTS.
"FAT COBRA... HIS SIZE AND STRENGTH ARE ONLY OUTCLASSED BY HIS SPEED.
"THE BRIDE OF NINE SPIDERS... HER HEART PUMPS THE COLDEST BLOOD IMAGINABLE...AND HORRORS INCONCEIVABLE TO MORTAL MEN.
"DOG BROTHER #1... HERO TO ALL THE STRAYS ON ALL THE STREETS OF THE WORLD...A PRANKSTER-ASSASSIN WHO RULES THE UNDER-CITY...

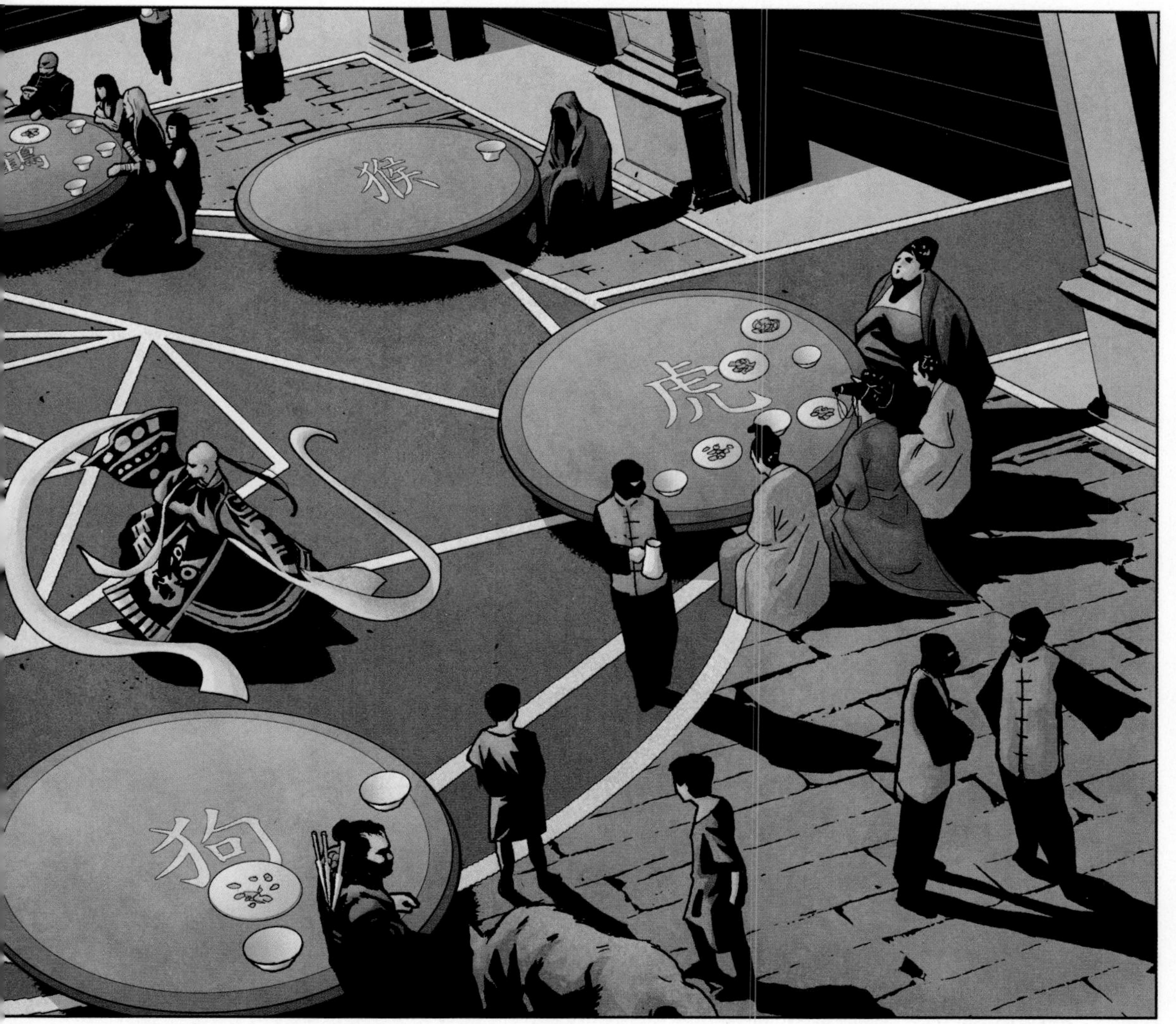
猴
虎
狗

"TIGER'S BEAUTIFUL DAUGHTER... MANY A MAN HAS FOUND HIS DOOM AT HER HAND OR IN HER BED.

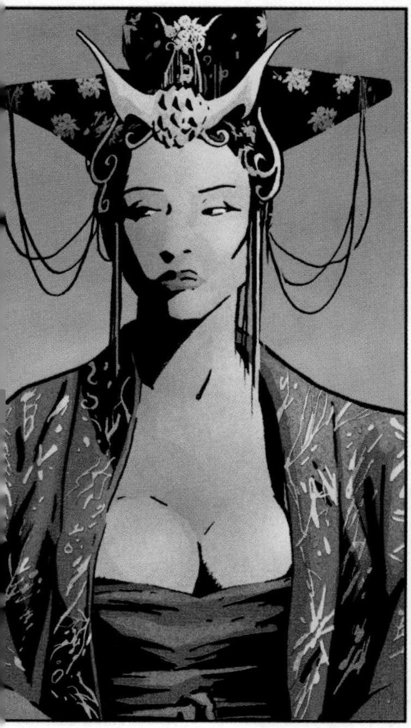

"THE PRINCE OF ORPHANS. MYSTERIOUS, EVEN TO WE WHO CULTIVATE UNENDING MYSTERY.

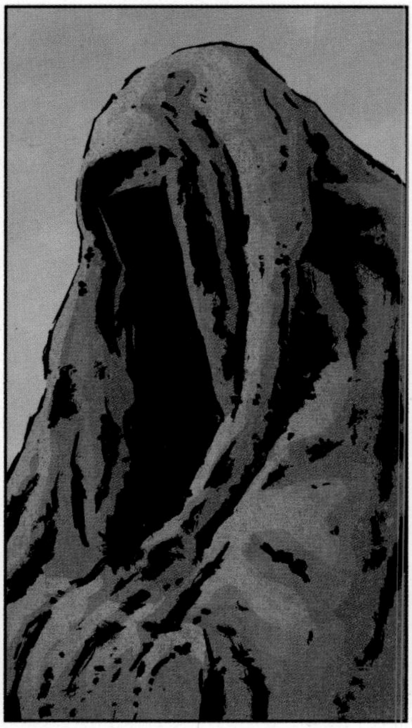

"AND THE NEW WEAPON OF K'UN-ZI...DAVOS. THE STEEL SERPENT... MASTER OF THE CRANES."

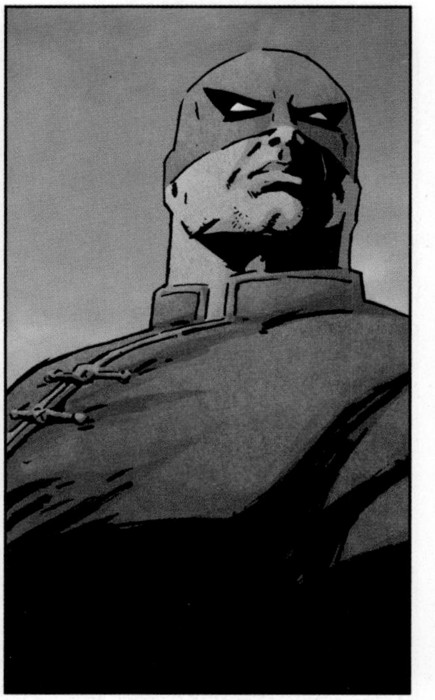

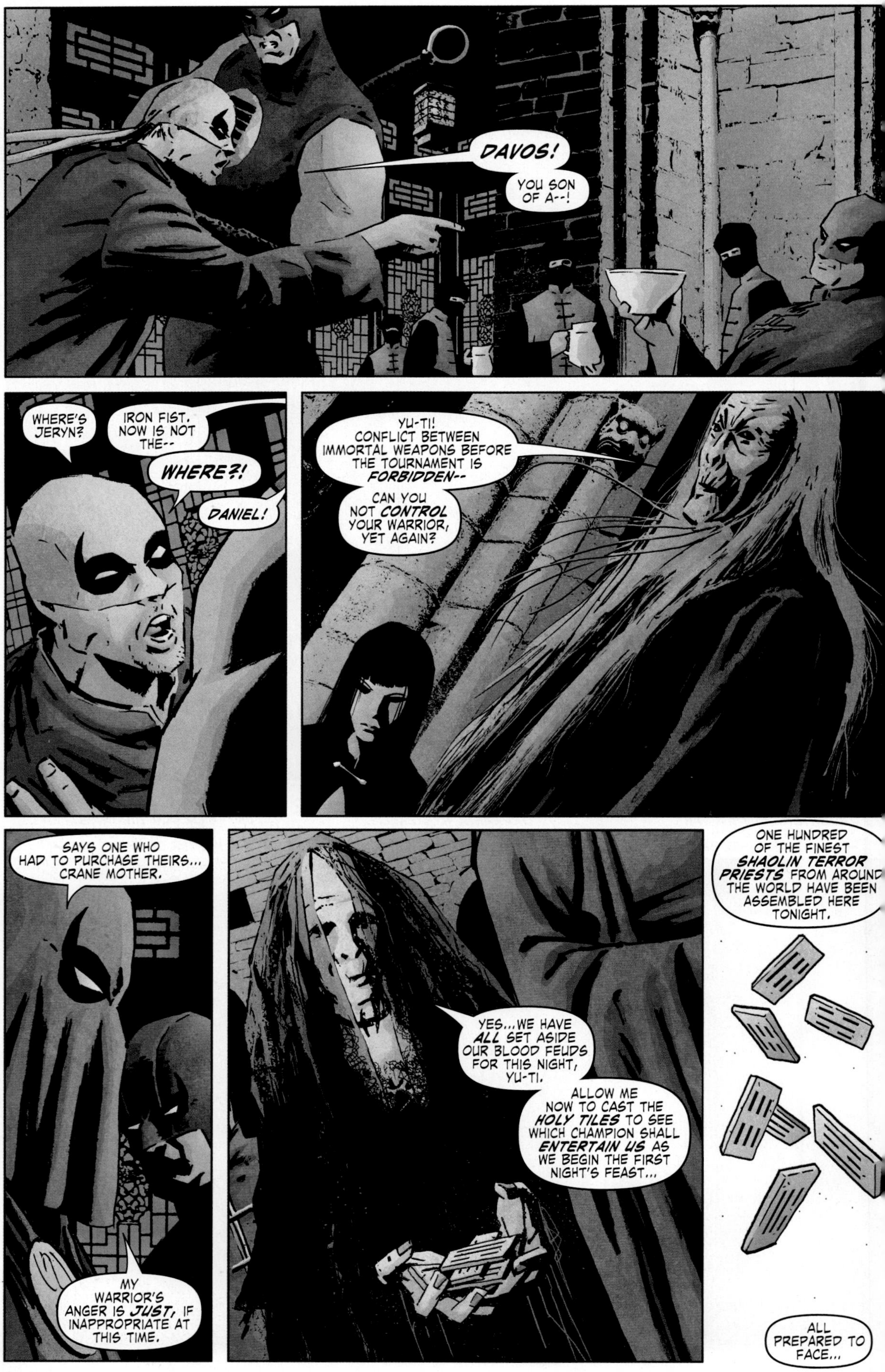
DAVOS!
YOU SON OF A--!
WHERE'S JERYN?
IRON FIST. NOW IS NOT THE--
WHERE?!
DANIEL!
YU-TI! CONFLICT BETWEEN IMMORTAL WEAPONS BEFORE THE TOURNAMENT IS FORBIDDEN--
CAN YOU NOT CONTROL YOUR WARRIOR, YET AGAIN?
SAYS ONE WHO HAD TO PURCHASE THEIRS... CRANE MOTHER.
MY WARRIOR'S ANGER IS JUST, IF INAPPROPRIATE AT THIS TIME.
YES...WE HAVE ALL SET ASIDE OUR BLOOD FEUDS FOR THIS NIGHT, YU-TI.
ALLOW ME NOW TO CAST THE HOLY TILES TO SEE WHICH CHAMPION SHALL ENTERTAIN US AS WE BEGIN THE FIRST NIGHT'S FEAST...
ONE HUNDRED OF THE FINEST SHAOLIN TERROR PRIESTS FROM AROUND THE WORLD HAVE BEEN ASSEMBLED HERE TONIGHT.
ALL PREPARED TO FACE...

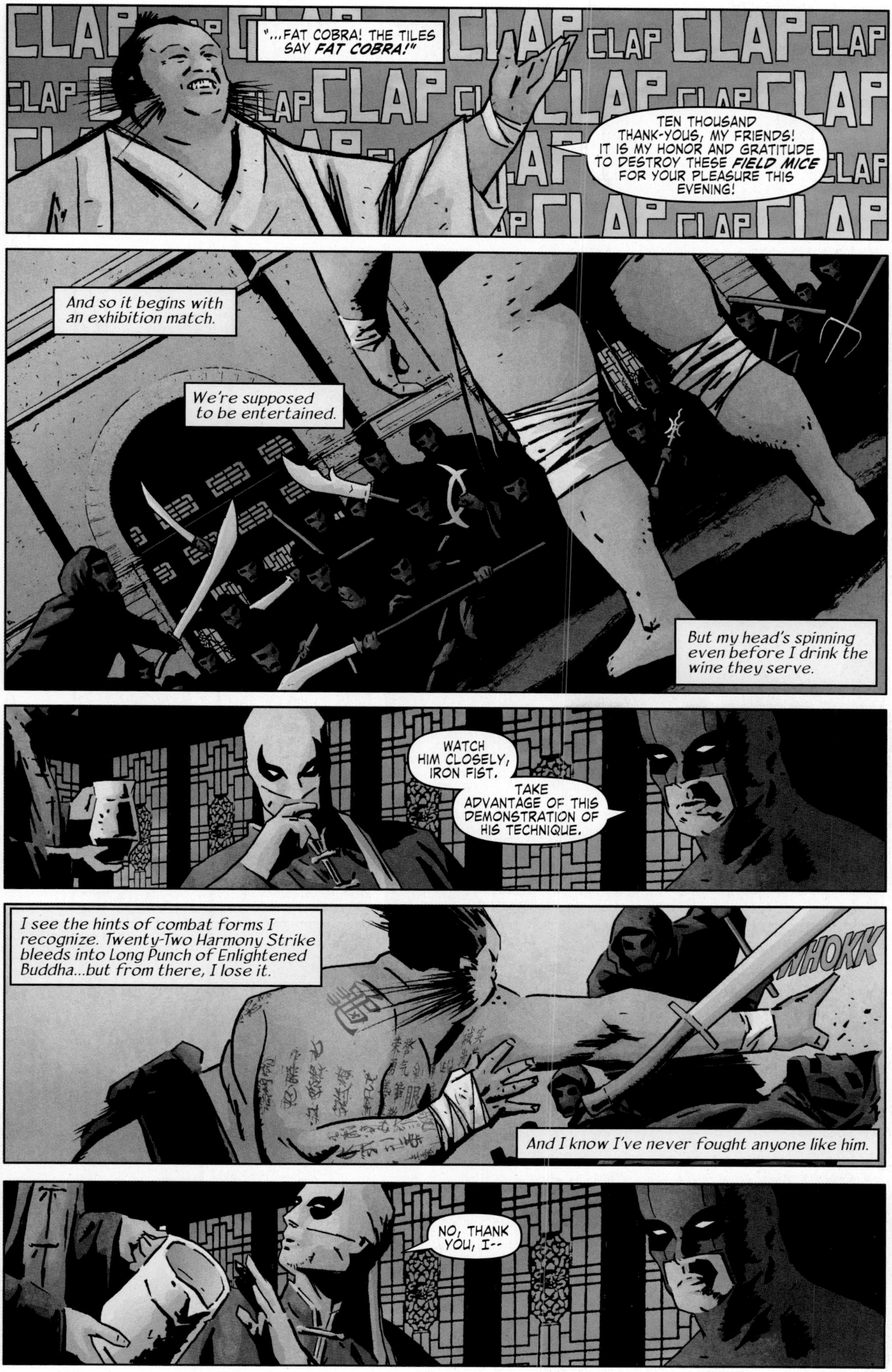

"...FAT COBRA! THE TILES SAY FAT COBRA!"
CLAP CLAP CLAP CLAP CLAP CLAP
TEN THOUSAND THANK-YOUS, MY FRIENDS! IT IS MY HONOR AND GRATITUDE TO DESTROY THESE FIELD MICE FOR YOUR PLEASURE THIS EVENING!
And so it begins with an exhibition match.
We're supposed to be entertained.
But my head's spinning even before I drink the wine they serve.
WATCH HIM CLOSELY, IRON FIST.
TAKE ADVANTAGE OF THIS DEMONSTRATION OF HIS TECHNIQUE.
I see the hints of combat forms I recognize. Twenty-Two Harmony Strike bleeds into Long Punch of Enlightened Buddha...but from there, I lose it.
WHOKK
And I know I've never fought anyone like him.
NO, THANK YOU, I--

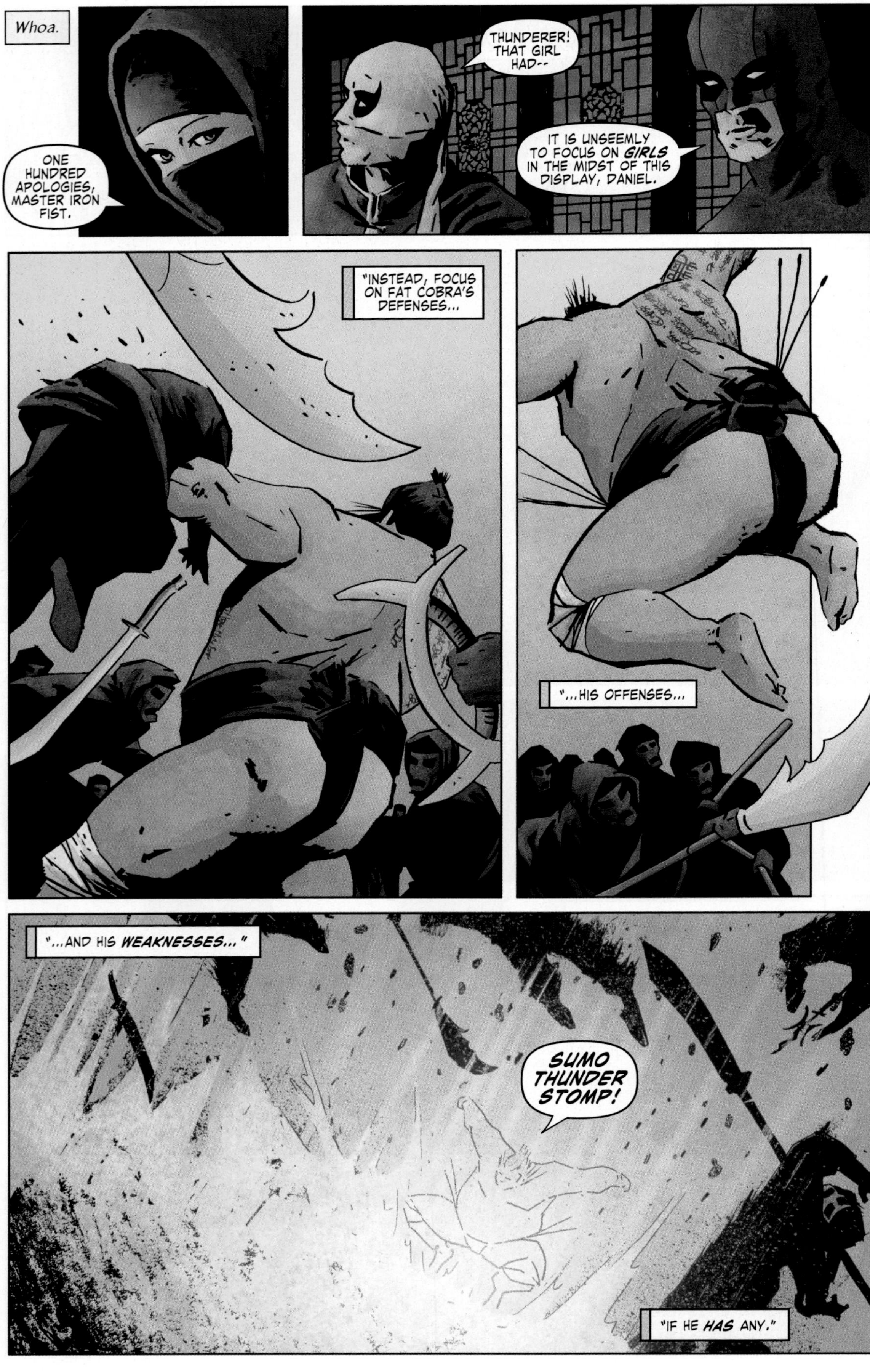
Whoa.
ONE HUNDRED APOLOGIES, MASTER IRON FIST.
THUNDERER! THAT GIRL HAD--
IT IS UNSEEMLY TO FOCUS ON GIRLS IN THE MIDST OF THIS DISPLAY, DANIEL.
"INSTEAD, FOCUS ON FAT COBRA'S DEFENSES...
"...HIS OFFENSES...
"...AND HIS WEAKNESSES..."
SUMO THUNDER STOMP!
"IF HE HAS ANY."

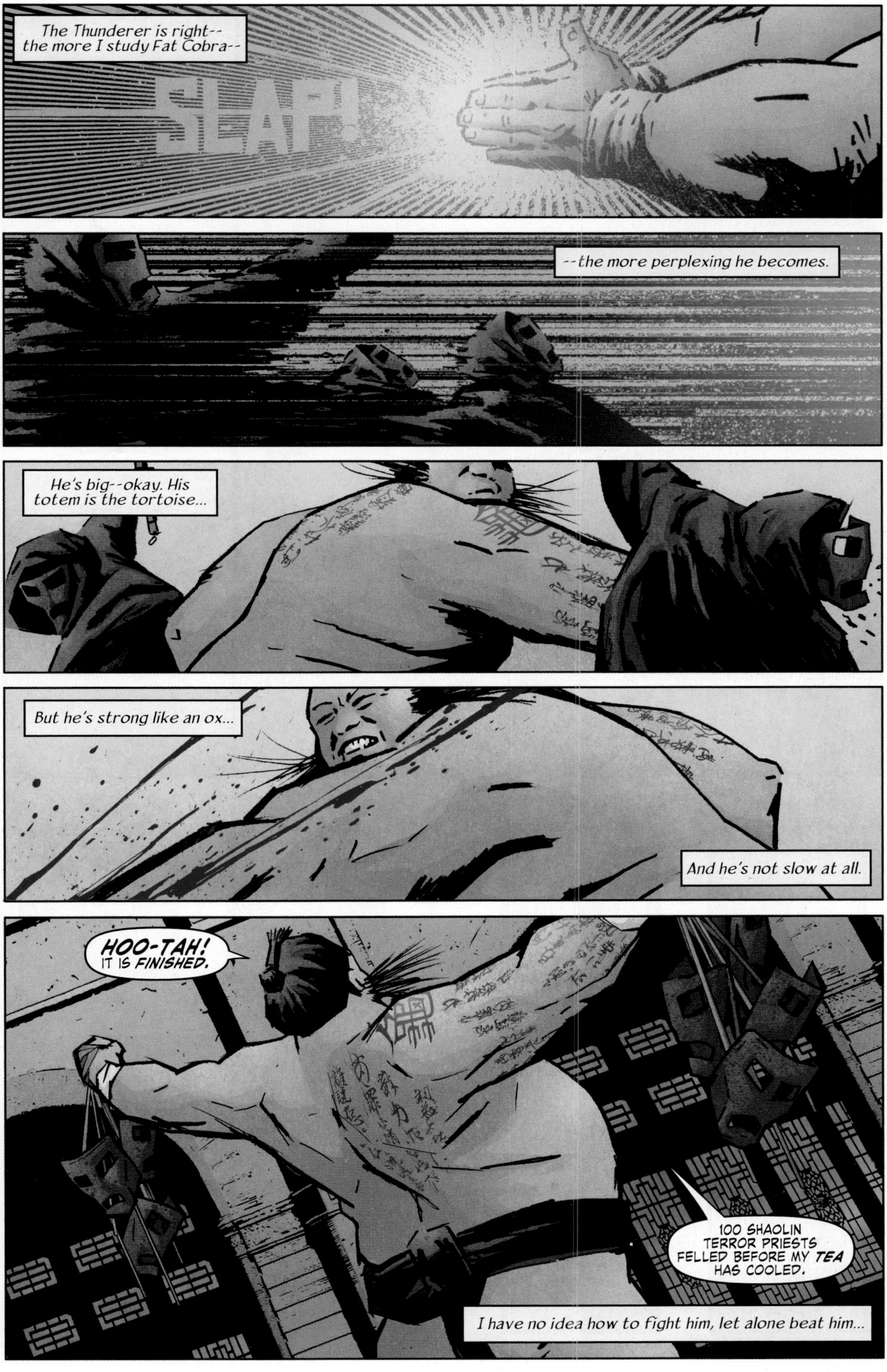
The Thunderer is right-- the more I study Fat Cobra--
SLAP!
--the more perplexing he becomes.
He's big--okay. His totem is the tortoise...
But he's strong like an ox...
And he's not slow at all.
HOO-TAH! IT IS FINISHED.
100 SHAOLIN TERROR PRIESTS FELLED BEFORE MY TEA HAS COOLED.
I have no idea how to fight him, let alone beat him...

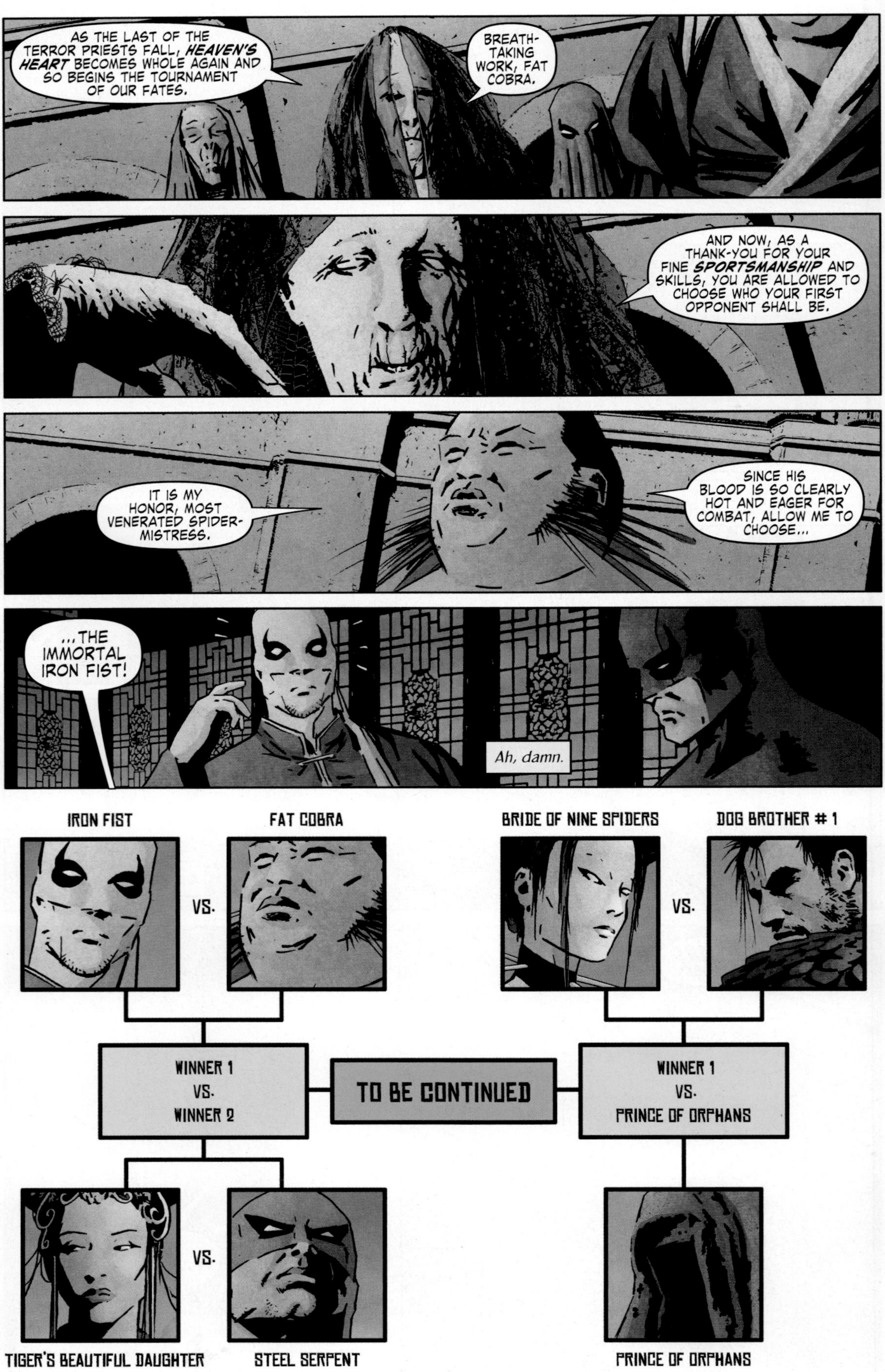
AS THE LAST OF THE TERROR PRIESTS FALL, HEAVEN'S HEART BECOMES WHOLE AGAIN AND SO BEGINS THE TOURNAMENT OF OUR FATES.
BREATH-TAKING WORK, FAT COBRA.
AND NOW, AS A THANK-YOU FOR YOUR FINE SPORTSMANSHIP AND SKILLS, YOU ARE ALLOWED TO CHOOSE WHO YOUR FIRST OPPONENT SHALL BE.
IT IS MY HONOR, MOST VENERATED SPIDER-MISTRESS.
SINCE HIS BLOOD IS SO CLEARLY HOT AND EAGER FOR COMBAT, ALLOW ME TO CHOOSE...
...THE IMMORTAL IRON FIST!
Ah, damn.
IRON FIST
FAT COBRA
VS.
BRIDE OF NINE SPIDERS
DOG BROTHER # 1
VS.
WINNER 1
VS.
WINNER 2
TO BE CONTINUED
WINNER 1
VS.
PRINCE OF ORPHANS
VS.
TIGER'S BEAUTIFUL DAUGHTER
STEEL SERPENT
PRINCE OF ORPHANS

鐵拳 9

五 三
蜘蛛 虎
七 一
猴 龍
天地
鶴 狗
二 六
龜
四
光栄
誠
忠
智
意
眼鏡蛇
冠軍

The 7 Capital Cities of Heaven

二

Round 2

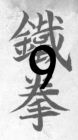

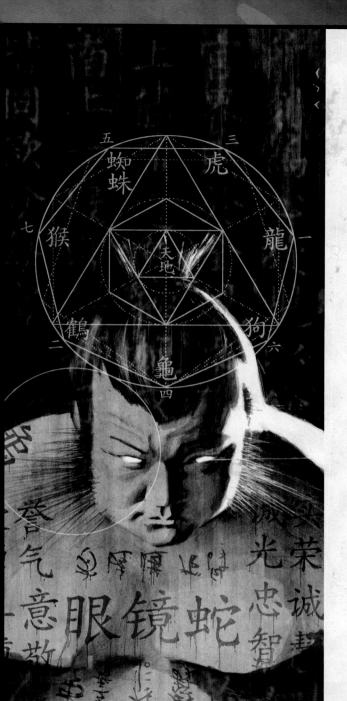

Many years ago.

NO MATTER HOW MANY TIMES YOU WISH THE BRUTAL WINTER WINDS WOULD **STOP,** THEY ONLY SERVE TO REMIND YOU:

K'UN-LUN IS NOW YOUR **HOME,** WENDELL RAND.

ITS WAYS ARE NOW **YOUR** WAYS.

ITS TRADITIONS, YOUR TRADITIONS.

AND ITS CITIZENS...

...ARE NOW YOUR BROTHERS.

AND IF YOU TRULY WANT TO FIT IN HERE...

YOU HAD BETTER START **BELIEVING** IT.

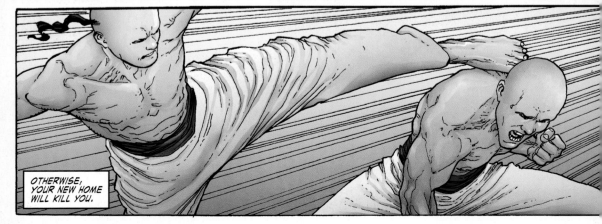

OTHERWISE, YOUR NEW HOME WILL KILL YOU.

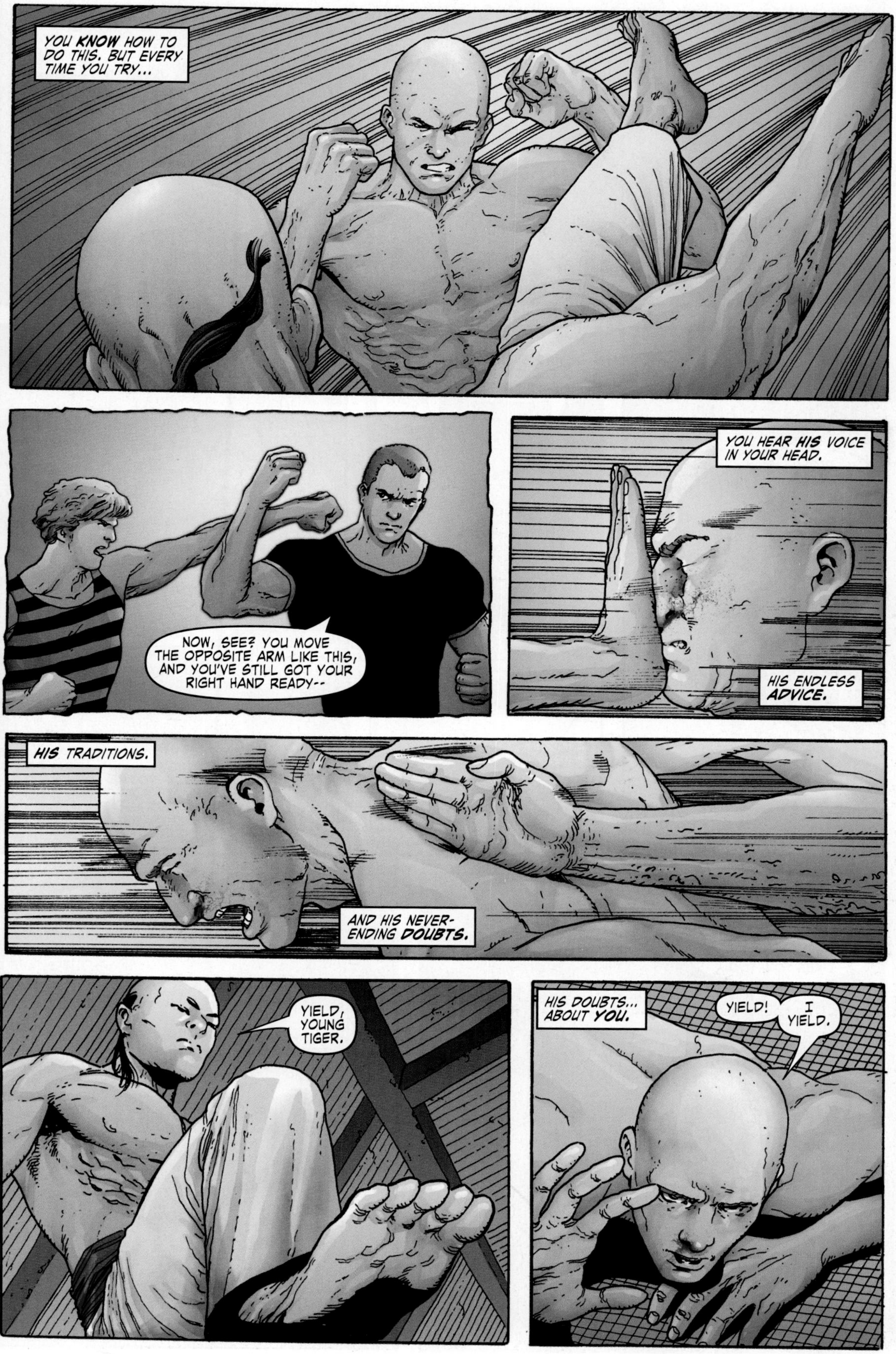
YOU KNOW HOW TO DO THIS. BUT EVERY TIME YOU TRY...
NOW, SEE? YOU MOVE THE OPPOSITE ARM LIKE THIS, AND YOU'VE STILL GOT YOUR RIGHT HAND READY--
YOU HEAR HIS VOICE IN YOUR HEAD.
HIS ENDLESS ADVICE.
HIS TRADITIONS.
AND HIS NEVER-ENDING DOUBTS.
YIELD, YOUNG TIGER.
HIS DOUBTS... ABOUT YOU.
YIELD!
I YIELD.

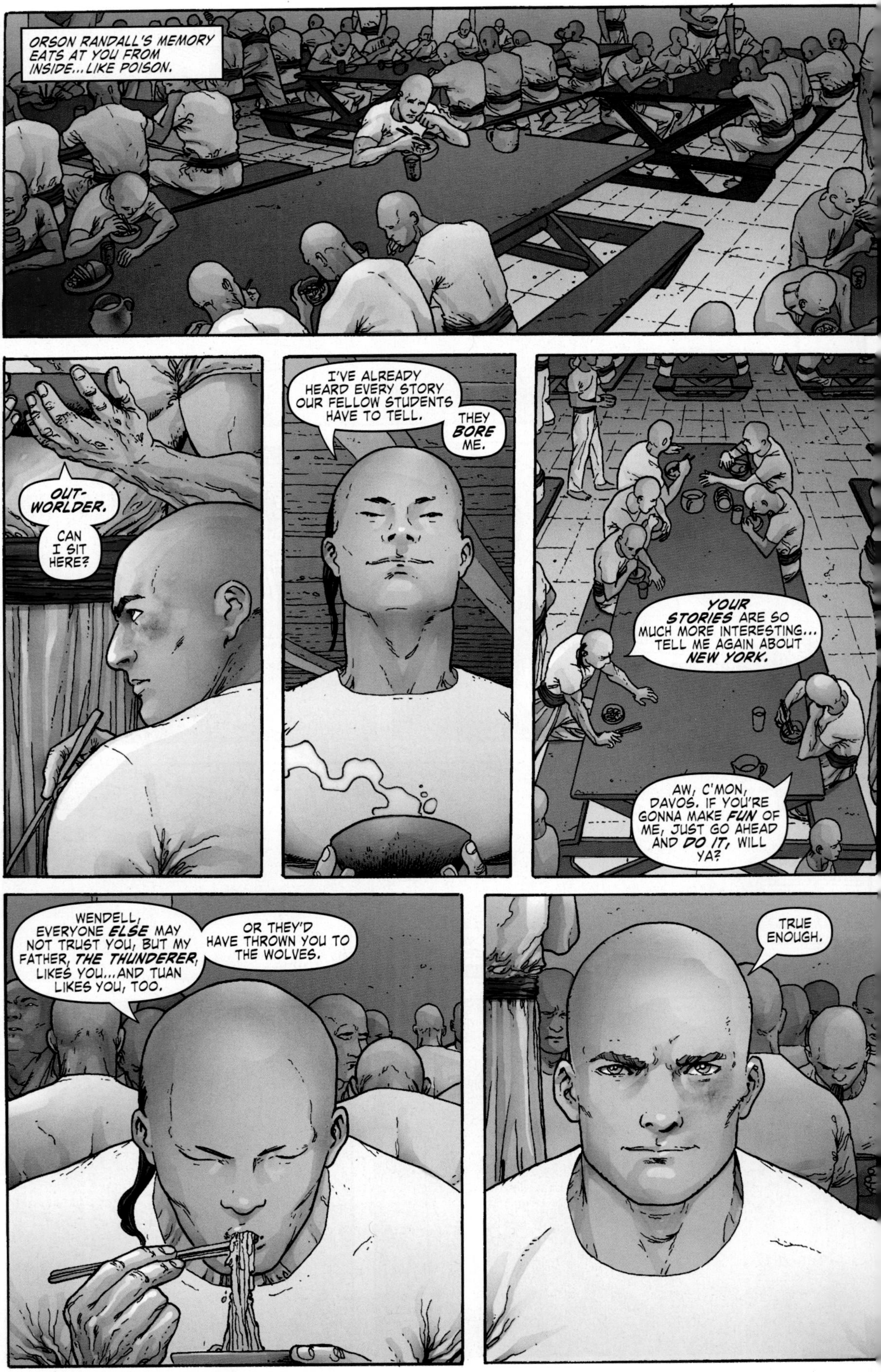
ORSON RANDALL'S MEMORY EATS AT YOU FROM INSIDE... LIKE POISON.
OUT-WORLDER.
CAN I SIT HERE?
I'VE ALREADY HEARD EVERY STORY OUR FELLOW STUDENTS HAVE TO TELL.
THEY BORE ME.
YOUR STORIES ARE SO MUCH MORE INTERESTING... TELL ME AGAIN ABOUT NEW YORK.
AW, C'MON, DAVOS. IF YOU'RE GONNA MAKE FUN OF ME, JUST GO AHEAD AND DO IT, WILL YA?
WENDELL, EVERYONE ELSE MAY NOT TRUST YOU, BUT MY FATHER, THE THUNDERER, LIKES YOU... AND TUAN LIKES YOU, TOO.
OR THEY'D HAVE THROWN YOU TO THE WOLVES.
TRUE ENOUGH.

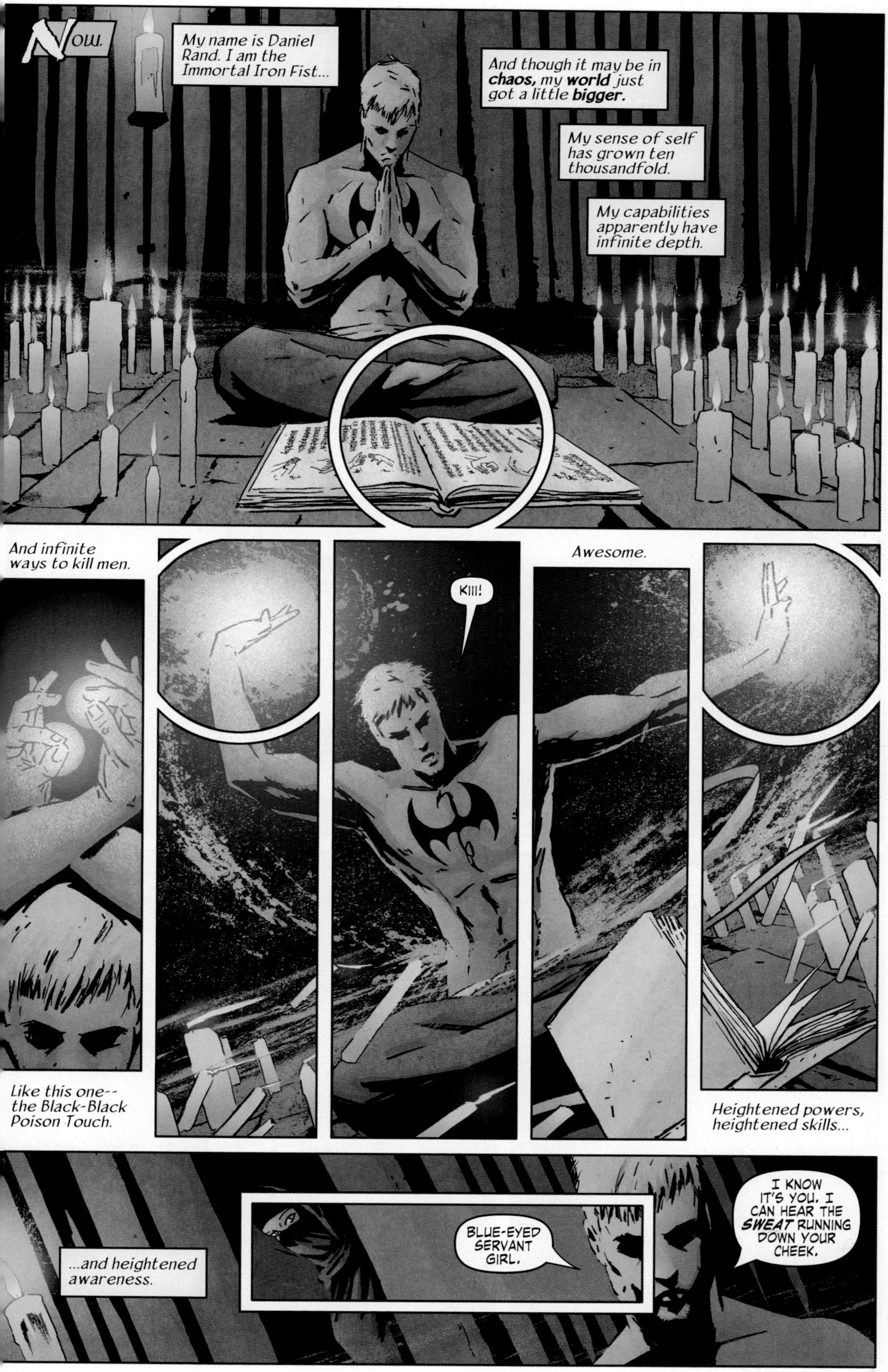
Now.
My name is Daniel Rand. I am the Immortal Iron Fist...
And though it may be in **chaos,** my **world** just got a little **bigger.**
My sense of self has grown ten thousandfold.
My capabilities apparently have infinite depth.
And infinite ways to kill men.
Like this one-- the Black-Black Poison Touch.
KIII!
Awesome.
Heightened powers, heightened skills...
...and heightened awareness.
BLUE-EYED SERVANT GIRL.
I KNOW IT'S YOU. I CAN HEAR THE ***SWEAT*** RUNNING DOWN YOUR CHEEK.

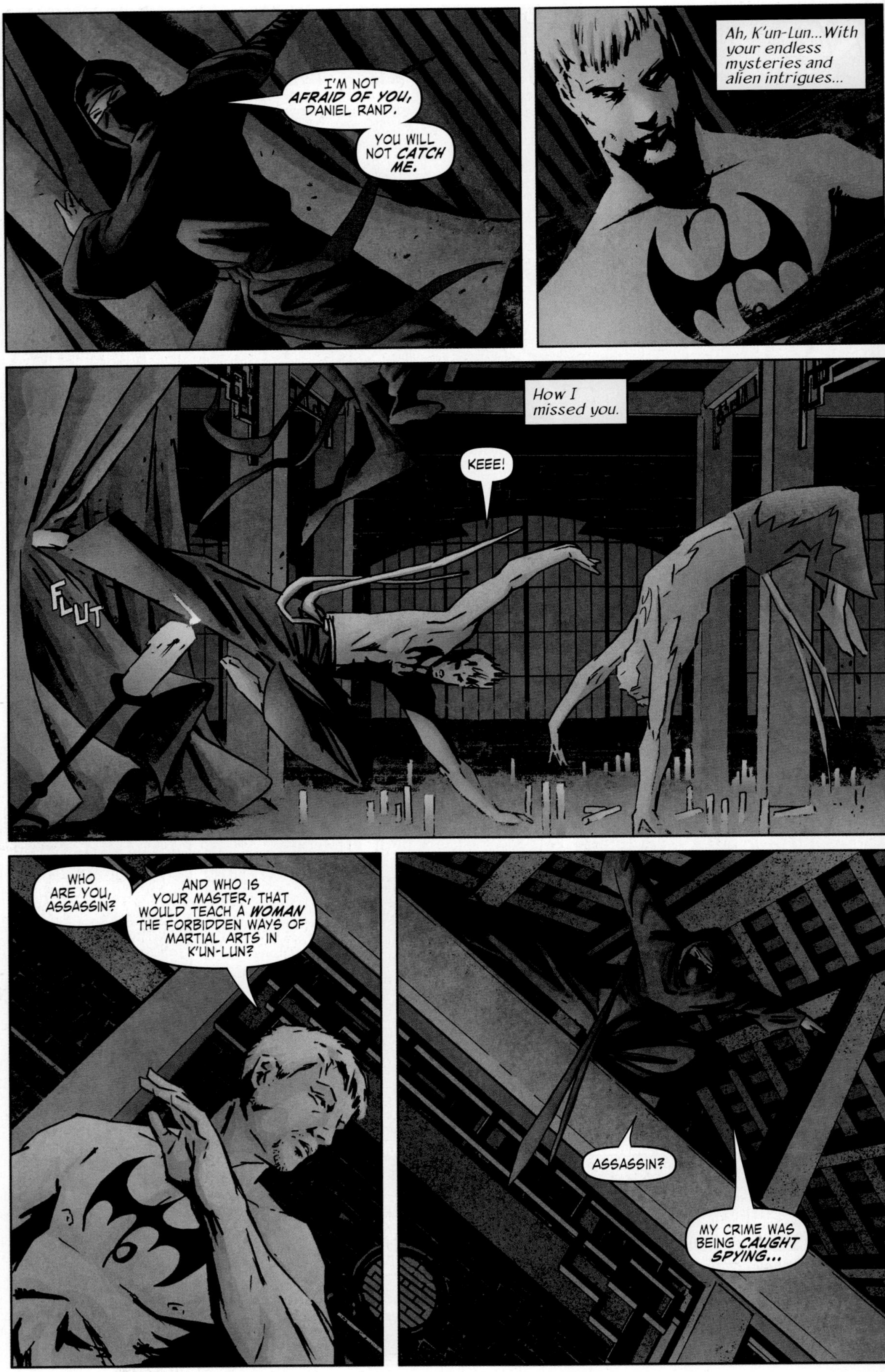
I'M NOT AFRAID OF YOU, DANIEL RAND.
YOU WILL NOT CATCH ME.
Ah, K'un-Lun... With your endless mysteries and alien intrigues...
How I missed you.
KEEE!
FLUT
WHO ARE YOU, ASSASSIN?
AND WHO IS YOUR MASTER, THAT WOULD TEACH A WOMAN THE FORBIDDEN WAYS OF MARTIAL ARTS IN K'UN-LUN?
ASSASSIN?
MY CRIME WAS BEING CAUGHT SPYING...

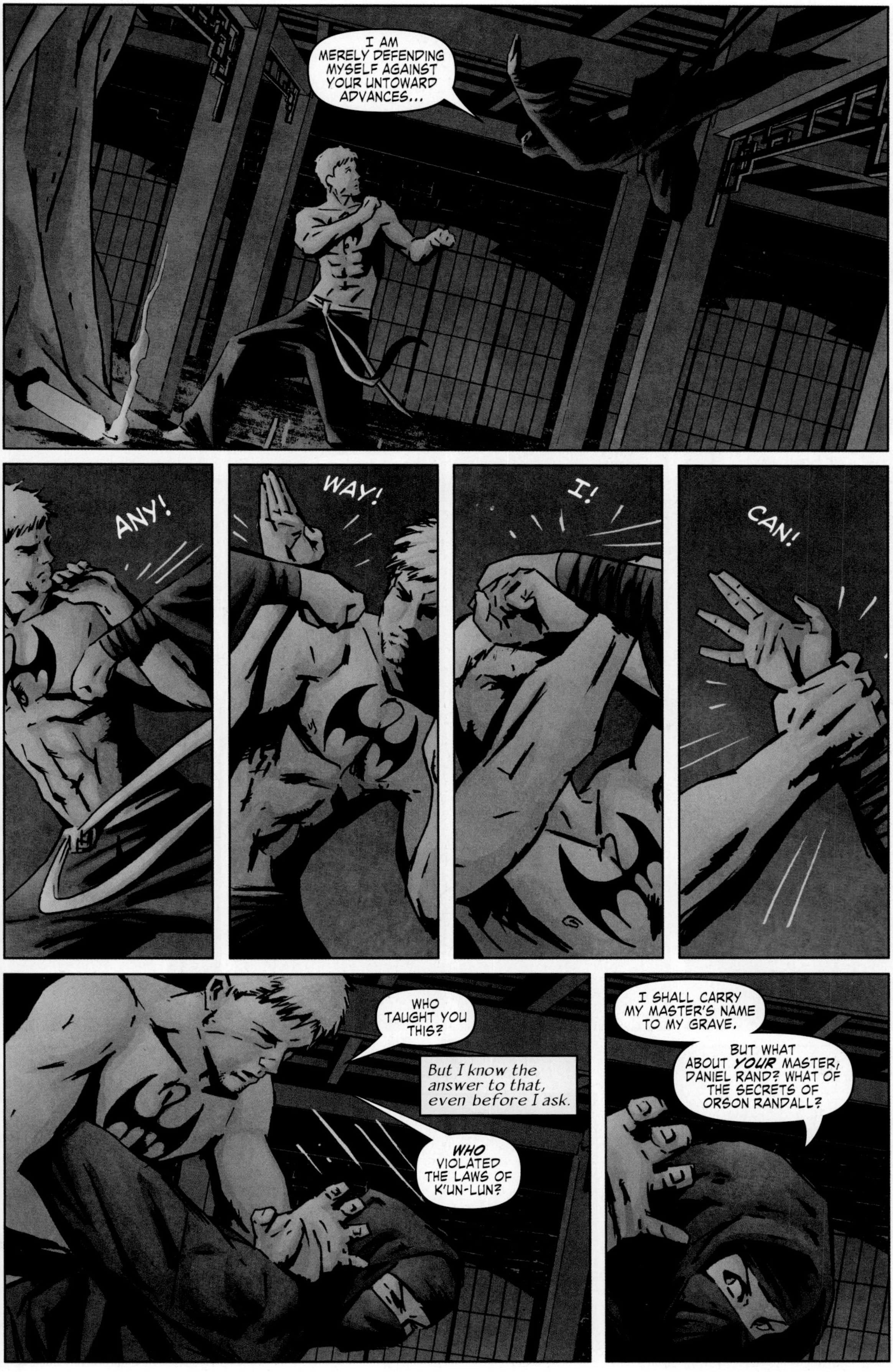
I AM MERELY DEFENDING MYSELF AGAINST YOUR UNTOWARD ADVANCES...
ANY!
WAY!
I!
CAN!
WHO TAUGHT YOU THIS?
But I know the answer to that, even before I ask.
WHO VIOLATED THE LAWS OF K'UN-LUN?
I SHALL CARRY MY MASTER'S NAME TO MY GRAVE.
BUT WHAT ABOUT YOUR MASTER, DANIEL RAND? WHAT OF THE SECRETS OF ORSON RANDALL?

WHAT SECRETS?

KRPK

KIII!

THERE ARE *LARGER THINGS* AT WORK...AND MISSING PIECES TO WHAT TROUBLES YOU.

AND I'VE BEEN SENT TO TELL YOU WHERE THE ANSWERS LIE.

ALL YOU MUST DO TO FIND THEM...IS *LOSE* YOUR UPCOMING MATCH.

DO *WHAT*? ARE YOU OUT OF YOUR *MIND*?

YOU MUST LEAVE THE *HEART OF HEAVEN* AND JOURNEY TO THE *WORLD* OF MEN.

YOU WON'T BE MISSED IF YOU'VE *LOST* AND AREN'T TO FIGHT AGAIN UNTIL THE *BATTLE ROYALE*...

...YOU MUST LET FAT COBRA DEFEAT YOU.

Nuts.

The girl is nuts.

That's not the way we *do things* in my line of work.

I've never deliberately lost *anything* in my *entire life*.

She's nuts.

Right?

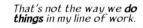

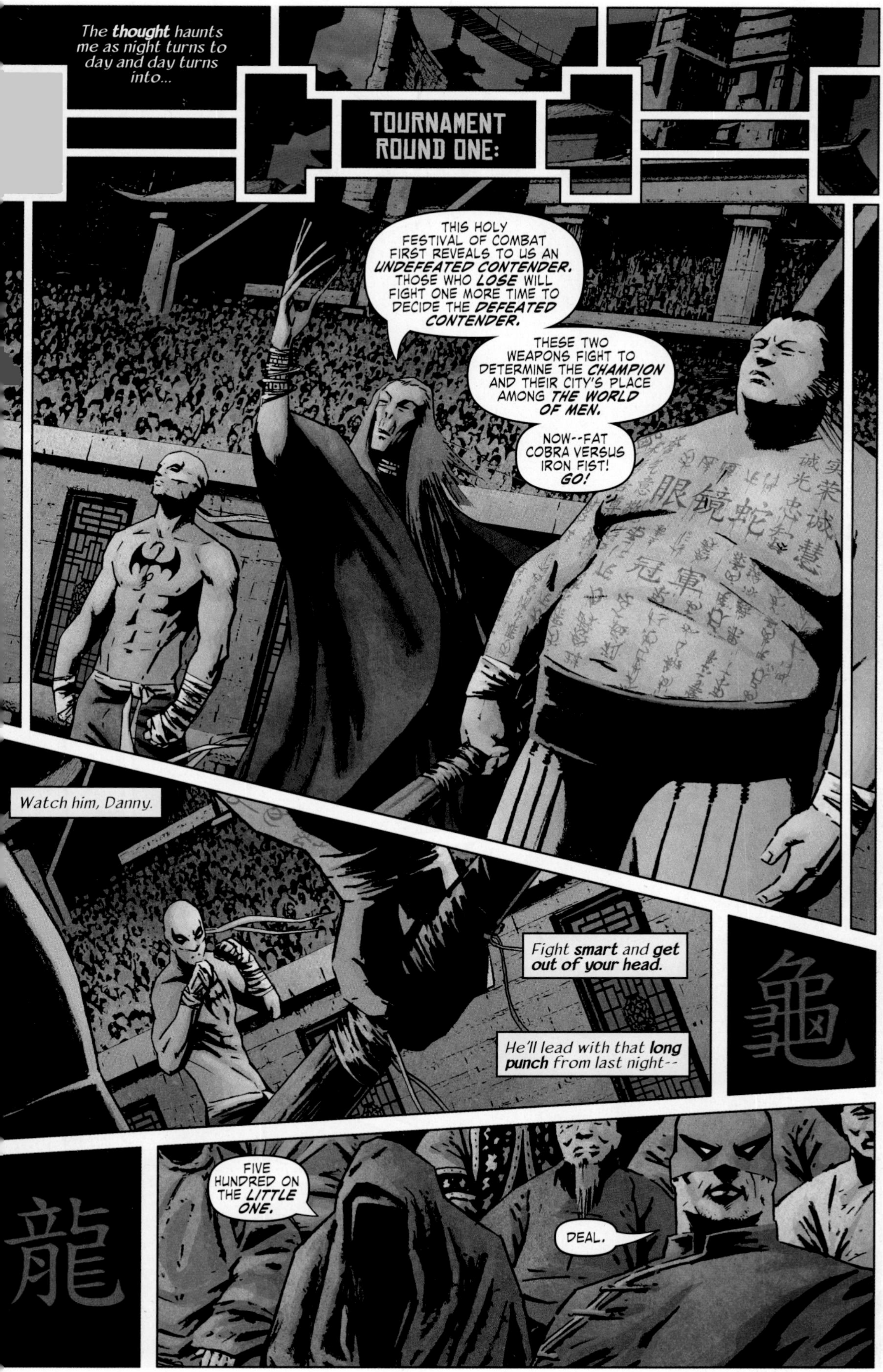
The **thought** haunts me as night turns to day and day turns into...
TOURNAMENT ROUND ONE:
THIS HOLY FESTIVAL OF COMBAT FIRST REVEALS TO US AN ***UNDEFEATED CONTENDER.*** THOSE WHO ***LOSE*** WILL FIGHT ONE MORE TIME TO DECIDE THE ***DEFEATED CONTENDER.***
THESE TWO WEAPONS FIGHT TO DETERMINE THE ***CHAMPION*** AND THEIR CITY'S PLACE AMONG ***THE WORLD OF MEN.***
NOW--FAT COBRA VERSUS IRON FIST! ***GO!***
Watch him, Danny.
Fight **smart** and **get out of your head.**
He'll lead with that **long punch** from last night--
FIVE HUNDRED ON THE ***LITTLE ONE.***
DEAL.

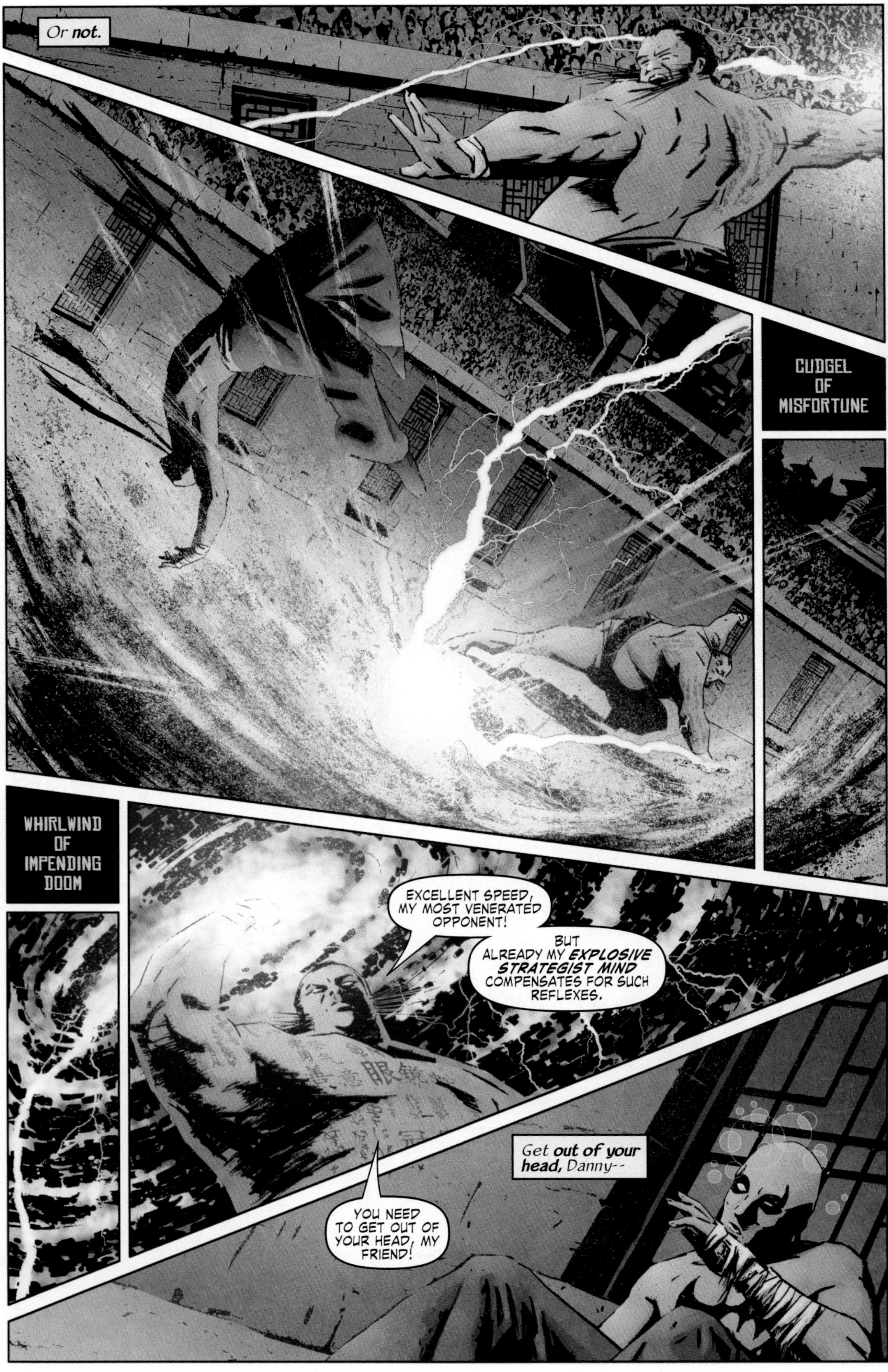
Or not.
CUDGEL OF MISFORTUNE
WHIRLWIND OF IMPENDING DOOM
EXCELLENT SPEED, MY MOST VENERATED OPPONENT!
BUT ALREADY MY EXPLOSIVE STRATEGIST MIND COMPENSATES FOR SUCH REFLEXES.
YOU NEED TO GET OUT OF YOUR HEAD, MY FRIEND!
Get out of your head, Danny--

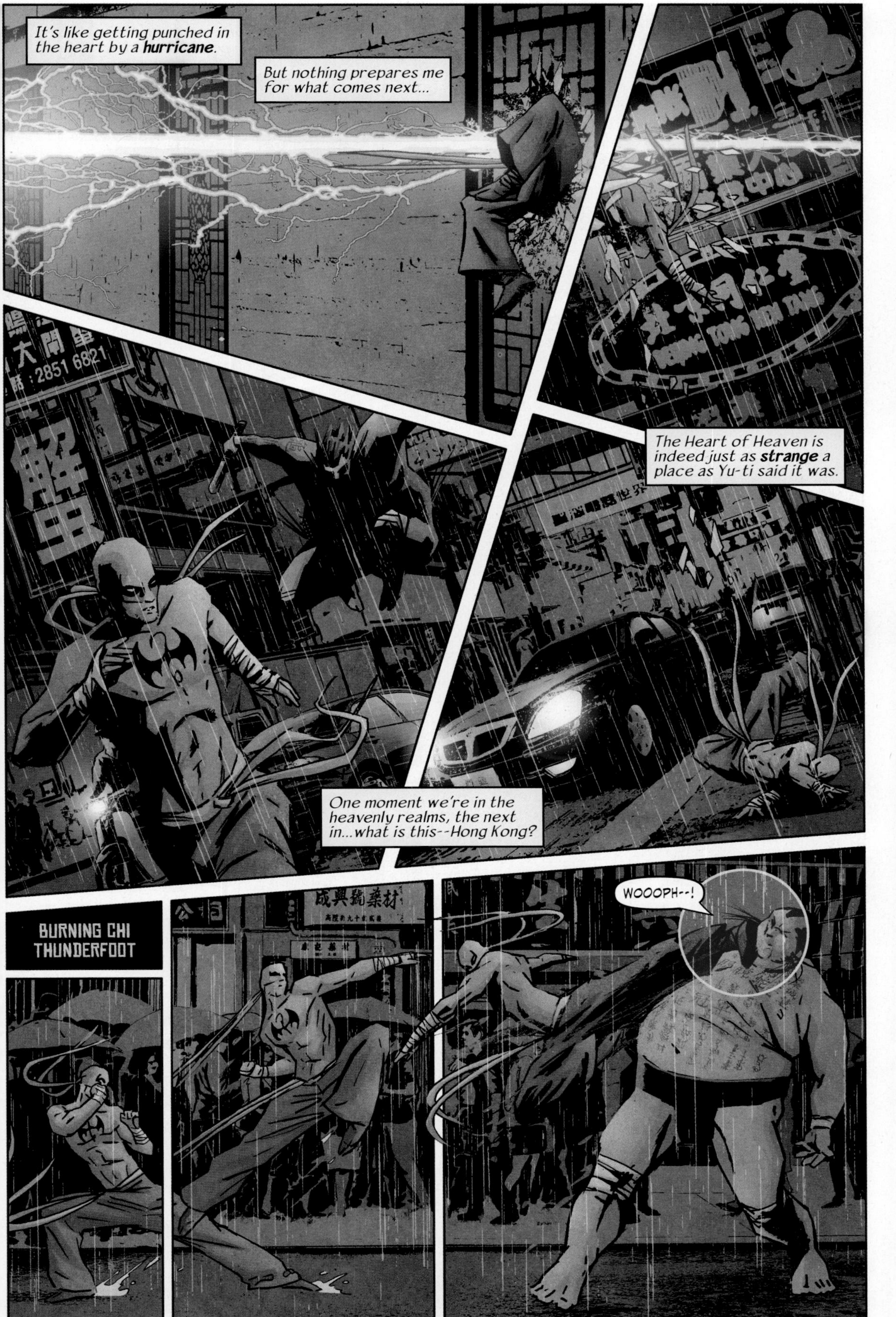
It's like getting punched in the heart by a **hurricane**.
But nothing prepares me for what comes next...
The Heart of Heaven is indeed just as **strange** a place as Yu-ti said it was.
One moment we're in the heavenly realms, the next in...what is this--Hong Kong?
BURNING CHI THUNDERFOOT
WOOOPH--!

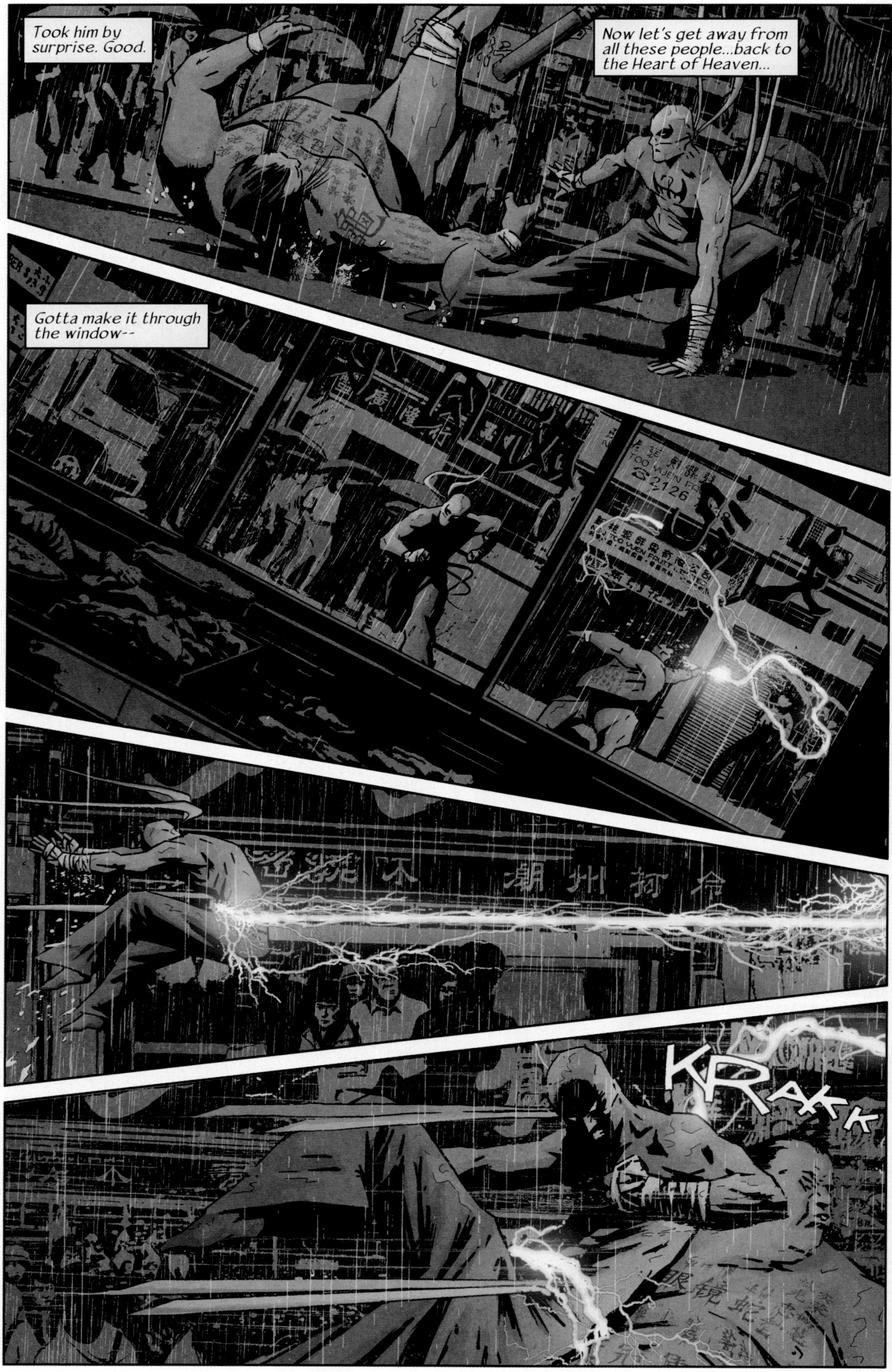
Took him by surprise. Good.
Now let's get away from all these people...back to the Heart of Heaven...
Gotta make it through the window--
KRAKK

YOU ARE A VENERATED OPPONENT...BUT YOU ARE GOING TO LOSE THIS FIGHT!

THE IRON FIST'S STREAK WILL BE BROKEN...

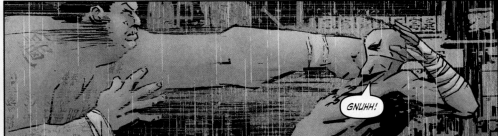

...AT LONG LAST!

I WOULDN'T COUNT ON--

THE DEVIL'S SKULLCRUSHER

GNUHH!

NOW...LET US TEST NOT YOUR SKILLS, BUT YOUR WISDOM...

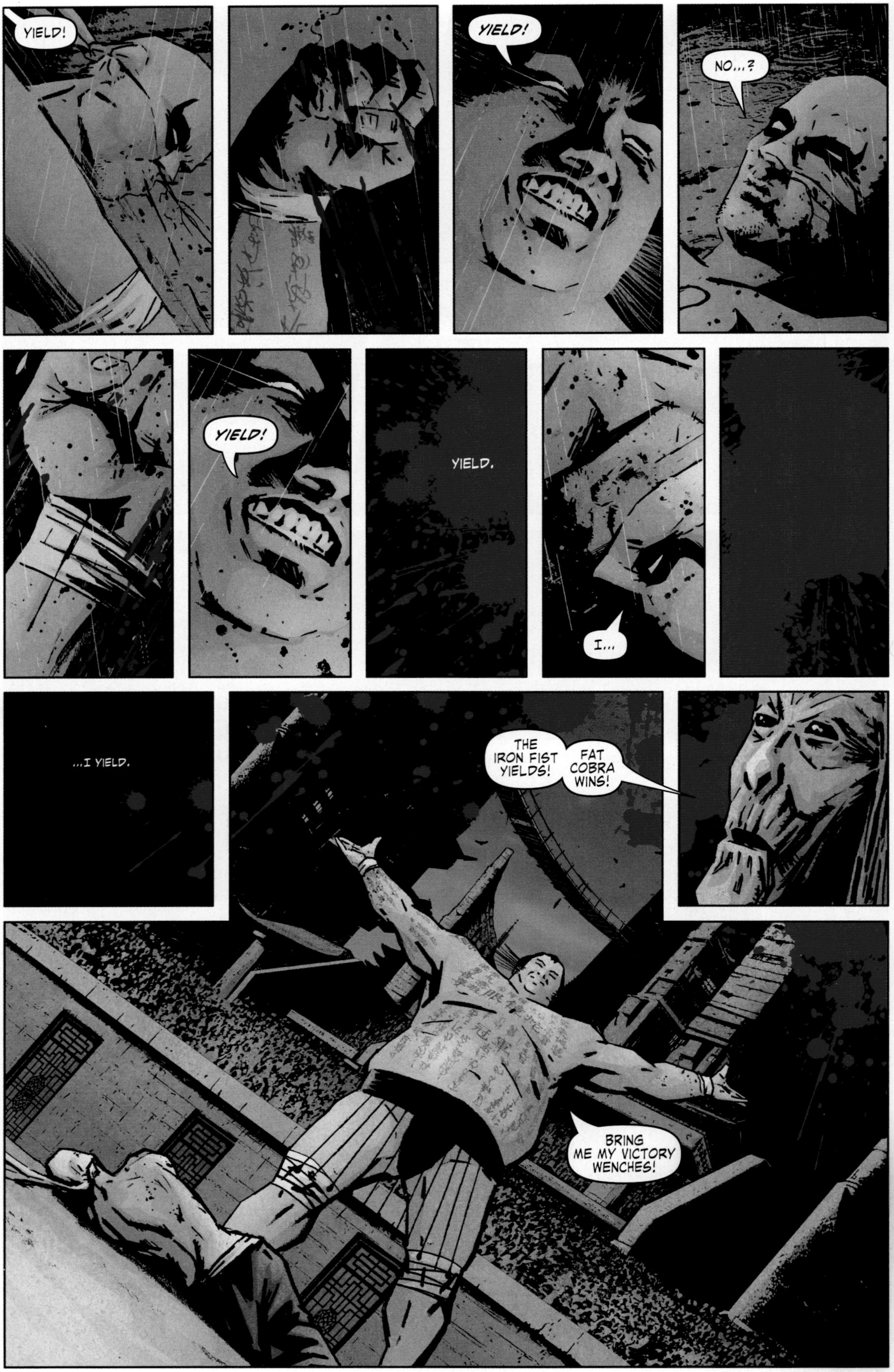
YIELD!
YIELD!
NO...?
YIELD!
YIELD.
I...
...I YIELD.
THE IRON FIST YIELDS!
FAT COBRA WINS!
BRING ME MY VICTORY WENCHES!

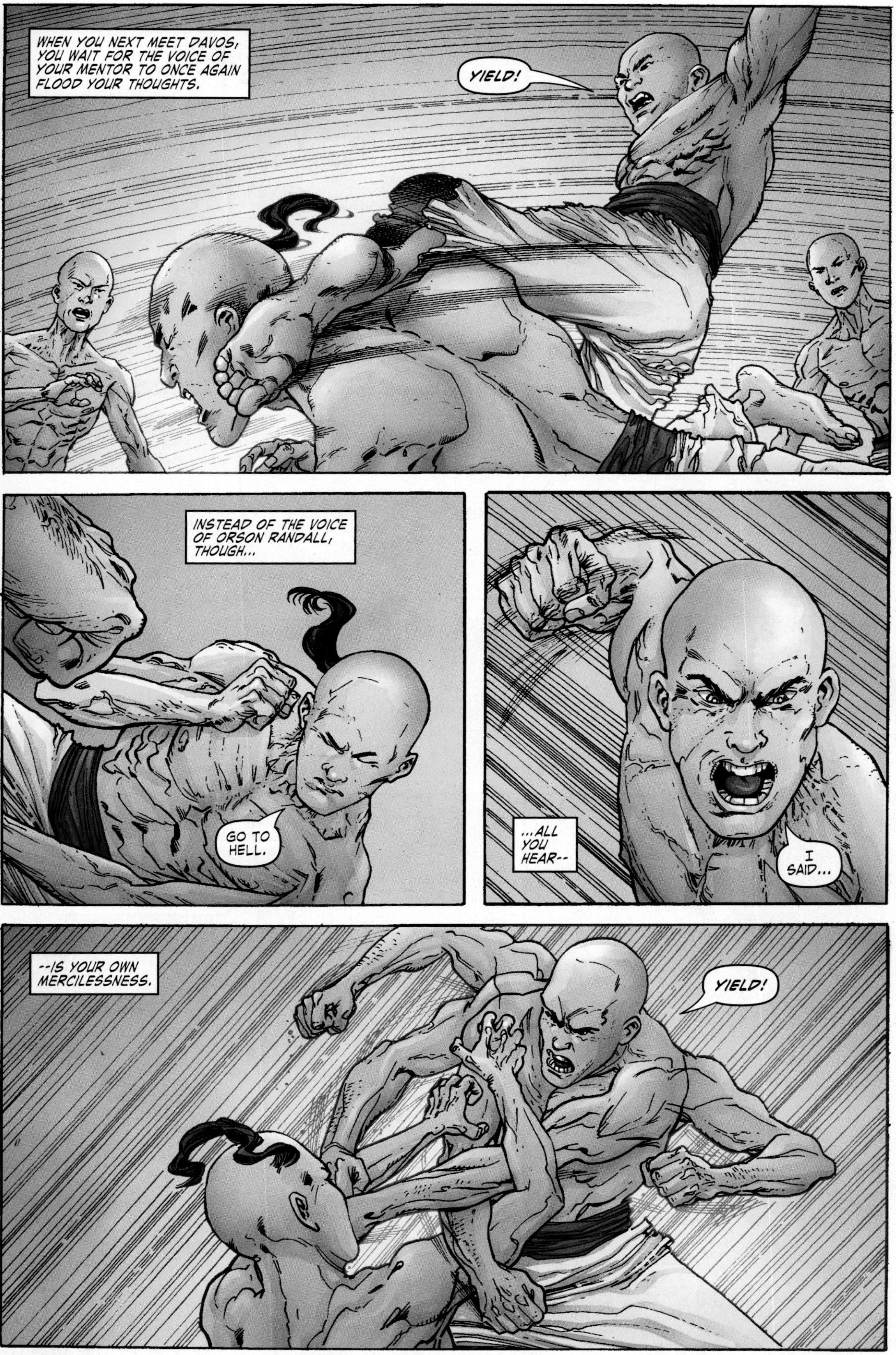
WHEN YOU NEXT MEET DAVOS, YOU WAIT FOR THE VOICE OF YOUR MENTOR TO ONCE AGAIN FLOOD YOUR THOUGHTS.
YIELD!
INSTEAD OF THE VOICE OF ORSON RANDALL, THOUGH...
GO TO HELL.
...ALL YOU HEAR--
I SAID...
--IS YOUR OWN MERCILESSNESS.
YIELD!

NEV... NEVER...

NNN--

YIELD!

PERHAPS YOU NO LONGER *NEED HIM* TO GUIDE YOU. OR PERHAPS YOU'VE REALIZED...

...

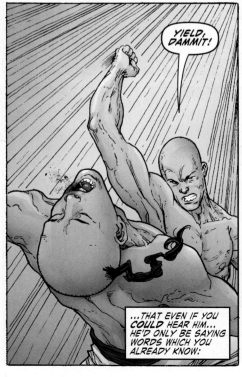

YIELD, DAMMIT!

...THAT EVEN IF YOU *COULD* HEAR HIM... HE'D ONLY BE SAYING WORDS WHICH YOU ALREADY KNOW:

YOU ARE WENDELL RAND.

AND YOU HAVE THE HEART OF A CHAMPION INSIDE YOU YET.

THE OTHERS ARE QUICK TO TURN THEIR BACKS ON ONE OF THEIR *OWN.*

WELL, IF YOU DON'T *LET ME* EAT WITH YOU, I THINK I'LL HAVE TO GO TO THE *STABLES.*

MAY I SIT?

ONLY THING WORSE THAN EATING WITH THE *OUTWORLDER* IS GETTING *BEATEN* BY HIM, HUNH?

SO...DID YOU THROW THAT MATCH?

DID YOU TAKE PITY ON ME, MAYBE?

...

I DIDN'T AND I NEVER WILL... I DEMAND THE *BEST* OF YOU, AND YOU SHALL KNOW ONLY THE BEST OF ME.

THE OTHER STUDENTS WILL *TALK,* OF COURSE. THE WAY STUDENTS OFTEN DO.

THE *SON OF THE THUNDERER* AND THE *OUTWORLDER.*

FRIENDS.

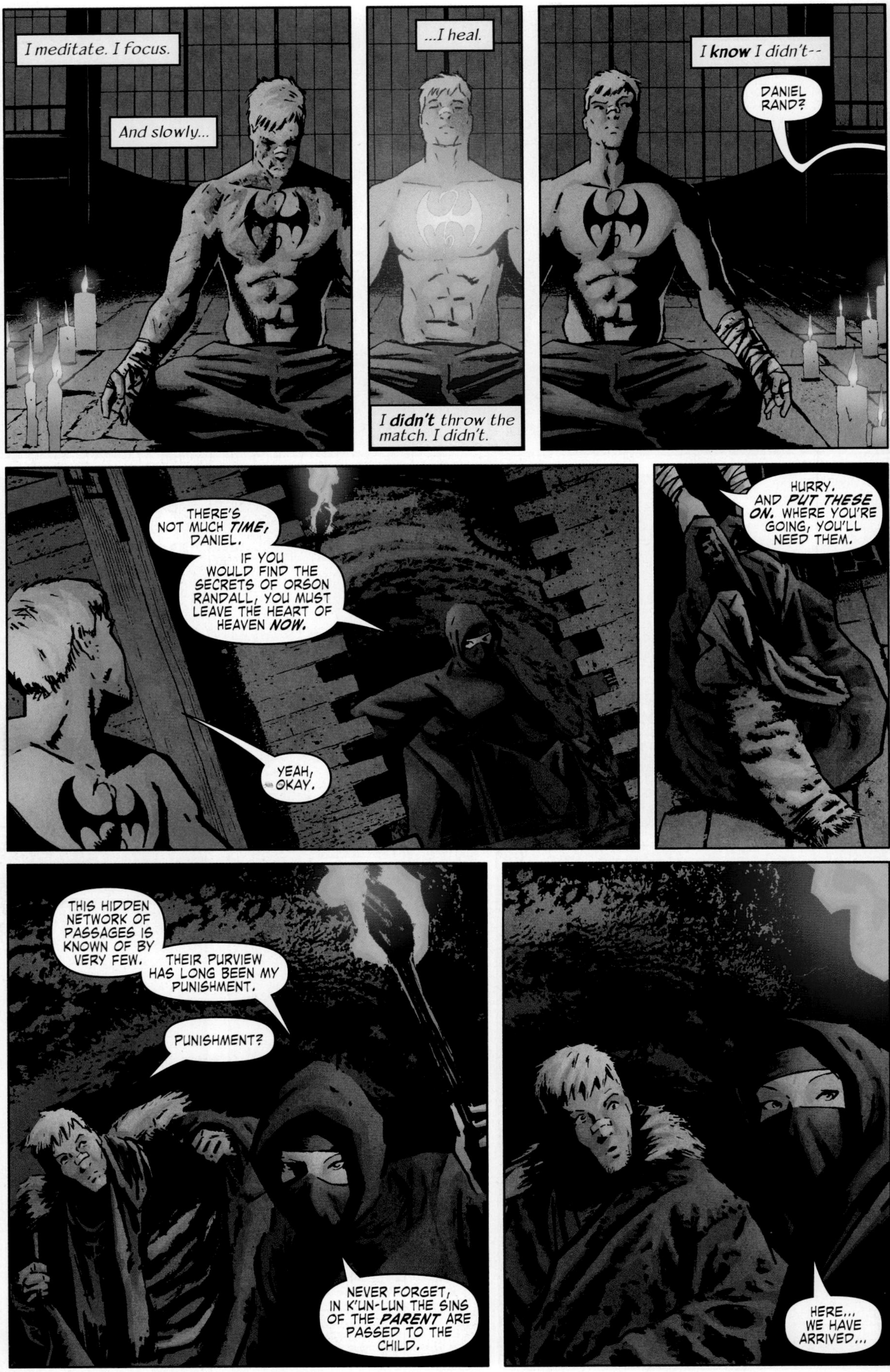
I meditate. I focus.
And slowly...
...I heal.
I didn't throw the match. I didn't.
I know I didn't--
DANIEL RAND?
THERE'S NOT MUCH TIME, DANIEL.
IF YOU WOULD FIND THE SECRETS OF ORSON RANDALL, YOU MUST LEAVE THE HEART OF HEAVEN NOW.
YEAH, OKAY.
HURRY. AND PUT THESE ON. WHERE YOU'RE GOING, YOU'LL NEED THEM.
THIS HIDDEN NETWORK OF PASSAGES IS KNOWN OF BY VERY FEW.
THEIR PURVIEW HAS LONG BEEN MY PUNISHMENT.
PUNISHMENT?
NEVER FORGET, IN K'UN-LUN THE SINS OF THE PARENT ARE PASSED TO THE CHILD.
HERE... WE HAVE ARRIVED...

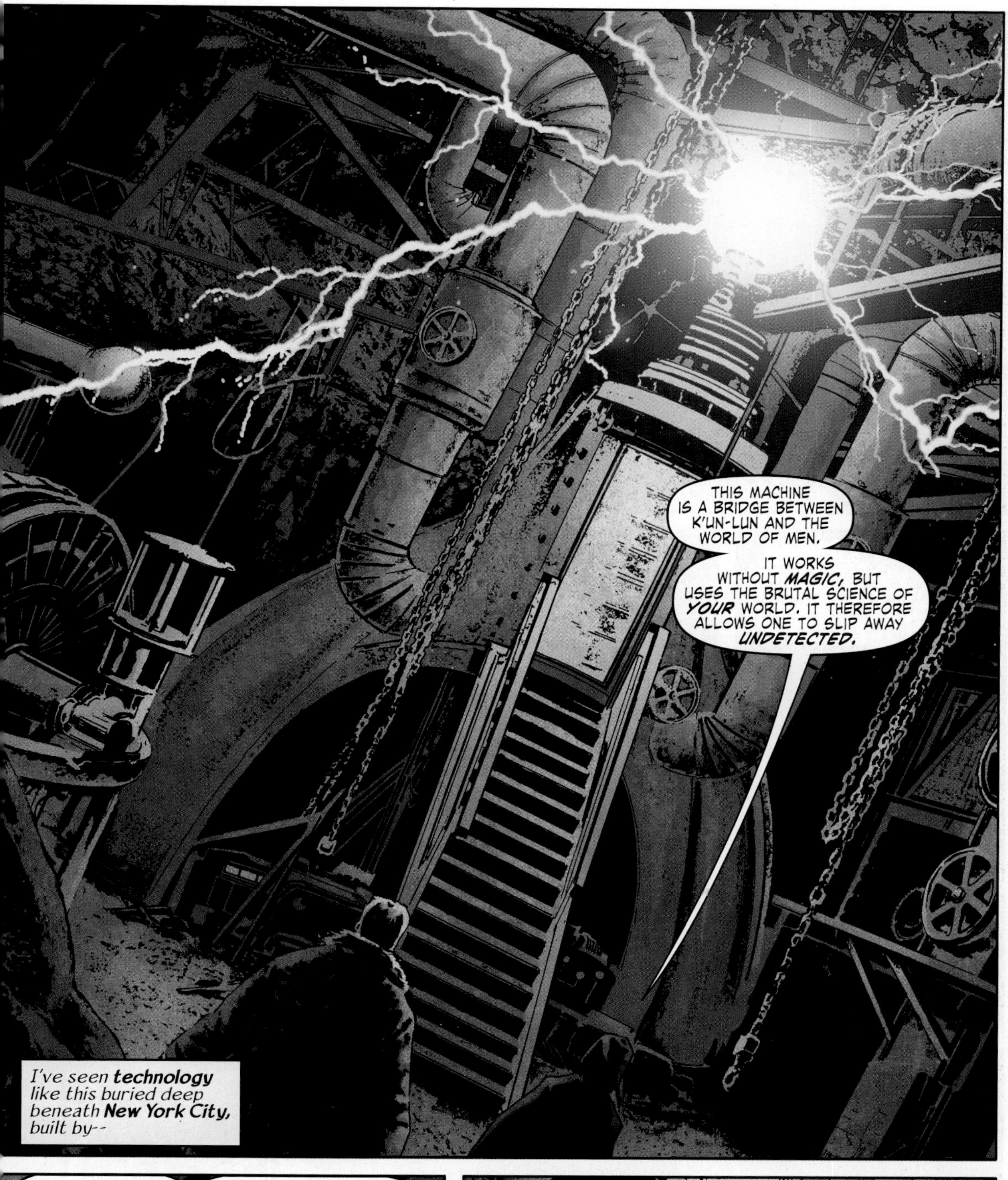
THIS MACHINE IS A BRIDGE BETWEEN K'UN-LUN AND THE WORLD OF MEN.
IT WORKS WITHOUT MAGIC, BUT USES THE BRUTAL SCIENCE OF YOUR WORLD. IT THEREFORE ALLOWS ONE TO SLIP AWAY UNDETECTED.
I've seen technology like this buried deep beneath New York City, built by--

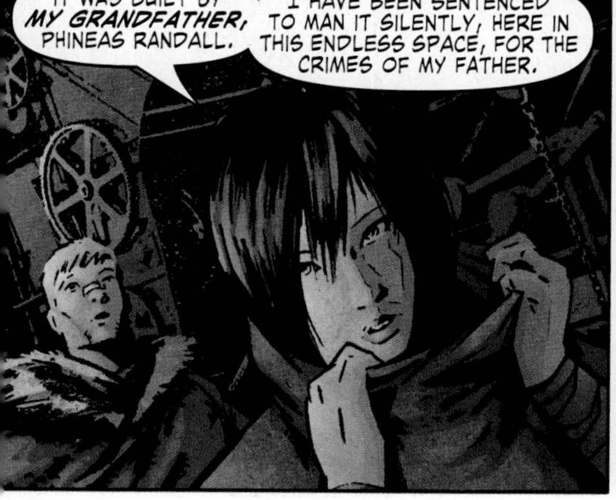
IT WAS BUILT BY MY GRANDFATHER, PHINEAS RANDALL.
I HAVE BEEN SENTENCED TO MAN IT SILENTLY, HERE IN THIS ENDLESS SPACE, FOR THE CRIMES OF MY FATHER.

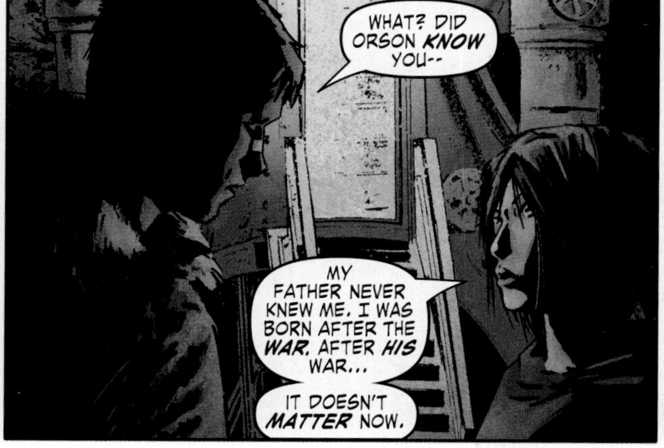
WHAT? DID ORSON KNOW YOU--
MY FATHER NEVER KNEW ME. I WAS BORN AFTER THE WAR. AFTER HIS WAR...
IT DOESN'T MATTER NOW.

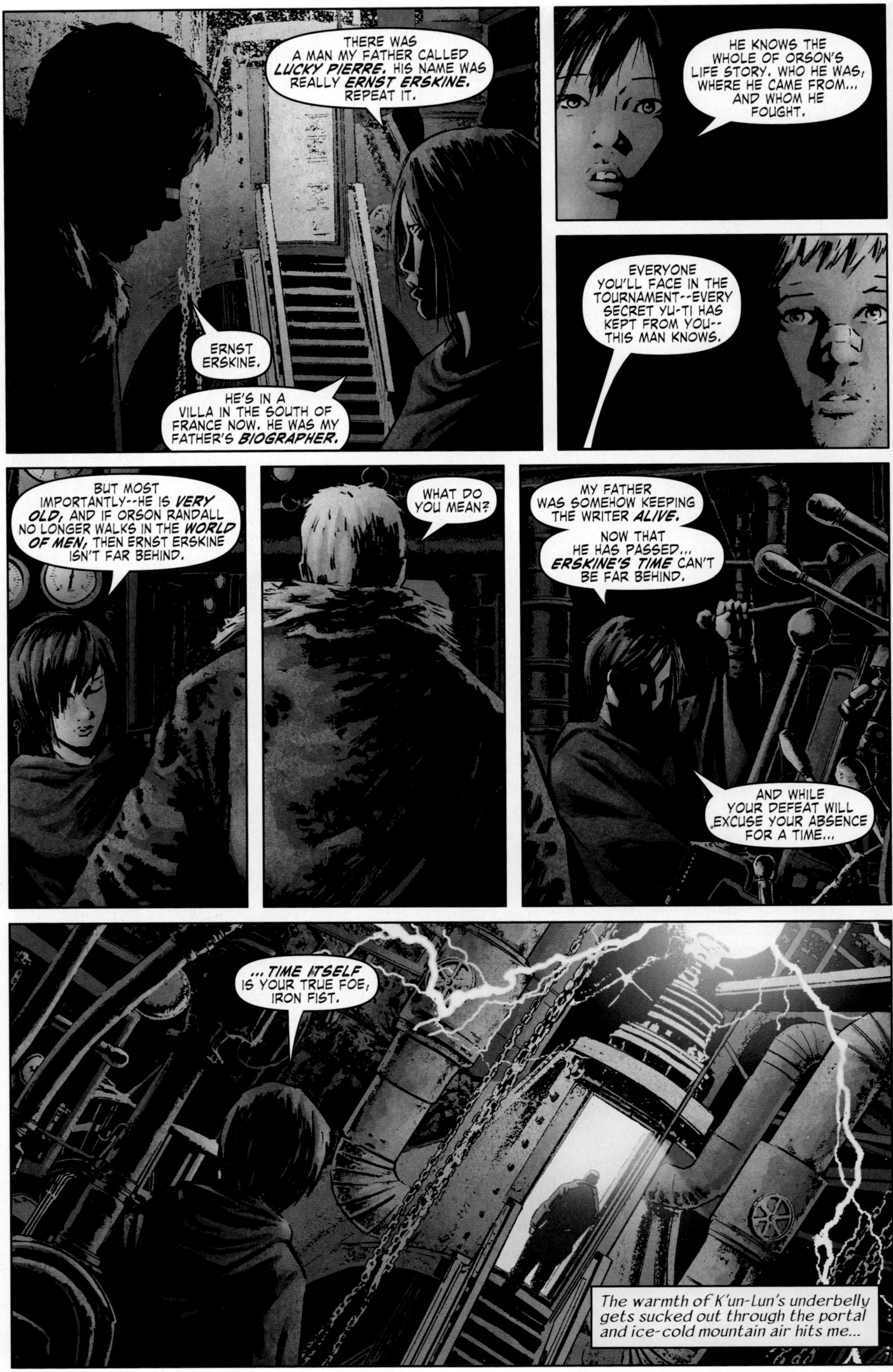
THERE WAS A MAN MY FATHER CALLED LUCKY PIERRE. HIS NAME WAS REALLY ERNST ERSKINE. REPEAT IT.
ERNST ERSKINE.
HE'S IN A VILLA IN THE SOUTH OF FRANCE NOW. HE WAS MY FATHER'S BIOGRAPHER.
HE KNOWS THE WHOLE OF ORSON'S LIFE STORY. WHO HE WAS, WHERE HE CAME FROM... AND WHOM HE FOUGHT.
EVERYONE YOU'LL FACE IN THE TOURNAMENT--EVERY SECRET YU-TI HAS KEPT FROM YOU--THIS MAN KNOWS.
BUT MOST IMPORTANTLY--HE IS VERY OLD, AND IF ORSON RANDALL NO LONGER WALKS IN THE WORLD OF MEN, THEN ERNST ERSKINE ISN'T FAR BEHIND.
WHAT DO YOU MEAN?
MY FATHER WAS SOMEHOW KEEPING THE WRITER ALIVE.
NOW THAT HE HAS PASSED... ERSKINE'S TIME CAN'T BE FAR BEHIND.
AND WHILE YOUR DEFEAT WILL EXCUSE YOUR ABSENCE FOR A TIME...
...TIME ITSELF IS YOUR TRUE FOE, IRON FIST.
The warmth of K'un-Lun's underbelly gets sucked out through the portal and ice-cold mountain air hits me...

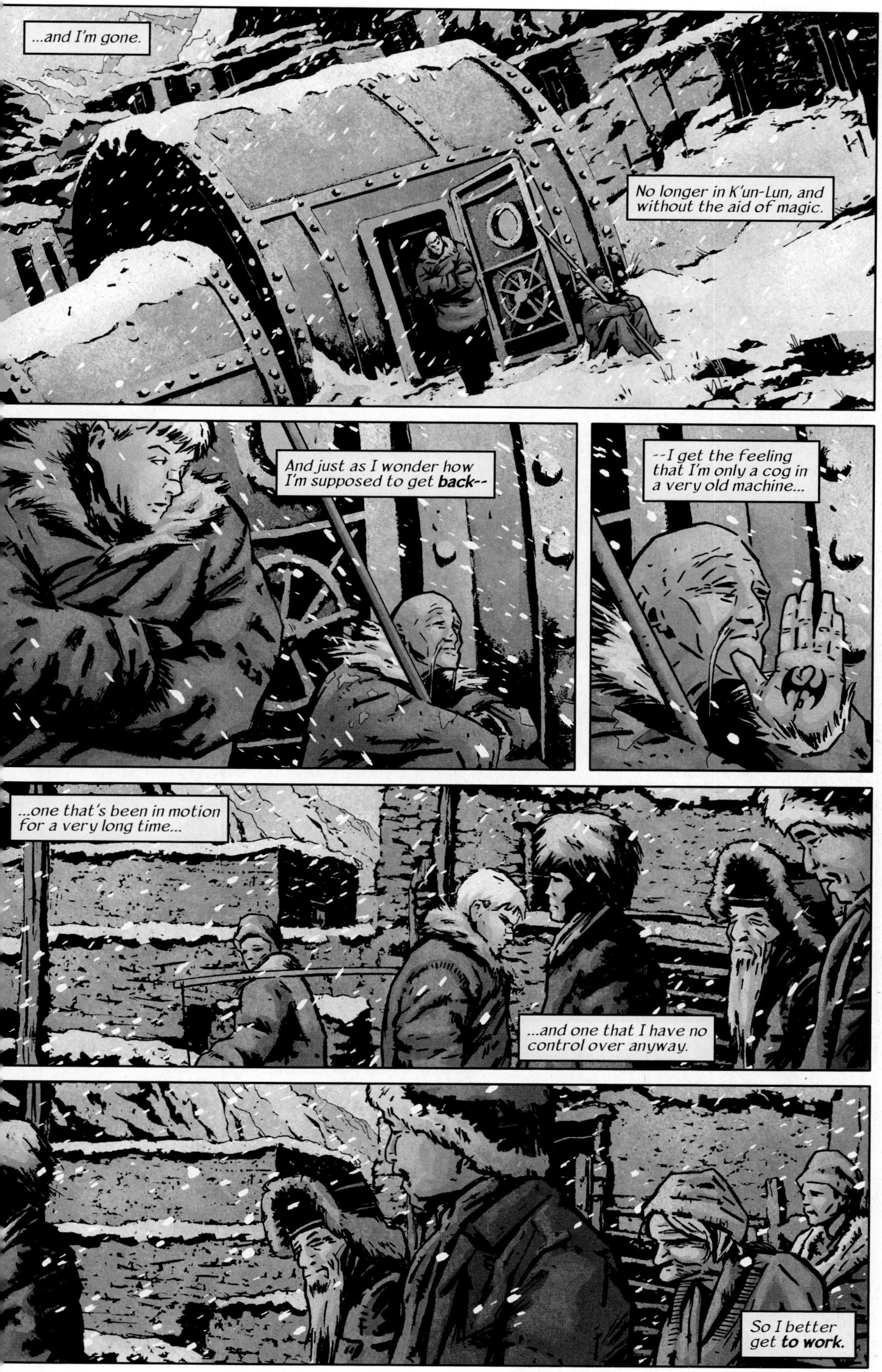
...and I'm gone.
No longer in K'un-Lun, and without the aid of magic.
And just as I wonder how I'm supposed to get back--
--I get the feeling that I'm only a cog in a very old machine...
...one that's been in motion for a very long time...
...and one that I have no control over anyway.
So I better get to work.

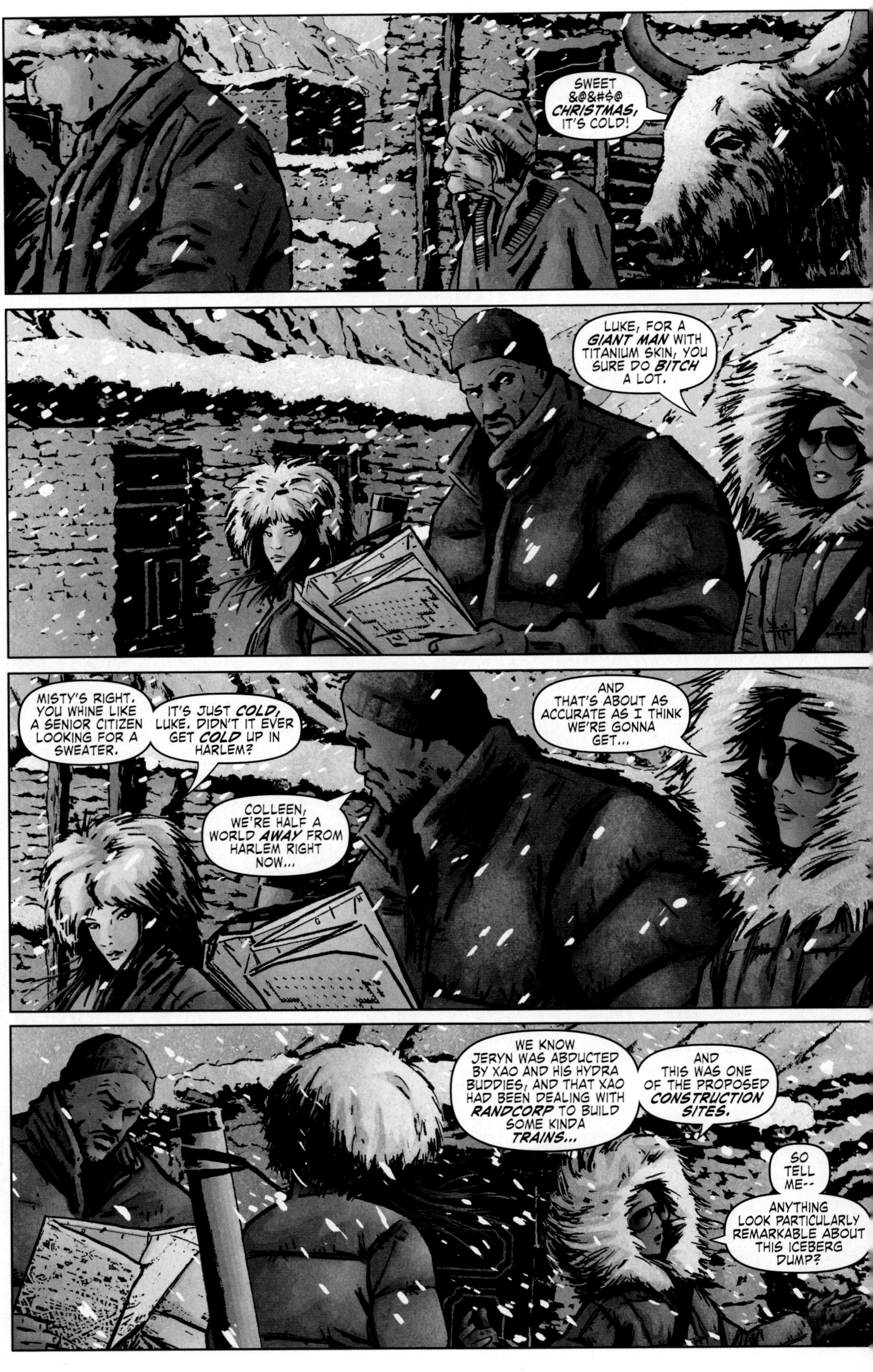
SWEET &@&#$@ CHRISTMAS, IT'S COLD!
LUKE, FOR A GIANT MAN WITH TITANIUM SKIN, YOU SURE DO BITCH A LOT.
MISTY'S RIGHT. YOU WHINE LIKE A SENIOR CITIZEN LOOKING FOR A SWEATER.
IT'S JUST COLD, LUKE. DIDN'T IT EVER GET COLD UP IN HARLEM?
COLLEEN, WE'RE HALF A WORLD AWAY FROM HARLEM RIGHT NOW...
AND THAT'S ABOUT AS ACCURATE AS I THINK WE'RE GONNA GET...
WE KNOW JERYN WAS ABDUCTED BY XAO AND HIS HYDRA BUDDIES, AND THAT XAO HAD BEEN DEALING WITH RANDCORP TO BUILD SOME KINDA TRAINS...
AND THIS WAS ONE OF THE PROPOSED CONSTRUCTION SITES.
SO TELL ME--
ANYTHING LOOK PARTICULARLY REMARKABLE ABOUT THIS ICEBERG DUMP?

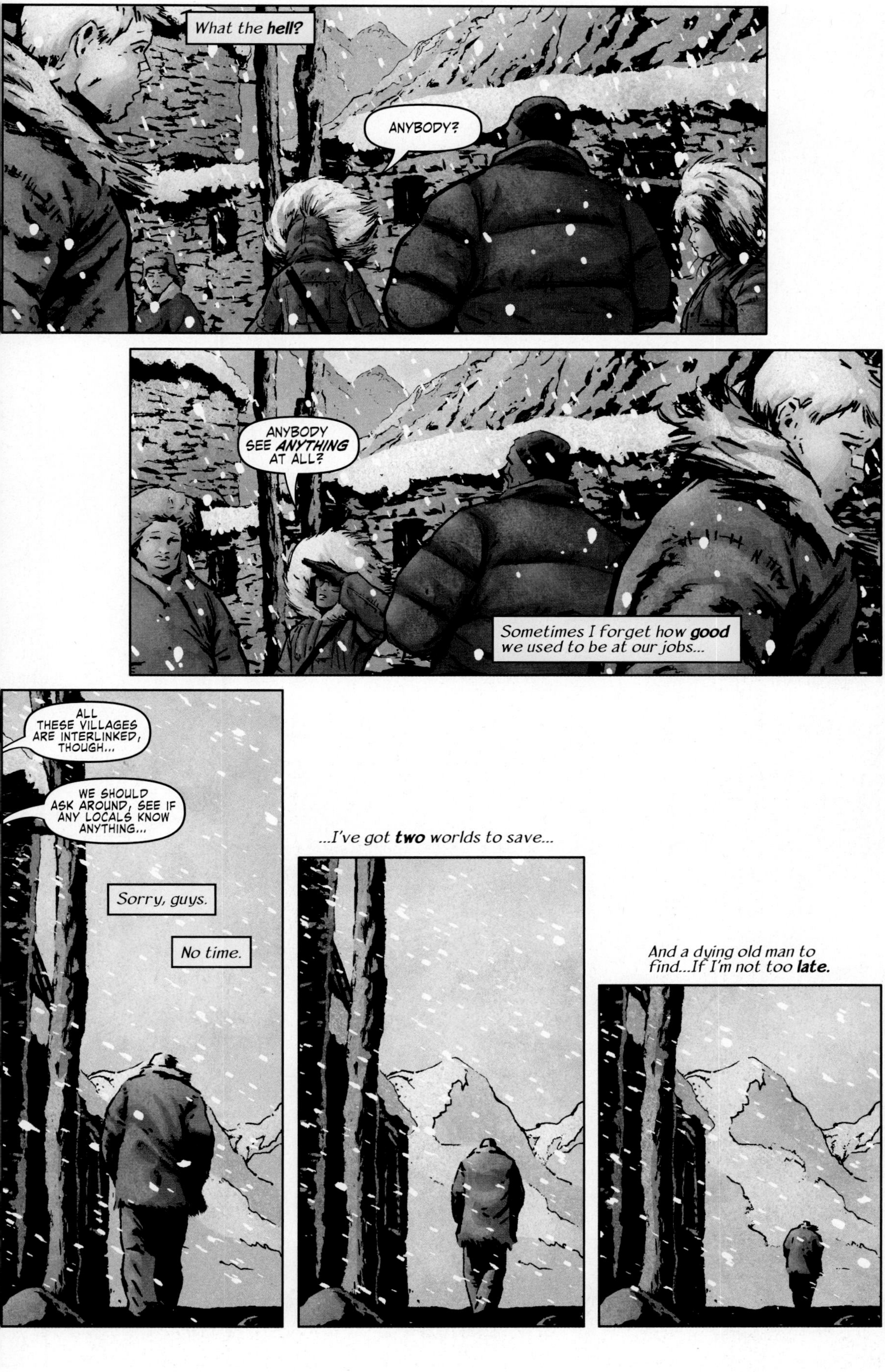

What the **hell?**
ANYBODY?
ANYBODY SEE ***ANYTHING*** AT ALL?
*Sometimes I forget how **good** we used to be at our jobs...*
ALL THESE VILLAGES ARE INTERLINKED, THOUGH...
WE SHOULD ASK AROUND, SEE IF ANY LOCALS KNOW ANYTHING...
Sorry, guys.
No time.
*...I've got **two** worlds to save...*
*And a dying old man to find...If I'm not too **late.***

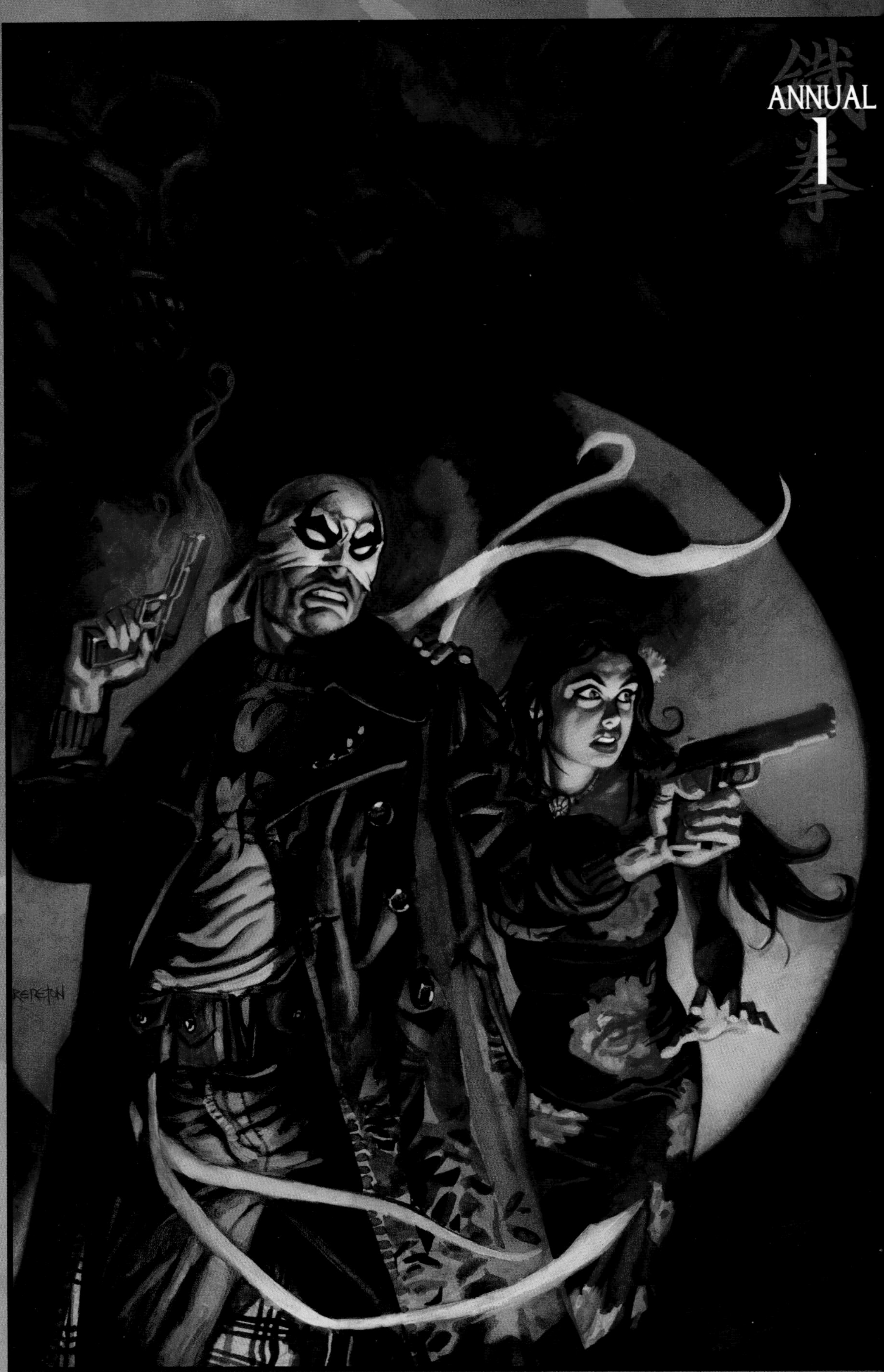

鐵
ANNUAL
1
拳
BRERETON

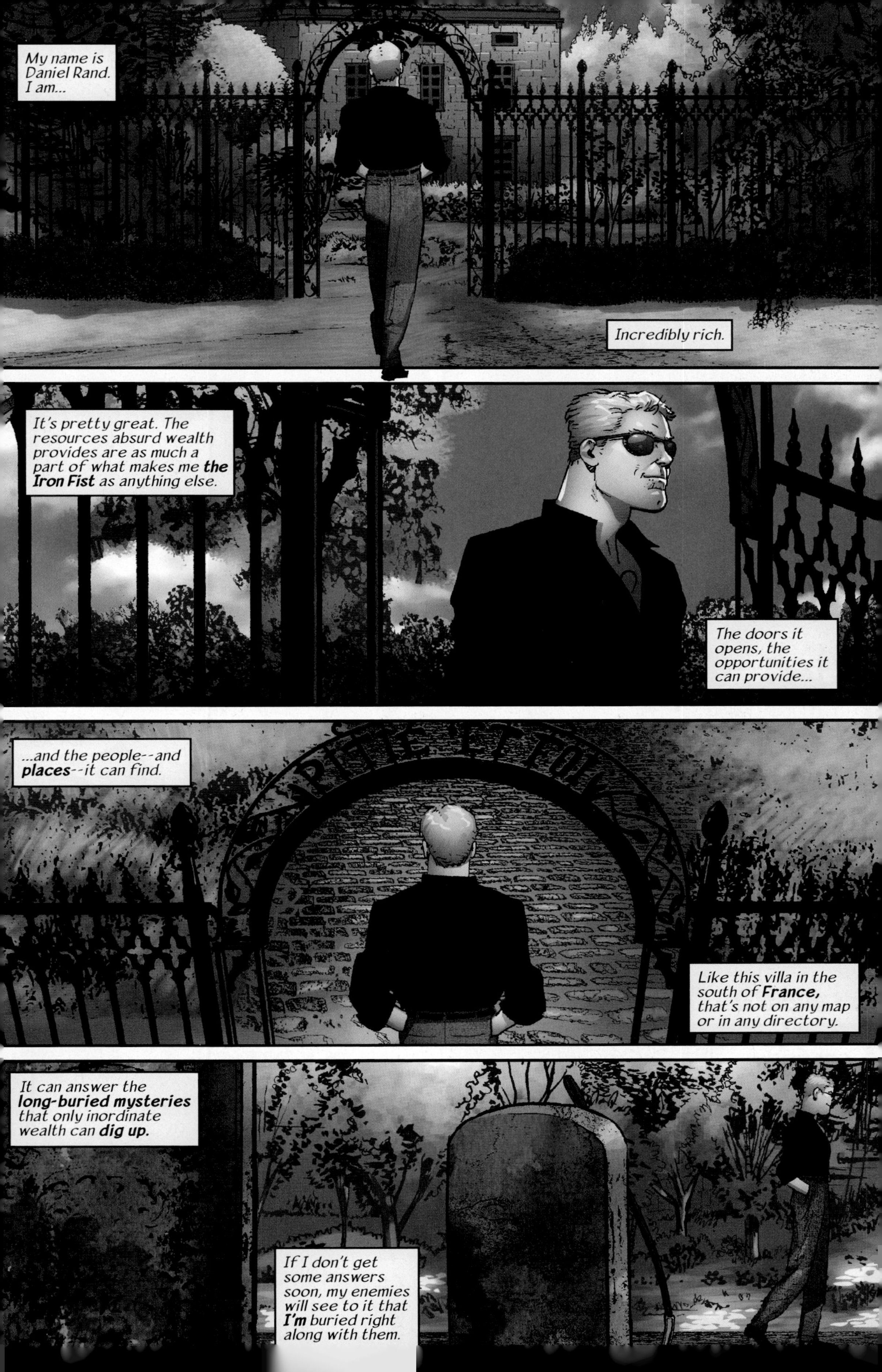

My name is Daniel Rand. I am...
Incredibly rich.
It's pretty great. The resources absurd wealth provides are as much a part of what makes me **the Iron Fist** as anything else.
The doors it opens, the opportunities it can provide...
...and the people--and **places**--it can find.
Like this villa in the south of **France,** that's not on any map or in any directory.
It can answer the **long-buried mysteries** that only inordinate wealth can **dig up.**
If I don't get some answers soon, my enemies will see to it that **I'm** buried right along with them.

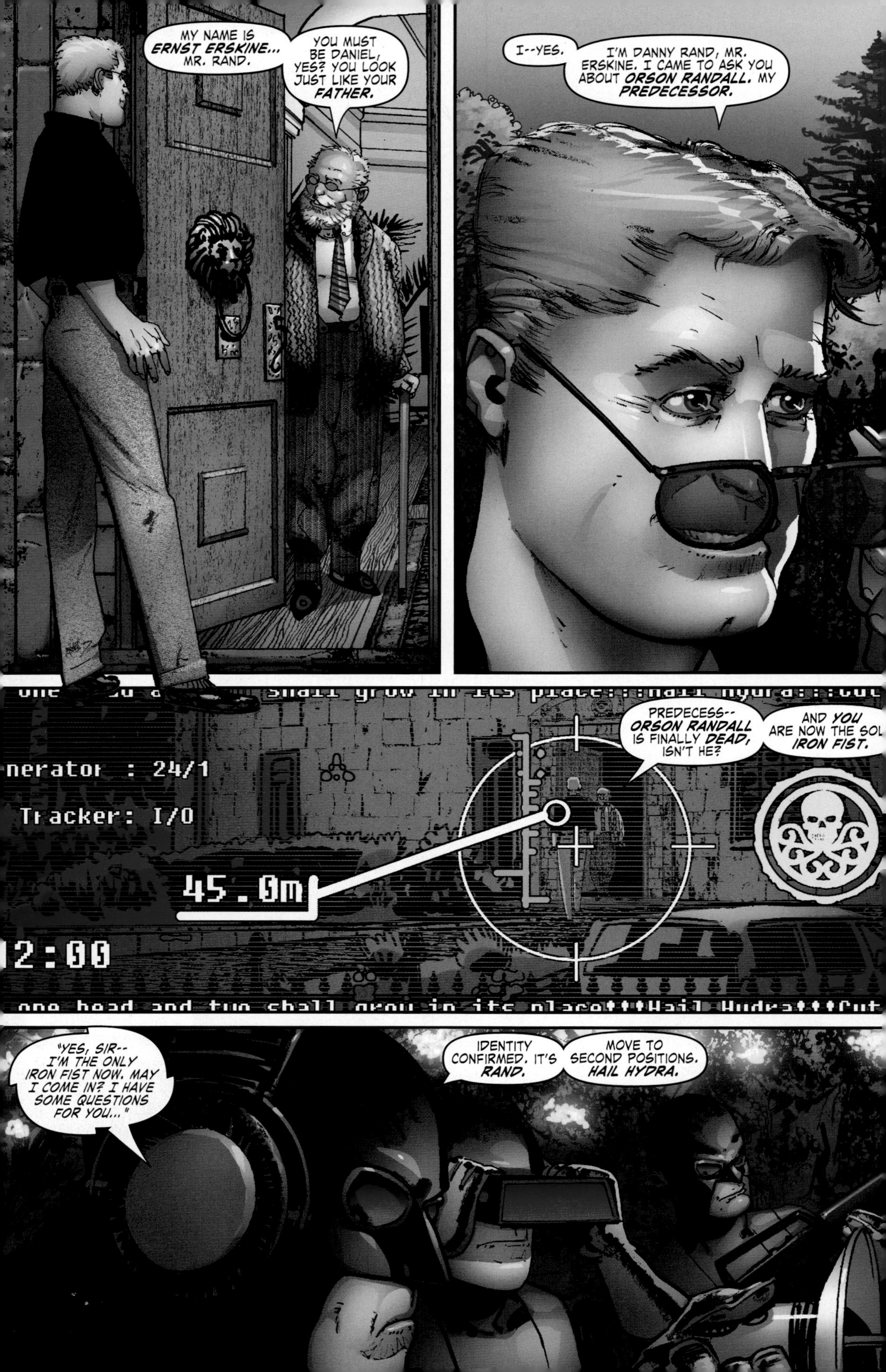

MY NAME IS ERNST ERSKINE... MR. RAND.
YOU MUST BE DANIEL, YES? YOU LOOK JUST LIKE YOUR FATHER.
I--YES.
I'M DANNY RAND, MR. ERSKINE. I CAME TO ASK YOU ABOUT ORSON RANDALL. MY PREDECESSOR.
nerator : 24/1
Tracker: I/O
45.0m
2:00
PREDECESS-- ORSON RANDALL IS FINALLY DEAD, ISN'T HE?
AND YOU ARE NOW THE SOL IRON FIST.
"YES, SIR-- I'M THE ONLY IRON FIST NOW. MAY I COME IN? I HAVE SOME QUESTIONS FOR YOU..."
IDENTITY CONFIRMED. IT'S RAND.
MOVE TO SECOND POSITIONS. HAIL HYDRA.

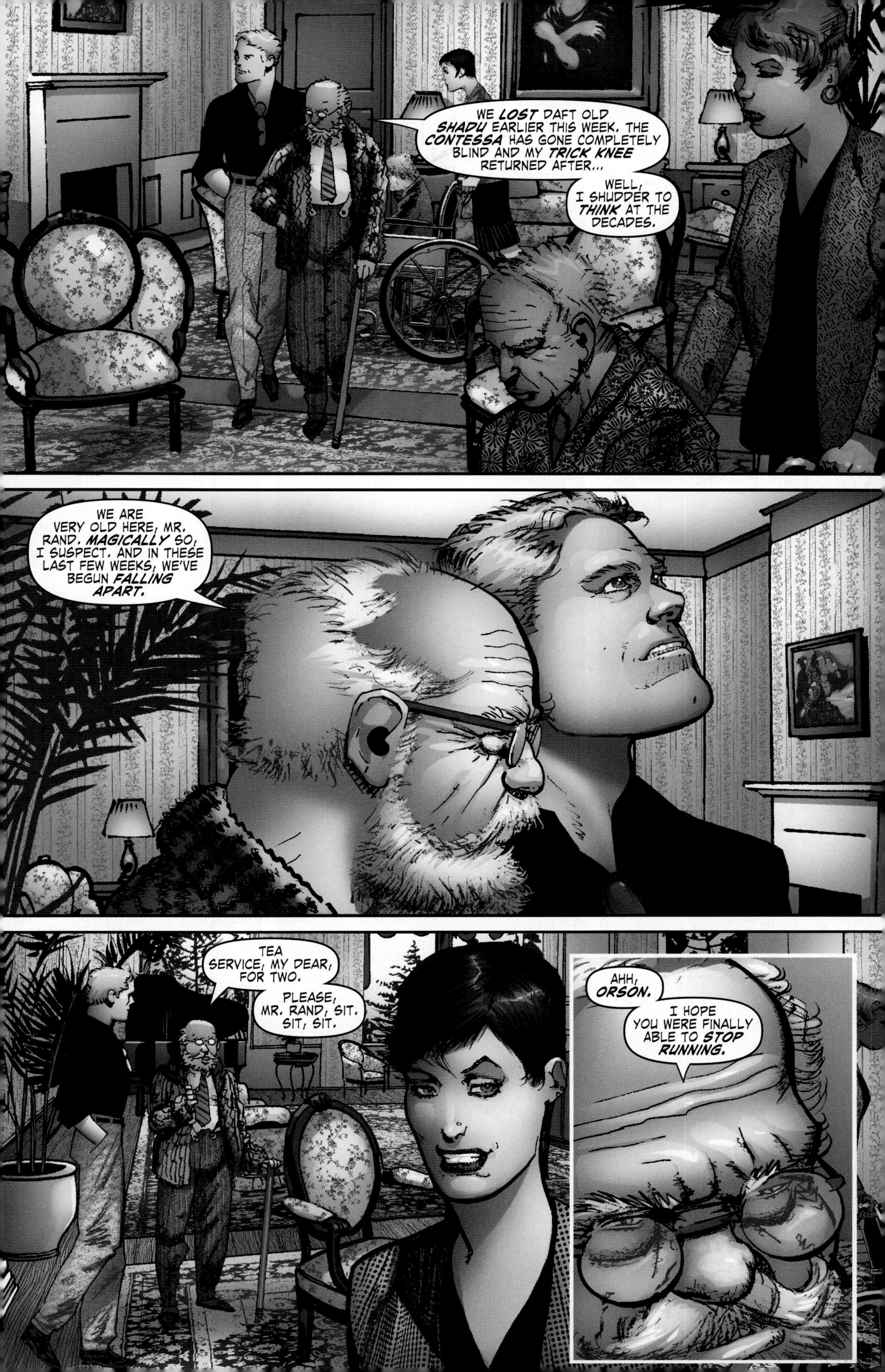
WE LOST DAFT OLD SHADU EARLIER THIS WEEK. THE CONTESSA HAS GONE COMPLETELY BLIND AND MY TRICK KNEE RETURNED AFTER...
WELL, I SHUDDER TO THINK AT THE DECADES.
WE ARE VERY OLD HERE, MR. RAND. MAGICALLY SO, I SUSPECT. AND IN THESE LAST FEW WEEKS, WE'VE BEGUN FALLING APART.
TEA SERVICE, MY DEAR, FOR TWO.
PLEASE, MR. RAND, SIT. SIT, SIT.
AHH, ORSON.
I HOPE YOU WERE FINALLY ABLE TO STOP RUNNING.

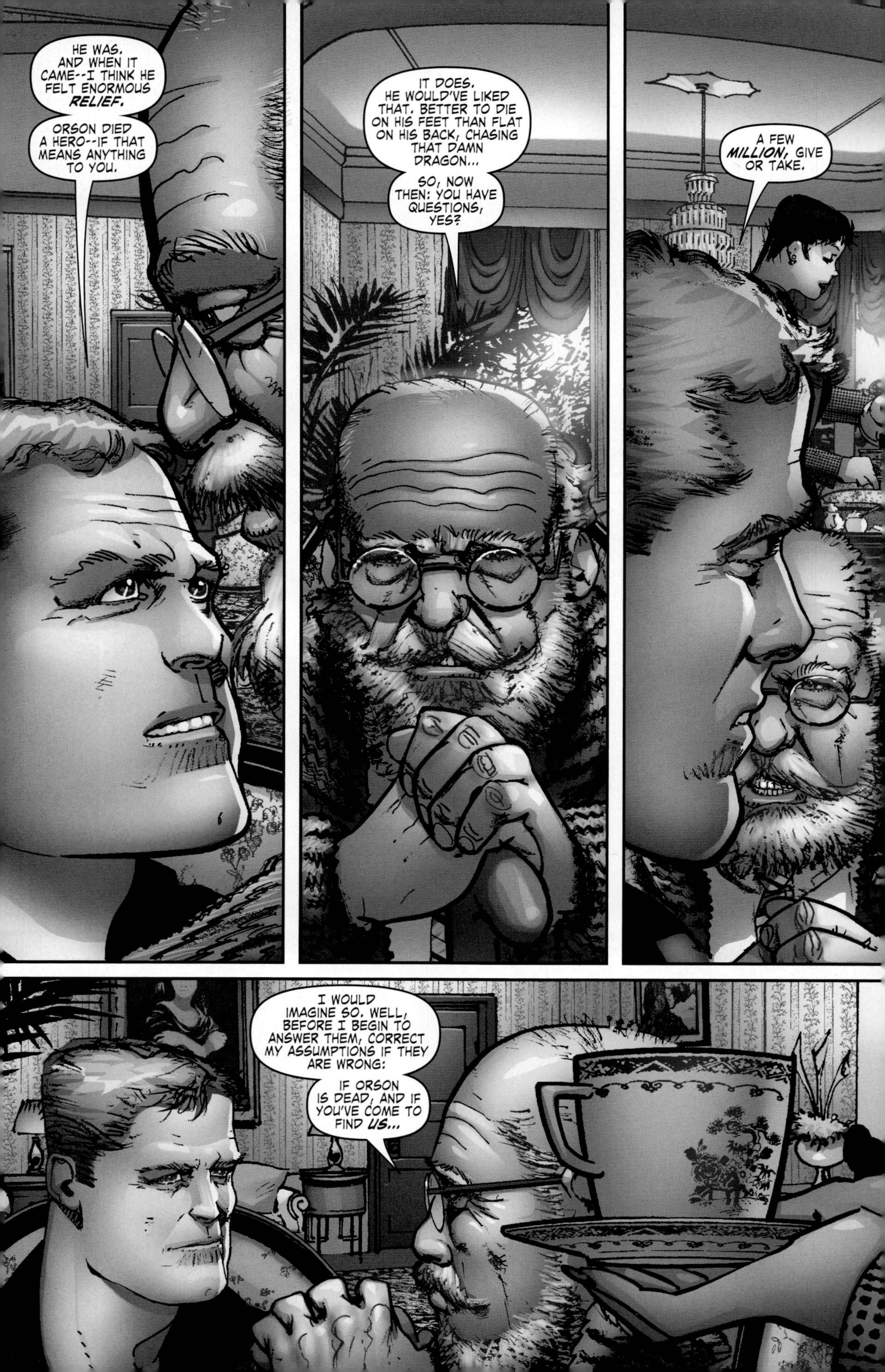
HE WAS. AND WHEN IT CAME--I THINK HE FELT ENORMOUS ***RELIEF.***
ORSON DIED A HERO--IF THAT MEANS ANYTHING TO YOU.
IT DOES. HE WOULD'VE LIKED THAT. BETTER TO DIE ON HIS FEET THAN FLAT ON HIS BACK, CHASING THAT DAMN DRAGON...
SO, NOW THEN: YOU HAVE QUESTIONS, YES?
A FEW ***MILLION,*** GIVE OR TAKE.
I WOULD IMAGINE SO. WELL, BEFORE I BEGIN TO ANSWER THEM, CORRECT MY ASSUMPTIONS IF THEY ARE WRONG:
IF ORSON IS DEAD, AND IF YOU'VE COME TO FIND ***US...***

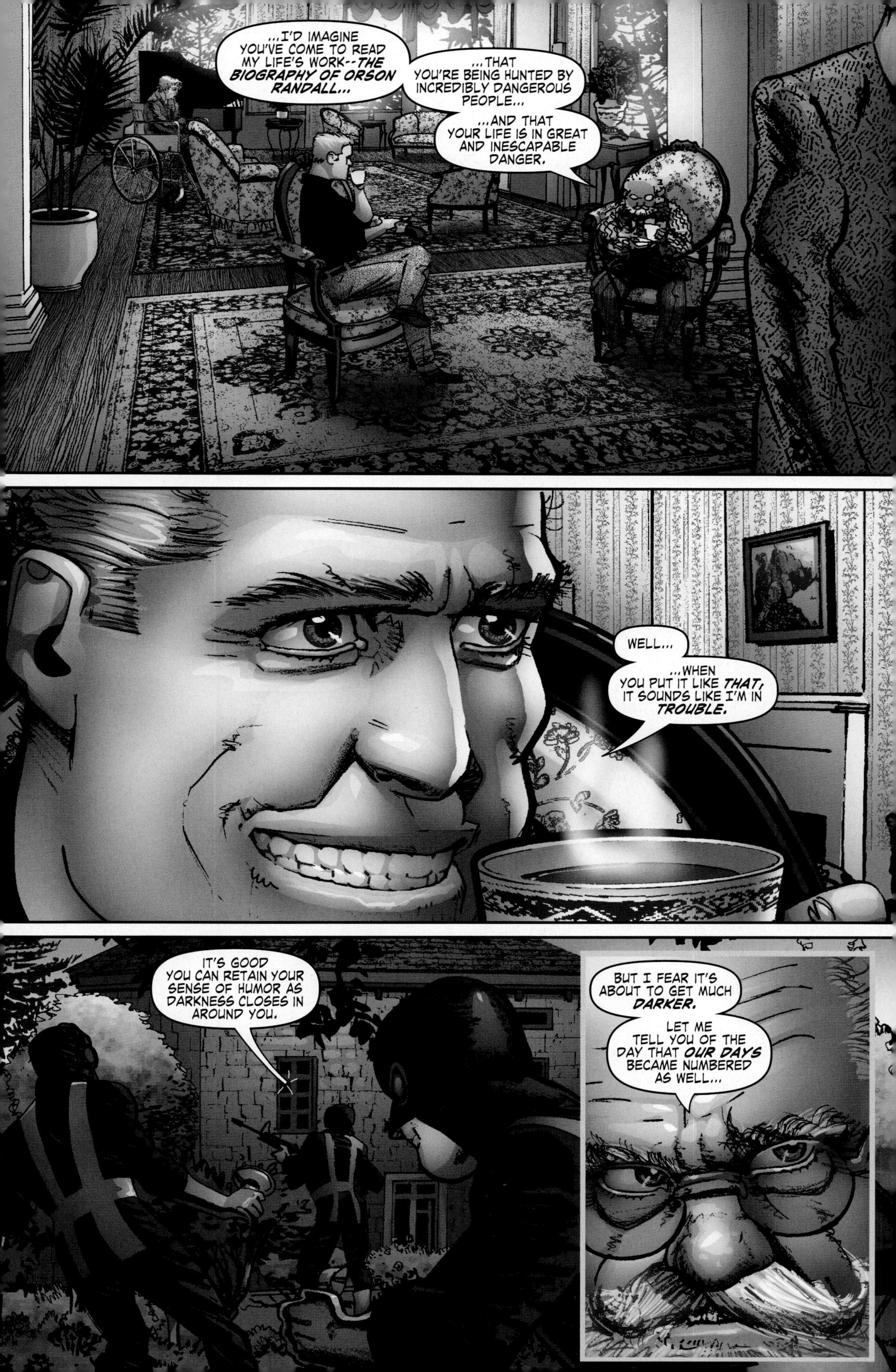
...I'D IMAGINE YOU'VE COME TO READ MY LIFE'S WORK--THE BIOGRAPHY OF ORSON RANDALL...
...THAT YOU'RE BEING HUNTED BY INCREDIBLY DANGEROUS PEOPLE...
...AND THAT YOUR LIFE IS IN GREAT AND INESCAPABLE DANGER.
WELL...
...WHEN YOU PUT IT LIKE THAT, IT SOUNDS LIKE I'M IN TROUBLE.
IT'S GOOD YOU CAN RETAIN YOUR SENSE OF HUMOR AS DARKNESS CLOSES IN AROUND YOU.
BUT I FEAR IT'S ABOUT TO GET MUCH DARKER.
LET ME TELL YOU OF THE DAY THAT OUR DAYS BECAME NUMBERED AS WELL...

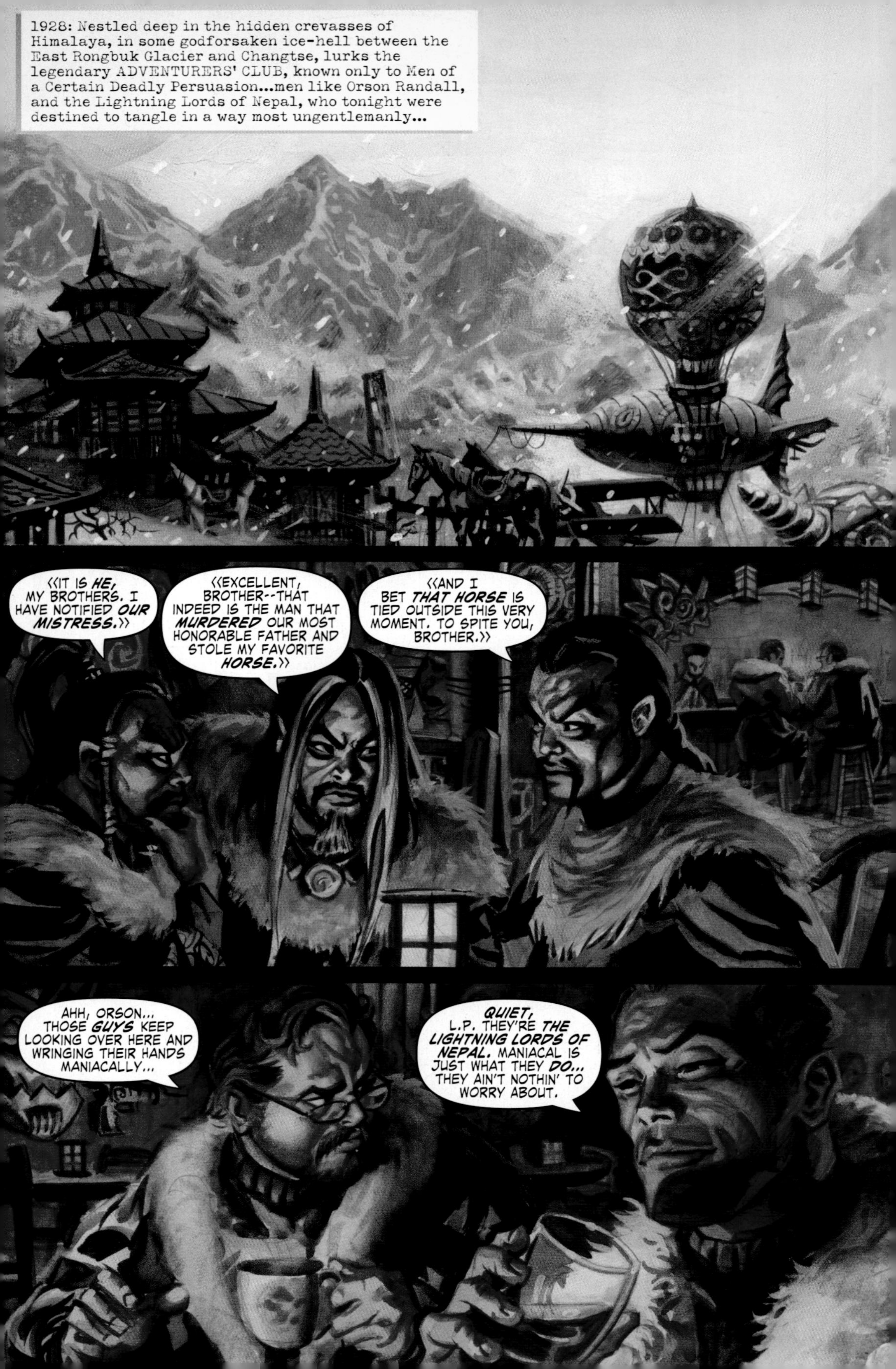
1928: Nestled deep in the hidden crevasses of Himalaya, in some godforsaken ice-hell between the East Rongbuk Glacier and Changtse, lurks the legendary ADVENTURERS' CLUB, known only to Men of a Certain Deadly Persuasion...men like Orson Randall, and the Lightning Lords of Nepal, who tonight were destined to tangle in a way most ungentlemanly...
<<IT IS HE, MY BROTHERS. I HAVE NOTIFIED OUR MISTRESS.>>
<<EXCELLENT, BROTHER--THAT INDEED IS THE MAN THAT MURDERED OUR MOST HONORABLE FATHER AND STOLE MY FAVORITE HORSE.>>
<<AND I BET THAT HORSE IS TIED OUTSIDE THIS VERY MOMENT. TO SPITE YOU, BROTHER.>>
AHH, ORSON... THOSE GUYS KEEP LOOKING OVER HERE AND WRINGING THEIR HANDS MANIACALLY...
QUIET, L.P. THEY'RE THE LIGHTNING LORDS OF NEPAL. MANIACAL IS JUST WHAT THEY DO... THEY AIN'T NOTHIN' TO WORRY ABOUT.

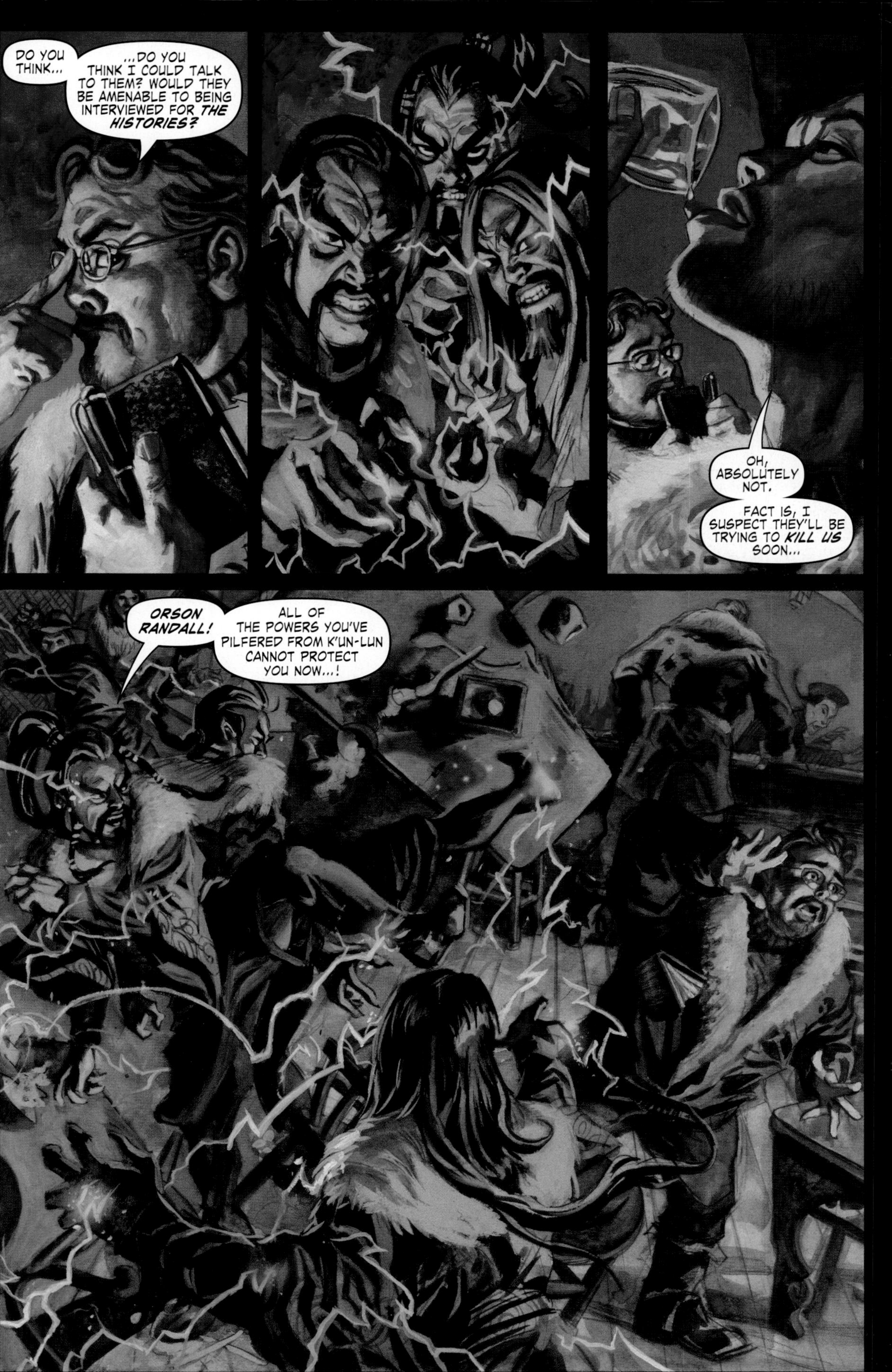
DO YOU THINK...
...DO YOU THINK I COULD TALK TO THEM? WOULD THEY BE AMENABLE TO BEING INTERVIEWED FOR *THE HISTORIES?*
OH, ABSOLUTELY NOT.
FACT IS, I SUSPECT THEY'LL BE TRYING TO *KILL US* SOON...
ORSON RANDALL!
ALL OF THE POWERS YOU'VE PILFERED FROM K'UN-LUN CANNOT PROTECT YOU NOW...!

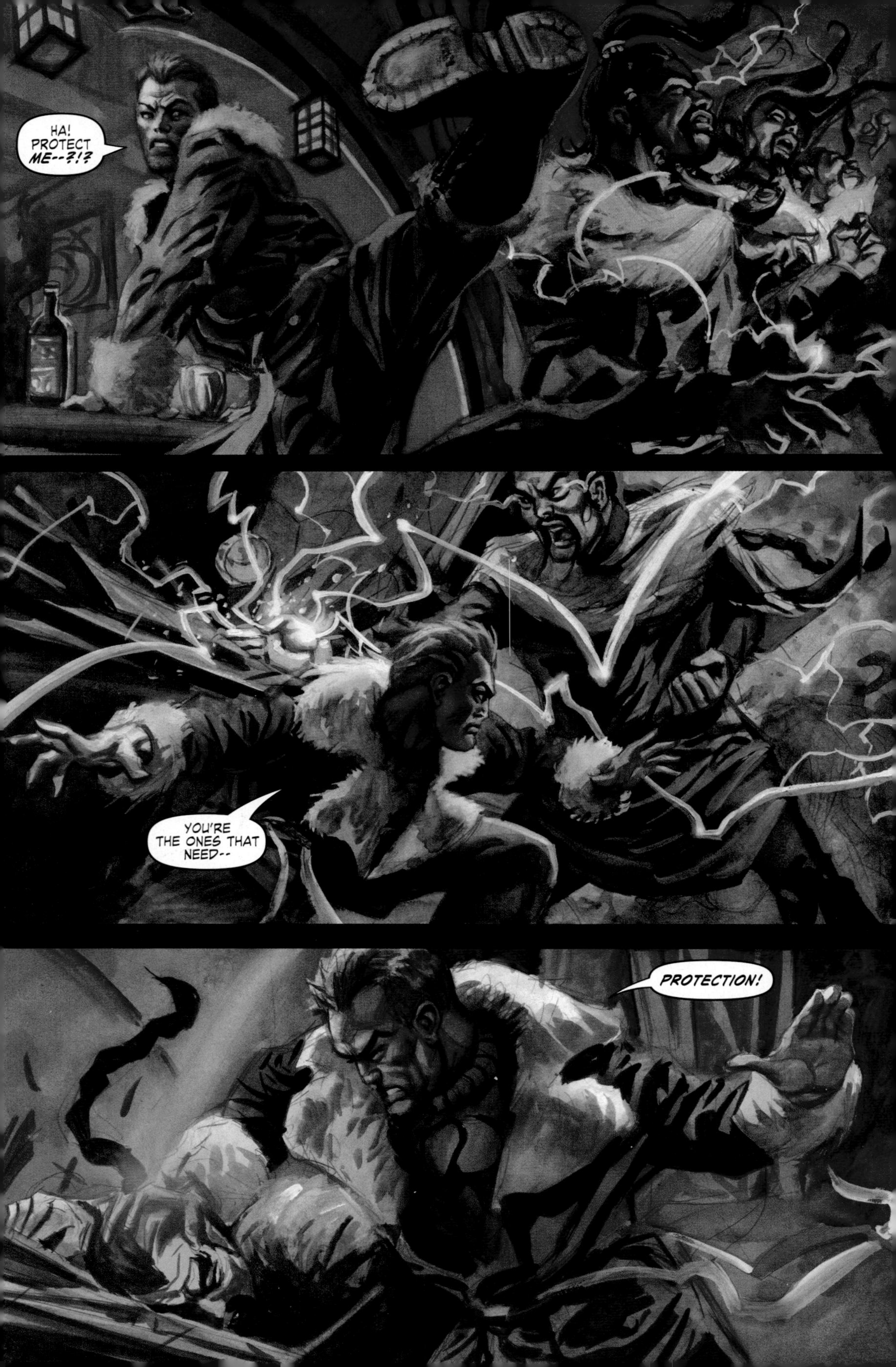
HA! PROTECT *ME*--?!?
YOU'RE THE ONES THAT NEED--
PROTECTION!

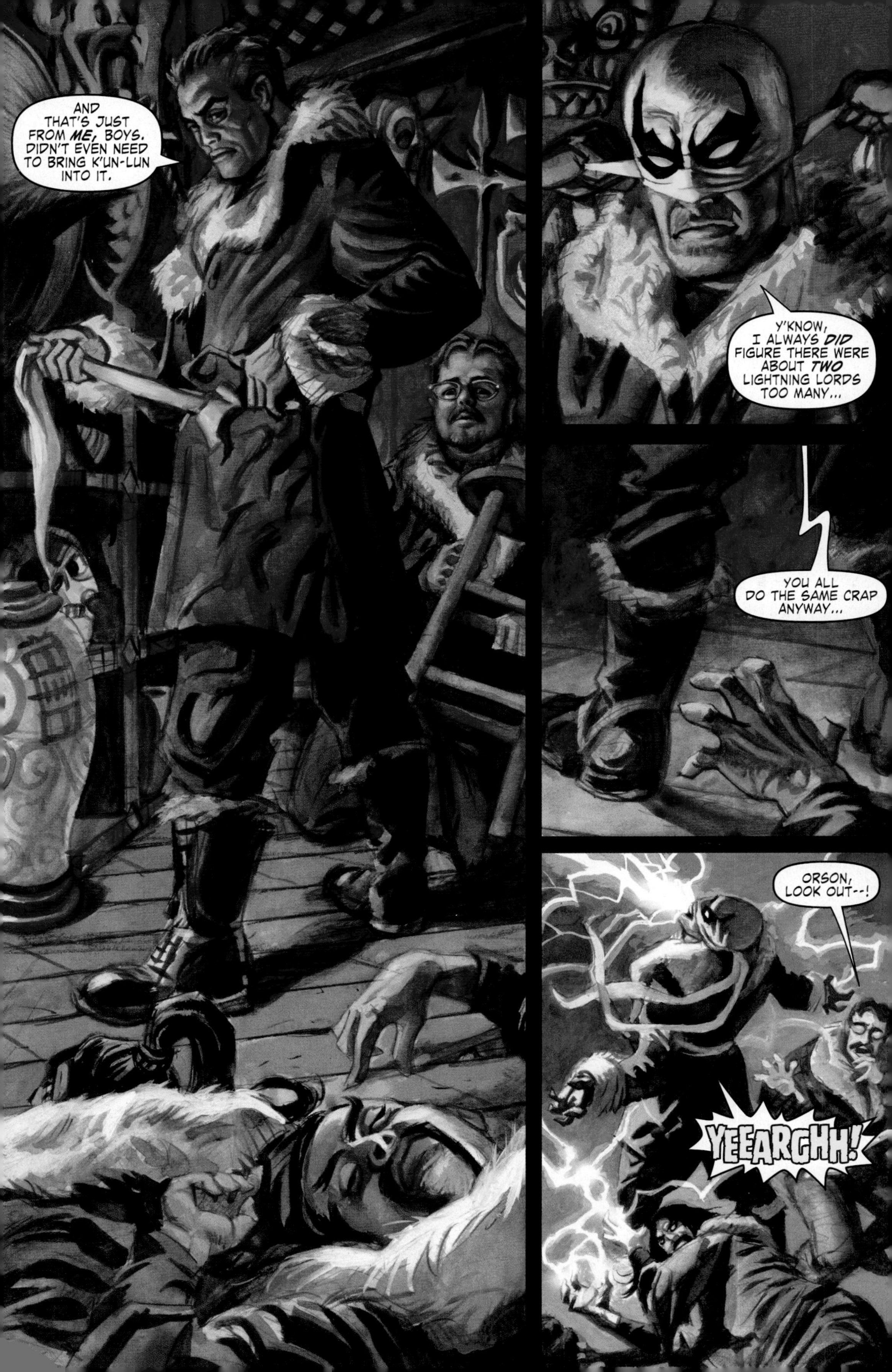
AND THAT'S JUST FROM ME, BOYS. DIDN'T EVEN NEED TO BRING K'UN-LUN INTO IT.
Y'KNOW, I ALWAYS DID FIGURE THERE WERE ABOUT TWO LIGHTNING LORDS TOO MANY...
YOU ALL DO THE SAME CRAP ANYWAY...
ORSON, LOOK OUT--!
YEEARGHH!

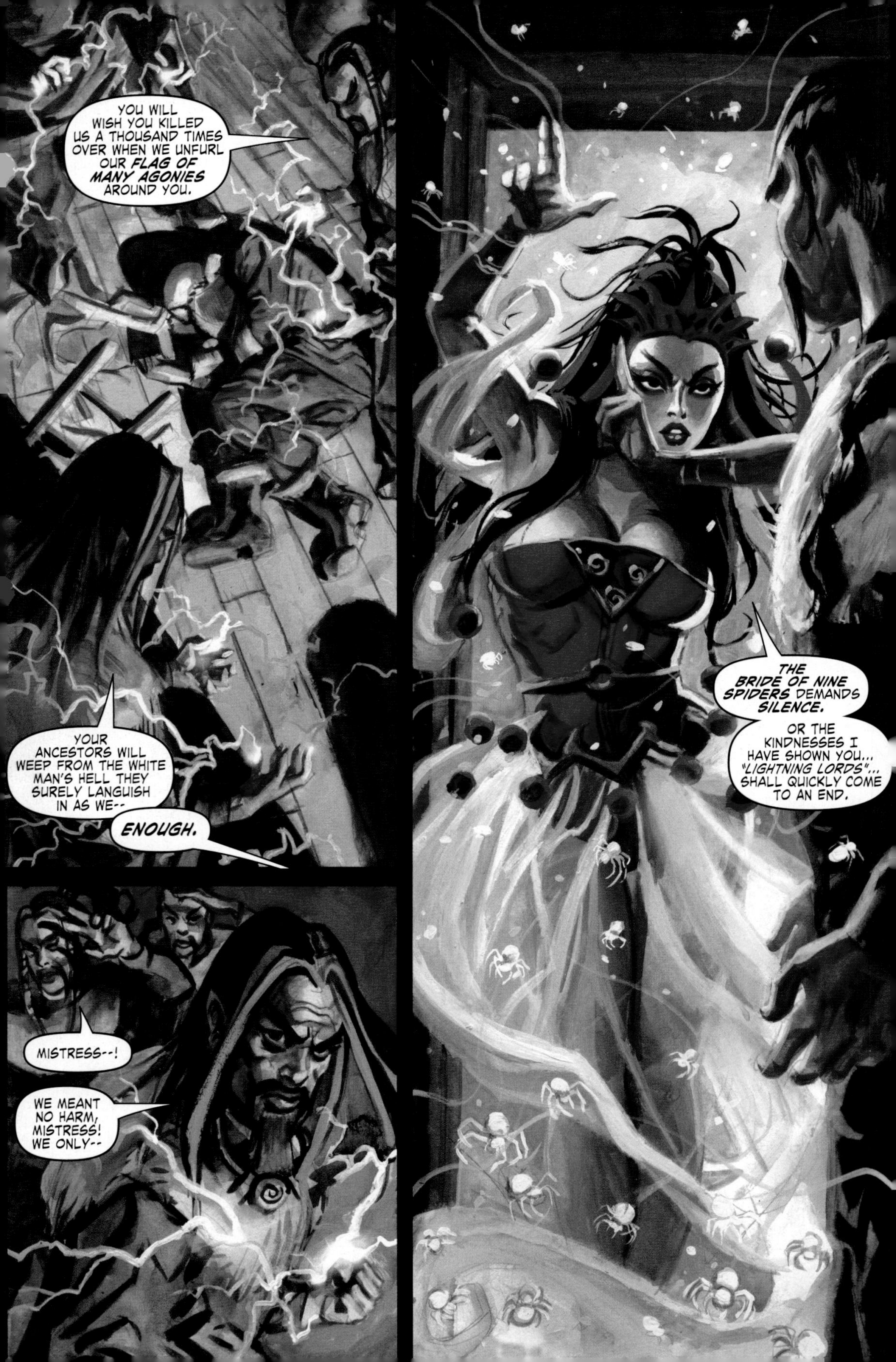
YOU WILL WISH YOU KILLED US A THOUSAND TIMES OVER WHEN WE UNFURL OUR FLAG OF MANY AGONIES AROUND YOU.
YOUR ANCESTORS WILL WEEP FROM THE WHITE MAN'S HELL THEY SURELY LANGUISH IN AS WE--
ENOUGH.
THE BRIDE OF NINE SPIDERS DEMANDS SILENCE.
OR THE KINDNESSES I HAVE SHOWN YOU... "LIGHTNING LORDS"... SHALL QUICKLY COME TO AN END.
MISTRESS--!
WE MEANT NO HARM, MISTRESS! WE ONLY--

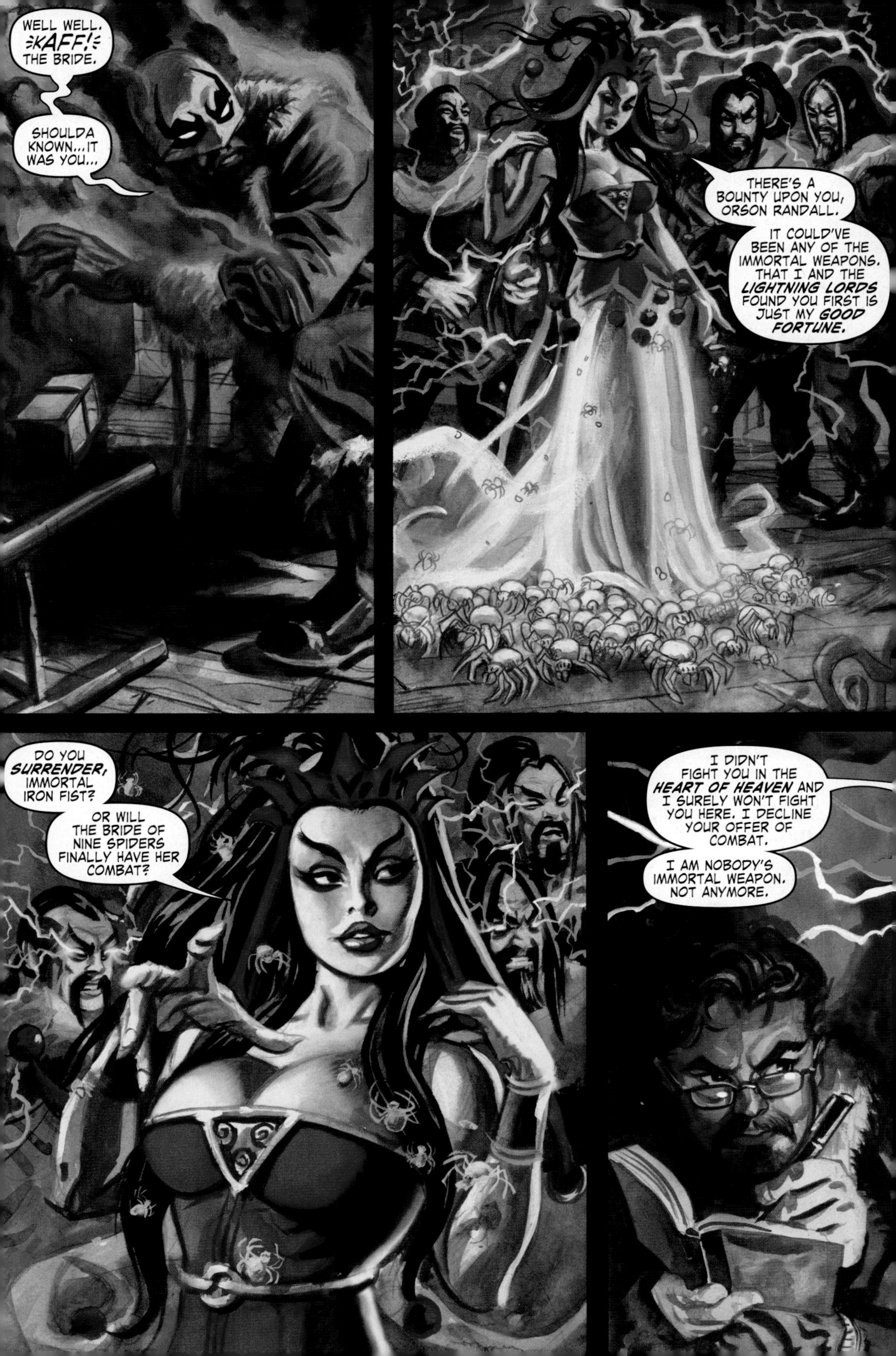
WELL WELL. *KAFF!* THE BRIDE.
SHOULDA KNOWN...IT WAS YOU...
THERE'S A BOUNTY UPON YOU, ORSON RANDALL.
IT COULD'VE BEEN ANY OF THE IMMORTAL WEAPONS. THAT I AND THE ***LIGHTNING LORDS*** FOUND YOU FIRST IS JUST MY ***GOOD FORTUNE.***
DO YOU ***SURRENDER,*** IMMORTAL IRON FIST?
OR WILL THE BRIDE OF NINE SPIDERS FINALLY HAVE HER COMBAT?
I DIDN'T FIGHT YOU IN THE ***HEART OF HEAVEN*** AND I SURELY WON'T FIGHT YOU HERE. I DECLINE YOUR OFFER OF COMBAT.
I AM NOBODY'S IMMORTAL WEAPON. NOT ANYMORE.

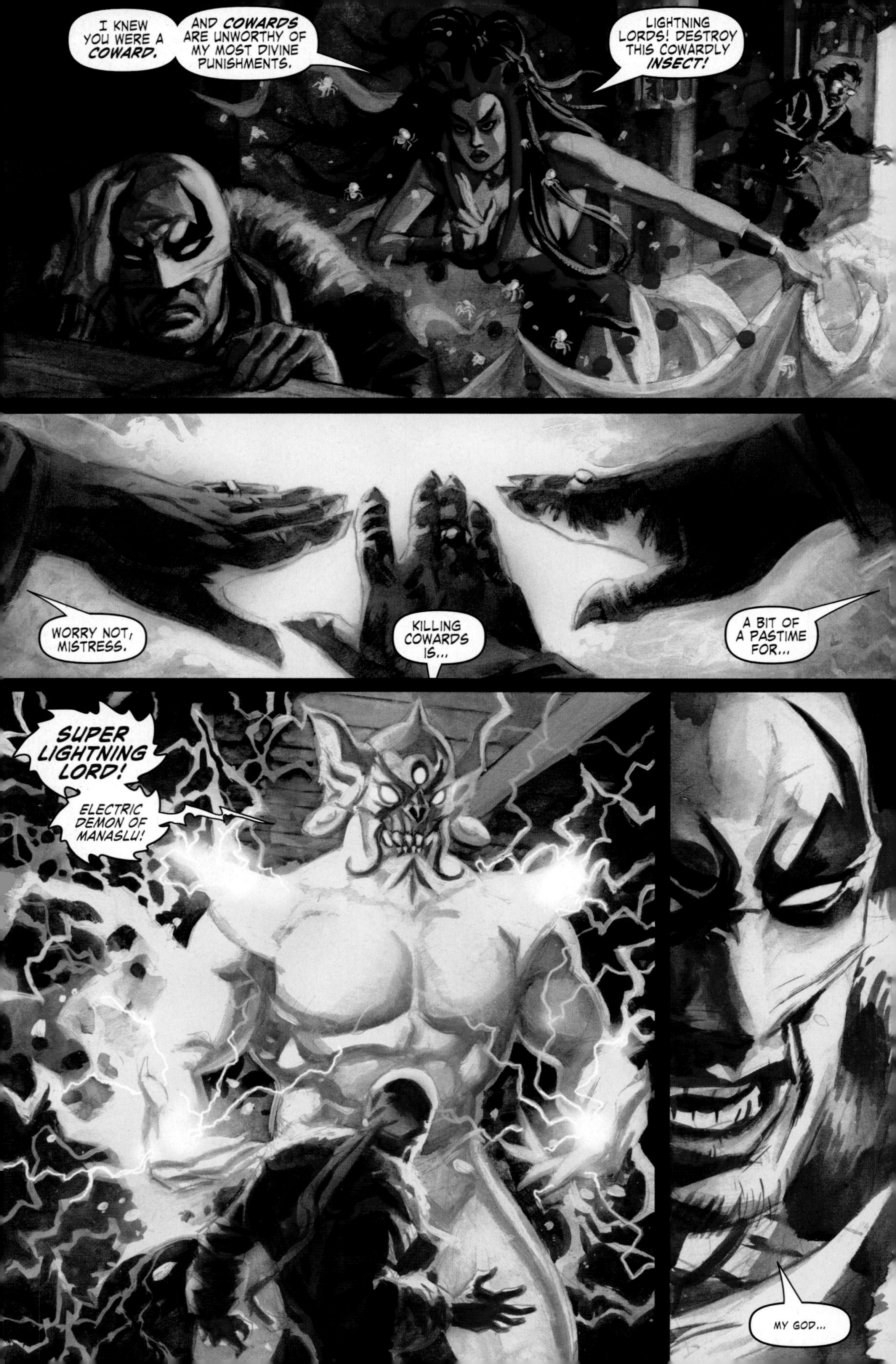
I KNEW YOU WERE A COWARD.
AND COWARDS ARE UNWORTHY OF MY MOST DIVINE PUNISHMENTS.
LIGHTNING LORDS! DESTROY THIS COWARDLY INSECT!
WORRY NOT, MISTRESS.
KILLING COWARDS IS...
A BIT OF A PASTIME FOR...
SUPER LIGHTNING LORD!
ELECTRIC DEMON OF MANASLU!
MY GOD...

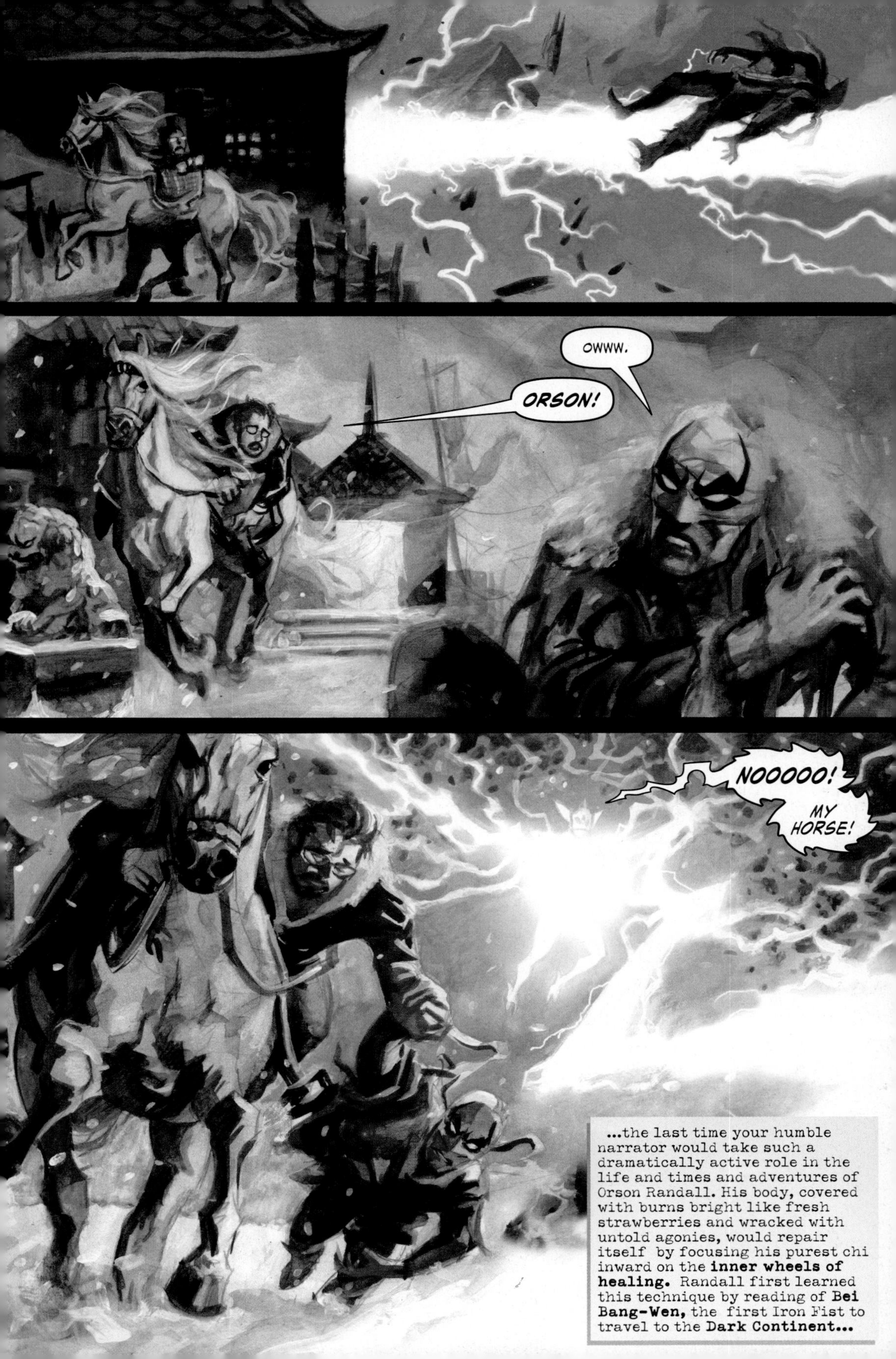
OWWW.
ORSON!
NOOOOO!
MY HORSE!
...the last time your humble narrator would take such a dramatically active role in the life and times and adventures of Orson Randall. His body, covered with burns bright like fresh strawberries and wracked with untold agonies, would repair itself by focusing his purest chi inward on the **inner wheels of healing.** Randall first learned this technique by reading of **Bei Bang-Wen,** the first Iron Fist to travel to the **Dark Continent...**

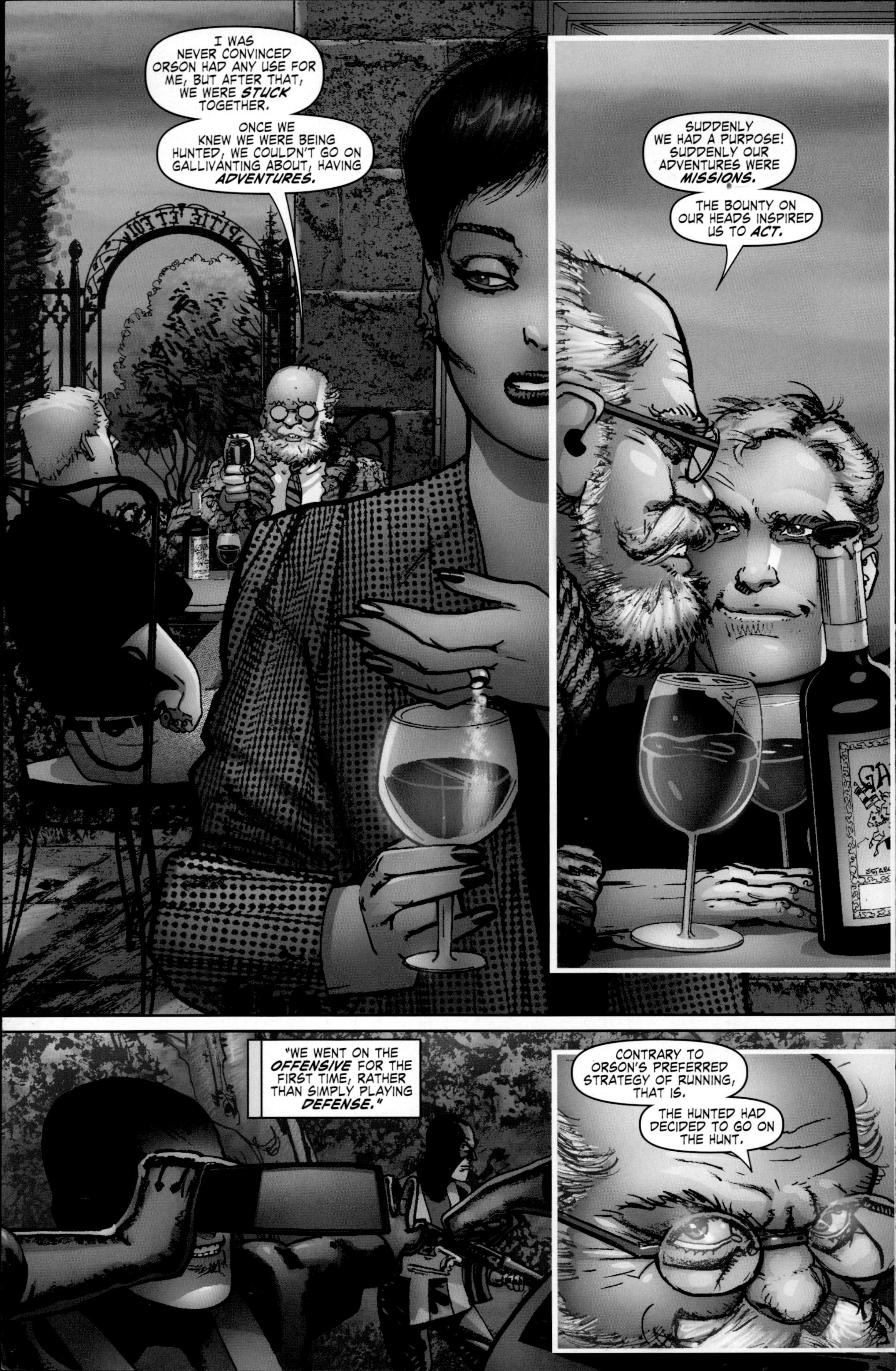

I WAS NEVER CONVINCED ORSON HAD ANY USE FOR ME, BUT AFTER THAT, WE WERE STUCK TOGETHER.
ONCE WE KNEW WE WERE BEING HUNTED, WE COULDN'T GO ON GALLIVANTING ABOUT, HAVING ADVENTURES.
SUDDENLY WE HAD A PURPOSE! SUDDENLY OUR ADVENTURES WERE MISSIONS.
THE BOUNTY ON OUR HEADS INSPIRED US TO ACT.
"WE WENT ON THE OFFENSIVE FOR THE FIRST TIME, RATHER THAN SIMPLY PLAYING DEFENSE."
CONTRARY TO ORSON'S PREFERRED STRATEGY OF RUNNING, THAT IS.
THE HUNTED HAD DECIDED TO GO ON THE HUNT.

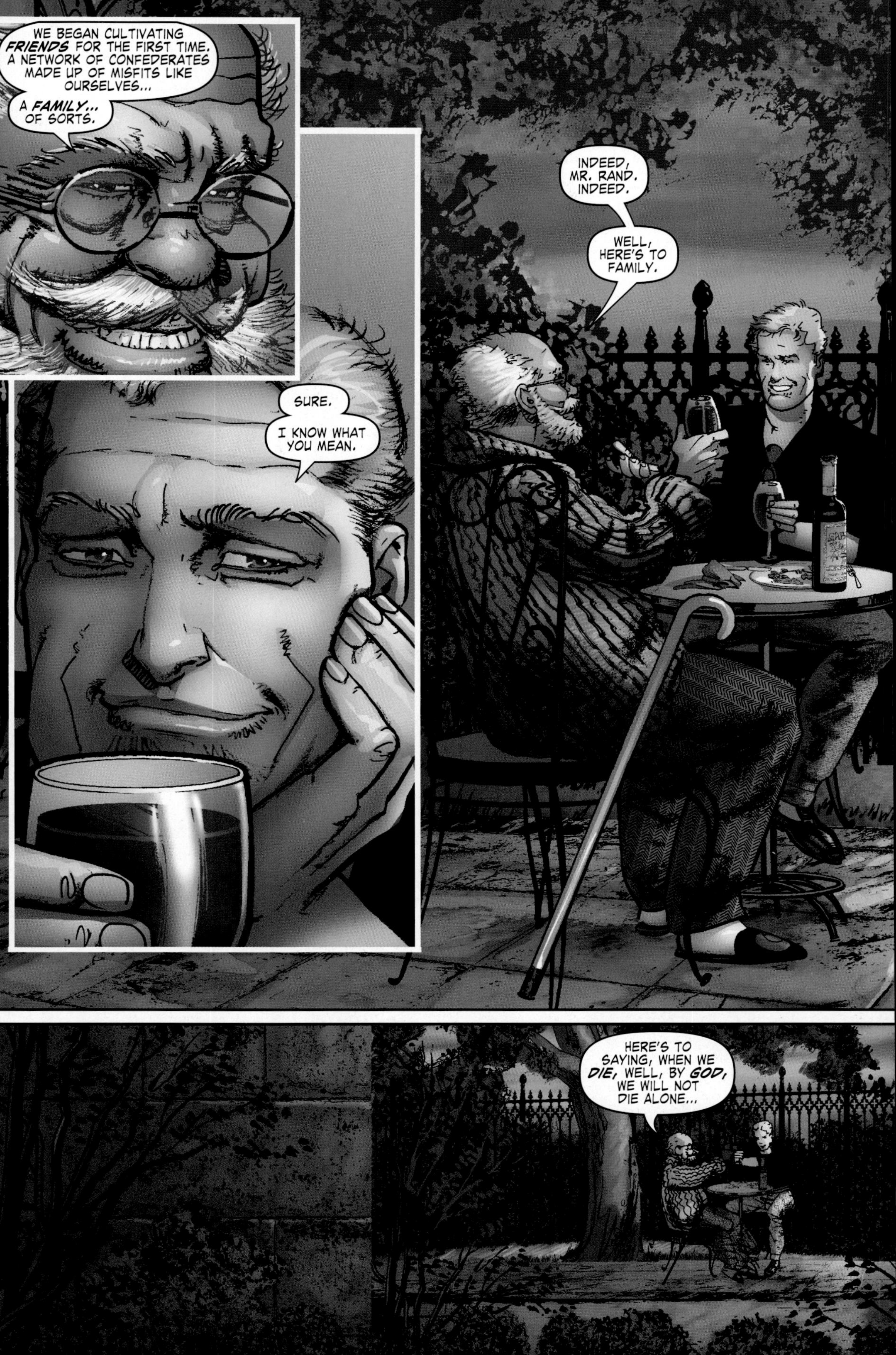
WE BEGAN CULTIVATING FRIENDS FOR THE FIRST TIME. A NETWORK OF CONFEDERATES MADE UP OF MISFITS LIKE OURSELVES...
A FAMILY... OF SORTS.
SURE.
I KNOW WHAT YOU MEAN.
INDEED, MR. RAND. INDEED.
WELL, HERE'S TO FAMILY.
HERE'S TO SAYING, WHEN WE DIE, WELL, BY GOD, WE WILL NOT DIE ALONE...

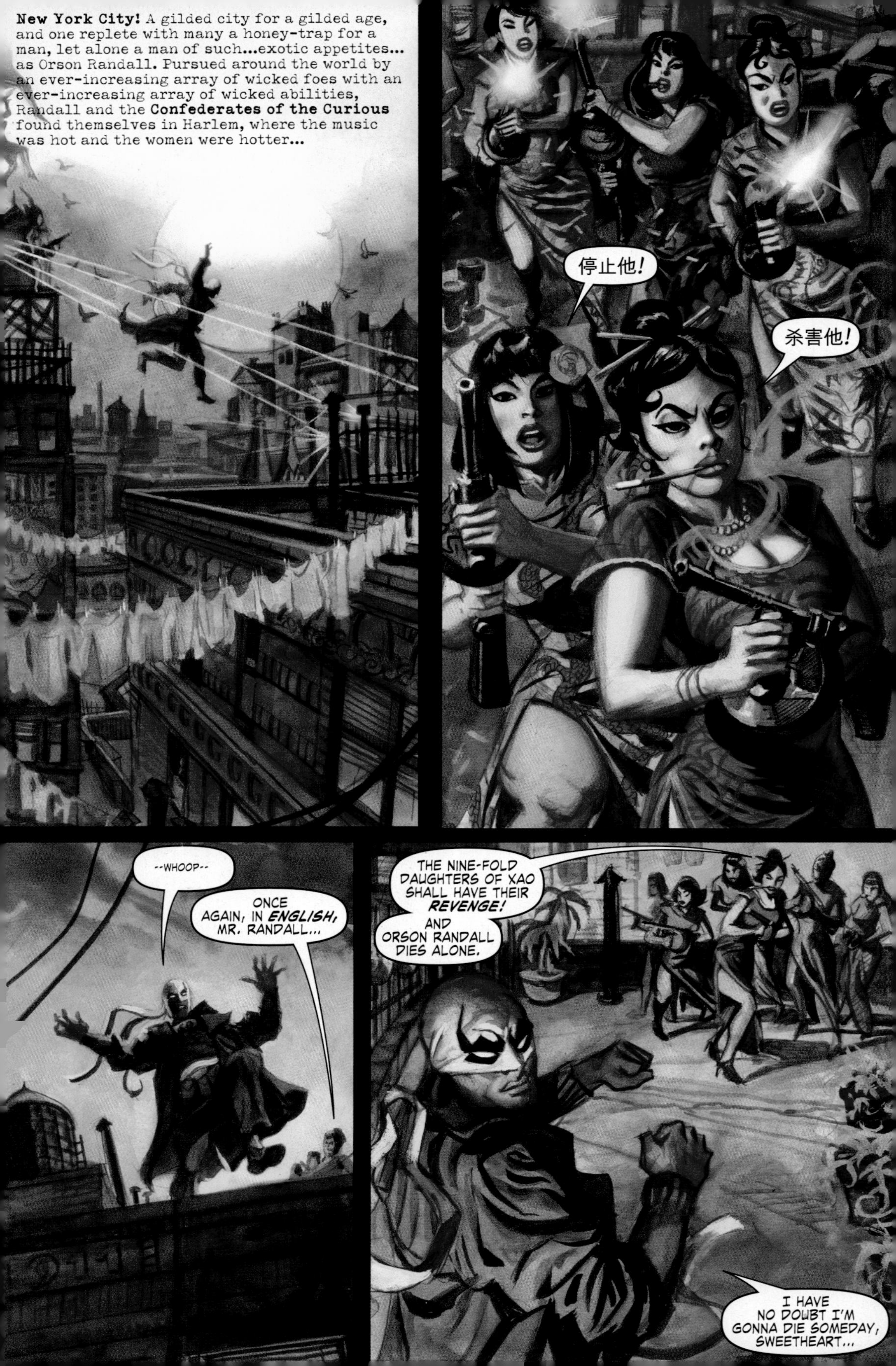
New York City! A gilded city for a gilded age, and one replete with many a honey-trap for a man, let alone a man of such...exotic appetites... as Orson Randall. Pursued around the world by an ever-increasing array of wicked foes with an ever-increasing array of wicked abilities, Randall and the **Confederates of the Curious** found themselves in Harlem, where the music was hot and the women were hotter...
停止他!
杀害他!
--WHOOP--
ONCE AGAIN, IN *ENGLISH,* MR. RANDALL...
THE NINE-FOLD DAUGHTERS OF XAO SHALL HAVE THEIR ***REVENGE!***
AND ORSON RANDALL DIES ALONE.
I HAVE NO DOUBT I'M GONNA DIE SOMEDAY, SWEETHEART...

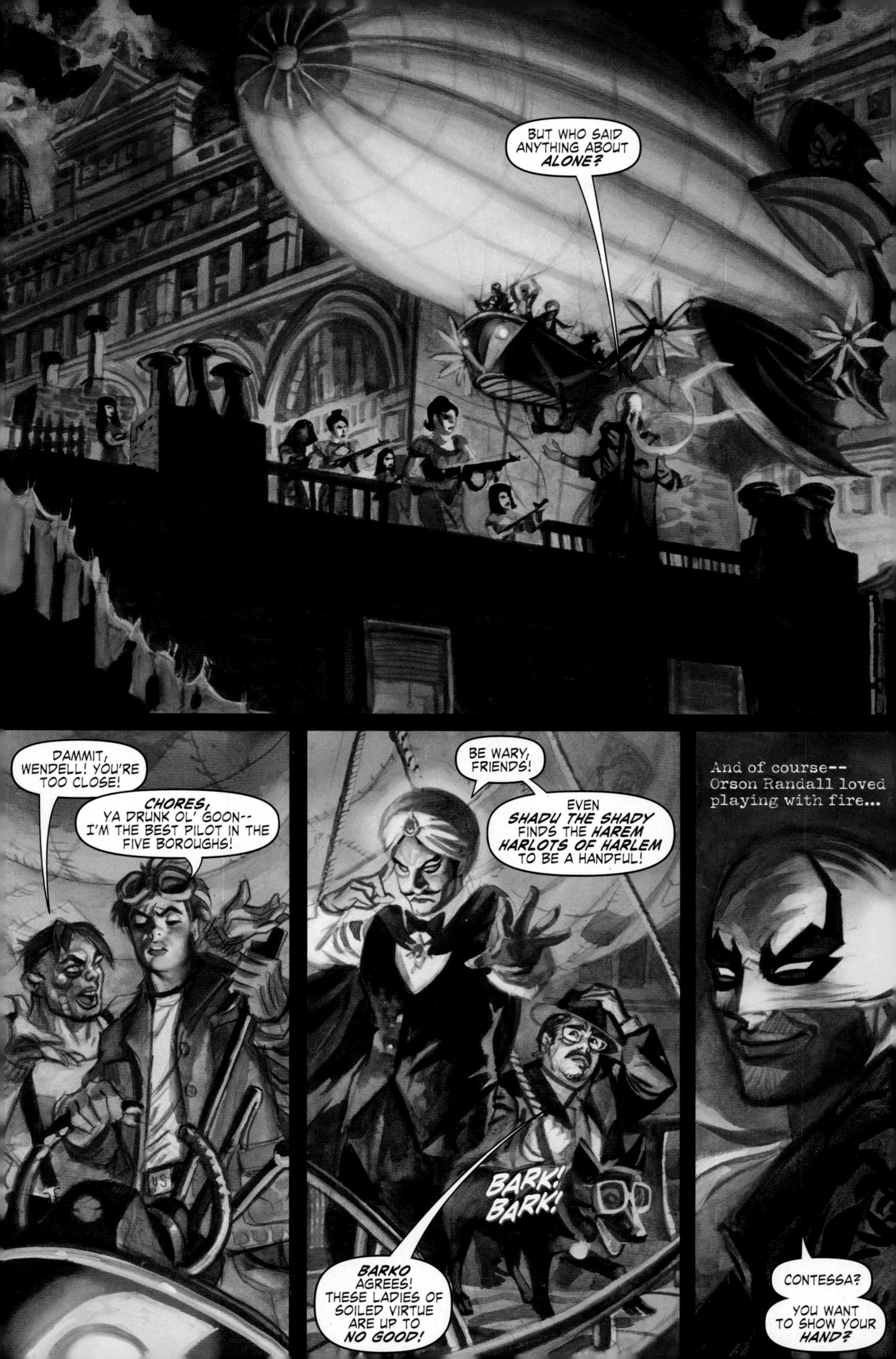
BUT WHO SAID ANYTHING ABOUT ALONE?
DAMMIT, WENDELL! YOU'RE TOO CLOSE!
CHORES, YA DRUNK OL' GOON-- I'M THE BEST PILOT IN THE FIVE BOROUGHS!
BE WARY, FRIENDS!
EVEN SHADU THE SHADY FINDS THE HAREM HARLOTS OF HARLEM TO BE A HANDFUL!
BARK! BARK!
BARKO AGREES! THESE LADIES OF SOILED VIRTUE ARE UP TO NO GOOD!
And of course-- Orson Randall loved playing with fire...
CONTESSA?
YOU WANT TO SHOW YOUR HAND?

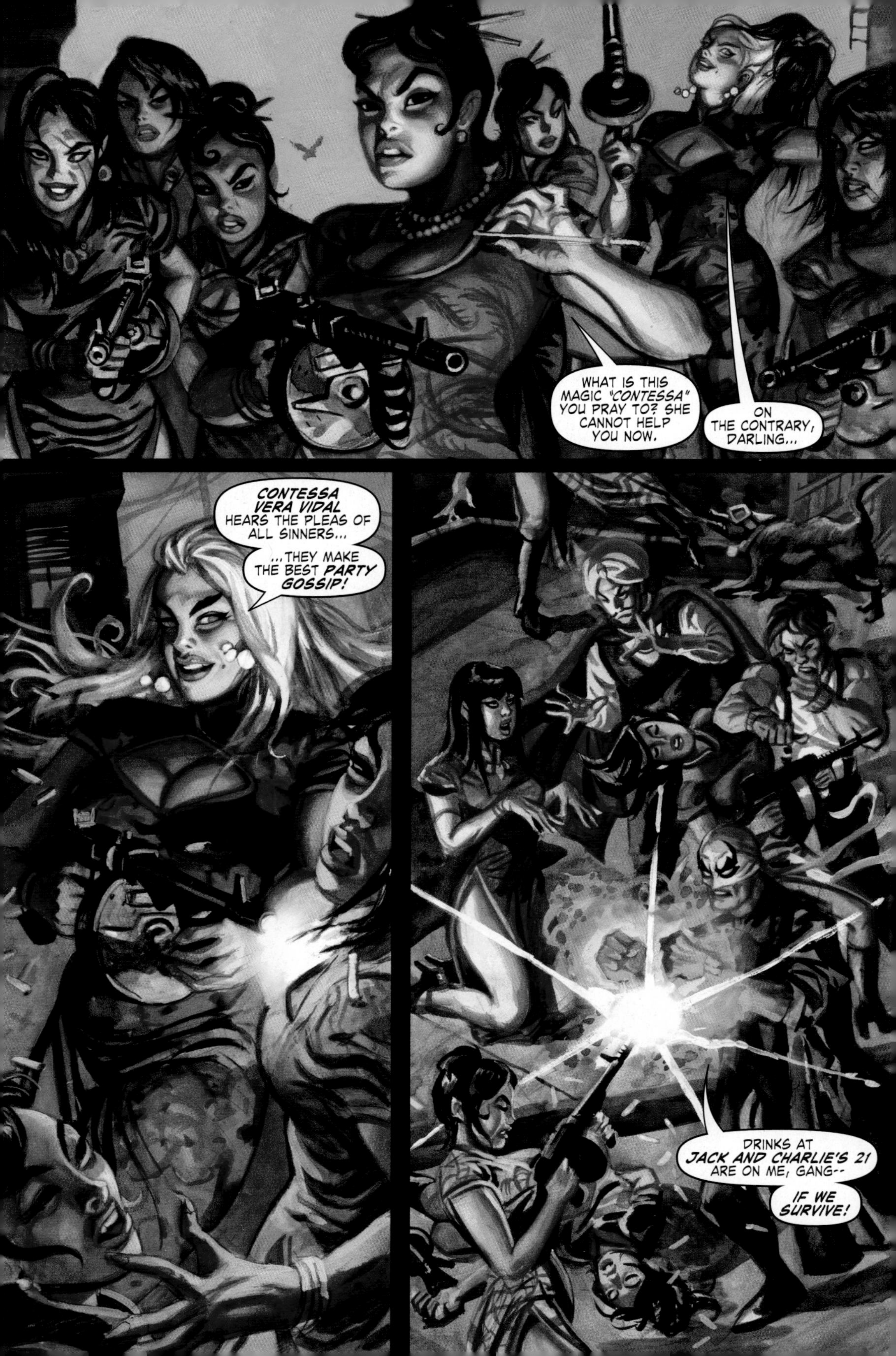
WHAT IS THIS MAGIC "CONTESSA" YOU PRAY TO? SHE CANNOT HELP YOU NOW.
ON THE CONTRARY, DARLING...
CONTESSA VERA VIDAL HEARS THE PLEAS OF ALL SINNERS...
...THEY MAKE THE BEST PARTY GOSSIP!
DRINKS AT JACK AND CHARLIE'S 21 ARE ON ME, GANG--
IF WE SURVIVE!

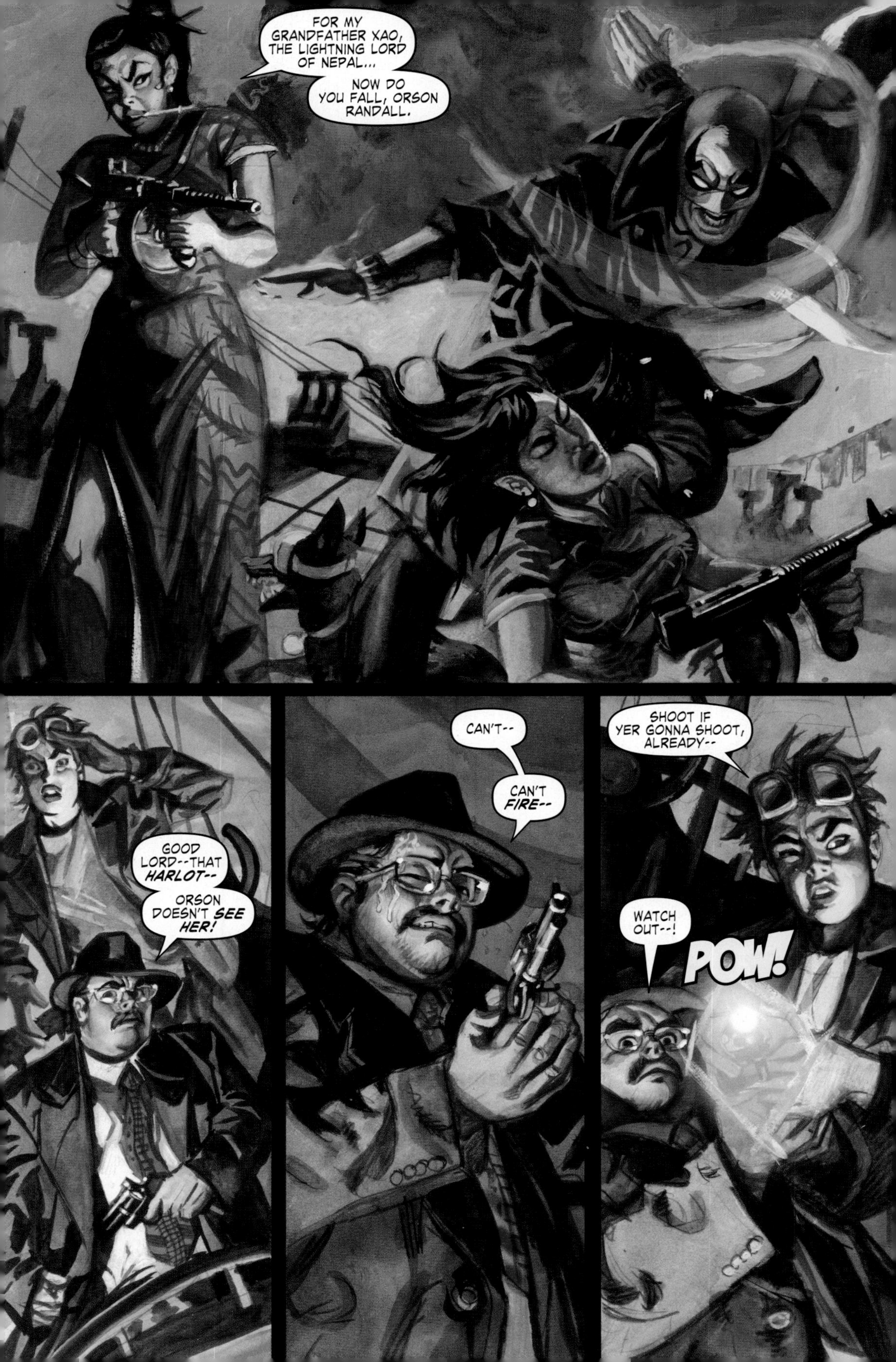
FOR MY GRANDFATHER XAO, THE LIGHTNING LORD OF NEPAL...
NOW DO YOU FALL, ORSON RANDALL.
GOOD LORD--THAT HARLOT--
ORSON DOESN'T SEE HER!
CAN'T--
CAN'T FIRE--
SHOOT IF YER GONNA SHOOT, ALREADY--
WATCH OUT--!
POW!

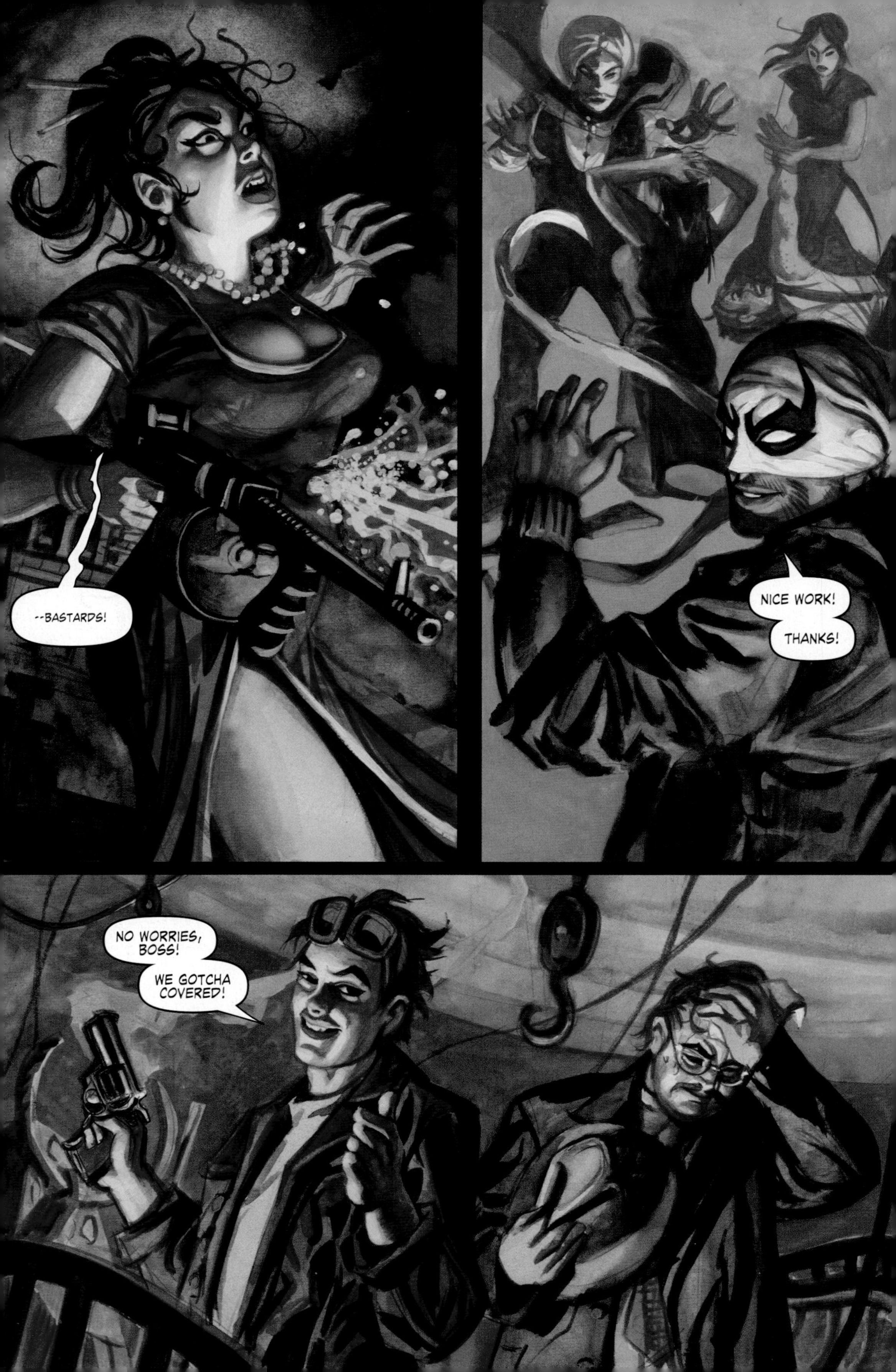
--BASTARDS!
NICE WORK!
THANKS!
NO WORRIES, BOSS!
WE GOTCHA COVERED!

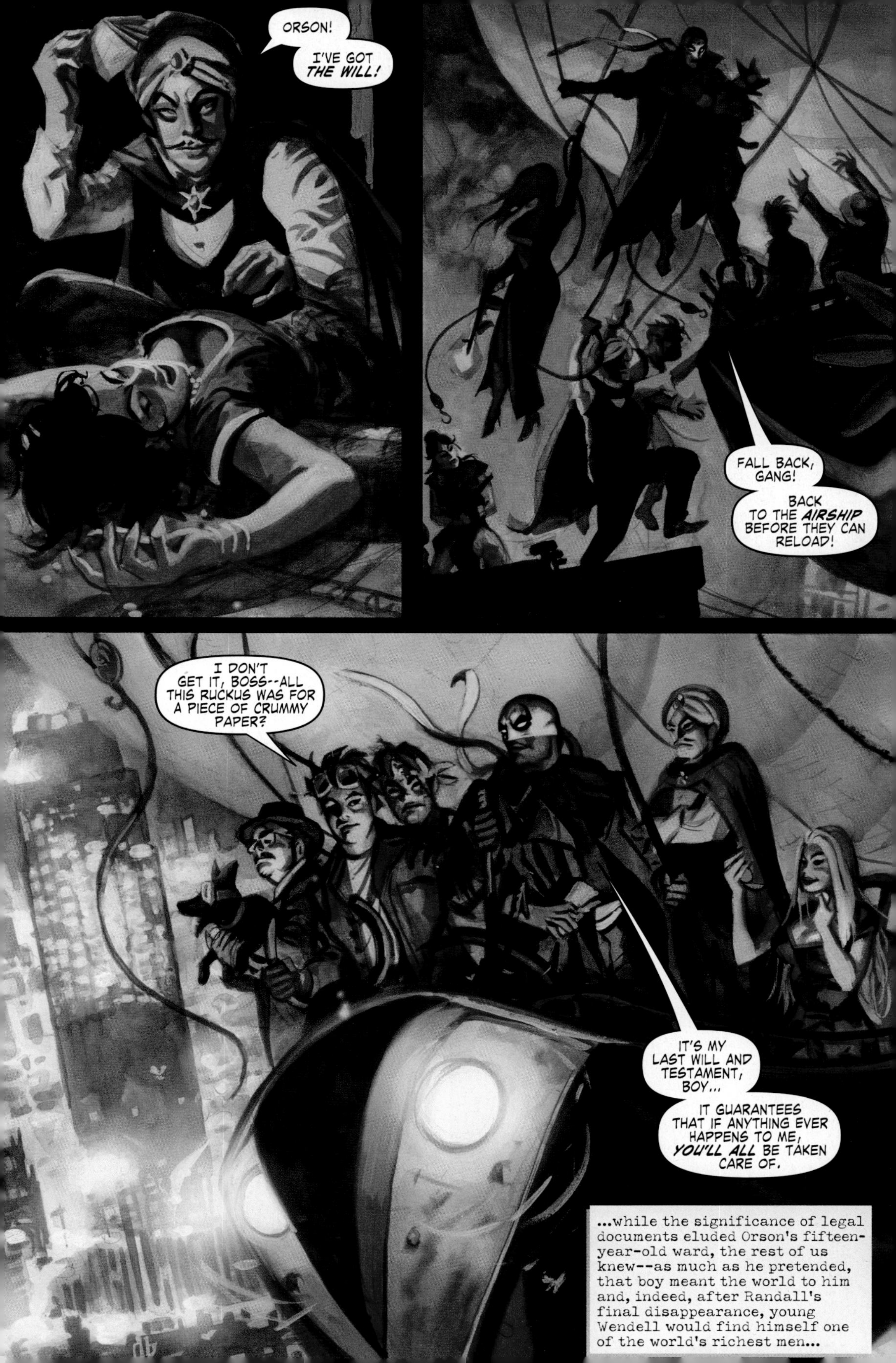

ORSON!
I'VE GOT THE WILL!
FALL BACK, GANG!
BACK TO THE AIRSHIP BEFORE THEY CAN RELOAD!
I DON'T GET IT, BOSS--ALL THIS RUCKUS WAS FOR A PIECE OF CRUMMY PAPER?
IT'S MY LAST WILL AND TESTAMENT, BOY...
IT GUARANTEES THAT IF ANYTHING EVER HAPPENS TO ME, YOU'LL ALL BE TAKEN CARE OF.
...while the significance of legal documents eluded Orson's fifteen-year-old ward, the rest of us knew--as much as he pretended, that boy meant the world to him and, indeed, after Randall's final disappearance, young Wendell would find himself one of the world's richest men...

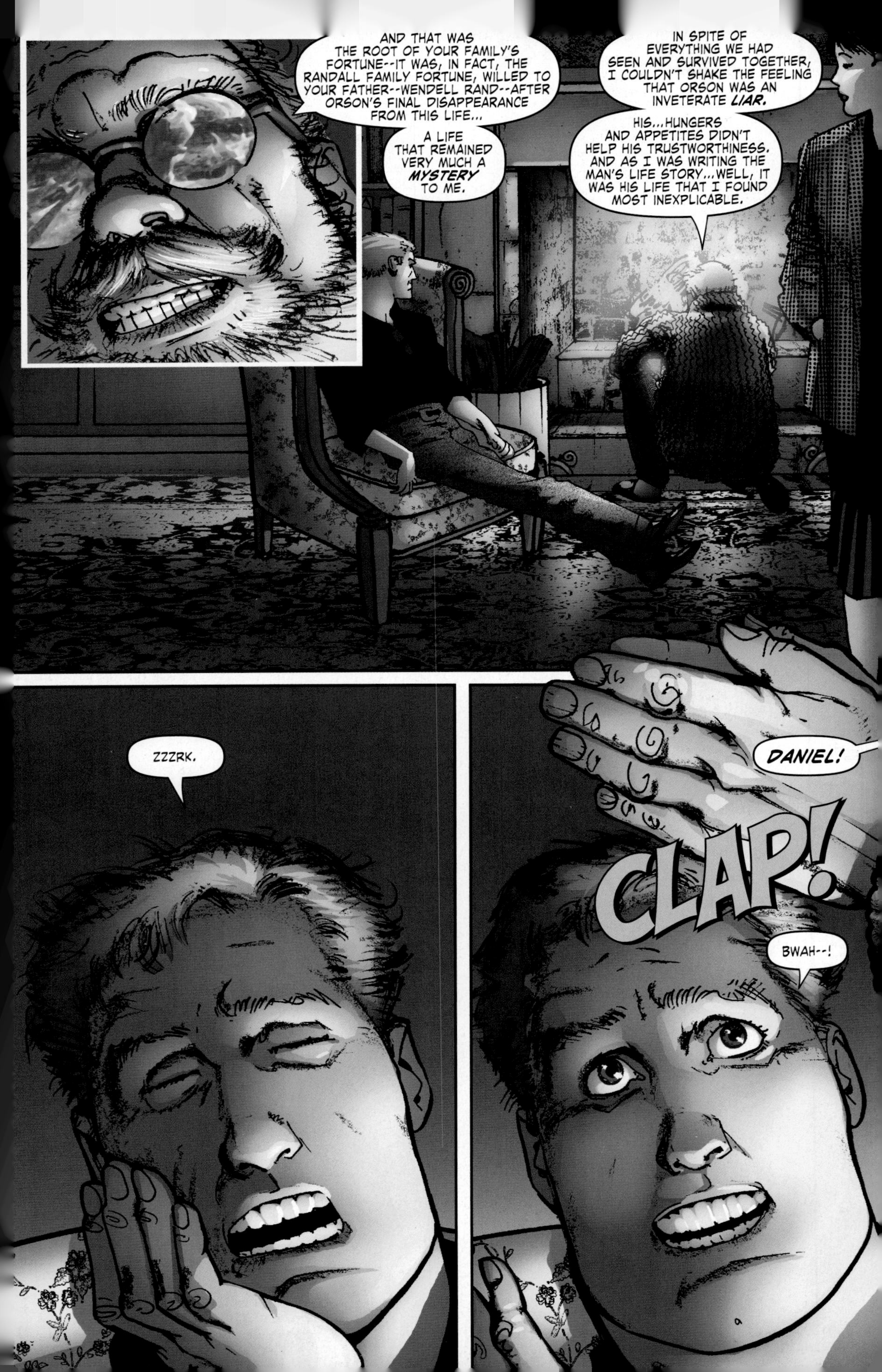
AND THAT WAS THE ROOT OF YOUR FAMILY'S FORTUNE--IT WAS, IN FACT, THE RANDALL FAMILY FORTUNE, WILLED TO YOUR FATHER--WENDELL RAND--AFTER ORSON'S FINAL DISAPPEARANCE FROM THIS LIFE...
A LIFE THAT REMAINED VERY MUCH A *MYSTERY* TO ME.
IN SPITE OF EVERYTHING WE HAD SEEN AND SURVIVED TOGETHER, I COULDN'T SHAKE THE FEELING THAT ORSON WAS AN INVETERATE *LIAR.*
HIS...HUNGERS AND APPETITES DIDN'T HELP HIS TRUSTWORTHINESS. AND AS I WAS WRITING THE MAN'S LIFE STORY...WELL, IT WAS HIS LIFE THAT I FOUND MOST INEXPLICABLE.
ZZZRK.
DANIEL!
CLAP!
BWAH--!

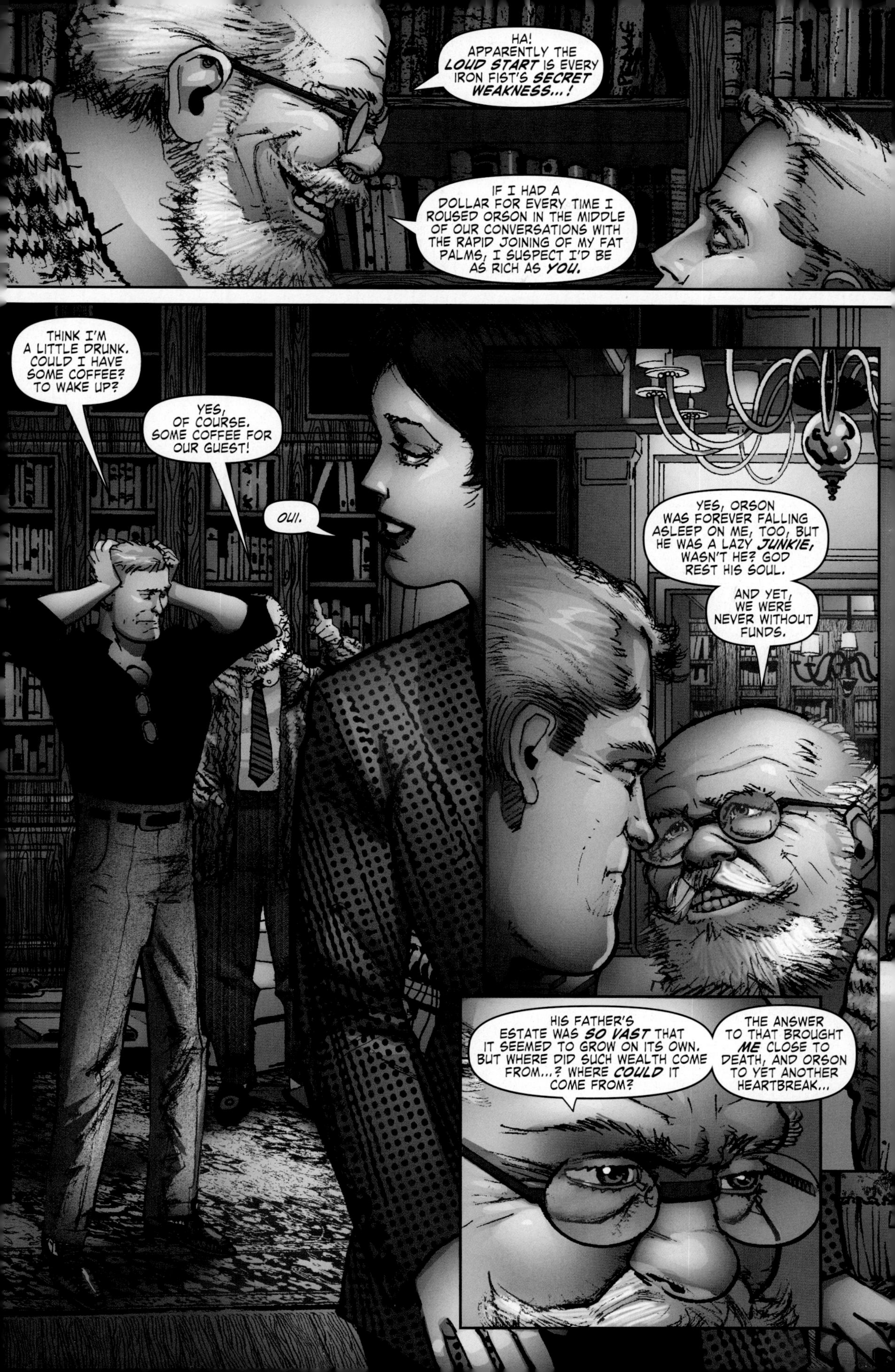
HA! APPARENTLY THE LOUD START IS EVERY IRON FIST'S SECRET WEAKNESS...!
IF I HAD A DOLLAR FOR EVERY TIME I ROUSED ORSON IN THE MIDDLE OF OUR CONVERSATIONS WITH THE RAPID JOINING OF MY FAT PALMS, I SUSPECT I'D BE AS RICH AS YOU.
THINK I'M A LITTLE DRUNK. COULD I HAVE SOME COFFEE? TO WAKE UP?
YES, OF COURSE. SOME COFFEE FOR OUR GUEST!
OUI.
YES, ORSON WAS FOREVER FALLING ASLEEP ON ME, TOO, BUT HE WAS A LAZY JUNKIE, WASN'T HE? GOD REST HIS SOUL.
AND YET, WE WERE NEVER WITHOUT FUNDS.
HIS FATHER'S ESTATE WAS SO VAST THAT IT SEEMED TO GROW ON ITS OWN. BUT WHERE DID SUCH WEALTH COME FROM...? WHERE COULD IT COME FROM?
THE ANSWER TO THAT BROUGHT ME CLOSE TO DEATH, AND ORSON TO YET ANOTHER HEARTBREAK...

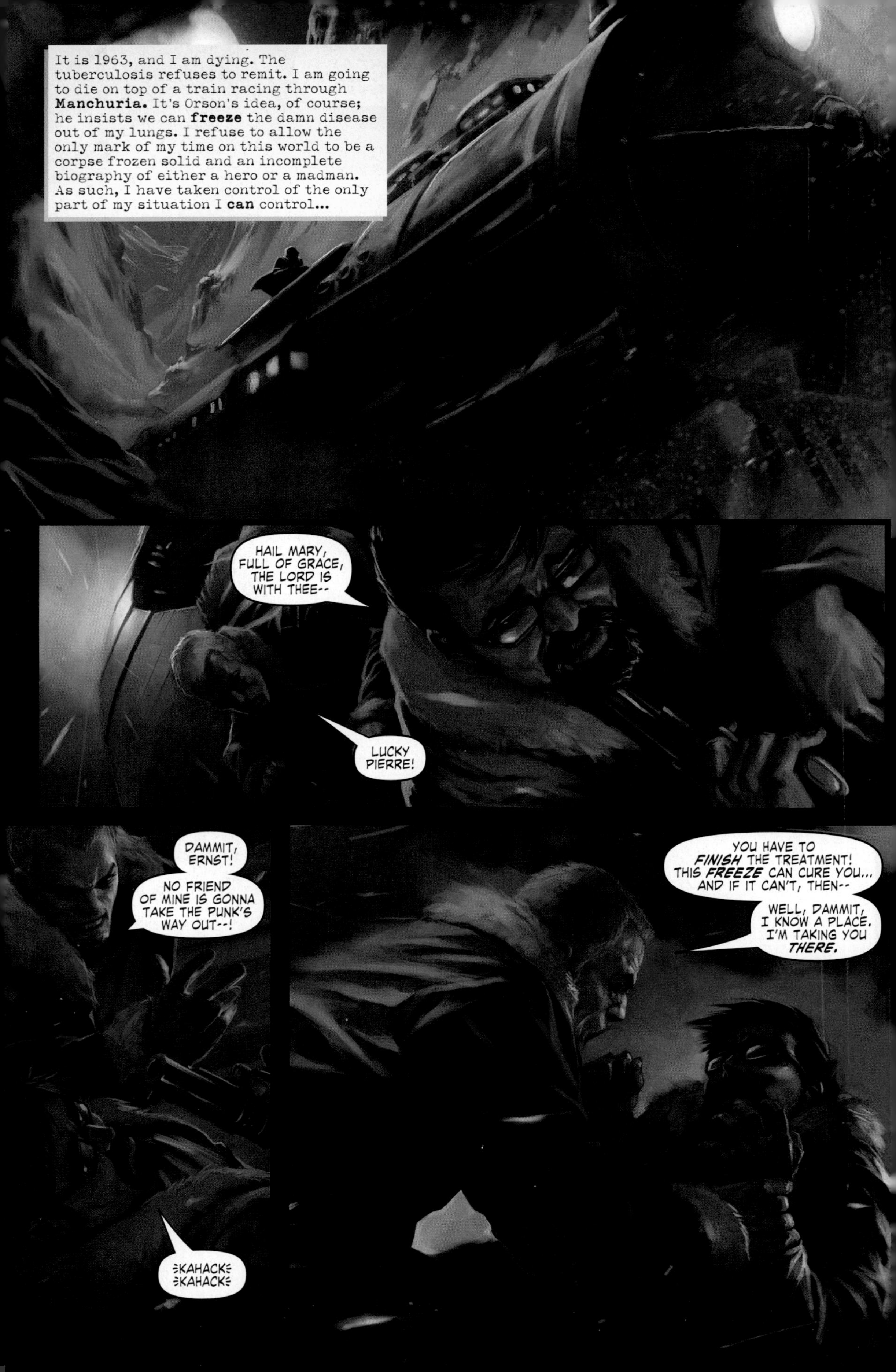

It is 1963, and I am dying. The tuberculosis refuses to remit. I am going to die on top of a train racing through **Manchuria.** It's Orson's idea, of course; he insists we can **freeze** the damn disease out of my lungs. I refuse to allow the only mark of my time on this world to be a corpse frozen solid and an incomplete biography of either a hero or a madman. As such, I have taken control of the only part of my situation I **can** control...
HAIL MARY, FULL OF GRACE, THE LORD IS WITH THEE--
LUCKY PIERRE!
DAMMIT, ERNST!
NO FRIEND OF MINE IS GONNA TAKE THE PUNK'S WAY OUT--!
KAHACK KAHACK
YOU HAVE TO *FINISH* THE TREATMENT! THIS *FREEZE* CAN CURE YOU... AND IF IT CAN'T, THEN--
WELL, DAMMIT, I KNOW A PLACE. I'M TAKING YOU *THERE.*

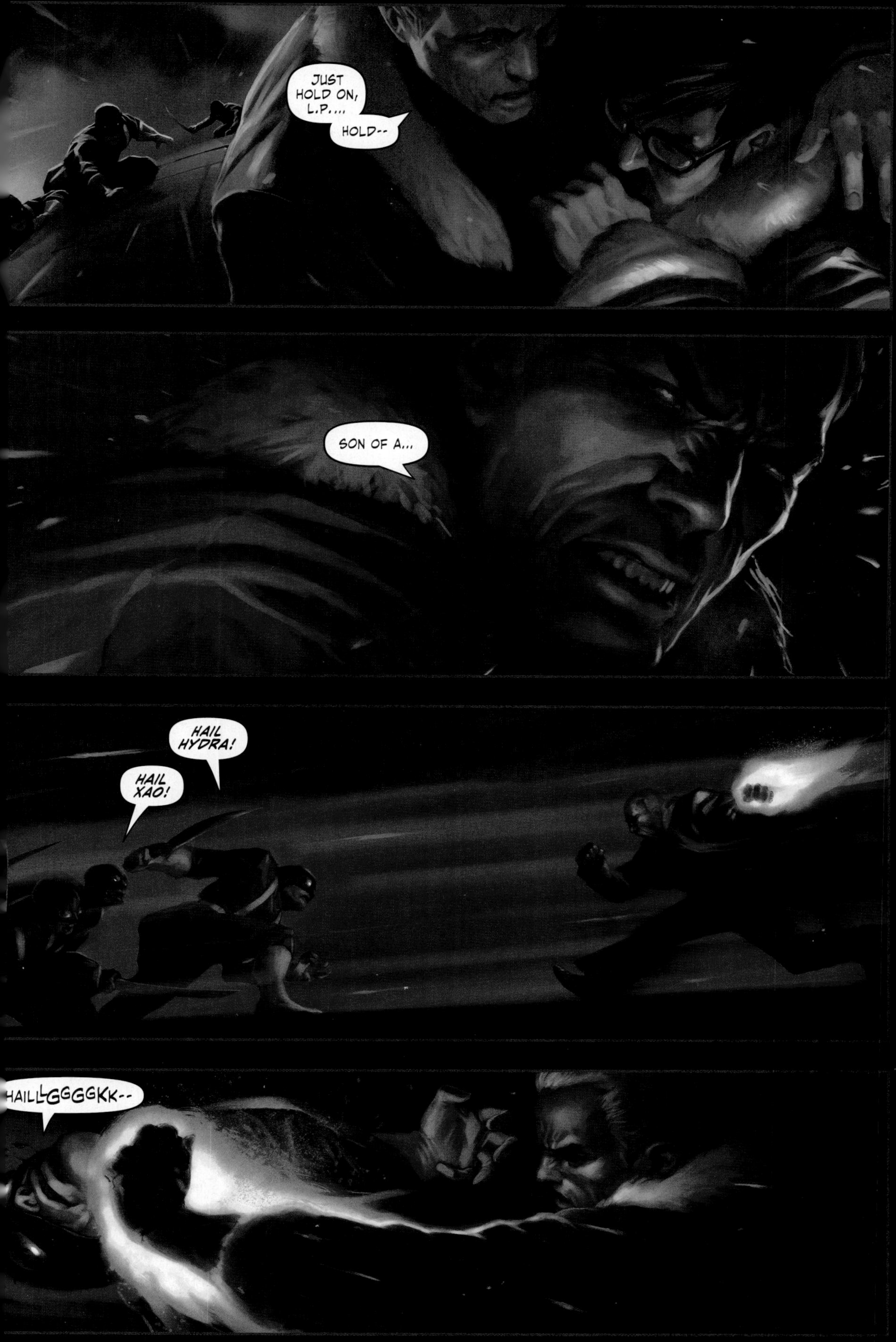
JUST HOLD ON, L.P....
HOLD--
SON OF A...
HAIL HYDRA!
HAIL XAO!
HAILLLGGGGKK--

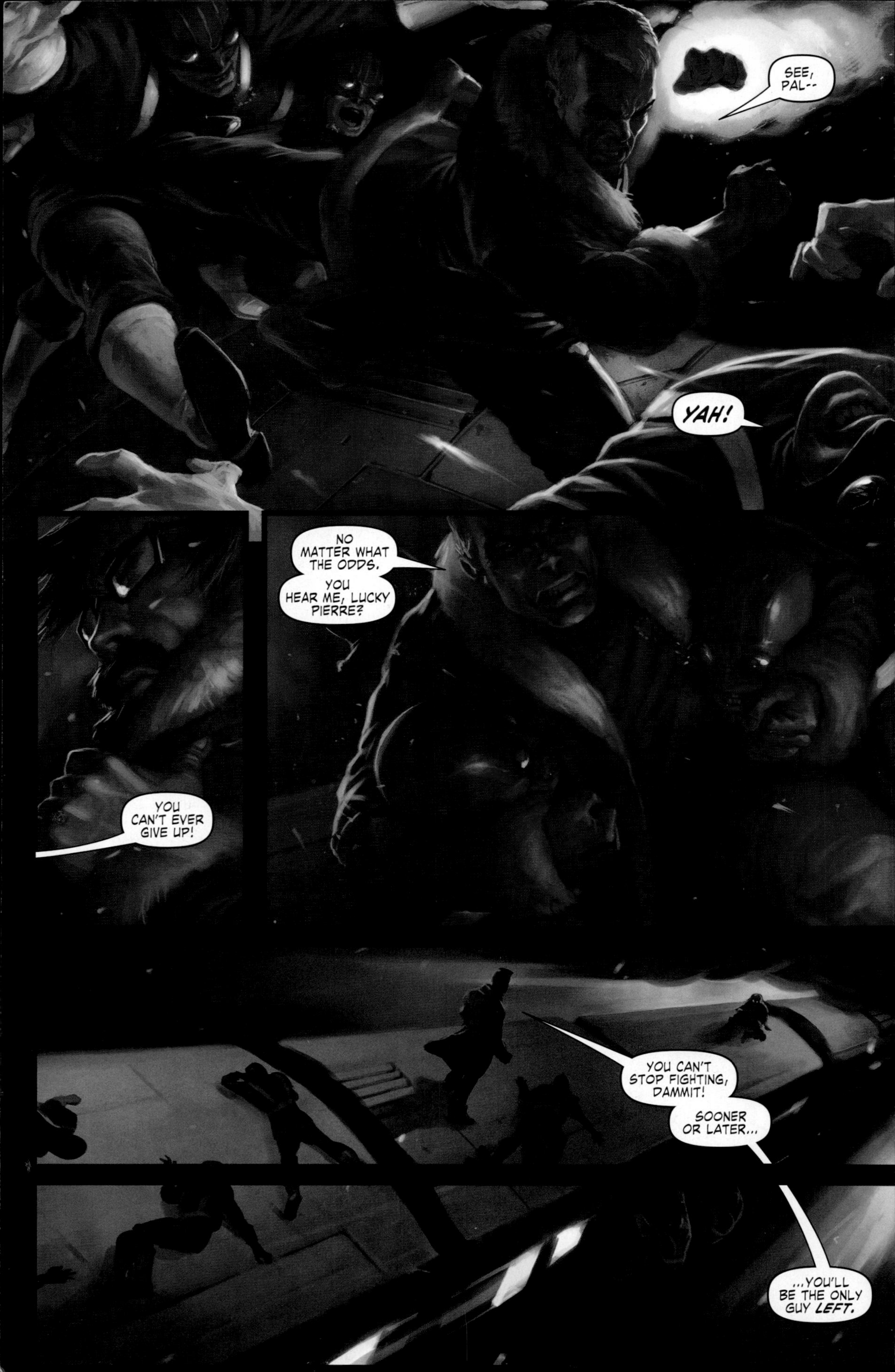
SEE, PAL--
YAH!
YOU CAN'T EVER GIVE UP!
NO MATTER WHAT THE ODDS.
YOU HEAR ME, LUCKY PIERRE?
YOU CAN'T STOP FIGHTING, DAMMIT!
SOONER OR LATER...
...YOU'LL BE THE ONLY GUY LEFT.

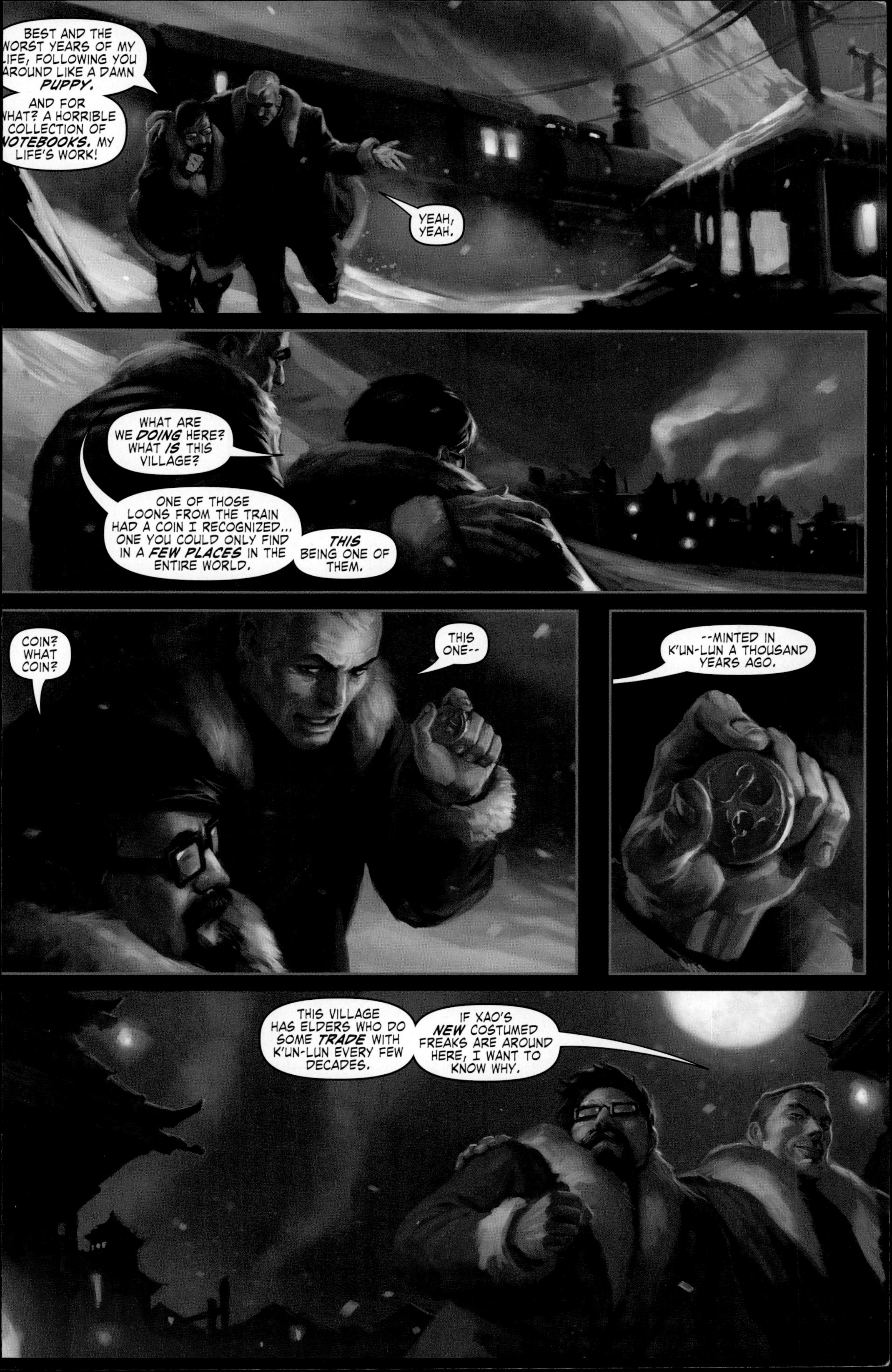
BEST AND THE WORST YEARS OF MY LIFE, FOLLOWING YOU AROUND LIKE A DAMN PUPPY.
AND FOR WHAT? A HORRIBLE COLLECTION OF NOTEBOOKS. MY LIFE'S WORK!
YEAH, YEAH.
WHAT ARE WE DOING HERE? WHAT IS THIS VILLAGE?
ONE OF THOSE LOONS FROM THE TRAIN HAD A COIN I RECOGNIZED... ONE YOU COULD ONLY FIND IN A FEW PLACES IN THE ENTIRE WORLD.
THIS BEING ONE OF THEM.
COIN? WHAT COIN?
THIS ONE--
--MINTED IN K'UN-LUN A THOUSAND YEARS AGO.
THIS VILLAGE HAS ELDERS WHO DO SOME TRADE WITH K'UN-LUN EVERY FEW DECADES.
IF XAO'S NEW COSTUMED FREAKS ARE AROUND HERE, I WANT TO KNOW WHY.

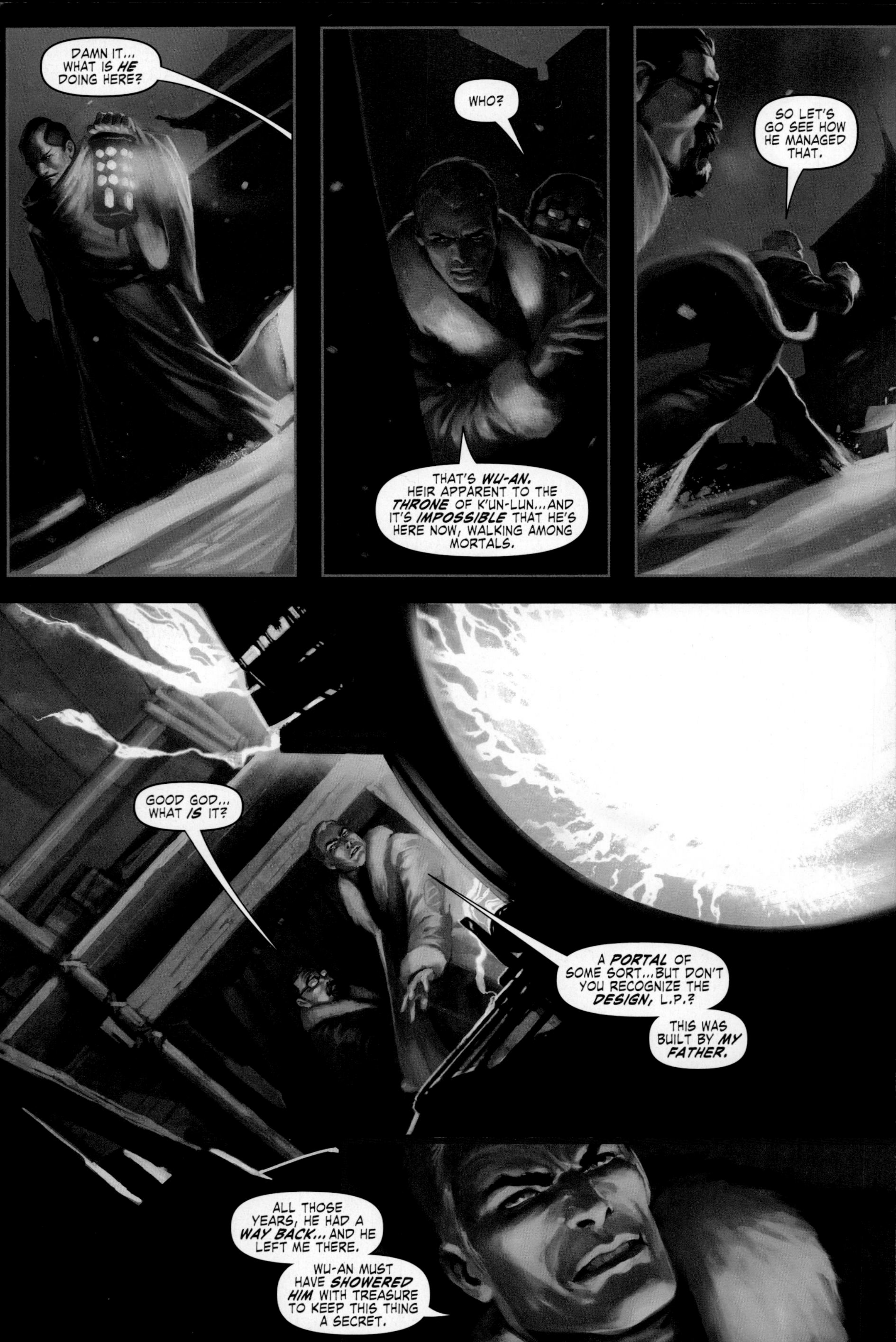
DAMN IT... WHAT IS *HE* DOING HERE?
WHO?
THAT'S ***WU-AN.*** HEIR APPARENT TO THE ***THRONE*** OF K'UN-LUN...AND IT'S ***IMPOSSIBLE*** THAT HE'S HERE NOW, WALKING AMONG MORTALS.
SO LET'S GO SEE HOW HE MANAGED THAT.
GOOD GOD... WHAT *IS* IT?
A ***PORTAL*** OF SOME SORT...BUT DON'T YOU RECOGNIZE THE ***DESIGN,*** L.P.?
THIS WAS BUILT BY ***MY FATHER.***
ALL THOSE YEARS, HE HAD A ***WAY BACK...*** AND HE LEFT ME THERE.
WU-AN MUST HAVE ***SHOWERED HIM*** WITH TREASURE TO KEEP THIS THING A SECRET.

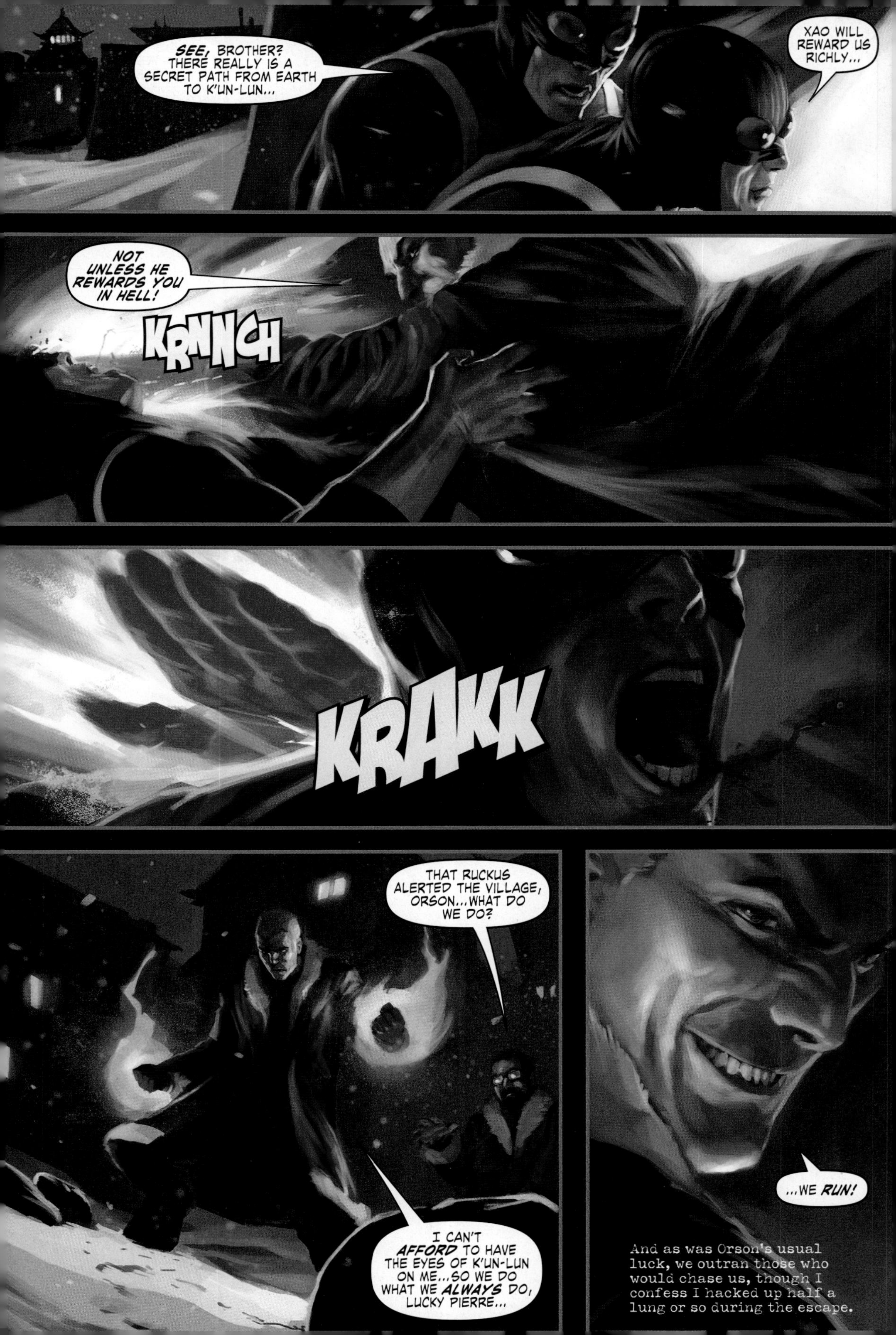
SEE, BROTHER? THERE REALLY IS A SECRET PATH FROM EARTH TO K'UN-LUN...
XAO WILL REWARD US RICHLY...
NOT UNLESS HE REWARDS YOU IN HELL!
KRNNCH
KRAKK
THAT RUCKUS ALERTED THE VILLAGE, ORSON...WHAT DO WE DO?
I CAN'T AFFORD TO HAVE THE EYES OF K'UN-LUN ON ME...SO WE DO WHAT WE ALWAYS DO, LUCKY PIERRE...
...WE RUN!
And as was Orson's usual luck, we outran those who would chase us, though I confess I hacked up half a lung or so during the escape.

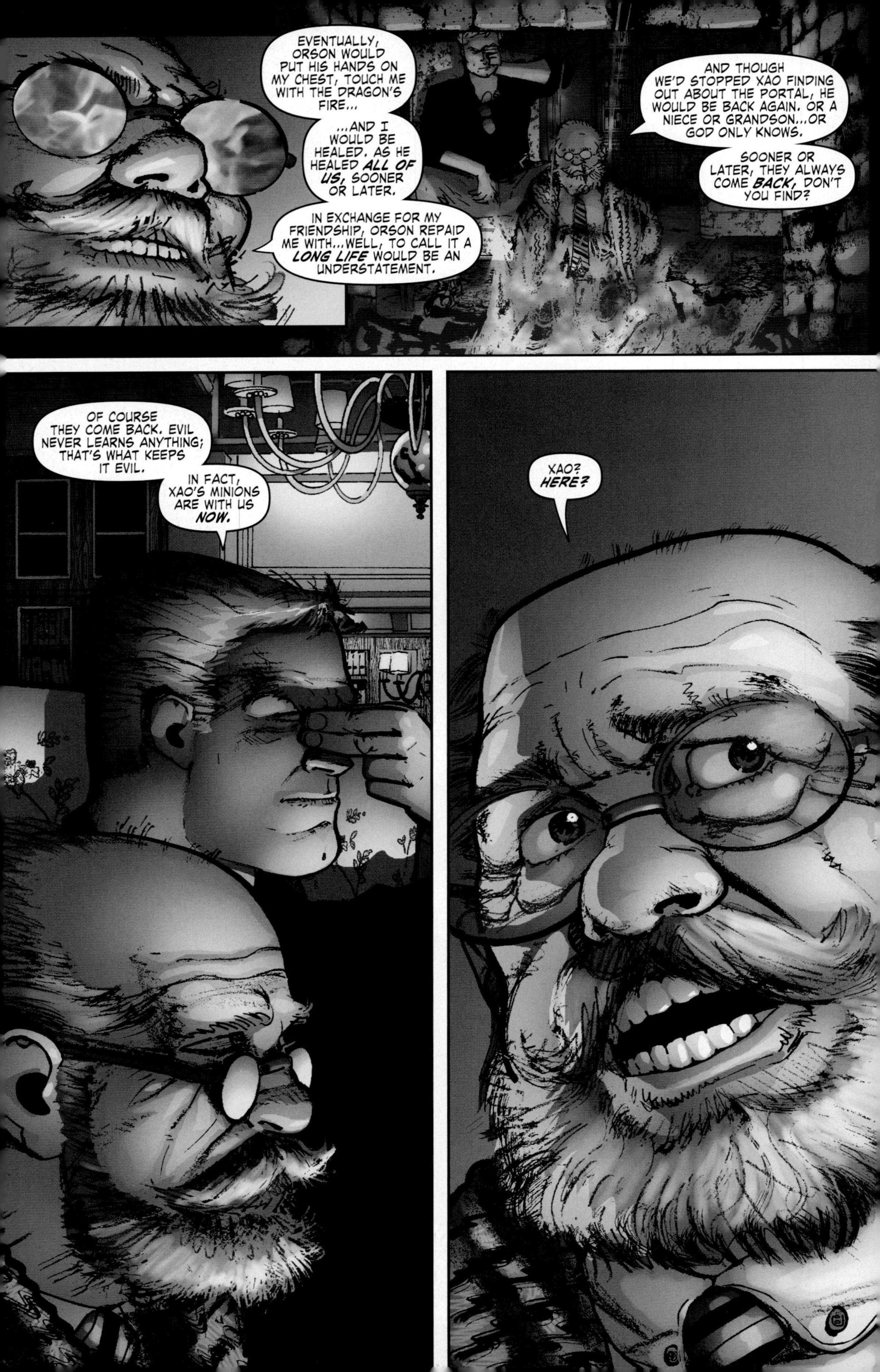
EVENTUALLY, ORSON WOULD PUT HIS HANDS ON MY CHEST, TOUCH ME WITH THE DRAGON'S FIRE...
...AND I WOULD BE HEALED. AS HE HEALED ALL OF US, SOONER OR LATER.
IN EXCHANGE FOR MY FRIENDSHIP, ORSON REPAID ME WITH...WELL, TO CALL IT A LONG LIFE WOULD BE AN UNDERSTATEMENT.
AND THOUGH WE'D STOPPED XAO FINDING OUT ABOUT THE PORTAL, HE WOULD BE BACK AGAIN. OR A NIECE OR GRANDSON...OR GOD ONLY KNOWS.
SOONER OR LATER, THEY ALWAYS COME BACK, DON'T YOU FIND?
OF COURSE THEY COME BACK. EVIL NEVER LEARNS ANYTHING; THAT'S WHAT KEEPS IT EVIL.
IN FACT, XAO'S MINIONS ARE WITH US NOW.
XAO? HERE?

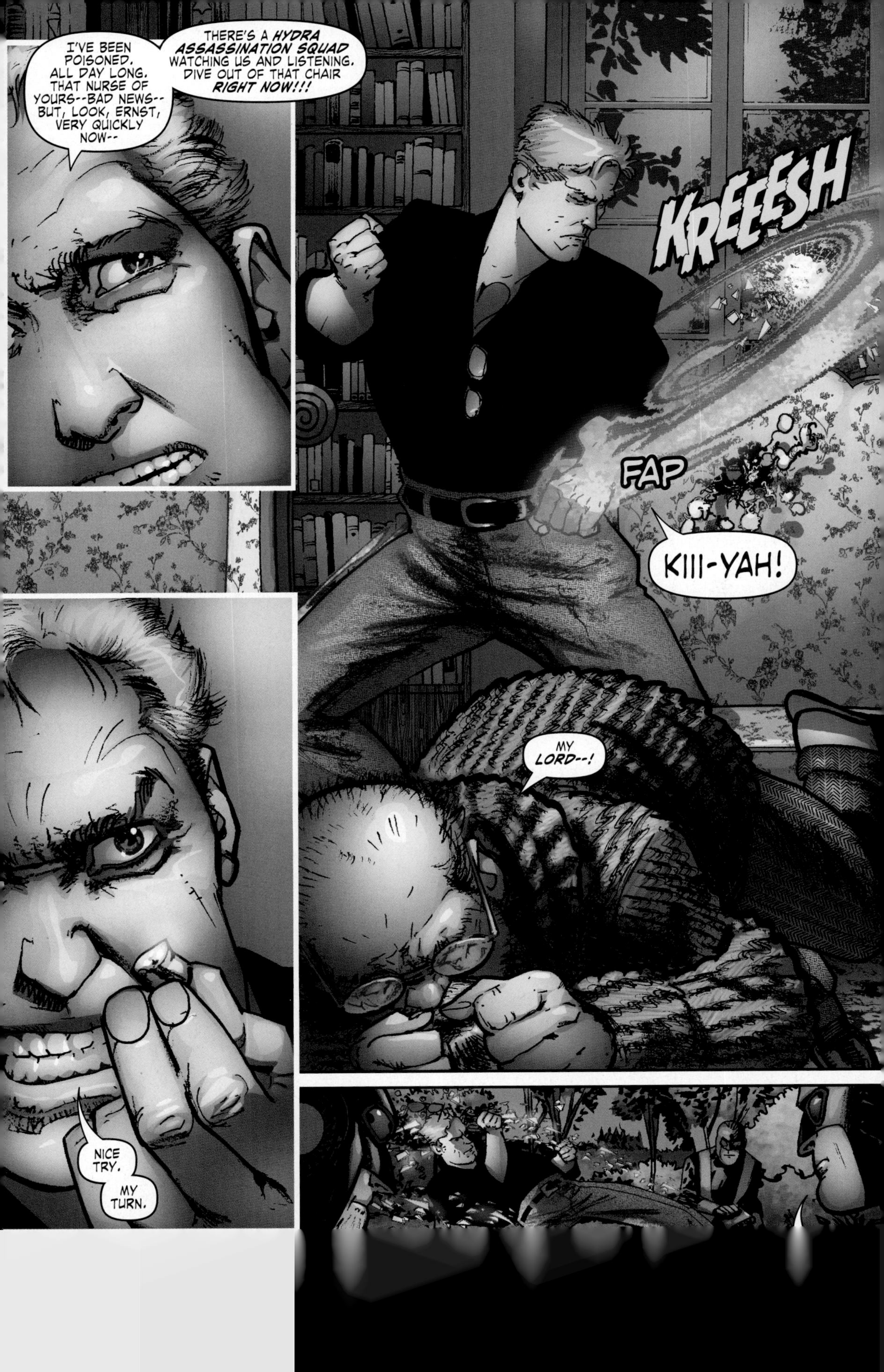
I'VE BEEN POISONED. ALL DAY LONG. THAT NURSE OF YOURS--BAD NEWS--BUT, LOOK, ERNST, VERY QUICKLY NOW--
THERE'S A HYDRA ASSASSINATION SQUAD WATCHING US AND LISTENING. DIVE OUT OF THAT CHAIR RIGHT NOW!!!
KREEESH
FAP
KIII-YAH!
MY LORD--!
NICE TRY.
MY TURN.

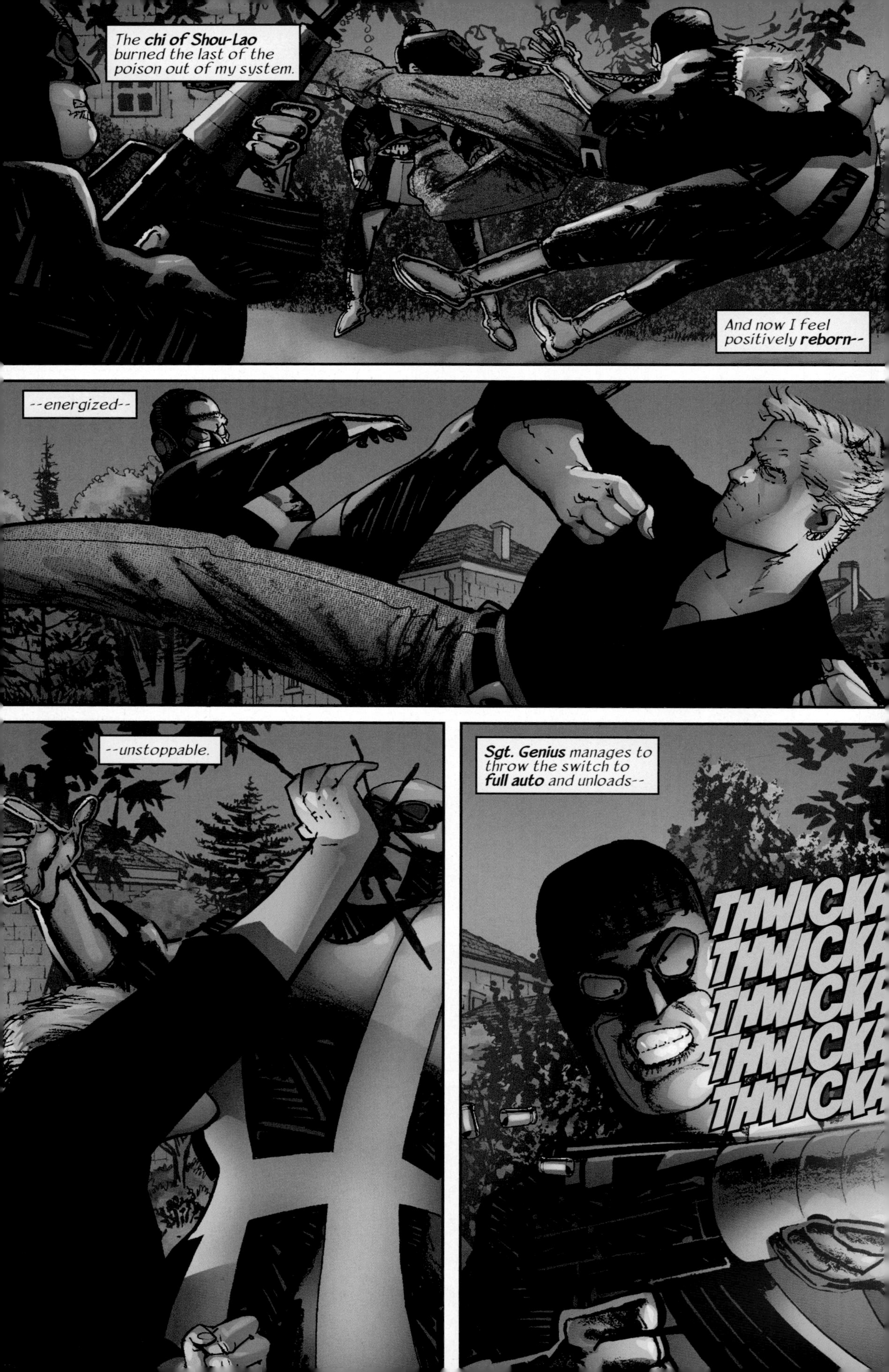
The chi of Shou-Lao burned the last of the poison out of my system.
And now I feel positively reborn--
--energized--
--unstoppable.
Sgt. Genius manages to throw the switch to full auto and unloads--
THWICKA
THWICKA
THWICKA
THWICKA
THWICKA

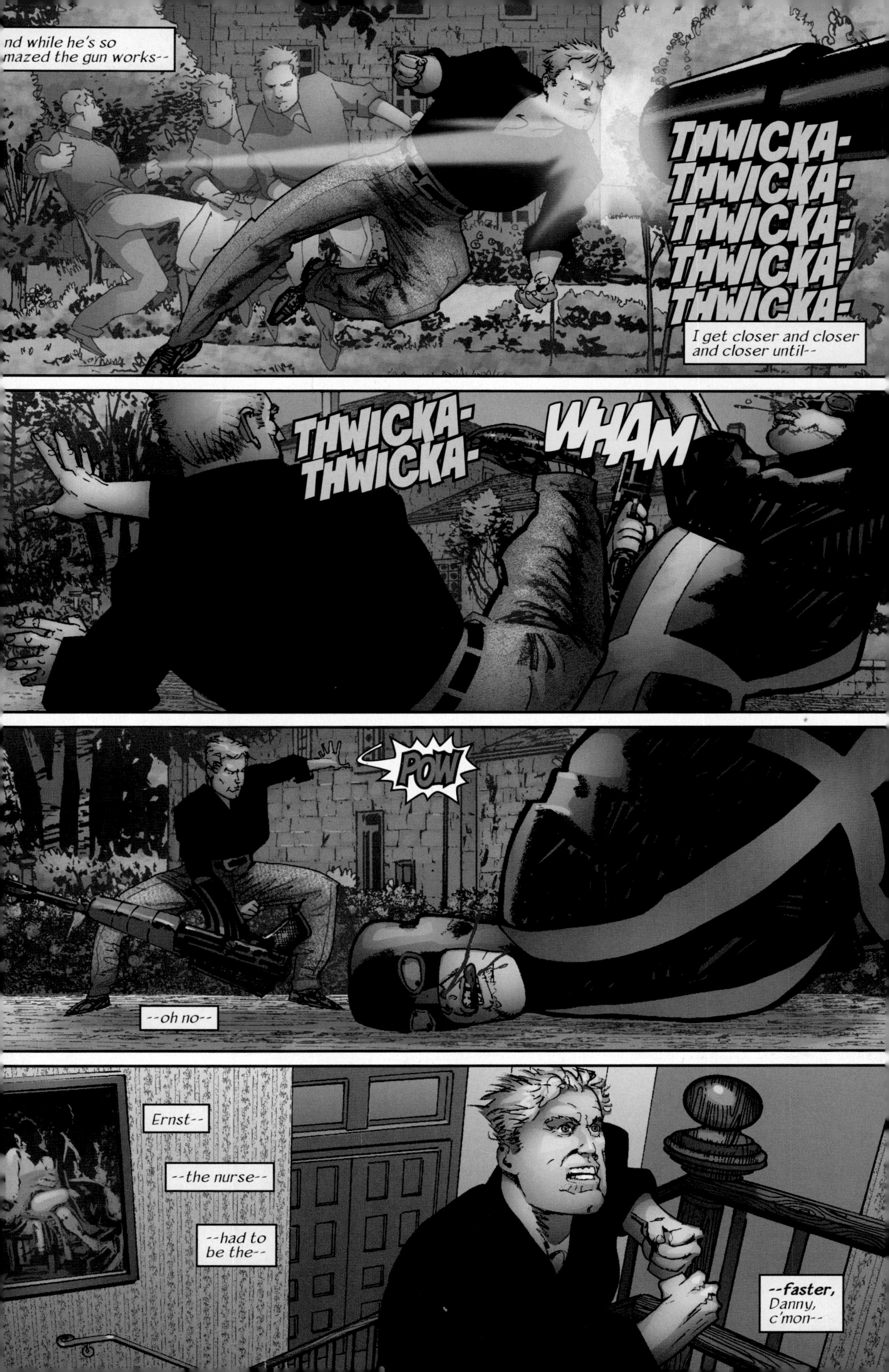
nd while he's so
mazed the gun works--
THWICKA-
THWICKA-
THWICKA-
THWICKA-
THWICKA-
I get closer and closer
and closer until--
THWICKA-
THWICKA-
WHAM
POW
--oh no--
Ernst--
--the nurse--
--had to
be the--
--faster,
Danny,
c'mon--

--faster--

SHE WAS TRYING TO SMOTHER POOR OLD *CHORES* HERE.

I *HAD* TO DO IT.

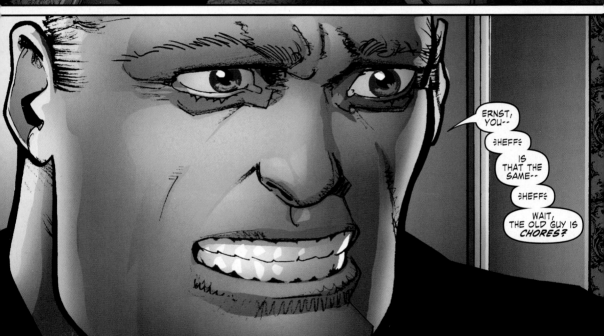

ERNST, YOU--

≥HEFF≤

IS THAT THE SAME--

≥HEFF≤

WAIT, THE OLD GUY IS *CHORES?*

I *TOLD YOU,* CALLING IT A *LONG LIFE* WOULD BE AN UNDER-STATEMENT. THE TIME WE SPENT WITH ORSON-- THE WOUNDS HE HEALED US OF--

WELL, ALLOW ME TO FORMALLY INTRODUCE MR. SEAMUS "CHORES" MACGILLICUDDY AND THE CONTESSA VERA VIDAL.

IS THAT *WENDELL?*

NO, SIR. I'M *DANNY...* HIS SON.

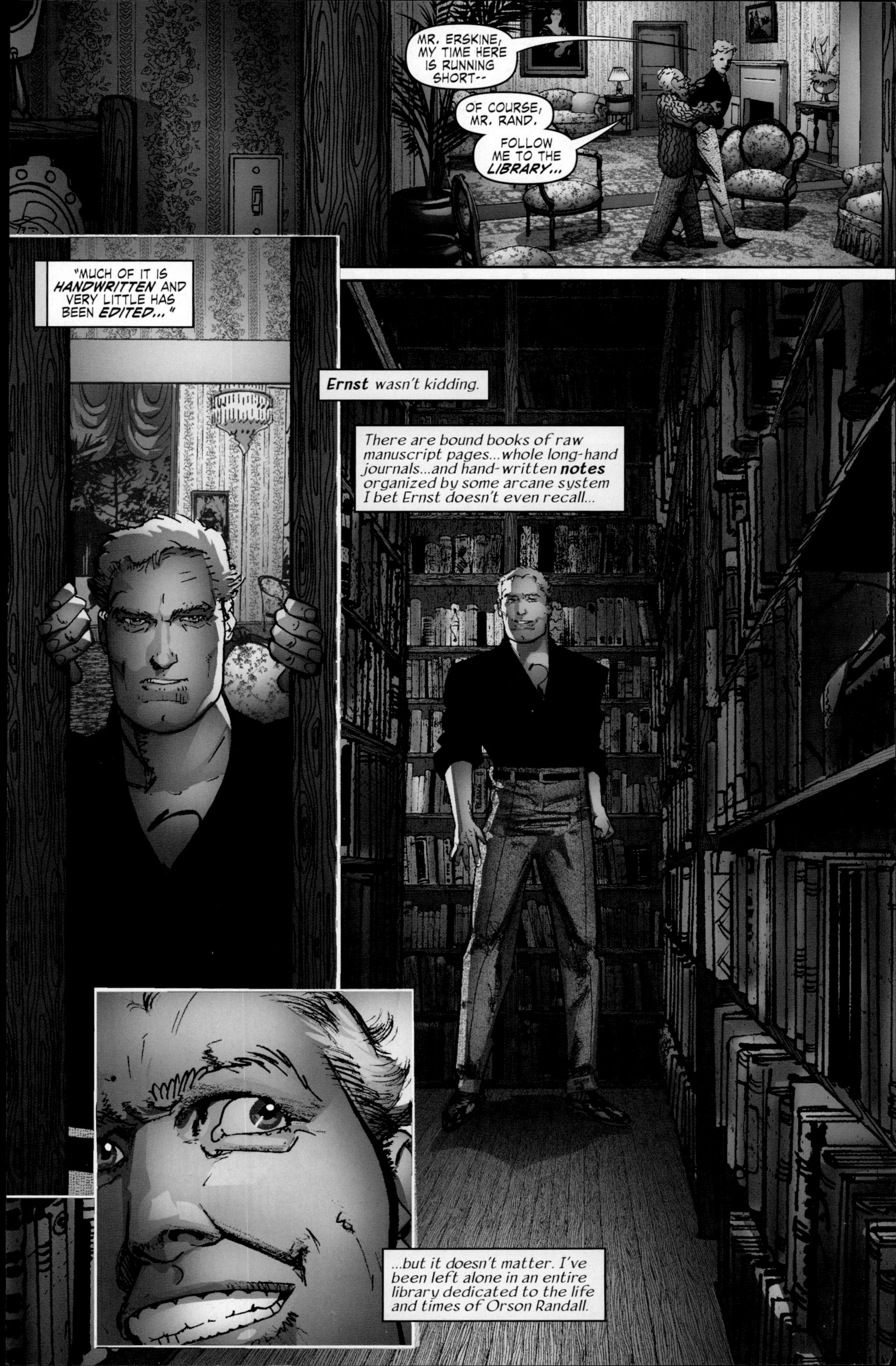
MR. ERSKINE, MY TIME HERE IS RUNNING SHORT--
OF COURSE, MR. RAND.
FOLLOW ME TO THE LIBRARY...
"MUCH OF IT IS HANDWRITTEN AND VERY LITTLE HAS BEEN EDITED..."
Ernst wasn't kidding.
There are bound books of raw manuscript pages...whole long-hand journals...and hand-written notes organized by some arcane system I bet Ernst doesn't even recall...
...but it doesn't matter. I've been left alone in an entire library dedicated to the life and times of Orson Randall.

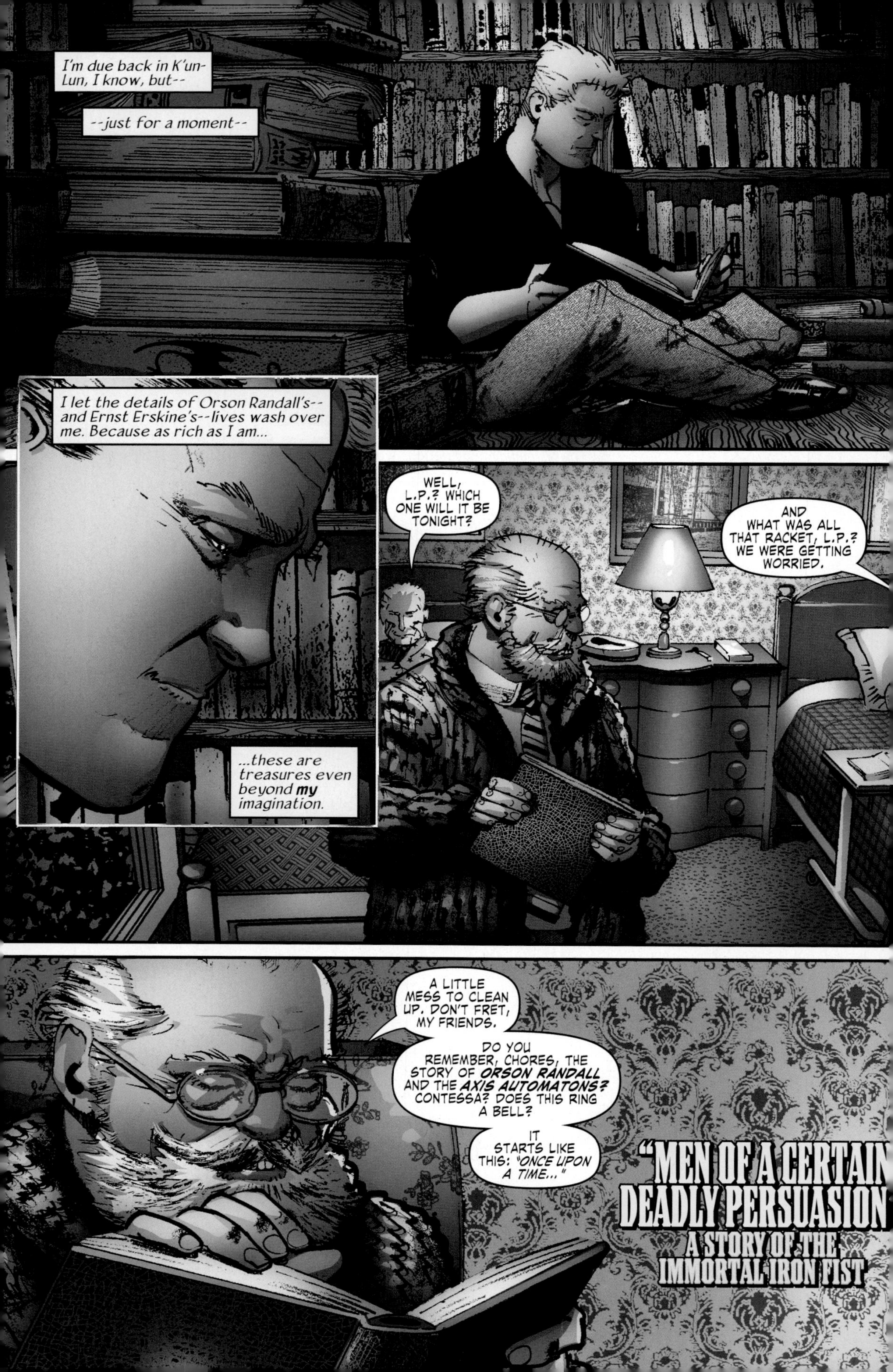
I'm due back in K'un-Lun, I know, but--
--just for a moment--
I let the details of Orson Randall's--and Ernst Erskine's--lives wash over me. Because as rich as I am...
...these are treasures even beyond **my** imagination.
WELL, L.P.? WHICH ONE WILL IT BE TONIGHT?
AND WHAT WAS ALL THAT RACKET, L.P.? WE WERE GETTING WORRIED.
A LITTLE MESS TO CLEAN UP. DON'T FRET, MY FRIENDS.
DO YOU REMEMBER, CHORES, THE STORY OF ***ORSON RANDALL*** AND THE ***AXIS AUTOMATONS?*** CONTESSA? DOES THIS RING A BELL?
IT STARTS LIKE THIS: *"ONCE UPON A TIME..."*
"MEN OF A CERTAIN DEADLY PERSUASION"
A STORY OF THE IMMORTAL IRON FIST

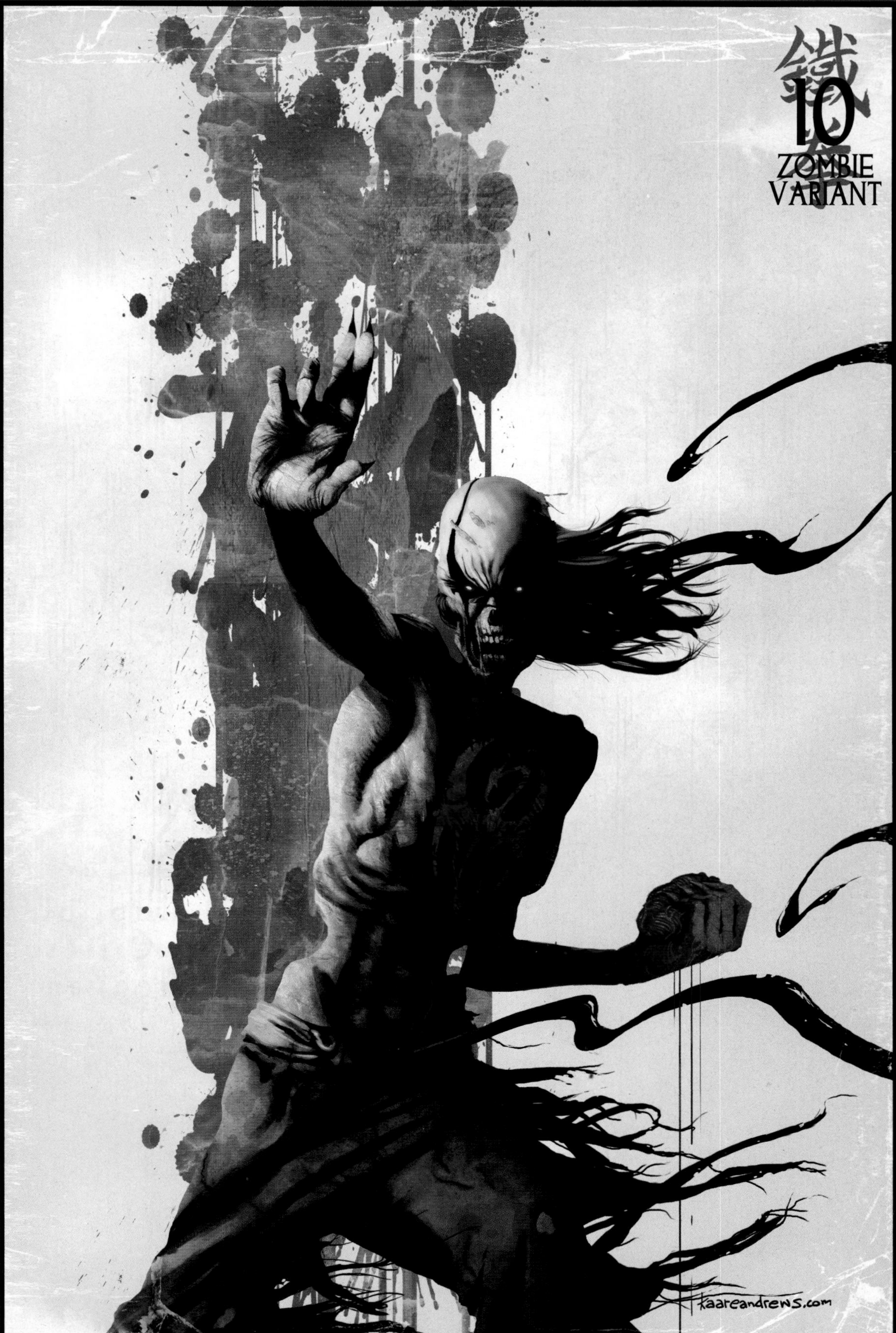
鐵拳
10
ZOMBIE
VARIANT
kaareandrews.com

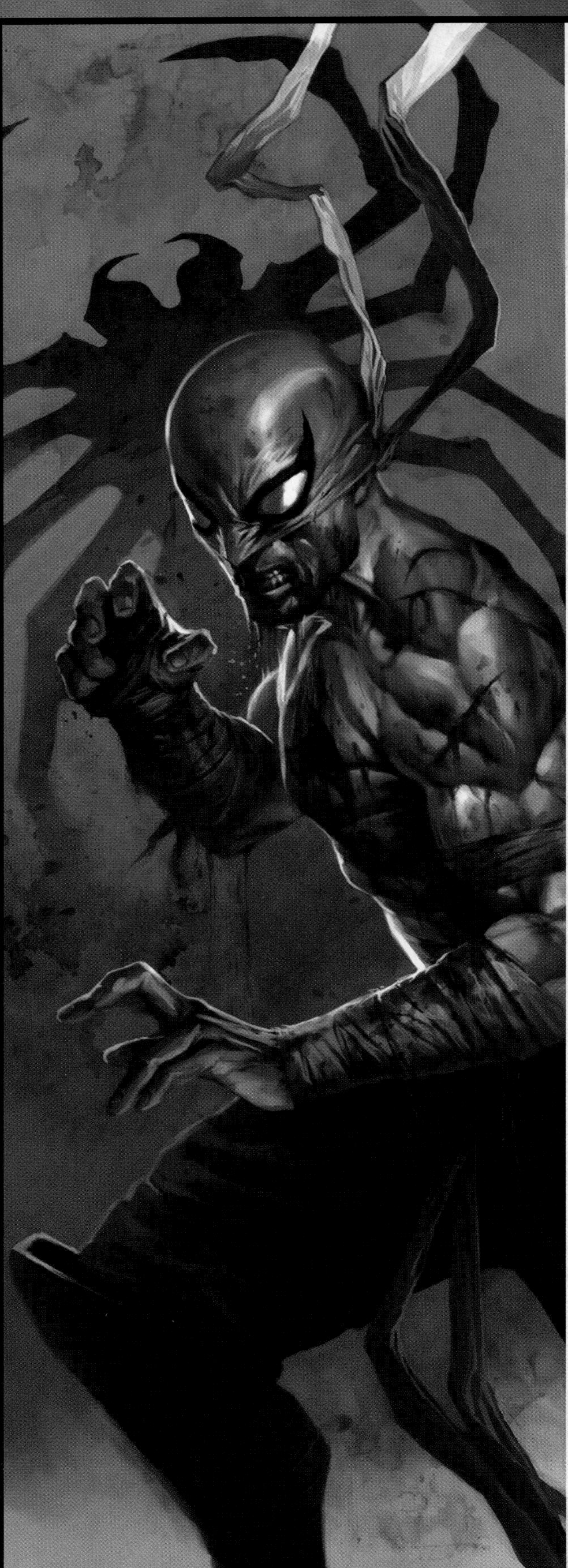

鐵拳 10

The 七 Capital Cities of Heaven

三

Round 3

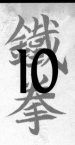

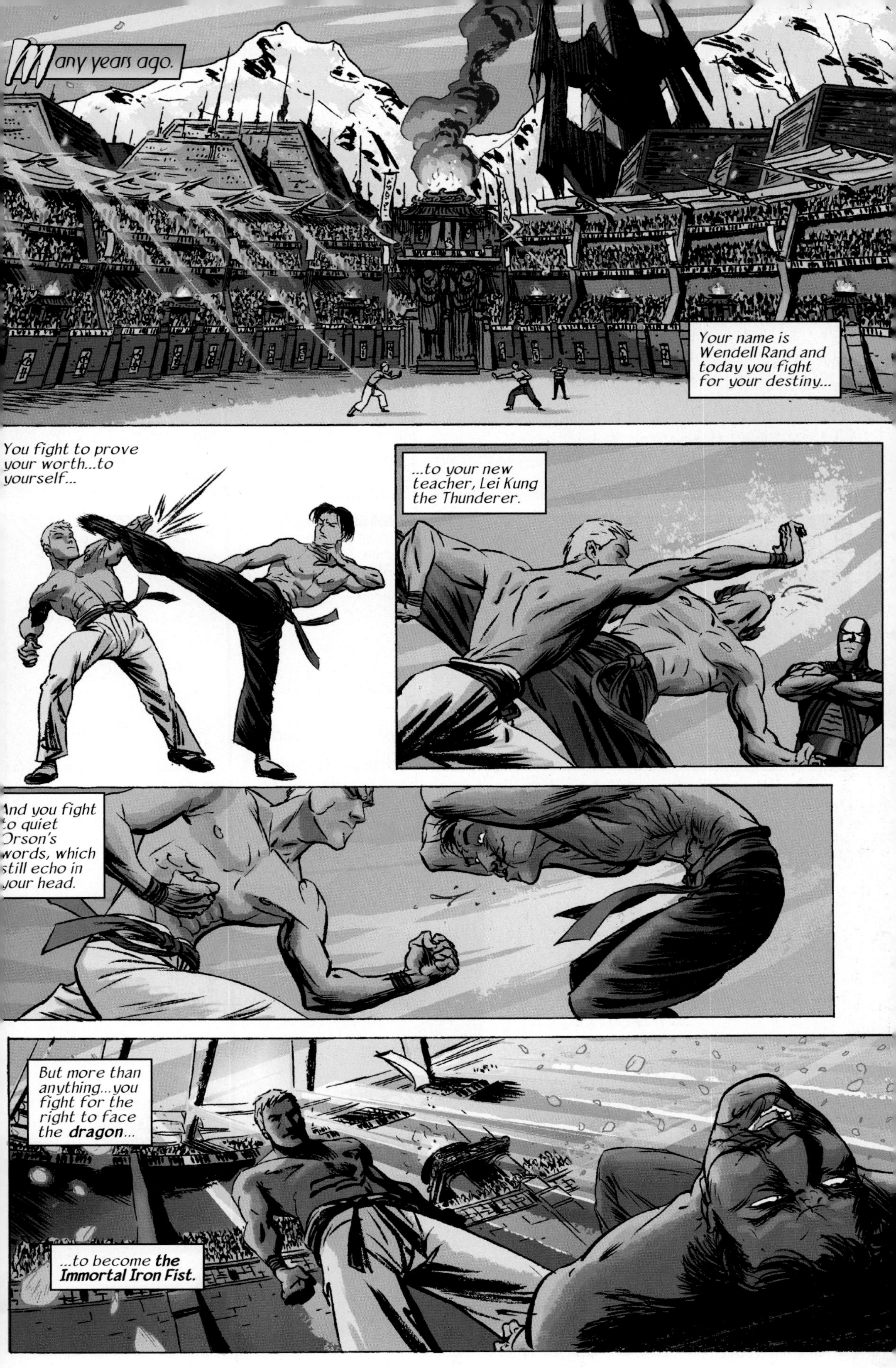
Many years ago.
Your name is Wendell Rand and today you fight for your destiny...
You fight to prove your worth...to yourself...
...to your new teacher, Lei Kung the Thunderer.
And you fight to quiet Orson's words, which still echo in your head.
But more than anything...you fight for the right to face the **dragon**...
...to become **the Immortal Iron Fist**.

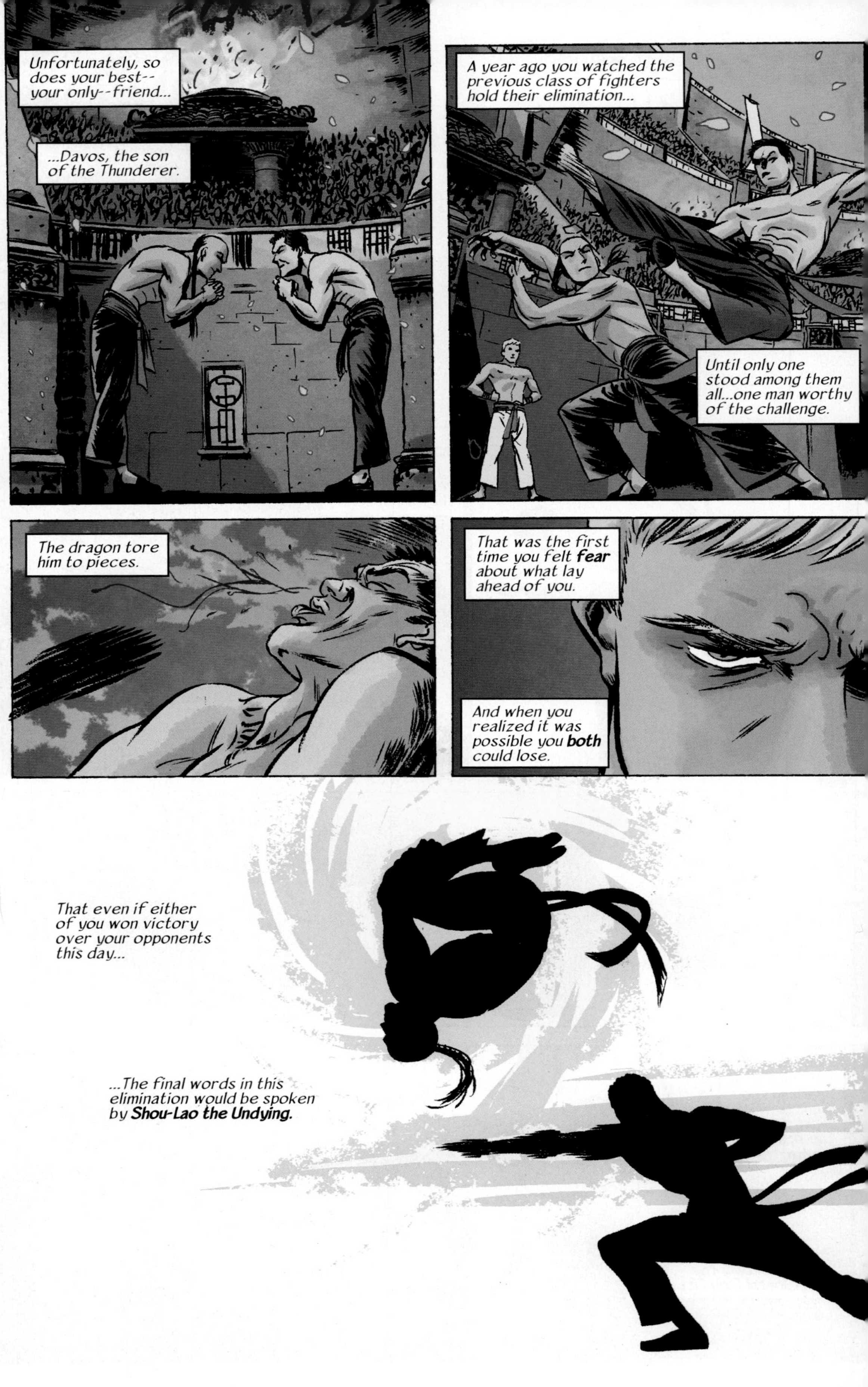
Unfortunately, so does your best--your only--friend...
...Davos, the son of the Thunderer.
A year ago you watched the previous class of fighters hold their elimination...
Until only one stood among them all...one man worthy of the challenge.
The dragon tore him to pieces.
That was the first time you felt **fear** about what lay ahead of you.
And when you realized it was possible you **both** could lose.
That even if either of you won victory over your opponents this day...
...The final words in this elimination would be spoken by **Shou-Lao the Undying.**

So it's an unpleasant mixture of feelings you struggle with this day.

You cheer on Davos in his bouts, as he does you in yours.

You pray you won't face him.

But you study his moves. You look for flaws.

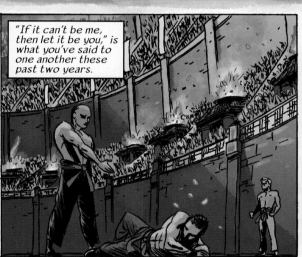
"If it can't be me, then let it be you," is what you've said to one another these past two years.

But do you truly mean that...?

THE FINAL BOUT WILL BE FOUGHT AT SUNRISE TOMORROW.

DAVOS VERSUS WENDELL... UNTIL ONE YIELDS.

Are you truly ready...?

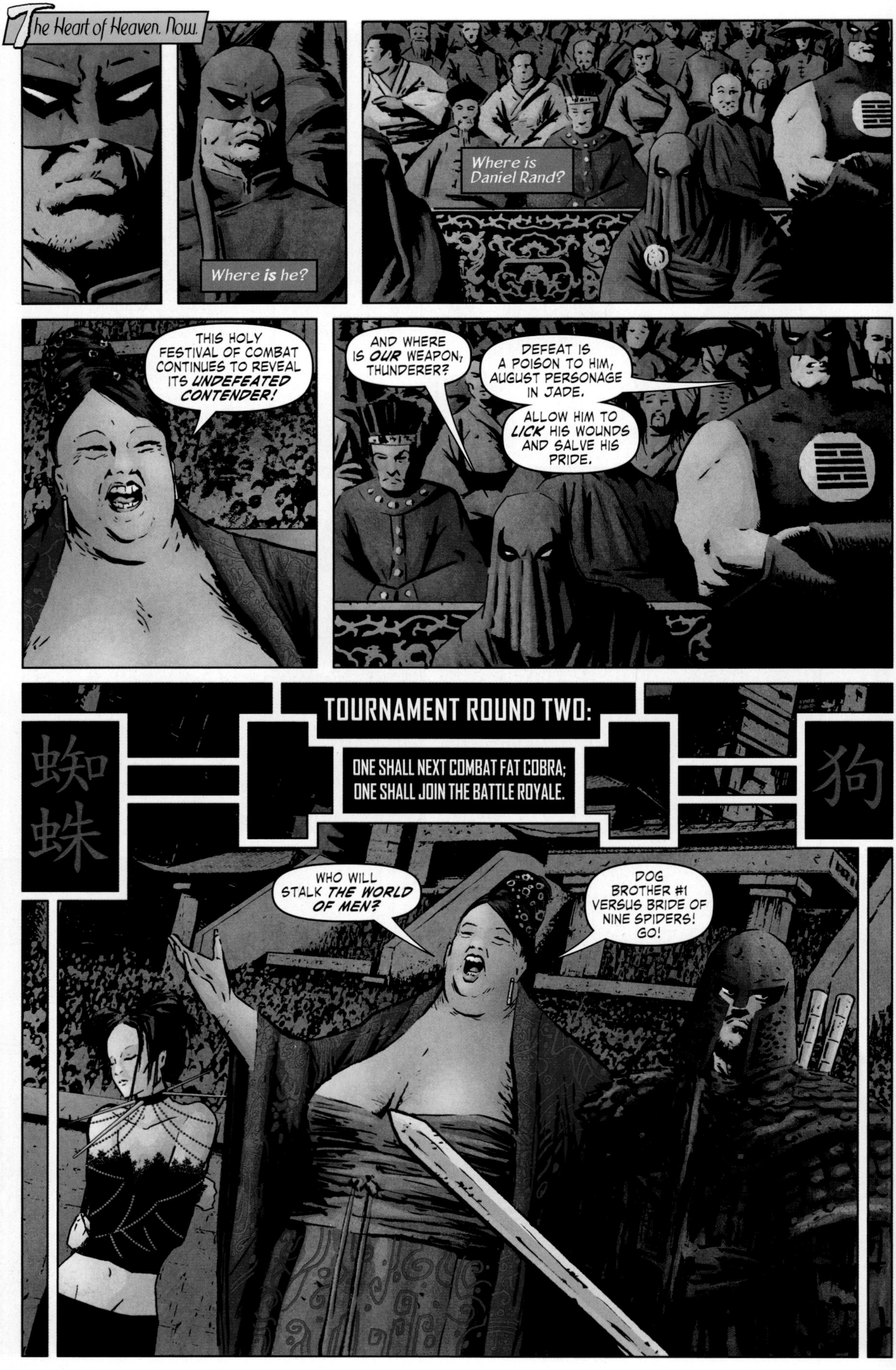
The Heart of Heaven. Now.
Where is he?
Where is Daniel Rand?
THIS HOLY FESTIVAL OF COMBAT CONTINUES TO REVEAL ITS UNDEFEATED CONTENDER!
AND WHERE IS OUR WEAPON, THUNDERER?
DEFEAT IS A POISON TO HIM, AUGUST PERSONAGE IN JADE.
ALLOW HIM TO LICK HIS WOUNDS AND SALVE HIS PRIDE.
TOURNAMENT ROUND TWO:
ONE SHALL NEXT COMBAT FAT COBRA; ONE SHALL JOIN THE BATTLE ROYALE.
蜘蛛
狗
WHO WILL STALK THE WORLD OF MEN?
DOG BROTHER #1 VERSUS BRIDE OF NINE SPIDERS! GO!

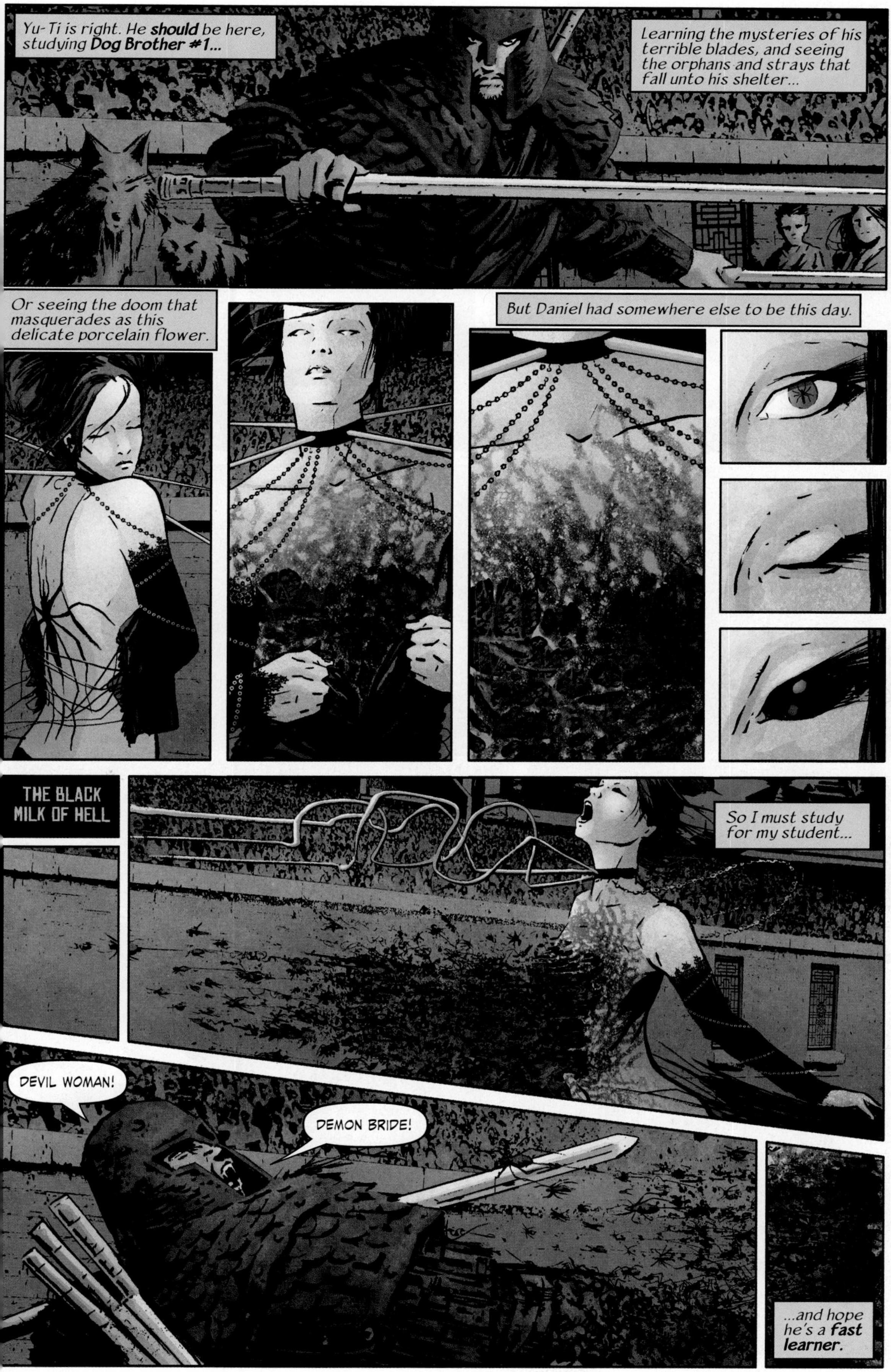
Yu-Ti is right. He **should** be here, studying **Dog Brother #1**...
Learning the mysteries of his terrible blades, and seeing the orphans and strays that fall unto his shelter...
Or seeing the doom that masquerades as this delicate porcelain flower.
But Daniel had somewhere else to be this day.
THE BLACK MILK OF HELL
So I must study for my student...
DEVIL WOMAN!
DEMON BRIDE!
...and hope he's a **fast learner**.

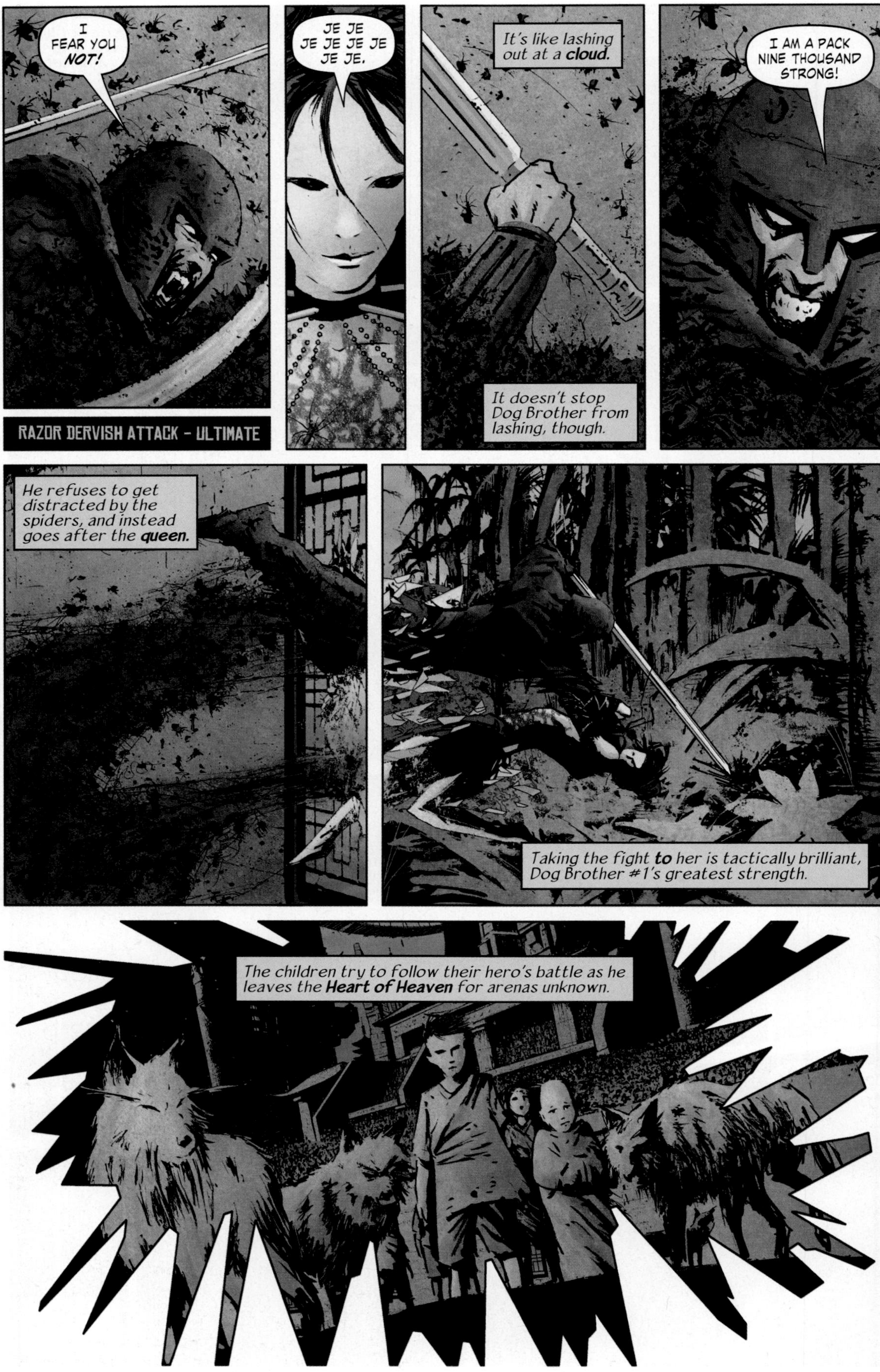
I FEAR YOU NOT!
RAZOR DERVISH ATTACK - ULTIMATE
JE JE JE JE JE JE JE JE.
It's like lashing out at a cloud.
It doesn't stop Dog Brother from lashing, though.
I AM A PACK NINE THOUSAND STRONG!
He refuses to get distracted by the spiders, and instead goes after the queen.
Taking the fight to her is tactically brilliant, Dog Brother #1's greatest strength.
The children try to follow their hero's battle as he leaves the Heart of Heaven for arenas unknown.

But they are children.

We veterans of the **tournament** know there is nothing to do but watch...

...and wait for a sign.

ARRROOOO OOOOONN NN

AARRRROOOOOOOO ONNNN AARRRROO OOOOOOONNNN AAR RRRO OOOOOOOOOONN NN RRRROOOOO NN AA RR

The **dogs** tell us all we need to know.

THESE *FAMILIARS* FINISH THE TALE.

THE *BRIDE OF NINE SPIDERS* WINS. TOMORROW'S MATCH SEES *CRANE CHAMPION* AGAINST *TIGER'S BEAUTIFUL DAUGHTER.*

MASTER?

LEAVE ME.

I'M GOING TO FIND OUR *CHAMPION.*

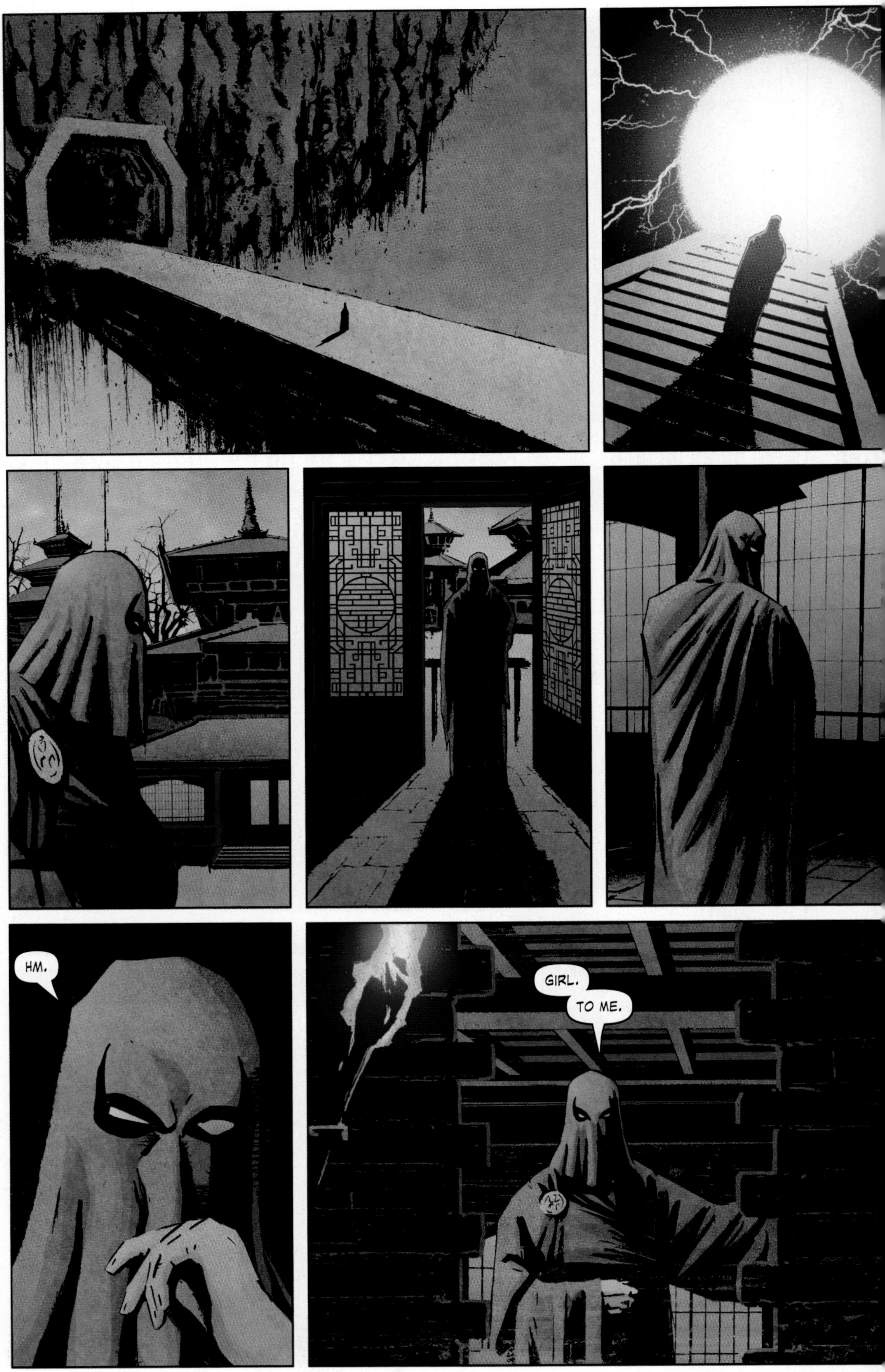
HM.
GIRL.
TO ME.

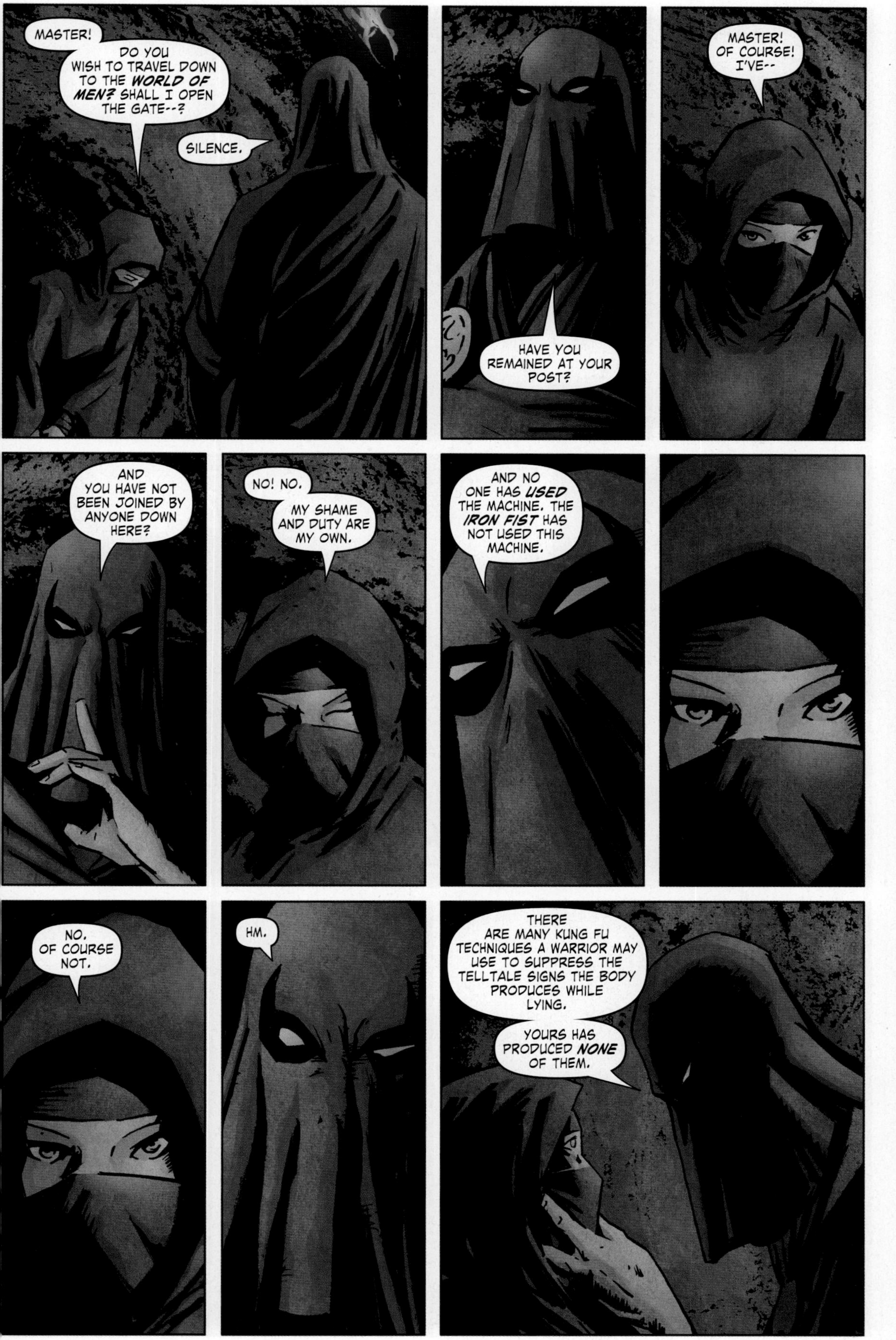
MASTER!
DO YOU WISH TO TRAVEL DOWN TO THE *WORLD OF MEN?* SHALL I OPEN THE GATE--?
SILENCE.
HAVE YOU REMAINED AT YOUR POST?
MASTER! OF COURSE! I'VE--
AND YOU HAVE NOT BEEN JOINED BY ANYONE DOWN HERE?
NO! NO.
MY SHAME AND DUTY ARE MY OWN.
AND NO ONE HAS *USED* THE MACHINE. THE *IRON FIST* HAS NOT USED THIS MACHINE.
NO. OF COURSE NOT.
HM.
THERE ARE MANY KUNG FU TECHNIQUES A WARRIOR MAY USE TO SUPPRESS THE TELLTALE SIGNS THE BODY PRODUCES WHILE LYING.
YOURS HAS PRODUCED *NONE* OF THEM.

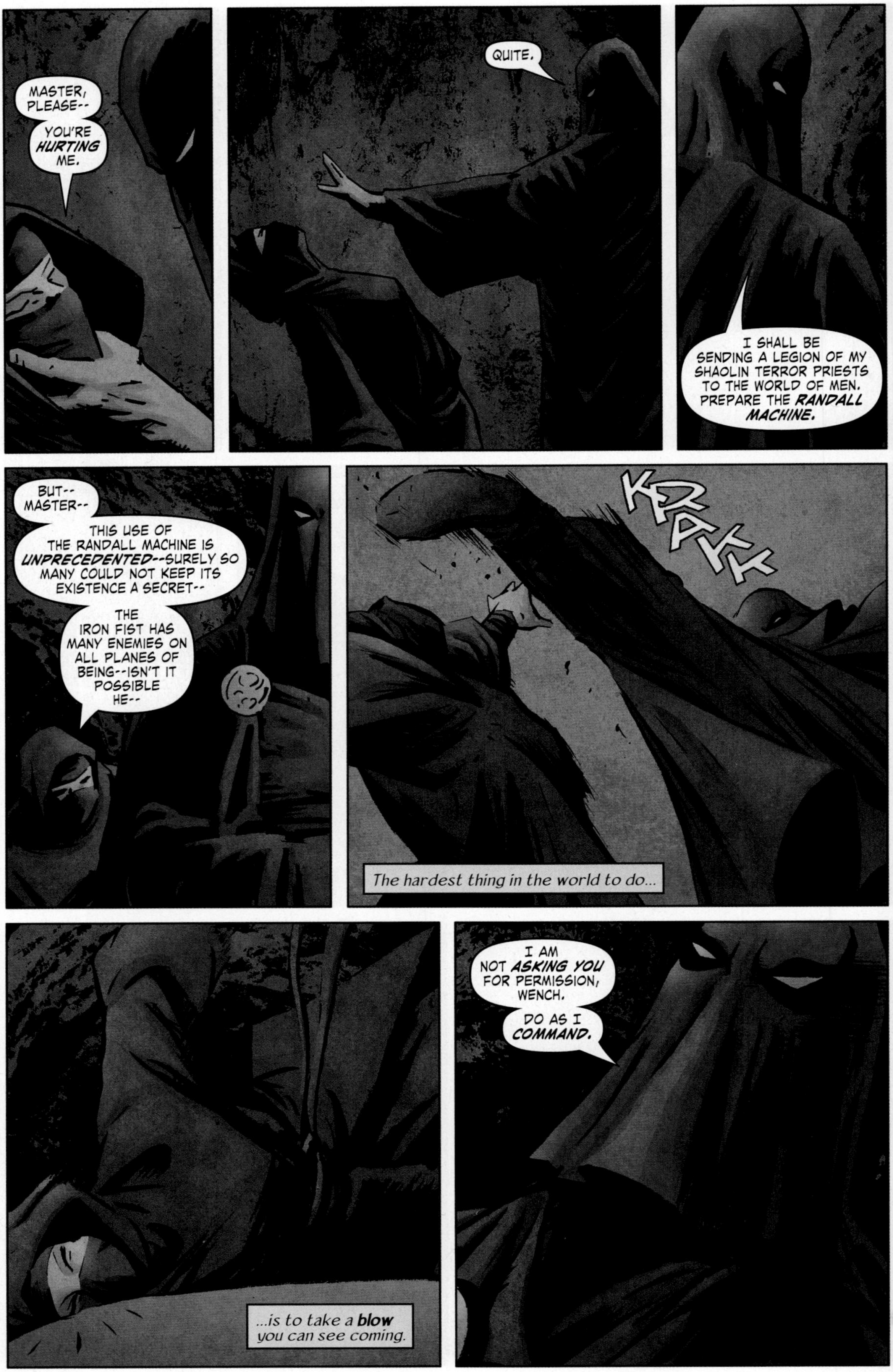
MASTER, PLEASE--
YOU'RE HURTING ME.
QUITE.
I SHALL BE SENDING A LEGION OF MY SHAOLIN TERROR PRIESTS TO THE WORLD OF MEN. PREPARE THE RANDALL MACHINE.
BUT-- MASTER--
THIS USE OF THE RANDALL MACHINE IS UNPRECEDENTED--SURELY SO MANY COULD NOT KEEP ITS EXISTENCE A SECRET--
THE IRON FIST HAS MANY ENEMIES ON ALL PLANES OF BEING--ISN'T IT POSSIBLE HE--
KRAKK
The hardest thing in the world to do...
...is to take a blow you can see coming.
I AM NOT ASKING YOU FOR PERMISSION, WENCH.
DO AS I COMMAND.

O! Iron Fist...

I pray you can see this blow coming...

For surely it will be hard not to *notice*.

XAO.

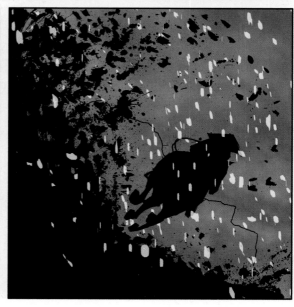

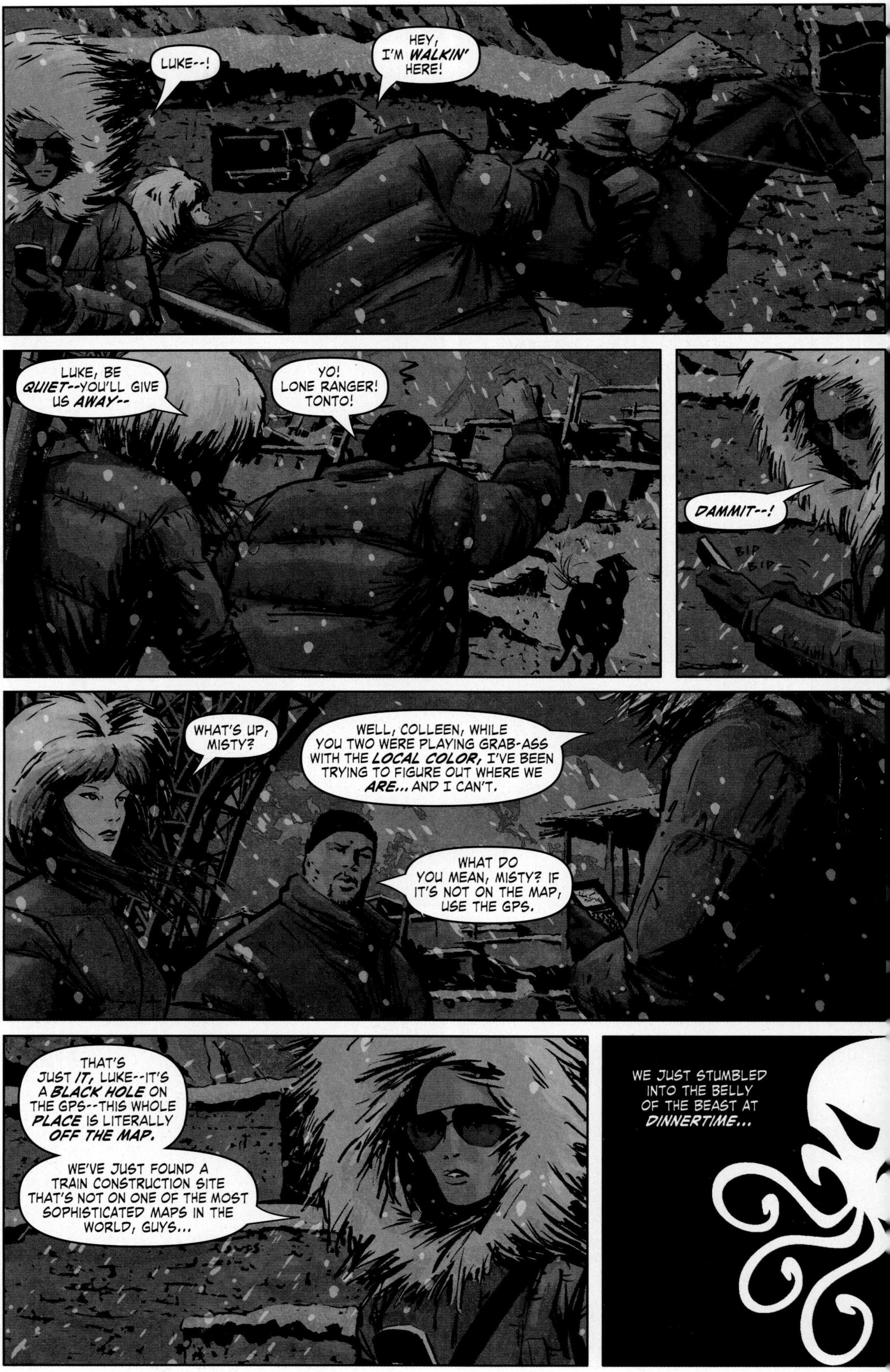
LUKE--!
HEY, I'M WALKIN' HERE!
LUKE, BE QUIET--YOU'LL GIVE US AWAY--
YO! LONE RANGER! TONTO!
DAMMIT--!
BIP BIP
WHAT'S UP, MISTY?
WELL, COLLEEN, WHILE YOU TWO WERE PLAYING GRAB-ASS WITH THE LOCAL COLOR, I'VE BEEN TRYING TO FIGURE OUT WHERE WE ARE... AND I CAN'T.
WHAT DO YOU MEAN, MISTY? IF IT'S NOT ON THE MAP, USE THE GPS.
THAT'S JUST IT, LUKE--IT'S A BLACK HOLE ON THE GPS--THIS WHOLE PLACE IS LITERALLY OFF THE MAP.
WE'VE JUST FOUND A TRAIN CONSTRUCTION SITE THAT'S NOT ON ONE OF THE MOST SOPHISTICATED MAPS IN THE WORLD, GUYS...
WE JUST STUMBLED INTO THE BELLY OF THE BEAST AT DINNERTIME...

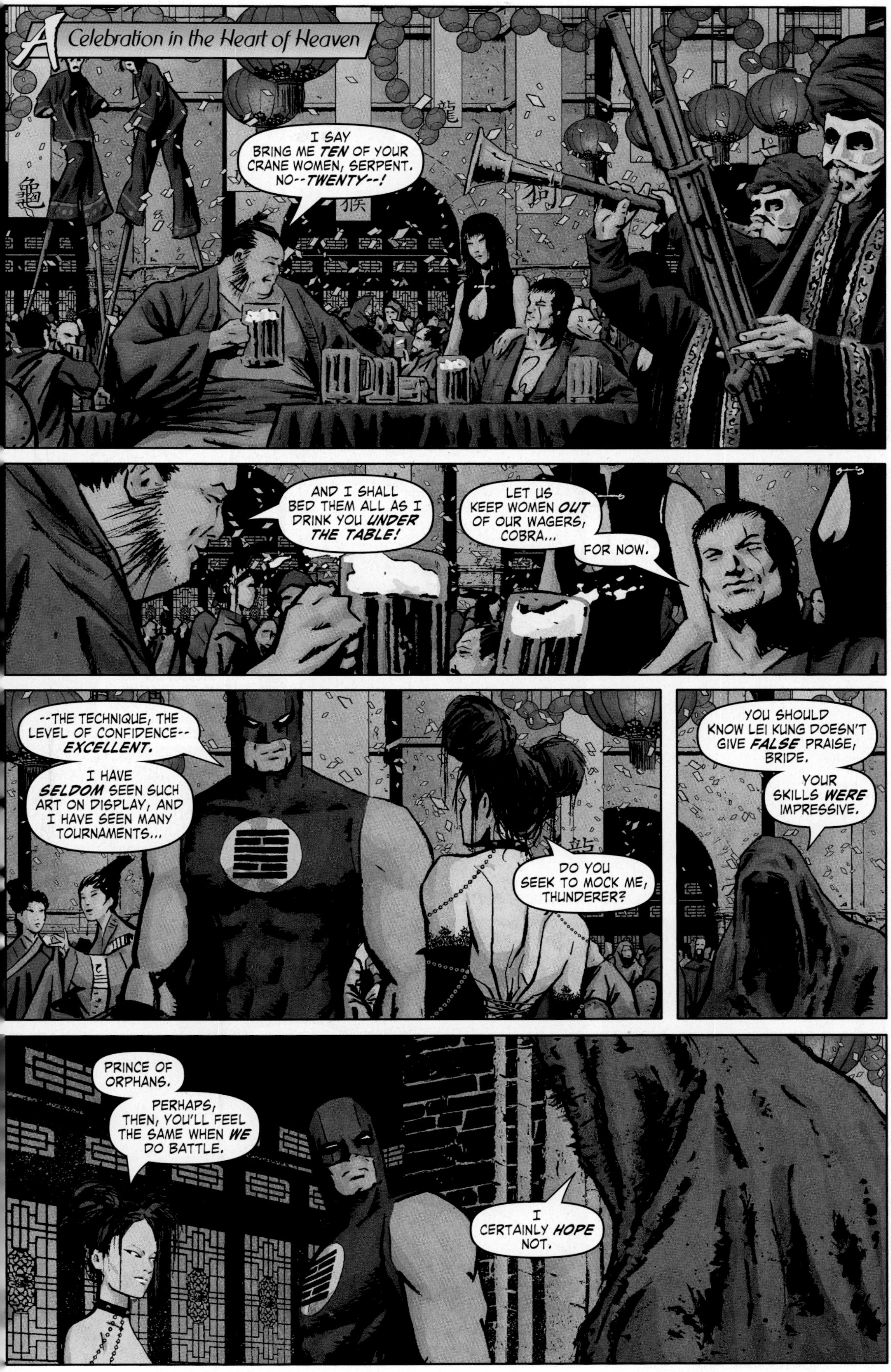
A Celebration in the Heart of Heaven
I SAY BRING ME TEN OF YOUR CRANE WOMEN, SERPENT. NO--TWENTY--!
AND I SHALL BED THEM ALL AS I DRINK YOU UNDER THE TABLE!
LET US KEEP WOMEN OUT OF OUR WAGERS, COBRA...
FOR NOW.
--THE TECHNIQUE, THE LEVEL OF CONFIDENCE-- EXCELLENT.
I HAVE SELDOM SEEN SUCH ART ON DISPLAY, AND I HAVE SEEN MANY TOURNAMENTS...
DO YOU SEEK TO MOCK ME, THUNDERER?
YOU SHOULD KNOW LEI KUNG DOESN'T GIVE FALSE PRAISE, BRIDE.
YOUR SKILLS WERE IMPRESSIVE.
PRINCE OF ORPHANS.
PERHAPS, THEN, YOU'LL FEEL THE SAME WHEN WE DO BATTLE.
I CERTAINLY HOPE NOT.

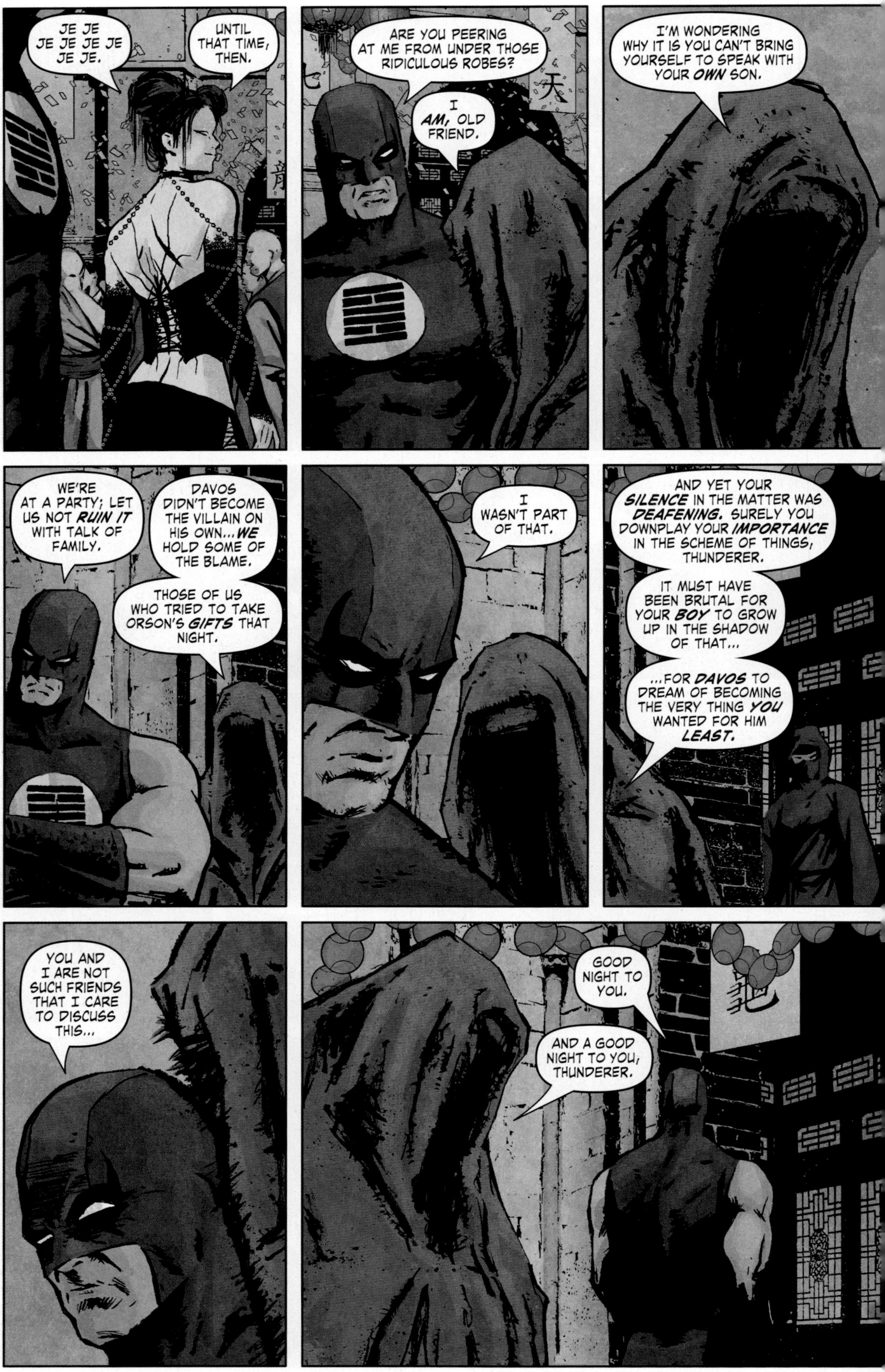
JE JE JE JE JE JE JE JE.
UNTIL THAT TIME, THEN.
ARE YOU PEERING AT ME FROM UNDER THOSE RIDICULOUS ROBES?
I AM, OLD FRIEND.
I'M WONDERING WHY IT IS YOU CAN'T BRING YOURSELF TO SPEAK WITH YOUR OWN SON.
WE'RE AT A PARTY; LET US NOT RUIN IT WITH TALK OF FAMILY.
DAVOS DIDN'T BECOME THE VILLAIN ON HIS OWN... WE HOLD SOME OF THE BLAME.
THOSE OF US WHO TRIED TO TAKE ORSON'S GIFTS THAT NIGHT.
I WASN'T PART OF THAT.
AND YET YOUR SILENCE IN THE MATTER WAS DEAFENING. SURELY YOU DOWNPLAY YOUR IMPORTANCE IN THE SCHEME OF THINGS, THUNDERER.
IT MUST HAVE BEEN BRUTAL FOR YOUR BOY TO GROW UP IN THE SHADOW OF THAT...
...FOR DAVOS TO DREAM OF BECOMING THE VERY THING YOU WANTED FOR HIM LEAST.
YOU AND I ARE NOT SUCH FRIENDS THAT I CARE TO DISCUSS THIS...
GOOD NIGHT TO YOU.
AND A GOOD NIGHT TO YOU, THUNDERER.

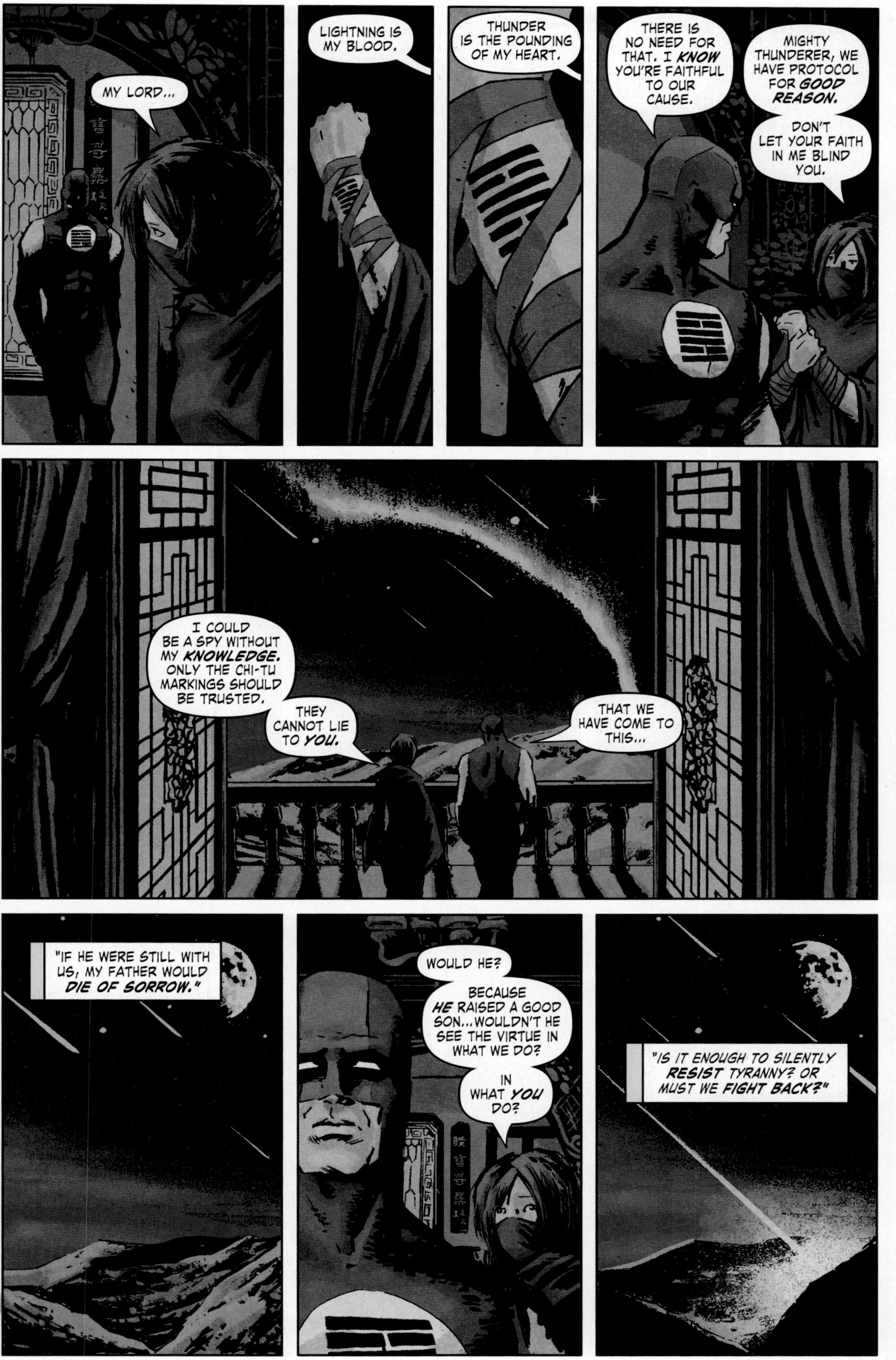
MY LORD...
LIGHTNING IS MY BLOOD.
THUNDER IS THE POUNDING OF MY HEART.
THERE IS NO NEED FOR THAT. I KNOW YOU'RE FAITHFUL TO OUR CAUSE.
MIGHTY THUNDERER, WE HAVE PROTOCOL FOR GOOD REASON.
DON'T LET YOUR FAITH IN ME BLIND YOU.
I COULD BE A SPY WITHOUT MY KNOWLEDGE. ONLY THE CHI-TU MARKINGS SHOULD BE TRUSTED.
THEY CANNOT LIE TO YOU.
THAT WE HAVE COME TO THIS...
"IF HE WERE STILL WITH US, MY FATHER WOULD DIE OF SORROW."
WOULD HE?
BECAUSE HE RAISED A GOOD SON...WOULDN'T HE SEE THE VIRTUE IN WHAT WE DO?
IN WHAT YOU DO?
"IS IT ENOUGH TO SILENTLY RESIST TYRANNY? OR MUST WE FIGHT BACK?"

SADLY, I'VE FOUND THAT SONS AND FATHERS ARE NOT *ALWAYS* A REFLECTION ON EACH OTHER...

...OR AT LEAST, NOT IN THE WAYS THEY WOULD *LIKE.*

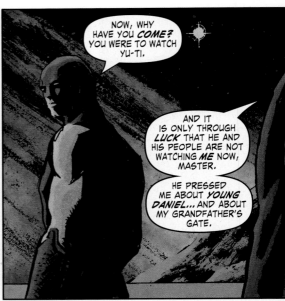

NOW, WHY HAVE YOU *COME?* YOU WERE TO WATCH YU-TI.

AND IT IS ONLY THROUGH *LUCK* THAT HE AND HIS PEOPLE ARE NOT WATCHING *ME* NOW, MASTER.

HE PRESSED ME ABOUT *YOUNG DANIEL*...AND ABOUT MY GRANDFATHER'S GATE.

HE DOES NOT *KNOW.*

BUT HE KNOWS.

WHAT HAS HE DONE?

TERROR PRIESTS HAVE BEEN SENT THROUGH THE GATE TO SEARCH FOR THE IRON FIST.

WE *MUST* GET DANIEL A MESSAGE, *SOMEHOW.* IF YU-TI'S MEN FIND HIM IN THE WORLD...

THERE IS NO SAFE WAY TO CONTACT HIM...

THE VEILS THAT SEPARATE K'UN-LUN FROM THE EARTHLY REALM ARE WATCHED *TOO CLOSELY* NOW.

IF HE IS SEEN, WE WILL LOSE EVERYTHING.

WE HAVEN'T LOST YET, LITTLE ONE...

AND YOU DON'T KNOW WHAT DANIEL RAND'KAI IS CAPABLE OF.

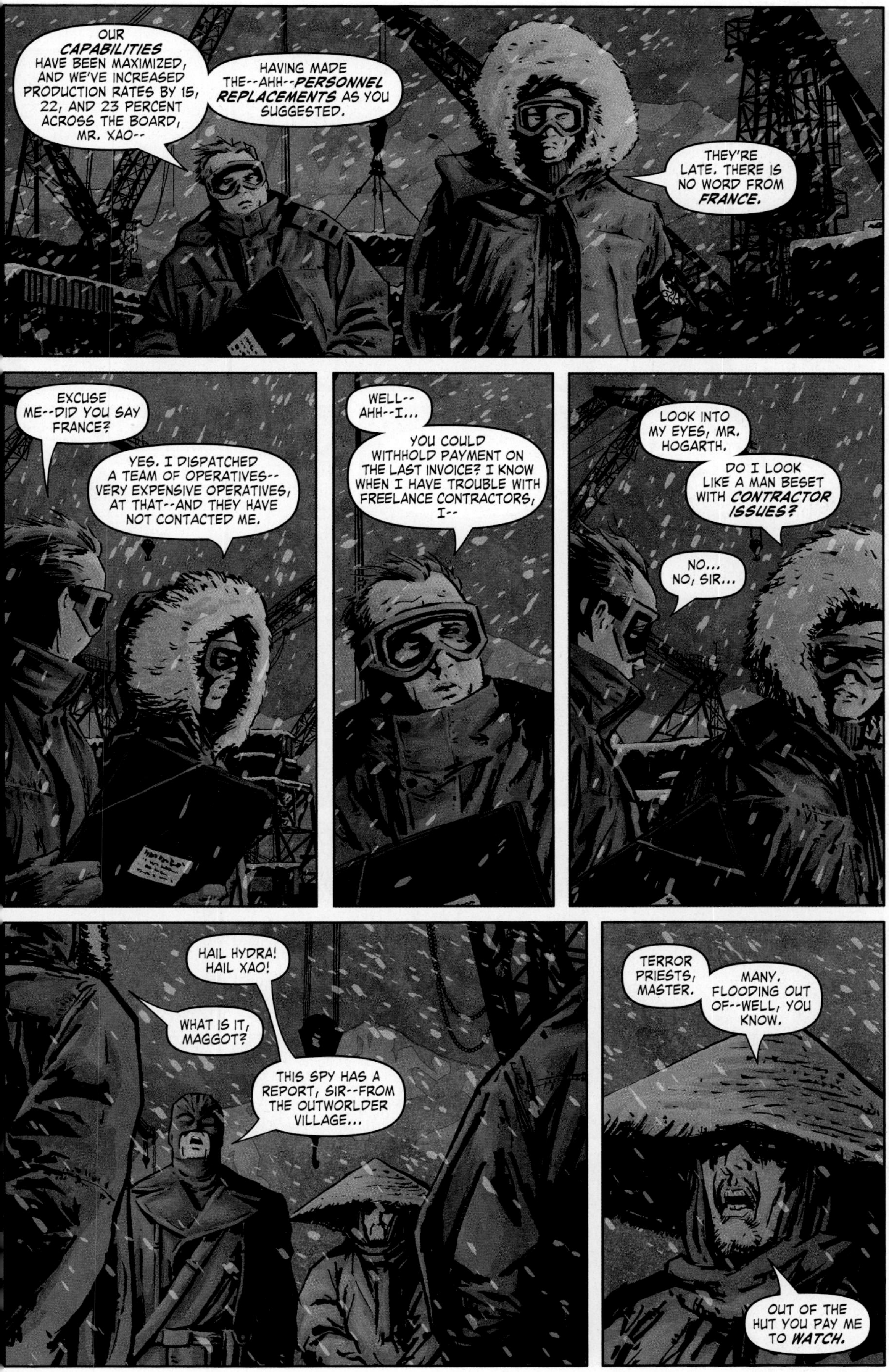
OUR *CAPABILITIES* HAVE BEEN MAXIMIZED, AND WE'VE INCREASED PRODUCTION RATES BY 15, 22, AND 23 PERCENT ACROSS THE BOARD, MR. XAO--
HAVING MADE THE--AHH--*PERSONNEL REPLACEMENTS* AS YOU SUGGESTED.
THEY'RE LATE. THERE IS NO WORD FROM *FRANCE.*
EXCUSE ME--DID YOU SAY FRANCE?
YES. I DISPATCHED A TEAM OF OPERATIVES--VERY EXPENSIVE OPERATIVES, AT THAT--AND THEY HAVE NOT CONTACTED ME.
WELL--AHH--I...
YOU COULD WITHHOLD PAYMENT ON THE LAST INVOICE? I KNOW WHEN I HAVE TROUBLE WITH FREELANCE CONTRACTORS, I--
LOOK INTO MY EYES, MR. HOGARTH.
DO I LOOK LIKE A MAN BESET WITH *CONTRACTOR ISSUES?*
NO... NO, SIR...
HAIL HYDRA! HAIL XAO!
WHAT IS IT, MAGGOT?
THIS SPY HAS A REPORT, SIR--FROM THE OUTWORLDER VILLAGE...
TERROR PRIESTS, MASTER.
MANY. FLOODING OUT OF--WELL, YOU KNOW.
OUT OF THE HUT YOU PAY ME TO *WATCH.*

MAGGOT, *KILL HIM.*

HAIL HYDRA!

BLAM! BLAM!

WHAT THE HELL ARE YOU DOING?!

DANIEL RAND HAS FLED THE HEART OF HEAVEN *AND* K'UN-LUN.

THERE'S ONLY ONE WAY FOR HIM TO RETURN. AND I'M GOING TO BE WAITING FOR HIM.

THIS IS A PLAN EIGHTY-EIGHT YEARS IN THE MAKING, AND IT'S ALL COMING TOGETHER FLAWLESSLY...

THIS IS *XAO.*

THE ORDER IS *GIVEN.* SECURE THE VILLAGE. NO SURVIVORS.

WAIT FOR IRON FIST.

HOLY HELL--!

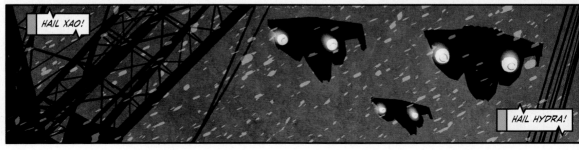

HAIL XAO!

HAIL HYDRA!

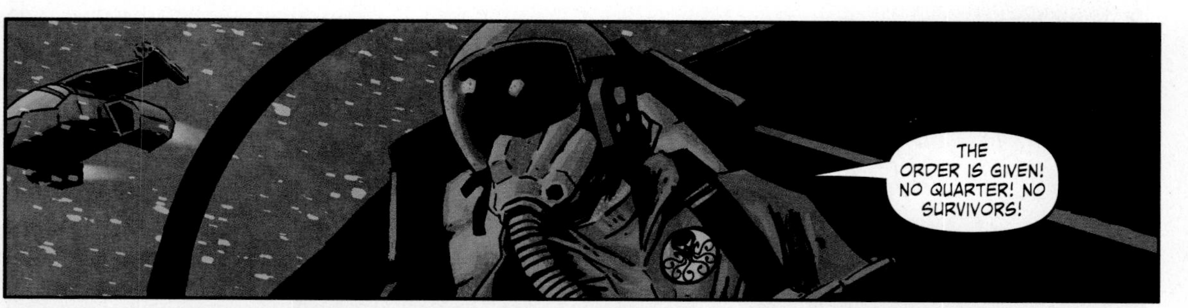
THE ORDER IS GIVEN! NO QUARTER! NO SURVIVORS!

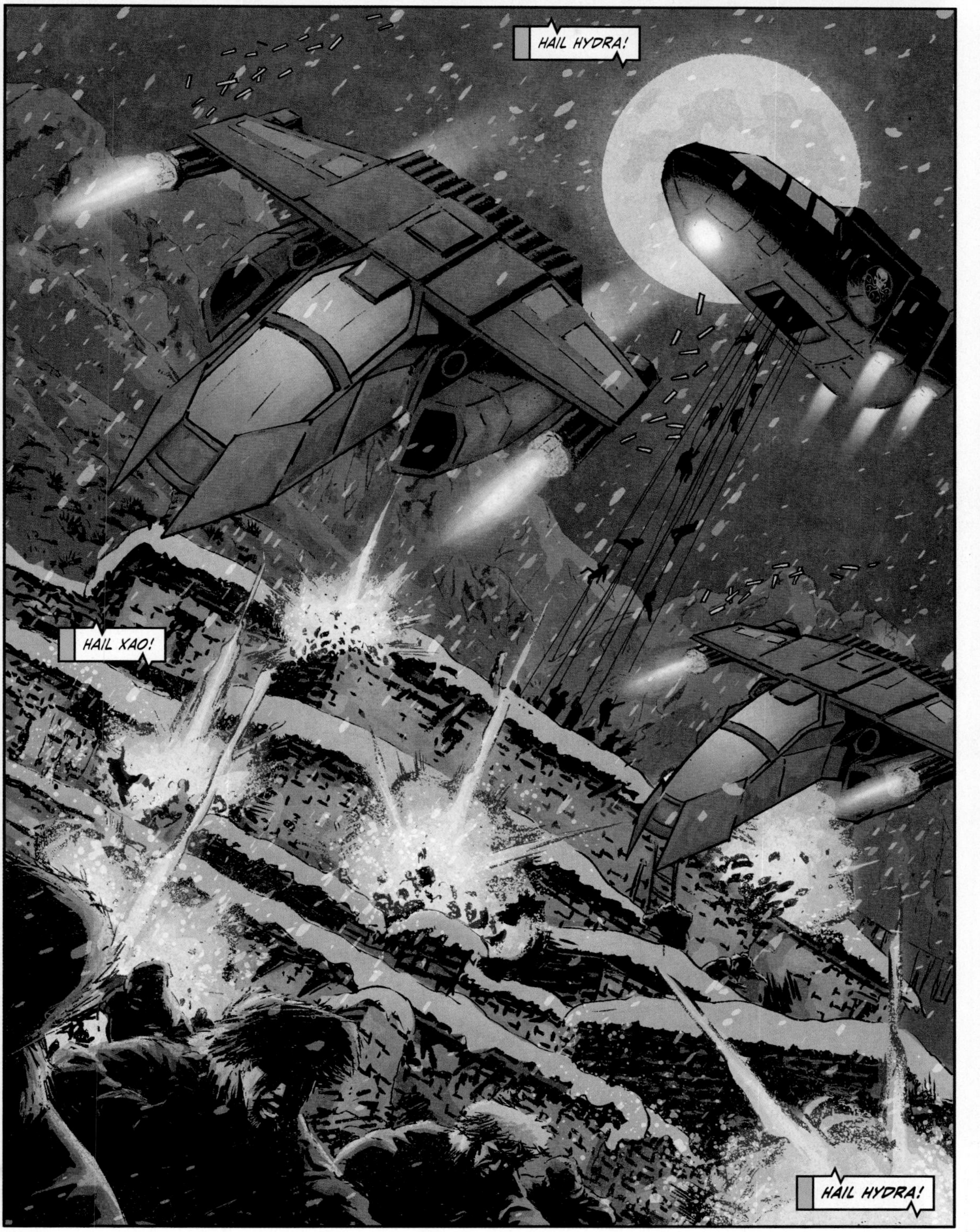
HAIL HYDRA!
HAIL XAO!
HAIL HYDRA!

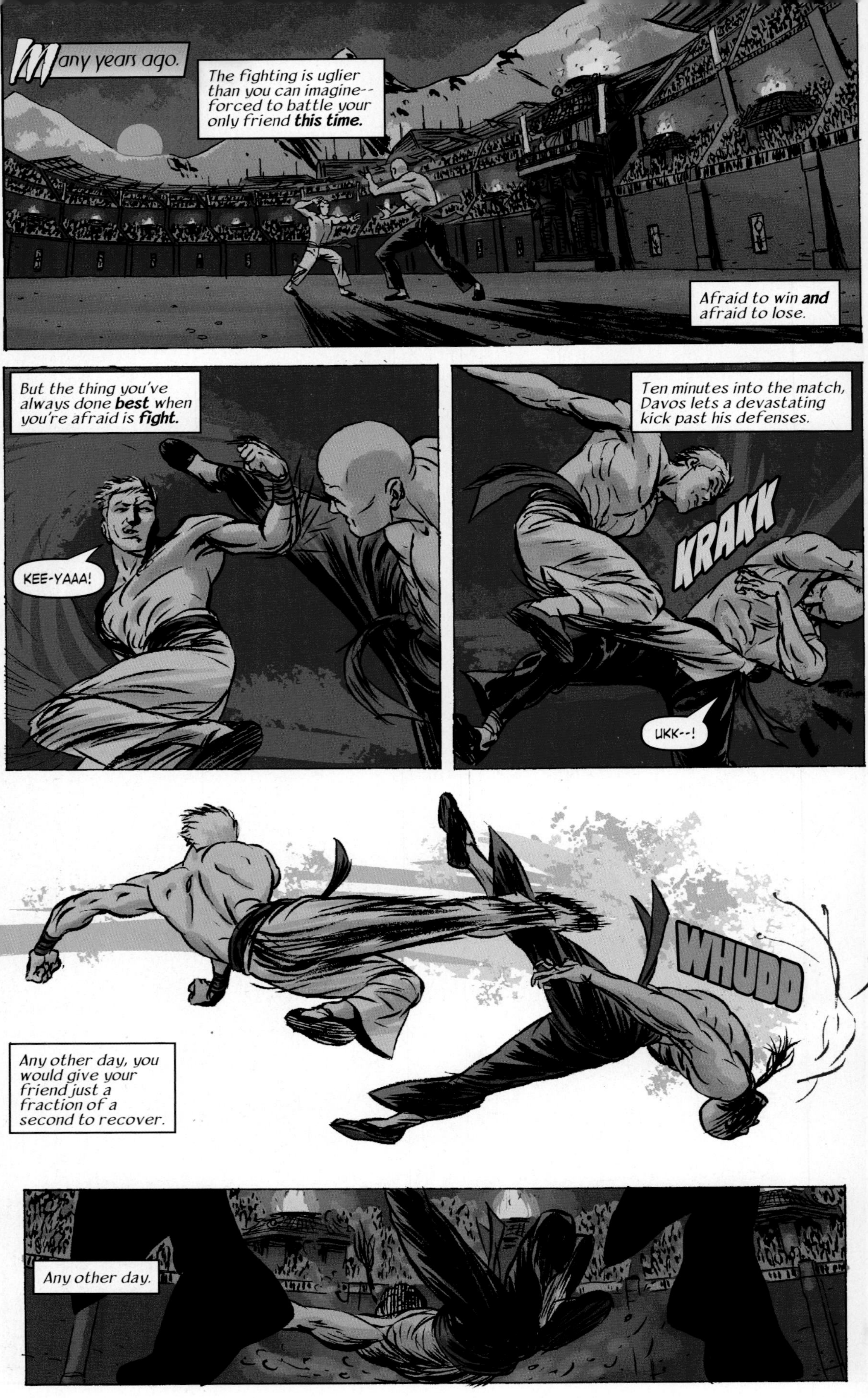
Many years ago.
The fighting is uglier than you can imagine--forced to battle your only friend **this time.**
Afraid to win **and** afraid to lose.
But the thing you've always done **best** when you're afraid is **fight.**
KEE-YAAA!
Ten minutes into the match, Davos lets a devastating kick past his defenses.
KRAKK
UKK--!
WHUDD
Any other day, you would give your friend just a fraction of a second to recover.
Any other day.

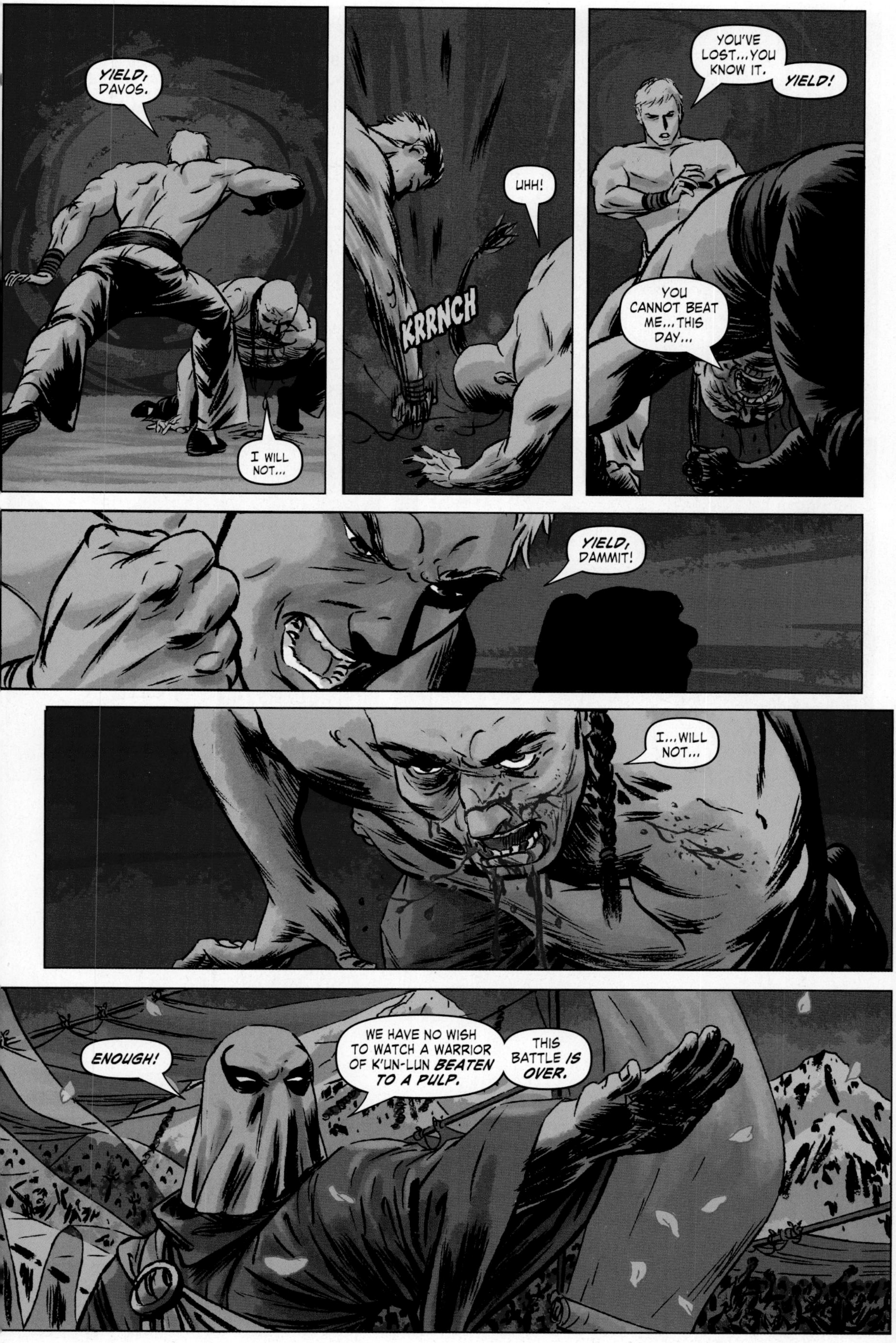
YIELD, DAVOS.
I WILL NOT...
UHH!
KRRNCH
YOU'VE LOST...YOU KNOW IT.
YIELD!
YOU CANNOT BEAT ME...THIS DAY...
YIELD, DAMMIT!
I...WILL NOT...
ENOUGH!
WE HAVE NO WISH TO WATCH A WARRIOR OF K'UN-LUN BEATEN TO A PULP.
THIS BATTLE IS OVER.

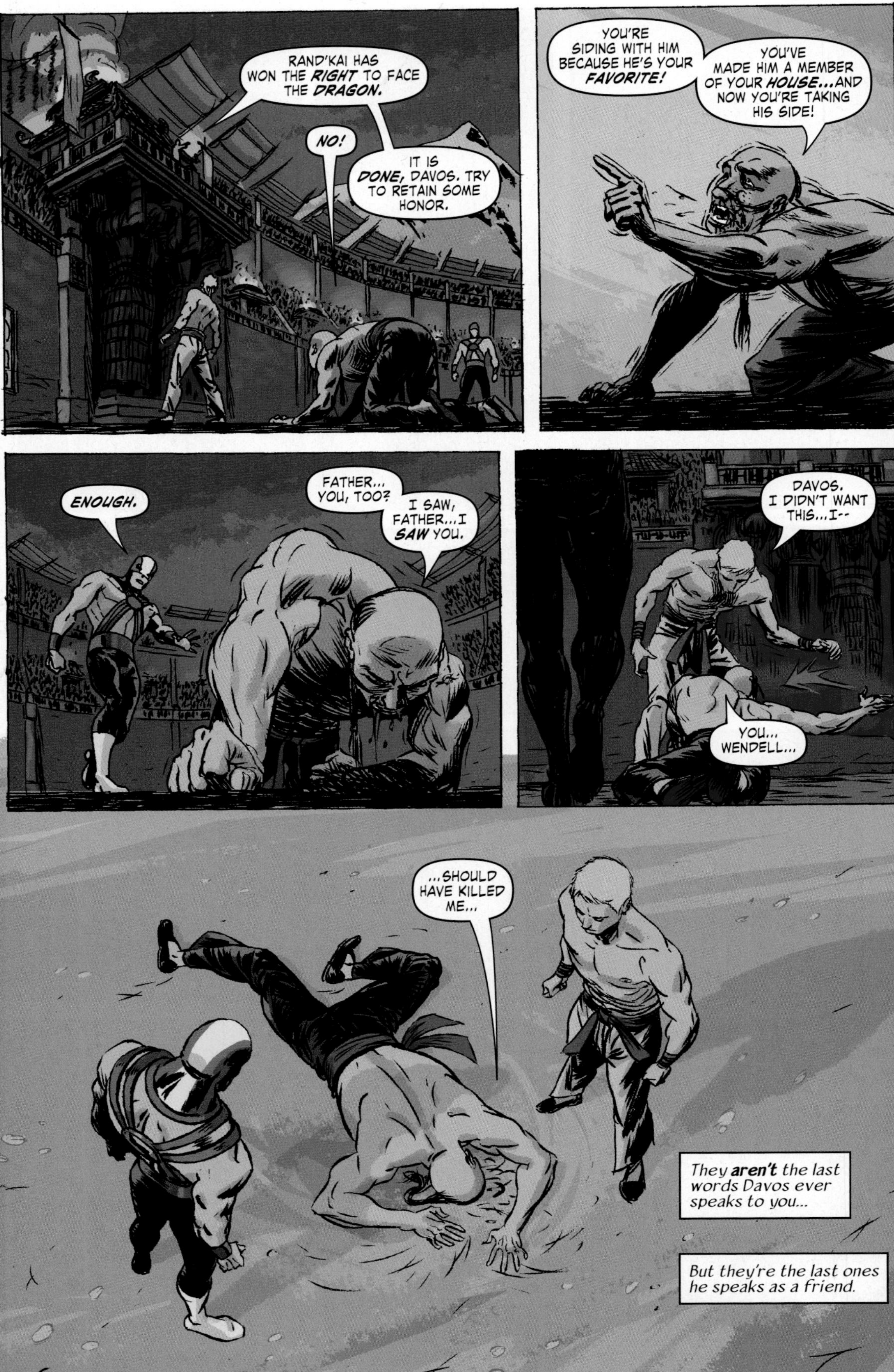

RAND'KAI HAS WON THE RIGHT TO FACE THE DRAGON.
NO!
IT IS DONE, DAVOS. TRY TO RETAIN SOME HONOR.
YOU'RE SIDING WITH HIM BECAUSE HE'S YOUR FAVORITE!
YOU'VE MADE HIM A MEMBER OF YOUR HOUSE...AND NOW YOU'RE TAKING HIS SIDE!
ENOUGH.
FATHER... YOU, TOO?
I SAW, FATHER...I SAW YOU.
DAVOS. I DIDN'T WANT THIS...I--
YOU... WENDELL...
...SHOULD HAVE KILLED ME...
They aren't the last words Davos ever speaks to you...
But they're the last ones he speaks as a friend.

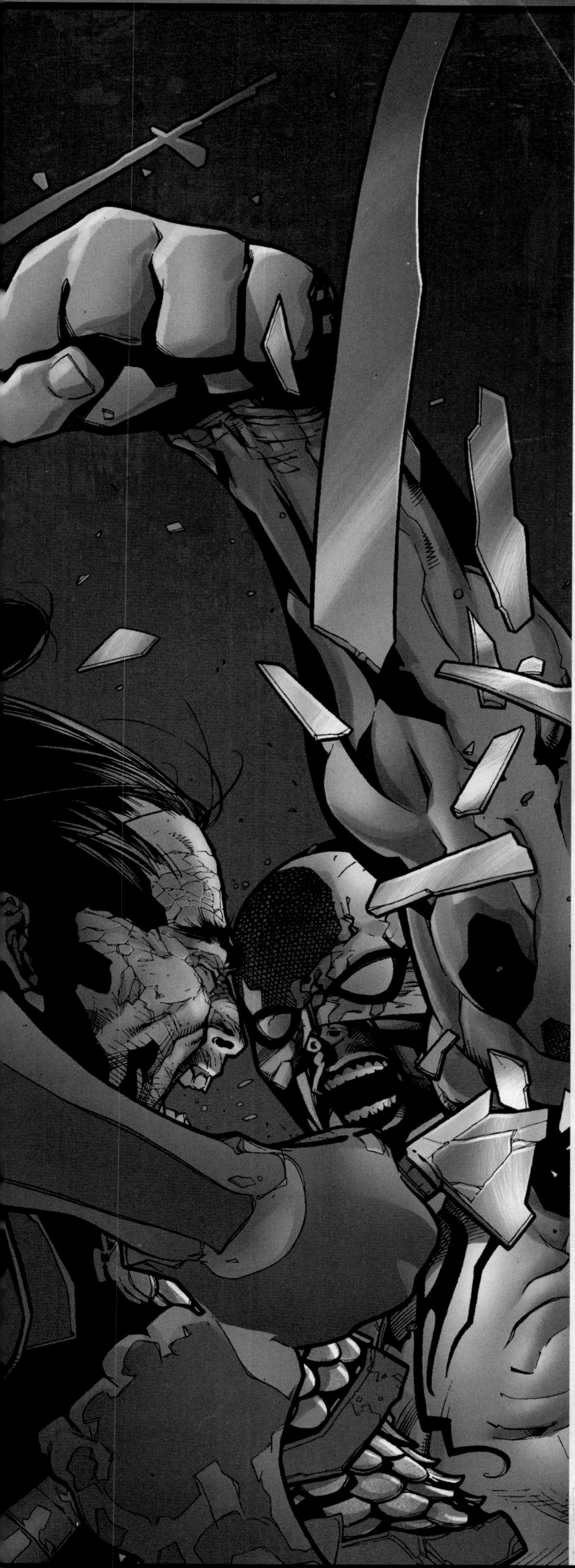

鐵拳 II

The 七 Capital Cities of Heaven

四 Round 4

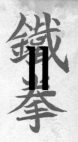

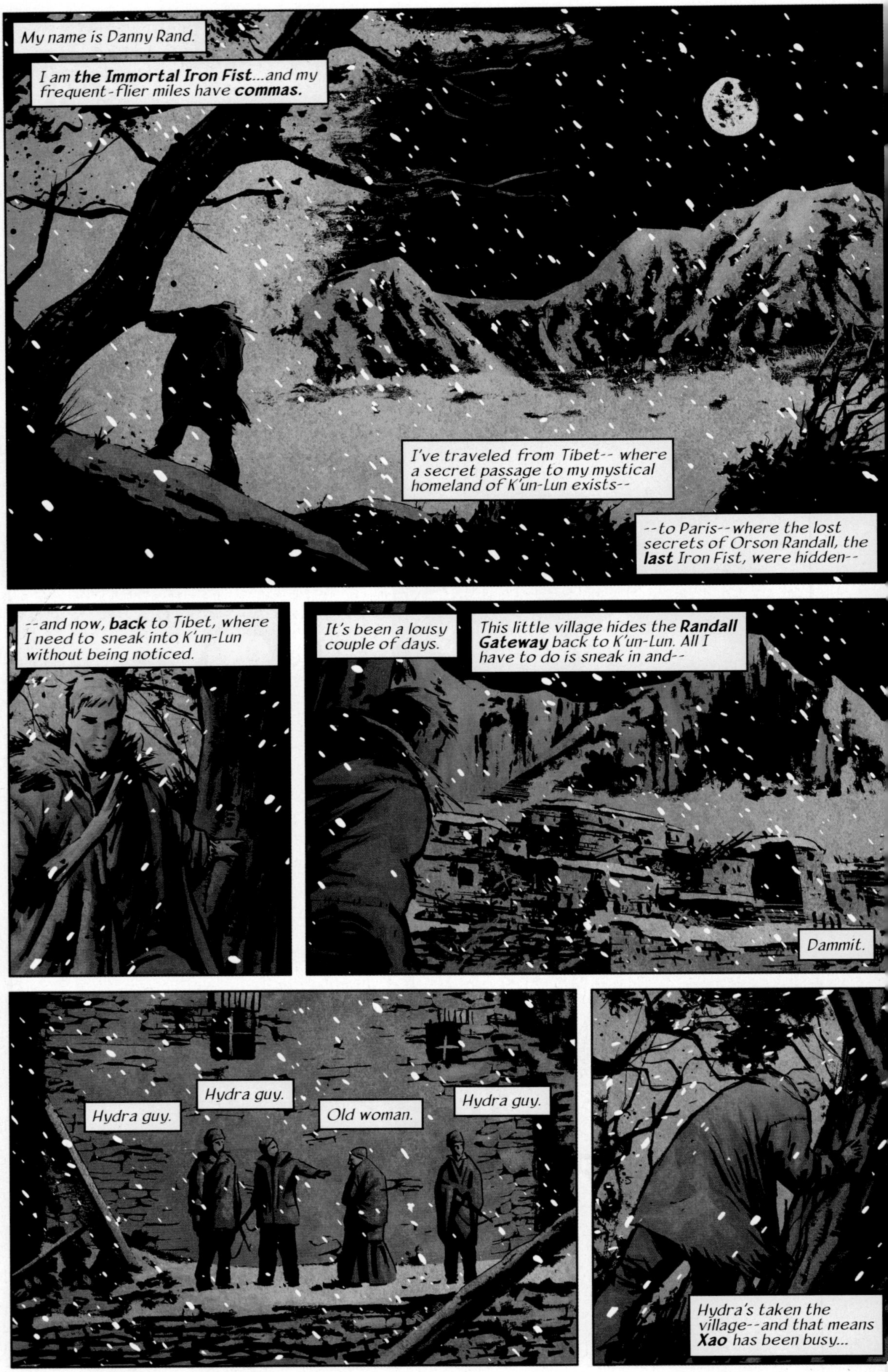
My name is Danny Rand.
I am **the Immortal Iron Fist**...and my frequent-flier miles have **commas.**
I've traveled from Tibet-- where a secret passage to my mystical homeland of K'un-Lun exists--
--to Paris--where the lost secrets of Orson Randall, the **last** Iron Fist, were hidden--
--and now, **back** to Tibet, where I need to sneak into K'un-Lun without being noticed.
It's been a lousy couple of days.
This little village hides the **Randall Gateway** back to K'un-Lun. All I have to do is sneak in and--
Dammit.
Hydra guy.
Hydra guy.
Old woman.
Hydra guy.
Hydra's taken the village--and that means **Xao** has been busy...

HURRY THEM UP.

HURRY THEM UP, HURRY THEM UP, HURRY THEM UP.

AHH--MR. XAO?

IT'S NOT A TOASTER. WE CAN'T JUST PLUG IT IN AND TURN IT ON.

ALSO--THIS IS A RIDICULOUS WAY TO WORK--YOU *HAVE* TO TELL ME WHAT THESE PLANS AND MODIFICATIONS YOU'VE MADE MEAN.

DON'T THINK I HAVEN'T NOTICED THE TRACK DOESN'T *GO* ANYWHERE.

TERROR, TORTURE, CONSPIRACY AND OBFUSCATION AREN'T MY *ONLY* TALENTS, MR. HOGARTH.

YOU MAKE THE TRAIN RUN. I'LL WORRY ABOUT TO WHERE.

WELL, GREAT.

THEN THE BEST I CAN TELL, YOUR HALF-BILLION-DOLLAR TRAIN IS READY TO GO FLYING OFF OF A HALF-CLICK OF TRACK.

EXCELLENT. YOU KNOW, IF THIS WORKS, I HAVE A GIFT FOR YOU.

IF IT FAILS, I HAVE A GIFT FROM YOUR *MOTHER*.

WHERE IS SHE? IS SHE HERE? IS SHE?

PLEASE, MR. HOGARTH. COMPORT YOURSELF WITH A MODICUM OF *DIGNITY*.

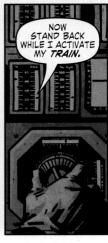

NOW STAND BACK WHILE I ACTIVATE MY *TRAIN*.

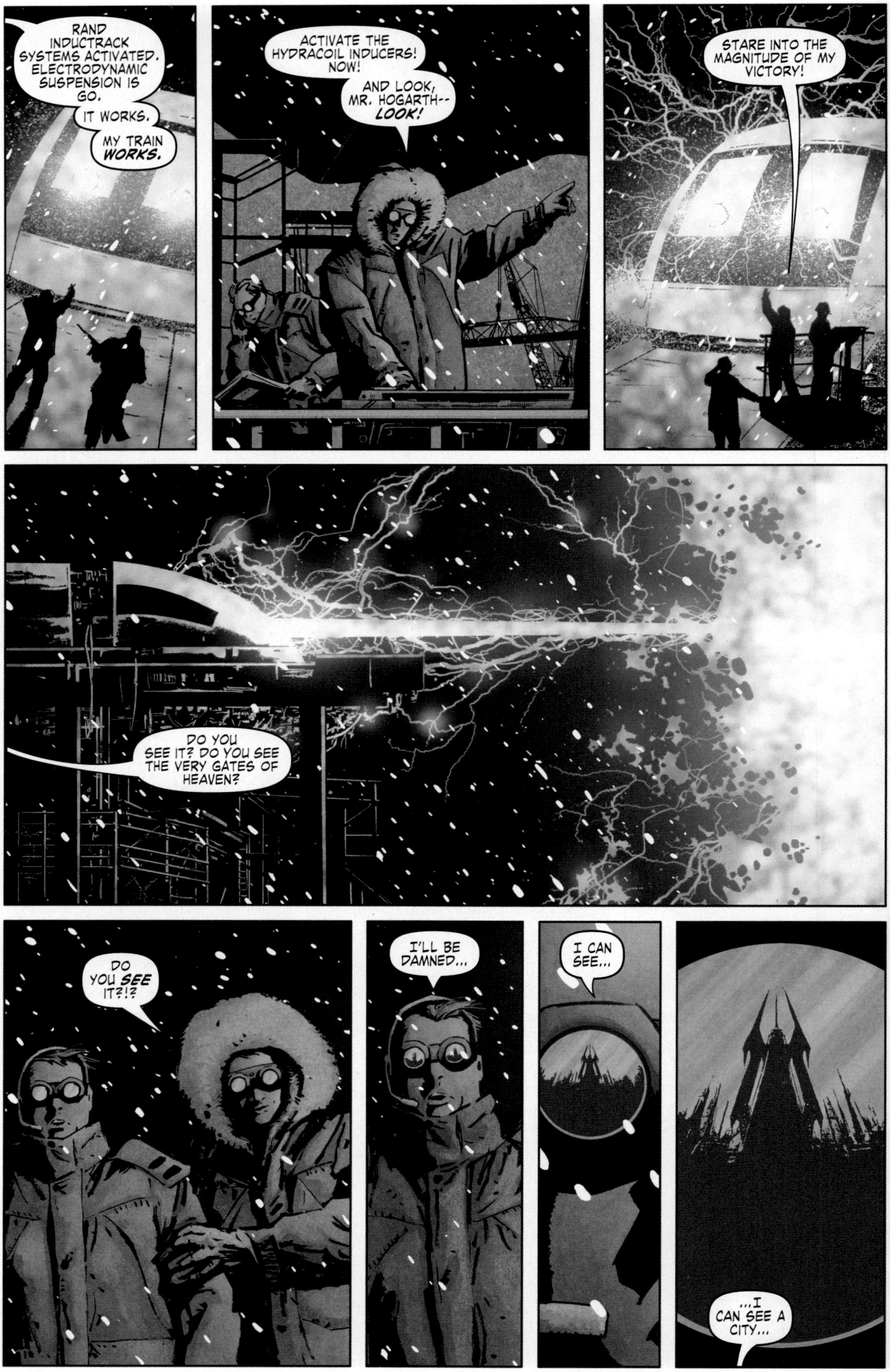
RAND INDUCTRACK SYSTEMS ACTIVATED. ELECTRODYNAMIC SUSPENSION IS GO.
IT WORKS.
MY TRAIN WORKS.
ACTIVATE THE HYDRACOIL INDUCERS! NOW!
AND LOOK, MR. HOGARTH-- LOOK!
STARE INTO THE MAGNITUDE OF MY VICTORY!
DO YOU SEE IT? DO YOU SEE THE VERY GATES OF HEAVEN?
DO YOU SEE IT?!?
I'LL BE DAMNED...
I CAN SEE...
...I CAN SEE A CITY...

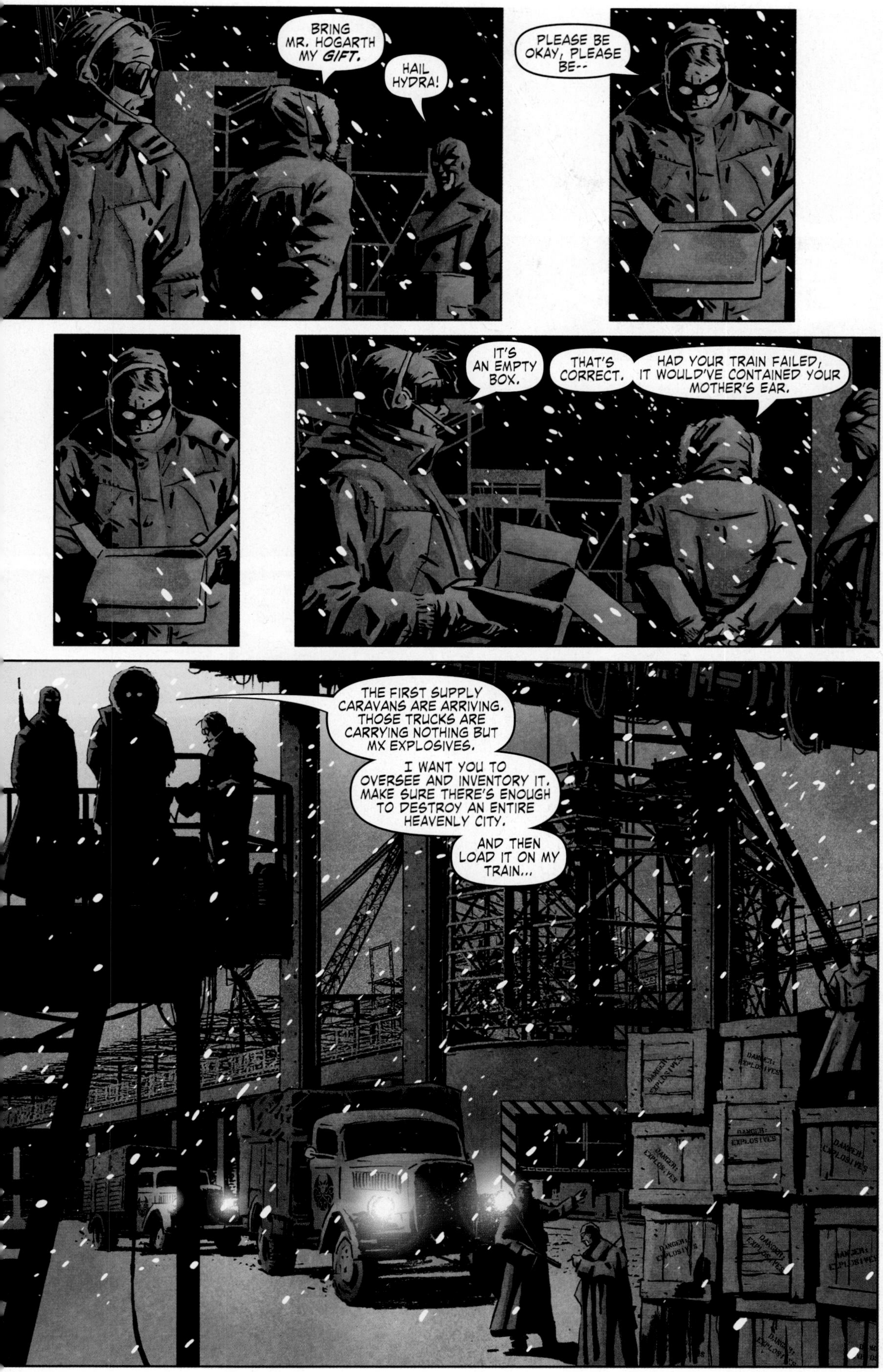
BRING MR. HOGARTH MY GIFT.
HAIL HYDRA!
PLEASE BE OKAY, PLEASE BE--
IT'S AN EMPTY BOX.
THAT'S CORRECT.
HAD YOUR TRAIN FAILED, IT WOULD'VE CONTAINED YOUR MOTHER'S EAR.
THE FIRST SUPPLY CARAVANS ARE ARRIVING. THOSE TRUCKS ARE CARRYING NOTHING BUT MX EXPLOSIVES.
I WANT YOU TO OVERSEE AND INVENTORY IT. MAKE SURE THERE'S ENOUGH TO DESTROY AN ENTIRE HEAVENLY CITY.
AND THEN LOAD IT ON MY TRAIN...
DANGER: EXPLOSIVES

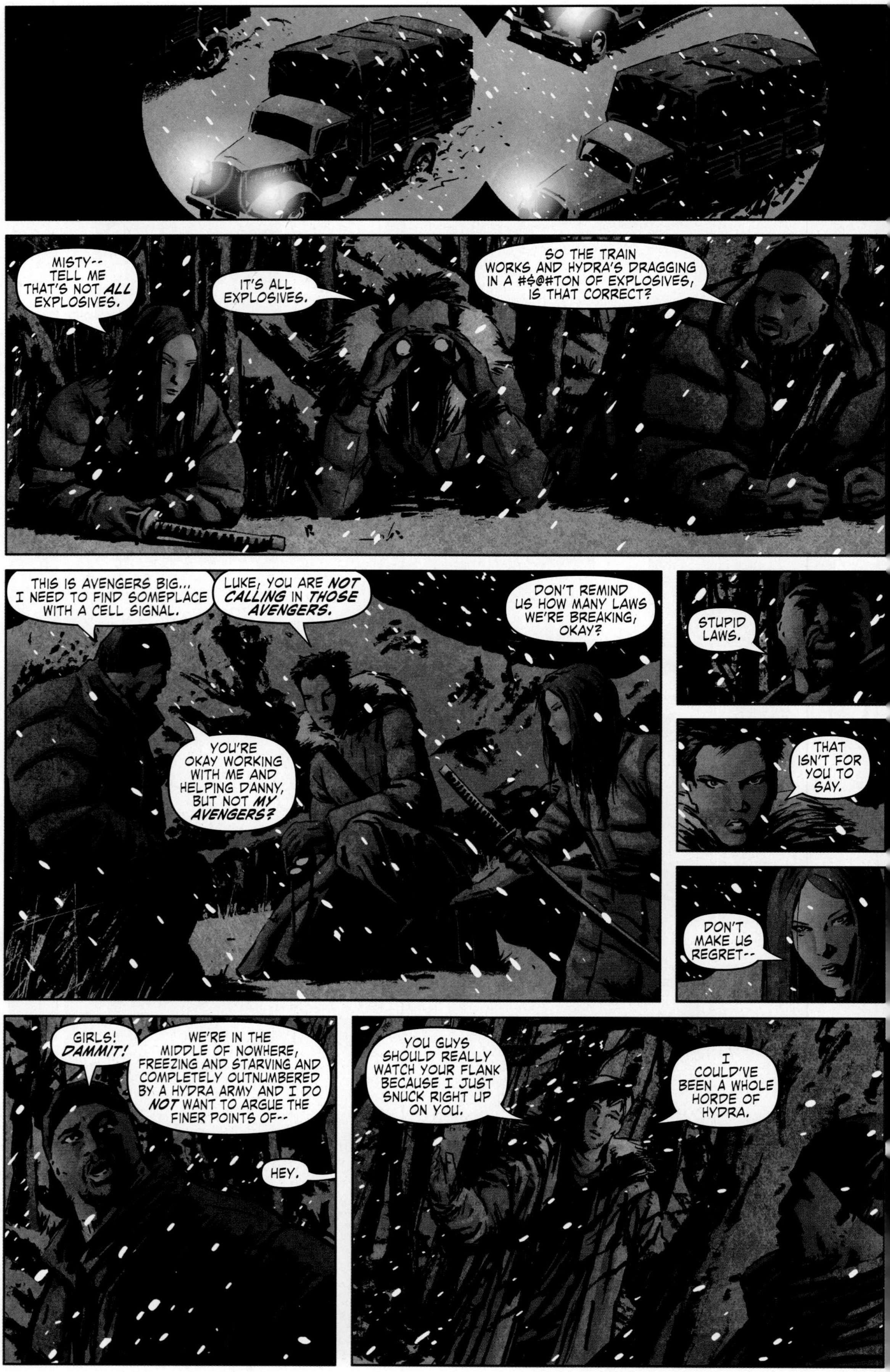
MISTY-- TELL ME THAT'S NOT ALL EXPLOSIVES.
IT'S ALL EXPLOSIVES.
SO THE TRAIN WORKS AND HYDRA'S DRAGGING IN A #$@#TON OF EXPLOSIVES, IS THAT CORRECT?
THIS IS AVENGERS BIG... I NEED TO FIND SOMEPLACE WITH A CELL SIGNAL.
LUKE, YOU ARE NOT CALLING IN THOSE AVENGERS.
DON'T REMIND US HOW MANY LAWS WE'RE BREAKING, OKAY?
YOU'RE OKAY WORKING WITH ME AND HELPING DANNY, BUT NOT MY AVENGERS?
STUPID LAWS.
THAT ISN'T FOR YOU TO SAY.
DON'T MAKE US REGRET--
GIRLS! DAMMIT!
WE'RE IN THE MIDDLE OF NOWHERE, FREEZING AND STARVING AND COMPLETELY OUTNUMBERED BY A HYDRA ARMY AND I DO NOT WANT TO ARGUE THE FINER POINTS OF--
HEY.
YOU GUYS SHOULD REALLY WATCH YOUR FLANK BECAUSE I JUST SNUCK RIGHT UP ON YOU.
I COULD'VE BEEN A WHOLE HORDE OF HYDRA.

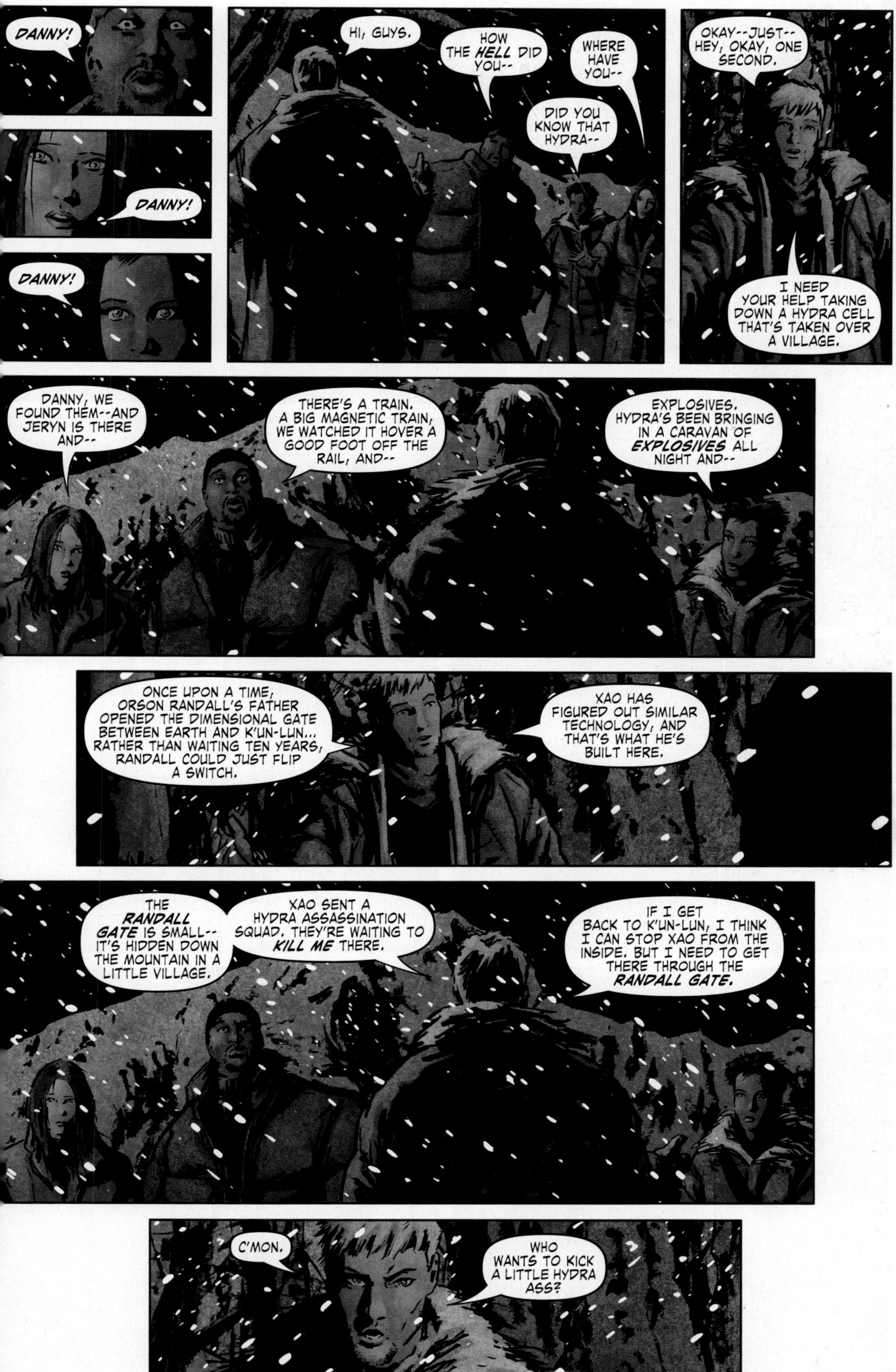
DANNY!
DANNY!
DANNY!
HI, GUYS.
HOW THE *HELL* DID YOU--
WHERE HAVE YOU--
DID YOU KNOW THAT HYDRA--
OKAY--JUST--HEY, OKAY, ONE SECOND.
I NEED YOUR HELP TAKING DOWN A HYDRA CELL THAT'S TAKEN OVER A VILLAGE.
DANNY, WE FOUND THEM--AND JERYN IS THERE AND--
THERE'S A TRAIN. A BIG MAGNETIC TRAIN, WE WATCHED IT HOVER A GOOD FOOT OFF THE RAIL, AND--
EXPLOSIVES. HYDRA'S BEEN BRINGING IN A CARAVAN OF *EXPLOSIVES* ALL NIGHT AND--
ONCE UPON A TIME, ORSON RANDALL'S FATHER OPENED THE DIMENSIONAL GATE BETWEEN EARTH AND K'UN-LUN... RATHER THAN WAITING TEN YEARS, RANDALL COULD JUST FLIP A SWITCH.
XAO HAS FIGURED OUT SIMILAR TECHNOLOGY, AND THAT'S WHAT HE'S BUILT HERE.
THE *RANDALL GATE* IS SMALL--IT'S HIDDEN DOWN THE MOUNTAIN IN A LITTLE VILLAGE.
XAO SENT A HYDRA ASSASSINATION SQUAD. THEY'RE WAITING TO *KILL ME* THERE.
IF I GET BACK TO K'UN-LUN, I THINK I CAN STOP XAO FROM THE INSIDE. BUT I NEED TO GET THERE THROUGH THE *RANDALL GATE.*
C'MON.
WHO WANTS TO KICK A LITTLE HYDRA ASS?

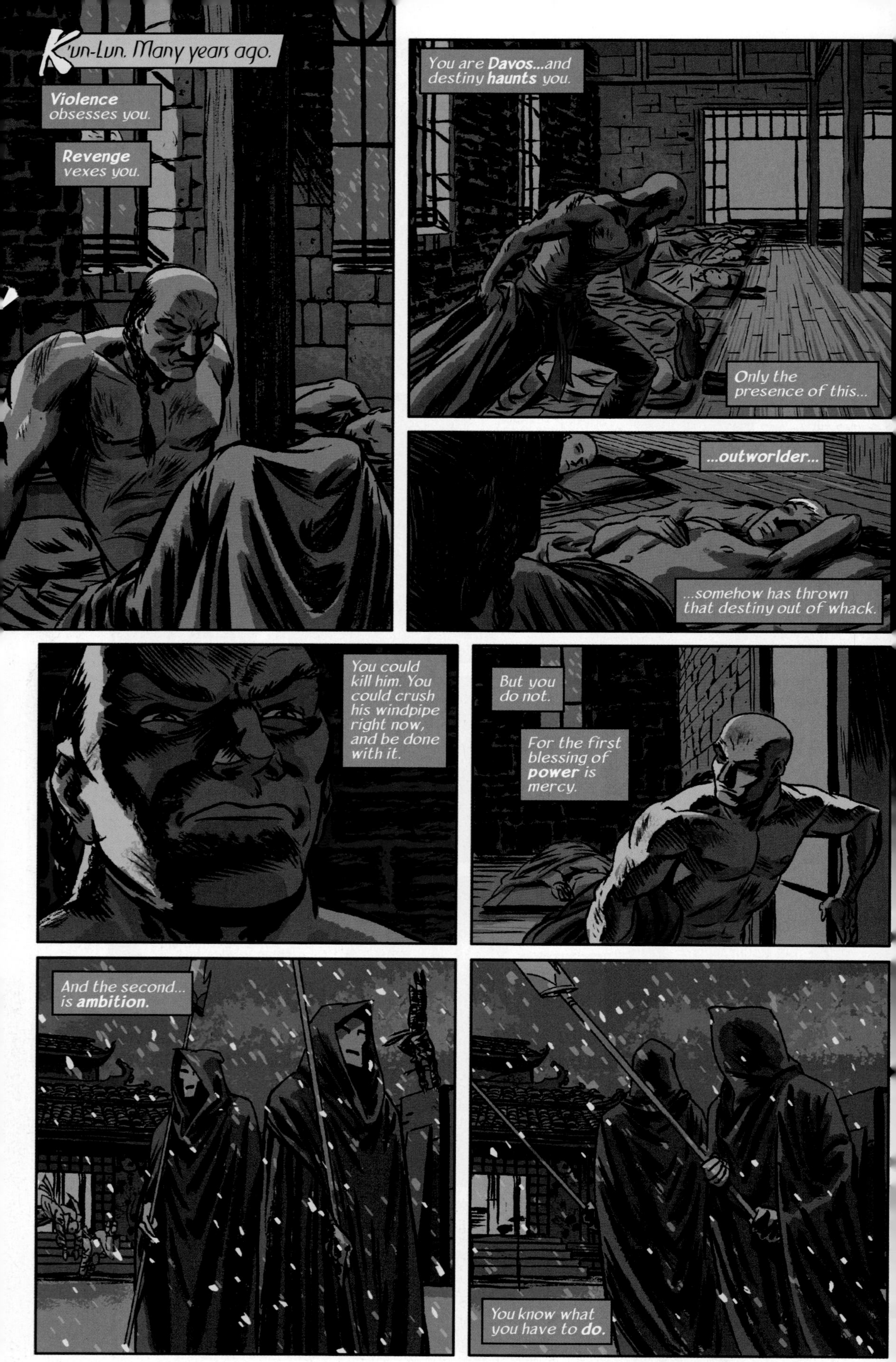
K'un-Lun. Many years ago.
Violence obsesses you.
Revenge vexes you.
You are Davos...and destiny haunts you.
Only the presence of this...
...outworlder...
...somehow has thrown that destiny out of whack.
You could kill him. You could crush his windpipe right now, and be done with it.
But you do not.
For the first blessing of power is mercy.
And the second... is ambition.
You know what you have to do.

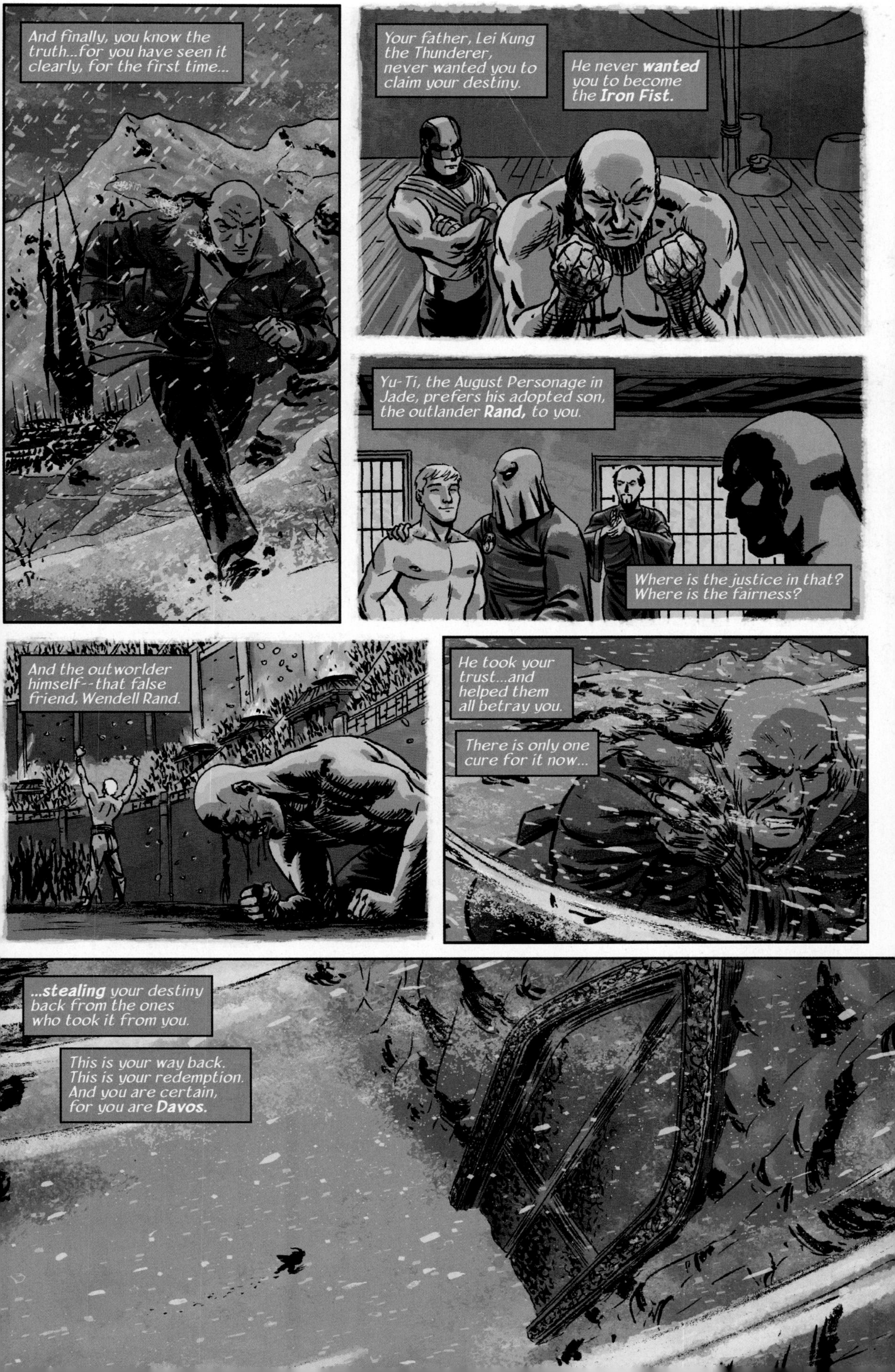
And finally, you know the truth...for you have seen it clearly, for the first time...
Your father, Lei Kung the Thunderer, never wanted you to claim your destiny.
He never **wanted** you to become the **Iron Fist.**
Yu-Ti, the August Personage in Jade, prefers his adopted son, the outlander **Rand,** to you.
Where is the justice in that? Where is the fairness?
And the outworlder himself--that false friend, Wendell Rand.
He took your trust...and helped them all betray you.
There is only one cure for it now...
...stealing your destiny back from the ones who took it from you.
This is your way back. This is your redemption. And you are certain, for you are **Davos.**

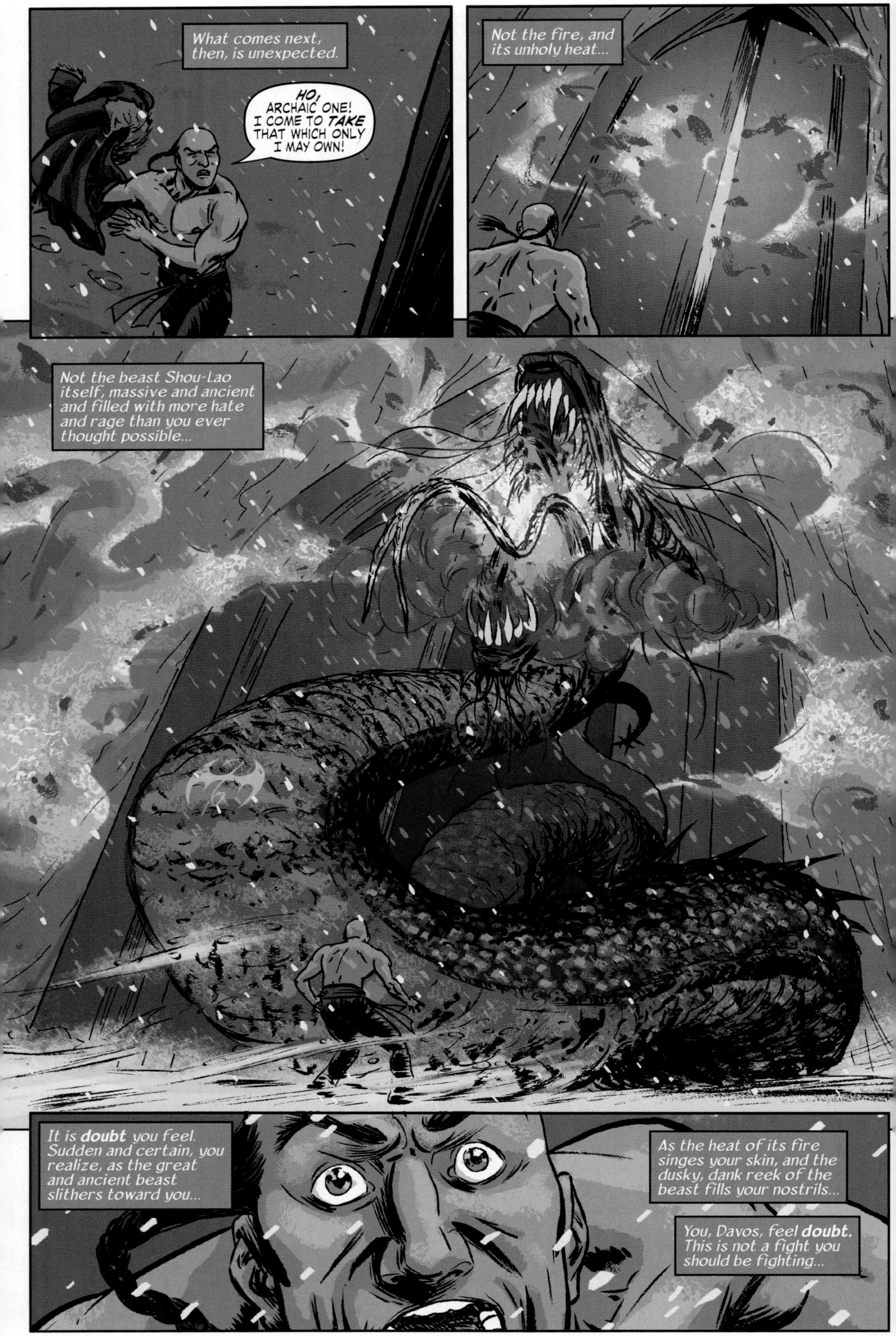
What comes next, then, is unexpected.
HO, ARCHAIC ONE! I COME TO TAKE THAT WHICH ONLY I MAY OWN!
Not the fire, and its unholy heat...
Not the beast Shou-Lao itself, massive and ancient and filled with more hate and rage than you ever thought possible...
It is doubt you feel. Sudden and certain, you realize, as the great and ancient beast slithers toward you...
As the heat of its fire singes your skin, and the dusky, dank reek of the beast fills your nostrils...
You, Davos, feel doubt. This is not a fight you should be fighting...

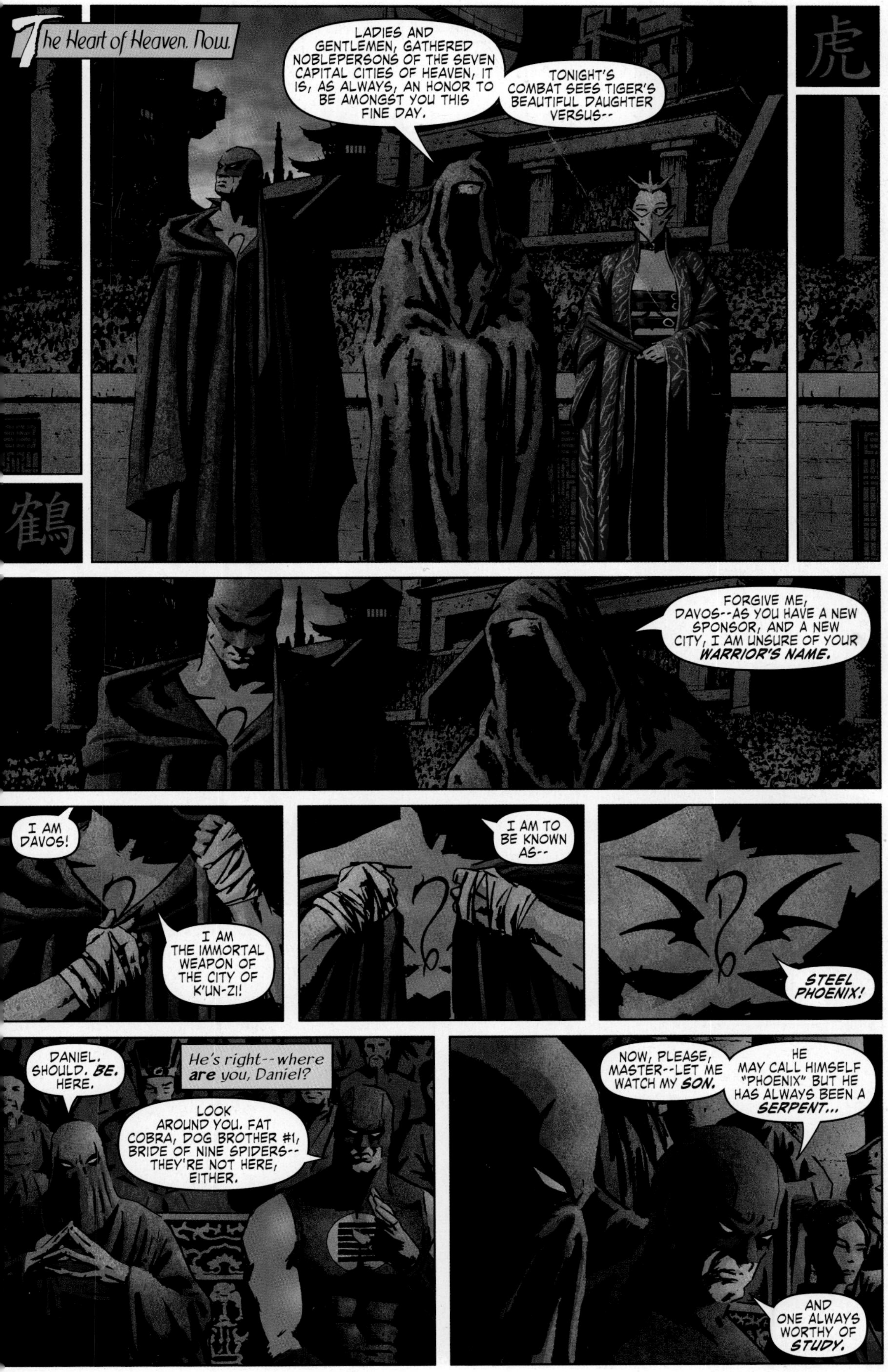
虎
鶴
The Heart of Heaven. Now.
LADIES AND GENTLEMEN, GATHERED NOBLEPERSONS OF THE SEVEN CAPITAL CITIES OF HEAVEN, IT IS, AS ALWAYS, AN HONOR TO BE AMONGST YOU THIS FINE DAY.
TONIGHT'S COMBAT SEES TIGER'S BEAUTIFUL DAUGHTER VERSUS--
FORGIVE ME, DAVOS--AS YOU HAVE A NEW SPONSOR, AND A NEW CITY, I AM UNSURE OF YOUR WARRIOR'S NAME.
I AM DAVOS!
I AM THE IMMORTAL WEAPON OF THE CITY OF K'UN-ZI!
I AM TO BE KNOWN AS--
STEEL PHOENIX!
DANIEL. SHOULD. BE. HERE.
He's right--where are you, Daniel?
LOOK AROUND YOU. FAT COBRA, DOG BROTHER #1, BRIDE OF NINE SPIDERS--THEY'RE NOT HERE, EITHER.
NOW, PLEASE, MASTER--LET ME WATCH MY SON.
HE MAY CALL HIMSELF "PHOENIX" BUT HE HAS ALWAYS BEEN A SERPENT...
AND ONE ALWAYS WORTHY OF STUDY.

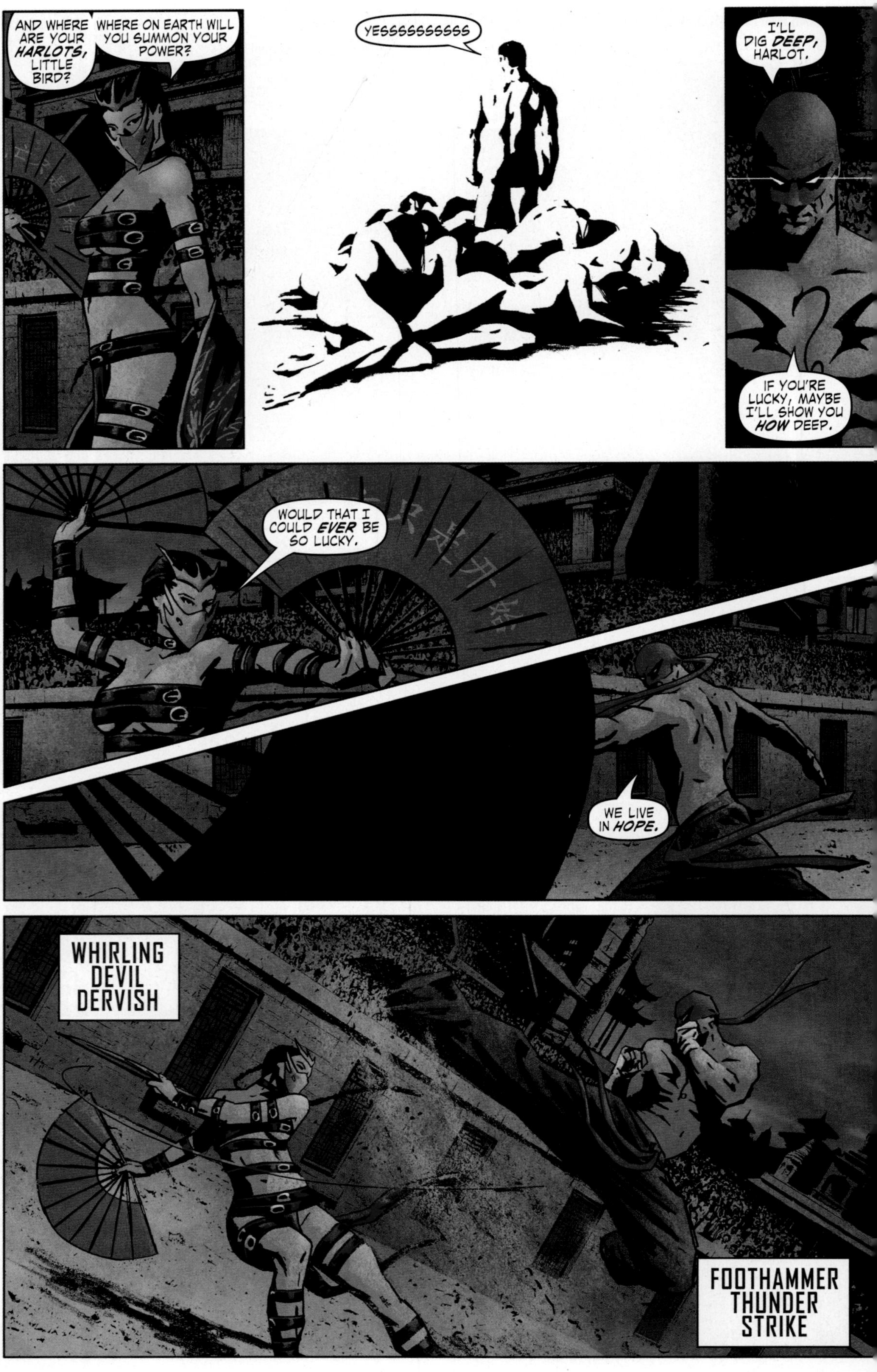
AND WHERE ARE YOUR HARLOTS, LITTLE BIRD?
WHERE ON EARTH WILL YOU SUMMON YOUR POWER?
YESSSSSSSSSS
I'LL DIG DEEP, HARLOT.
IF YOU'RE LUCKY, MAYBE I'LL SHOW YOU HOW DEEP.
WOULD THAT I COULD EVER BE SO LUCKY.
WE LIVE IN HOPE.
WHIRLING DEVIL DERVISH
FOOTHAMMER THUNDER STRIKE

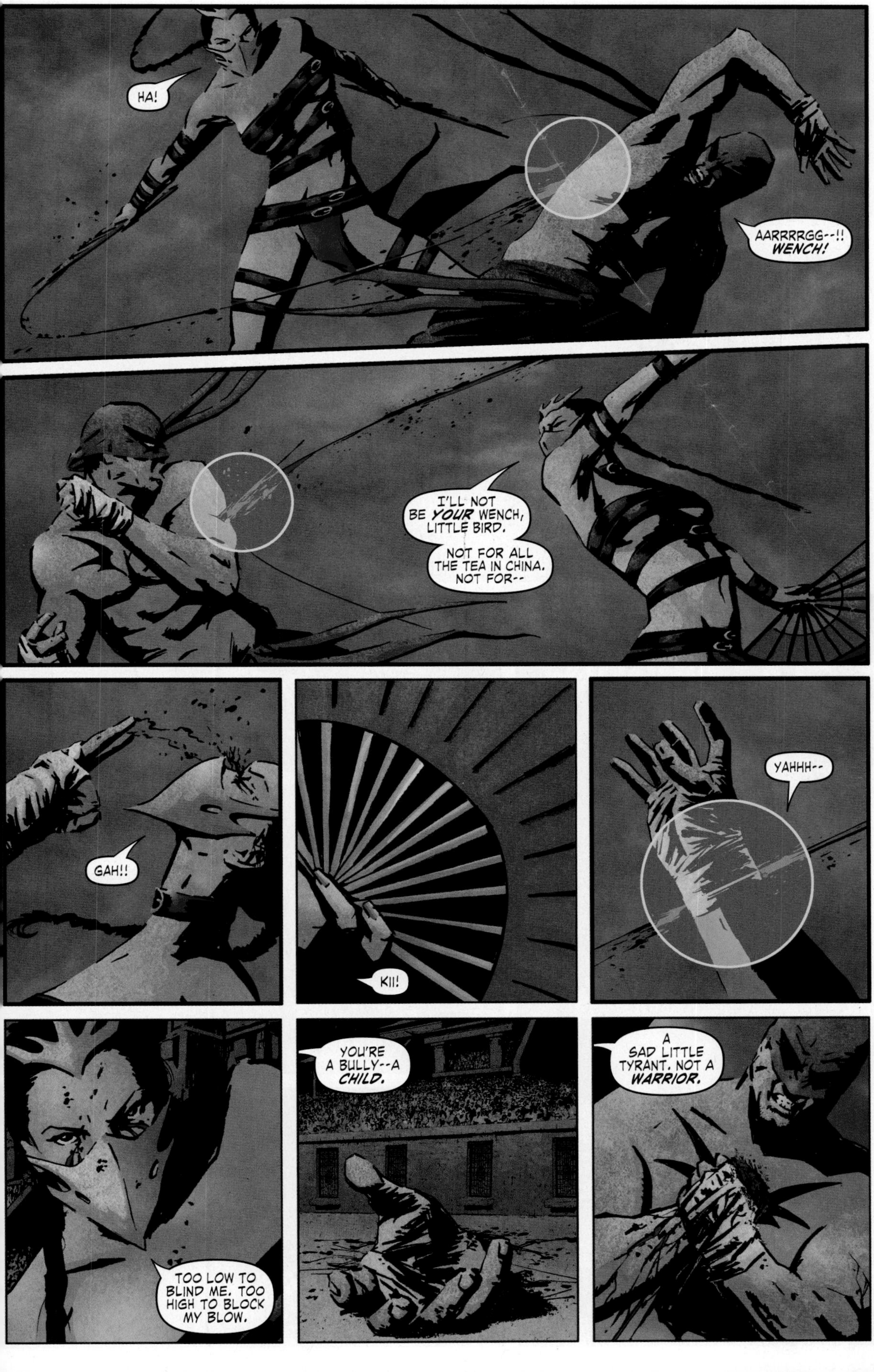
HA!
AARRRRGG--!! WENCH!
I'LL NOT BE YOUR WENCH, LITTLE BIRD.
NOT FOR ALL THE TEA IN CHINA. NOT FOR--
GAH!!
KII!
YAHHH--
TOO LOW TO BLIND ME. TOO HIGH TO BLOCK MY BLOW.
YOU'RE A BULLY--A CHILD.
A SAD LITTLE TYRANT. NOT A WARRIOR.

You--Davos, the warrior--suddenly fight not for your destiny, not to right a cosmic wrong, but rather...

...you fight to save your own life.

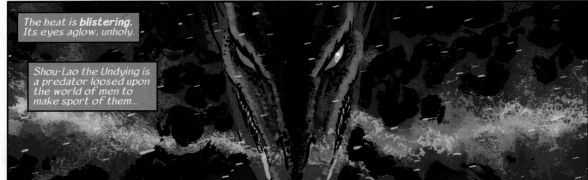

The heat is **blistering**. Its eyes aglow, unholy.

Shou-Lao the Undying is a predator loosed upon the world of men to make sport of them...

ROOAAARRRR!!

And its death-scream absolutely deafens you.

How did **Orson Randall** survive this? How did **anyone?**

ROOAAARRRR!!

DAVOS. DAMMIT.

MASTER--IT'S **DAVOS**--

I KNOW, OLD FRIEND, QUICKLY, NOW-- TO **THE CAVE!**

They'll be here soon-- they'll **all** be here soon, champion.

Your glory comes **now...**or **never.**

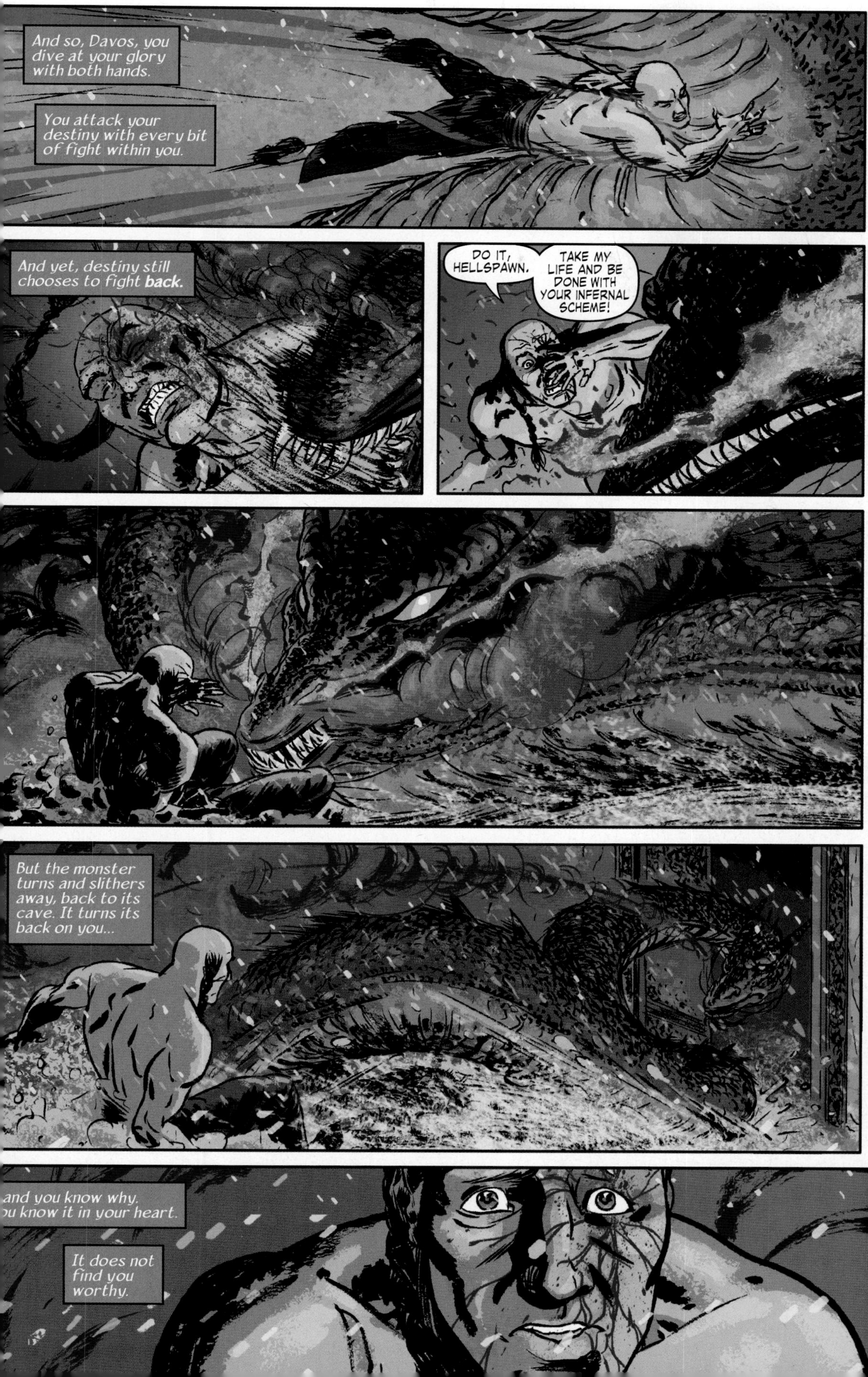
And so, Davos, you dive at your glory with both hands.
You attack your destiny with every bit of fight within you.
And yet, destiny still chooses to fight **back**.
DO IT, HELLSPAWN.
TAKE MY LIFE AND BE DONE WITH YOUR INFERNAL SCHEME!
But the monster turns and slithers away, back to its cave. It turns its back on you...
and you know why. ou know it in your heart.
It does not find you worthy.

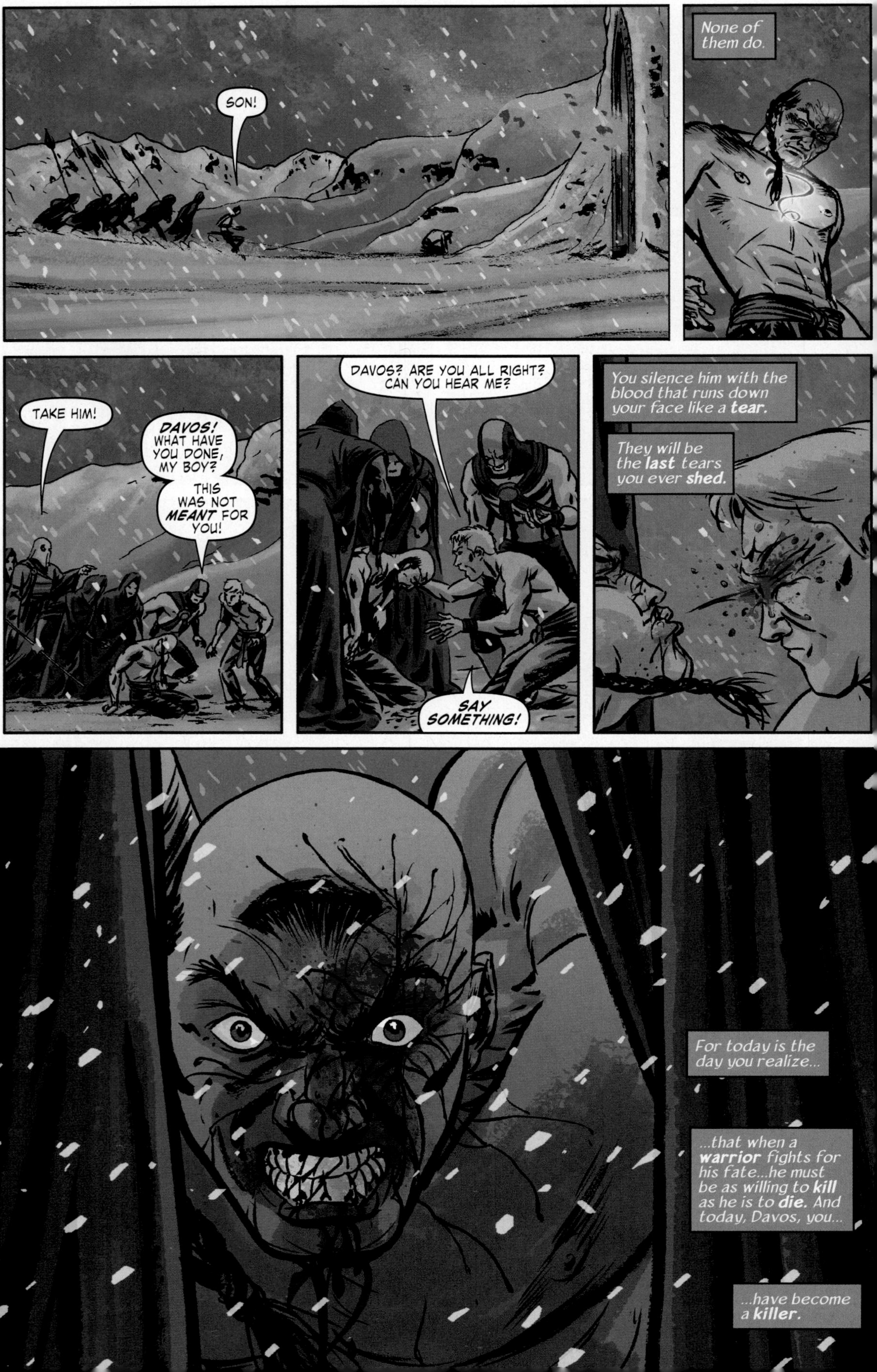
SON!
None of them do.
TAKE HIM!
DAVOS! WHAT HAVE YOU DONE, MY BOY?
THIS WAS NOT MEANT FOR YOU!
DAVOS? ARE YOU ALL RIGHT? CAN YOU HEAR ME?
SAY SOMETHING!
You silence him with the blood that runs down your face like a tear.
They will be the last tears you ever shed.
For today is the day you realize...
...that when a warrior fights for his fate...he must be as willing to kill as he is to die. And today, Davos, you...
...have become a killer.

I.... WILL....

KILL YOU....

FOR THIS TRANS-GRESSION.

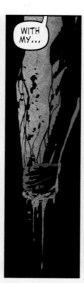

WITH MY...

...BARE...

...HANDS.

KFFFFFFWAM

STEEL PHOENIX BLOW (FIRST EXECUTION)

THIS ISN'T COMBAT...

THIS IS MURDER...!

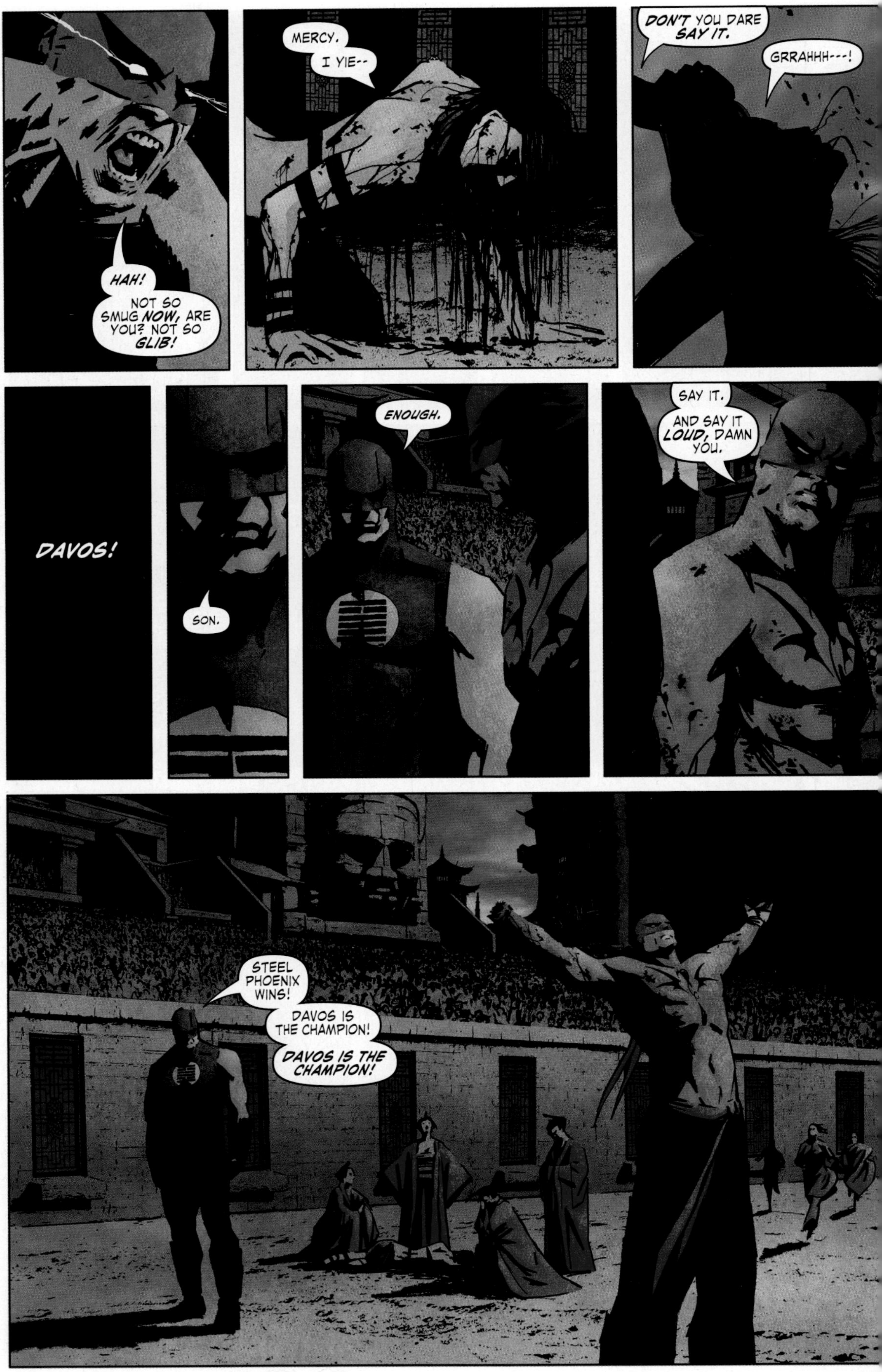
HAH!
NOT SO SMUG NOW, ARE YOU? NOT SO GLIB!
MERCY.
I YIE--
DON'T YOU DARE SAY IT.
GRRAHHH---!
DAVOS!
SON.
ENOUGH.
SAY IT.
AND SAY IT LOUD, DAMN YOU.
STEEL PHOENIX WINS!
DAVOS IS THE CHAMPION!
DAVOS IS THE CHAMPION!

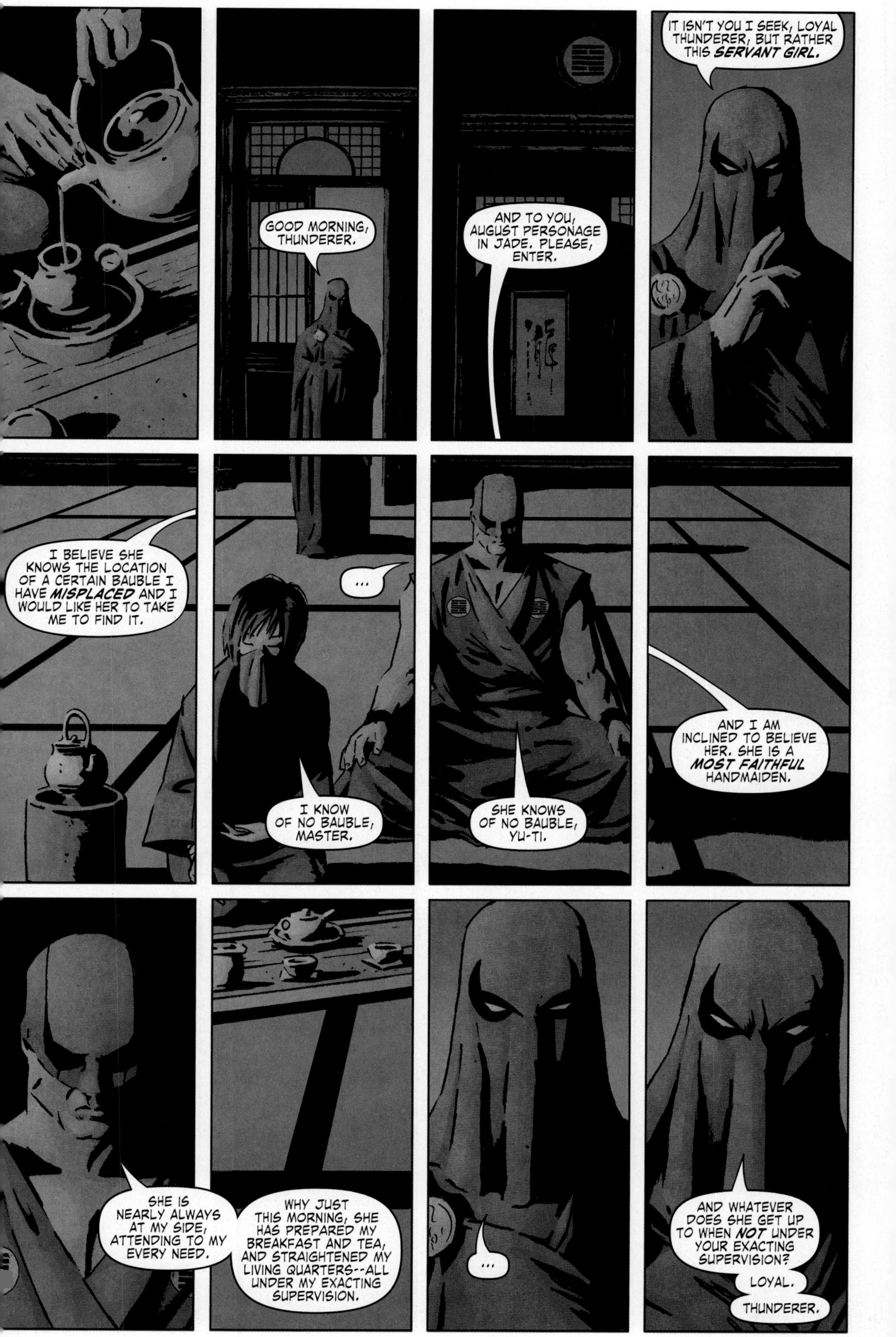
GOOD MORNING, THUNDERER.
AND TO YOU, AUGUST PERSONAGE IN JADE. PLEASE, ENTER.
IT ISN'T YOU I SEEK, LOYAL THUNDERER, BUT RATHER THIS SERVANT GIRL.
I BELIEVE SHE KNOWS THE LOCATION OF A CERTAIN BAUBLE I HAVE MISPLACED AND I WOULD LIKE HER TO TAKE ME TO FIND IT.
...
I KNOW OF NO BAUBLE, MASTER.
SHE KNOWS OF NO BAUBLE, YU-TI.
AND I AM INCLINED TO BELIEVE HER. SHE IS A MOST FAITHFUL HANDMAIDEN.
SHE IS NEARLY ALWAYS AT MY SIDE, ATTENDING TO MY EVERY NEED.
WHY JUST THIS MORNING, SHE HAS PREPARED MY BREAKFAST AND TEA, AND STRAIGHTENED MY LIVING QUARTERS--ALL UNDER MY EXACTING SUPERVISION.
...
AND WHATEVER DOES SHE GET UP TO WHEN NOT UNDER YOUR EXACTING SUPERVISION?
LOYAL.
THUNDERER.

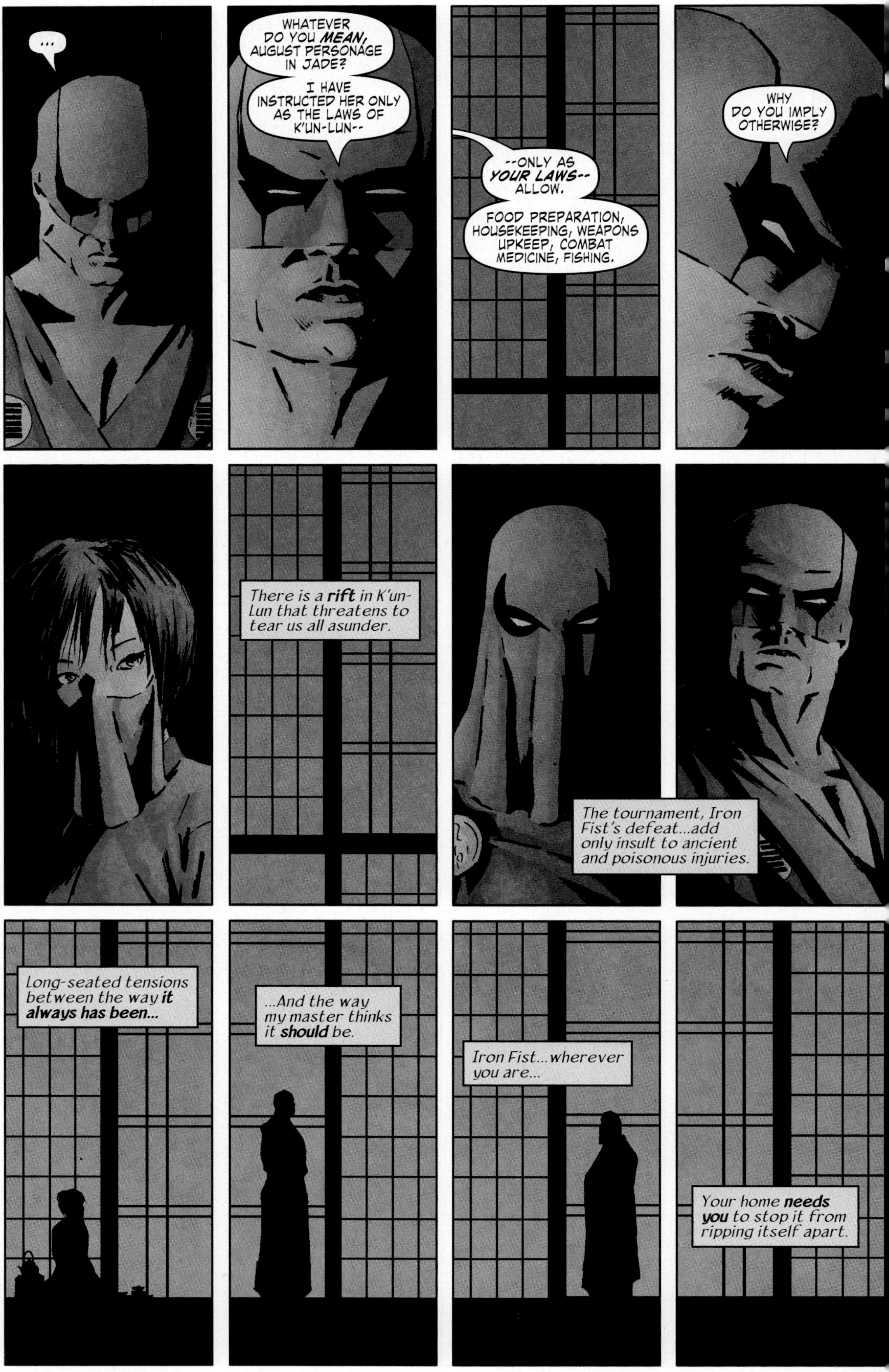
...
WHATEVER DO YOU MEAN, AUGUST PERSONAGE IN JADE?
I HAVE INSTRUCTED HER ONLY AS THE LAWS OF K'UN-LUN--
--ONLY AS YOUR LAWS-- ALLOW.
FOOD PREPARATION, HOUSEKEEPING, WEAPONS UPKEEP, COMBAT MEDICINE, FISHING.
WHY DO YOU IMPLY OTHERWISE?
There is a rift in K'un-Lun that threatens to tear us all asunder.
The tournament, Iron Fist's defeat...add only insult to ancient and poisonous injuries.
Long-seated tensions between the way it always has been...
...And the way my master thinks it should be.
Iron Fist...wherever you are...
Your home needs you to stop it from ripping itself apart.

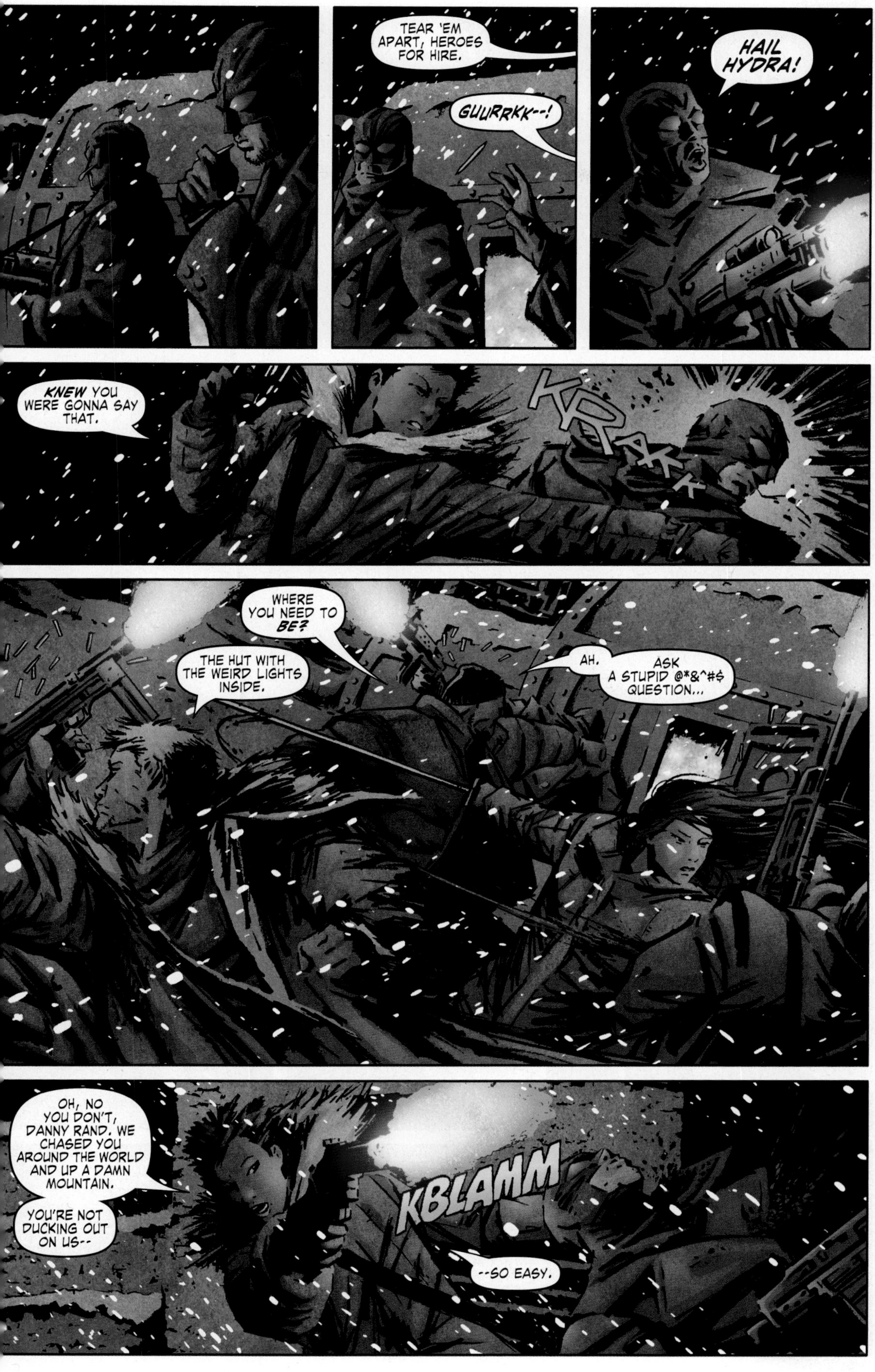
TEAR 'EM APART, HEROES FOR HIRE.
GUURRKK--!
HAIL HYDRA!
KNEW YOU WERE GONNA SAY THAT.
KRAKK
WHERE YOU NEED TO BE?
THE HUT WITH THE WEIRD LIGHTS INSIDE.
AH.
ASK A STUPID @*&^#$ QUESTION...
OH, NO YOU DON'T, DANNY RAND. WE CHASED YOU AROUND THE WORLD AND UP A DAMN MOUNTAIN.
YOU'RE NOT DUCKING OUT ON US--
KBLAMM
--SO EASY.

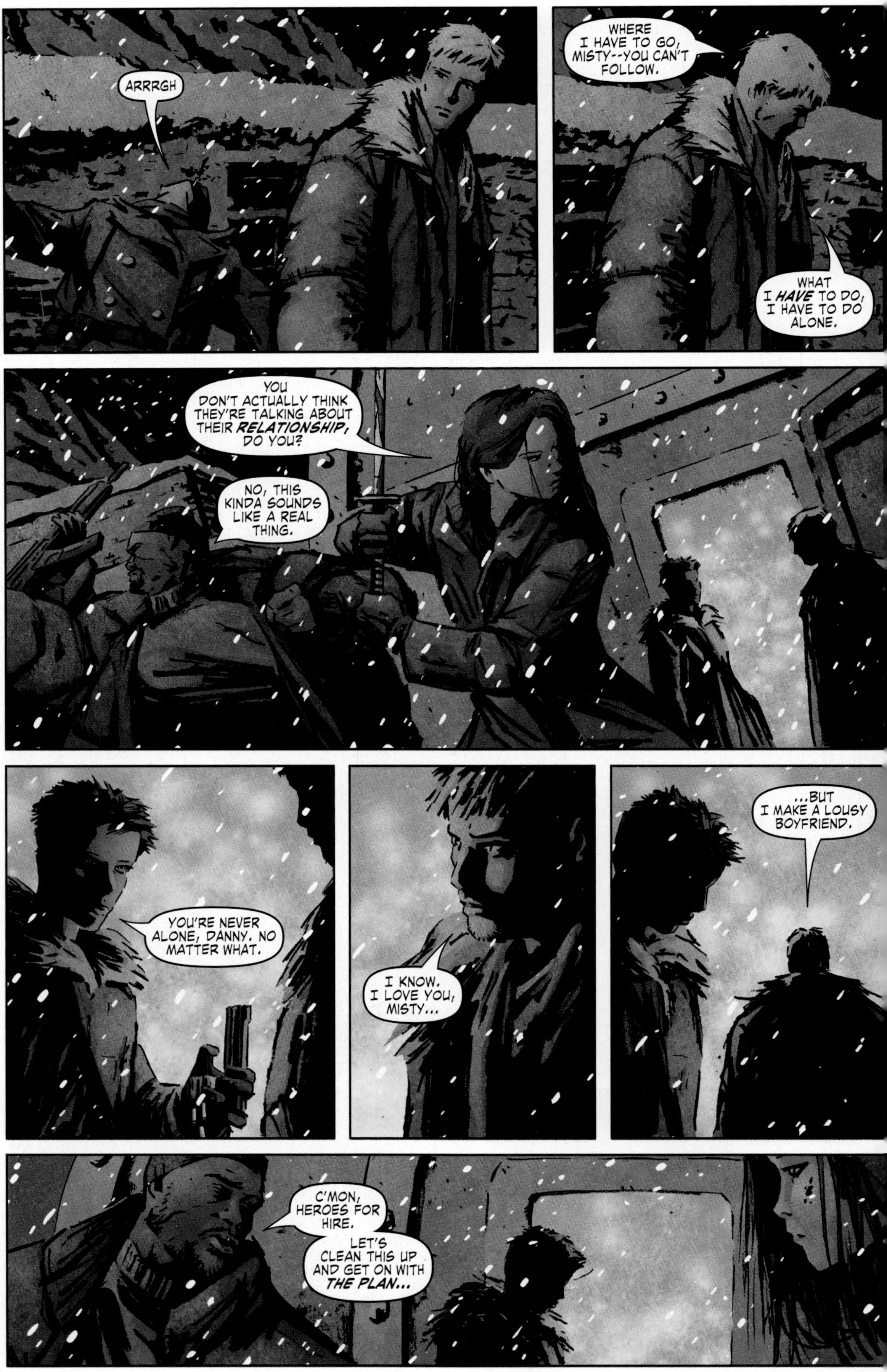
ARRRGH
WHERE I HAVE TO GO, MISTY--YOU CAN'T FOLLOW.
WHAT I *HAVE* TO DO, I HAVE TO DO ALONE.
YOU DON'T ACTUALLY THINK THEY'RE TALKING ABOUT THEIR *RELATIONSHIP*, DO YOU?
NO, THIS KINDA SOUNDS LIKE A REAL THING.
YOU'RE NEVER ALONE, DANNY. NO MATTER WHAT.
I KNOW. I LOVE YOU, MISTY...
...BUT I MAKE A LOUSY BOYFRIEND.
C'MON, HEROES FOR HIRE.
LET'S CLEAN THIS UP AND GET ON WITH *THE PLAN...*

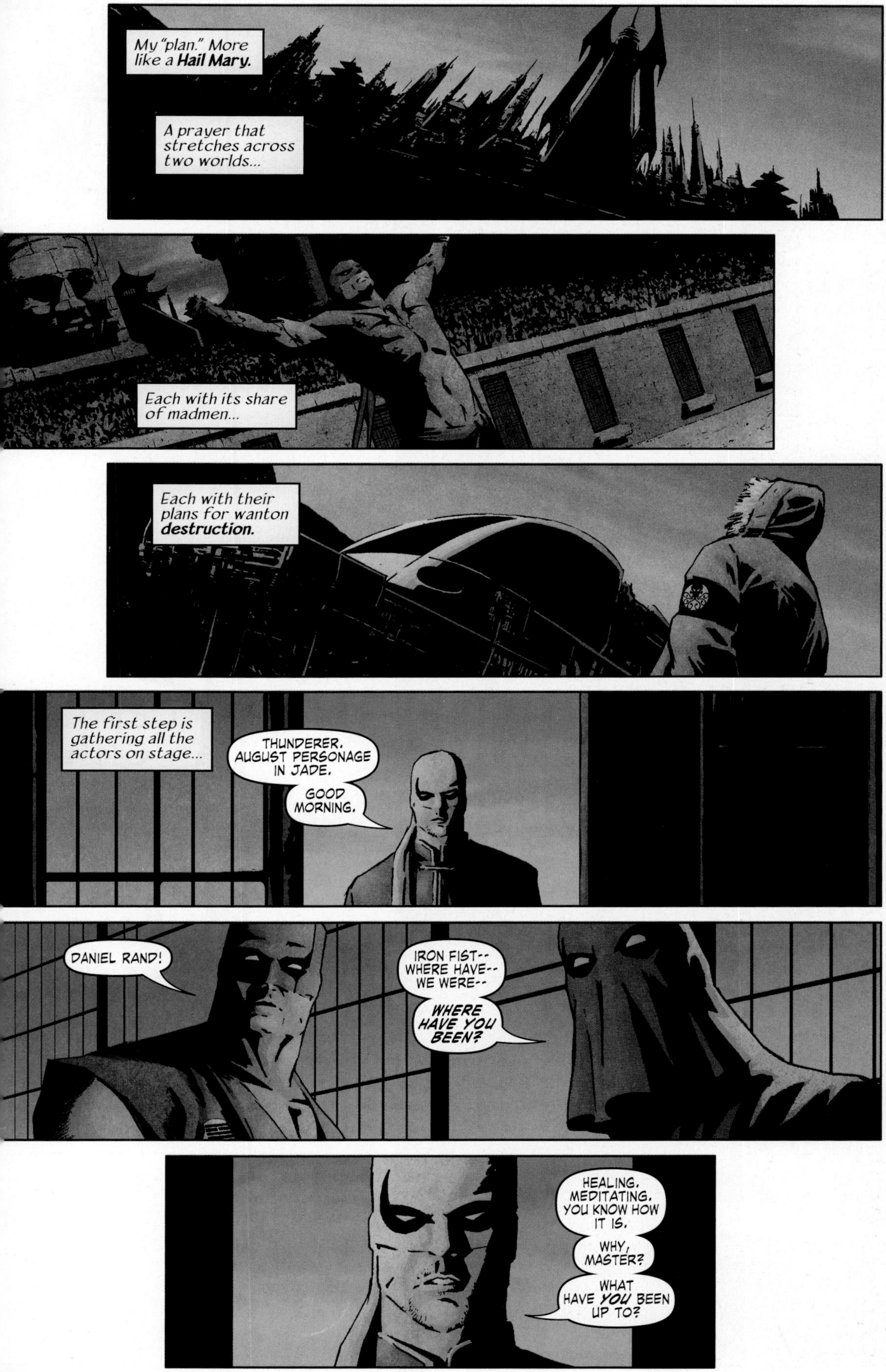
My "plan." More like a **Hail Mary.**
A prayer that stretches across two worlds...
Each with its share of madmen...
Each with their plans for wanton **destruction.**
The first step is gathering all the actors on stage...
THUNDERER. AUGUST PERSONAGE IN JADE.
GOOD MORNING.
DANIEL RAND!
IRON FIST-- WHERE HAVE-- WE WERE--
WHERE HAVE YOU BEEN?
HEALING. MEDITATING. YOU KNOW HOW IT IS.
WHY, MASTER?
WHAT HAVE ***YOU*** BEEN UP TO?

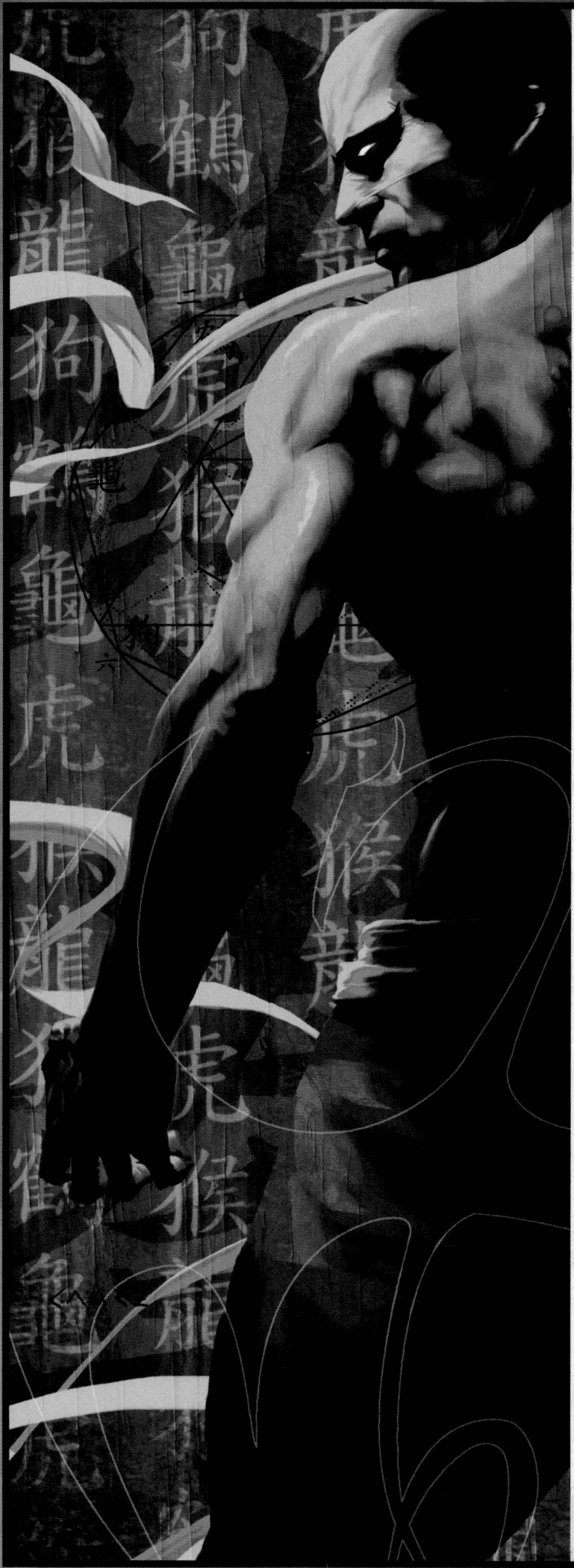

The 七 Capital Cities of Heaven

五

Round 5

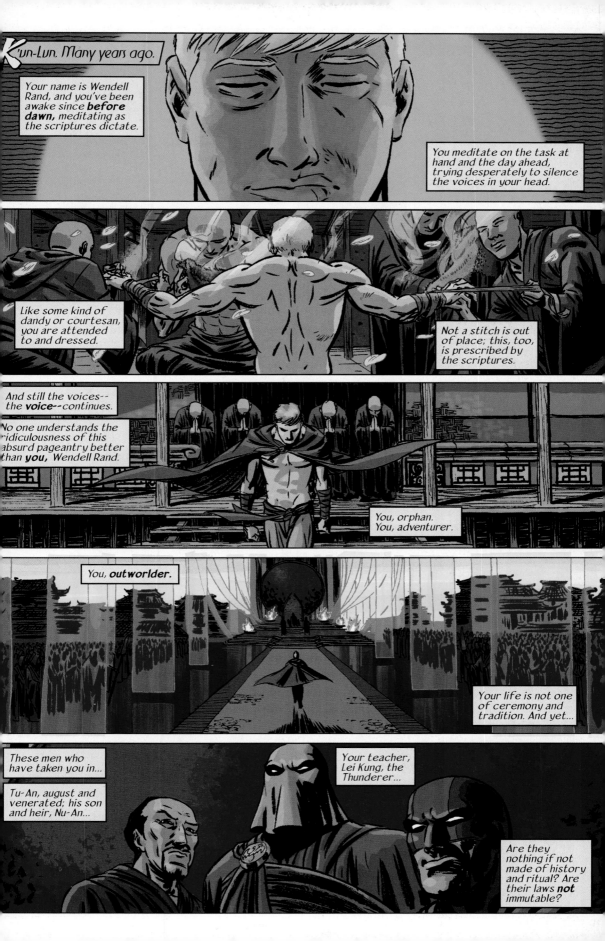

K'un-Lun. Many years ago.

Your name is Wendell Rand, and you've been awake since **before dawn,** meditating as the scriptures dictate.

You meditate on the task at hand and the day ahead, trying desperately to silence the voices in your head.

Like some kind of dandy or courtesan, you are attended to and dressed.

Not a stitch is out of place; this, too, is prescribed by the scriptures.

And still the voices-- the **voice**--continues.

No one understands the ridiculousness of this absurd pageantry better than **you,** Wendell Rand.

You, orphan. You, adventurer.

You, **outworlder.**

Your life is not one of ceremony and tradition. And yet...

These men who have taken you in...

Tu-An, august and venerated; his son and heir, Nu-An...

Your teacher, Lei Kung, the Thunderer...

Are they nothing if not made of history and ritual? Are their laws **not** immutable?

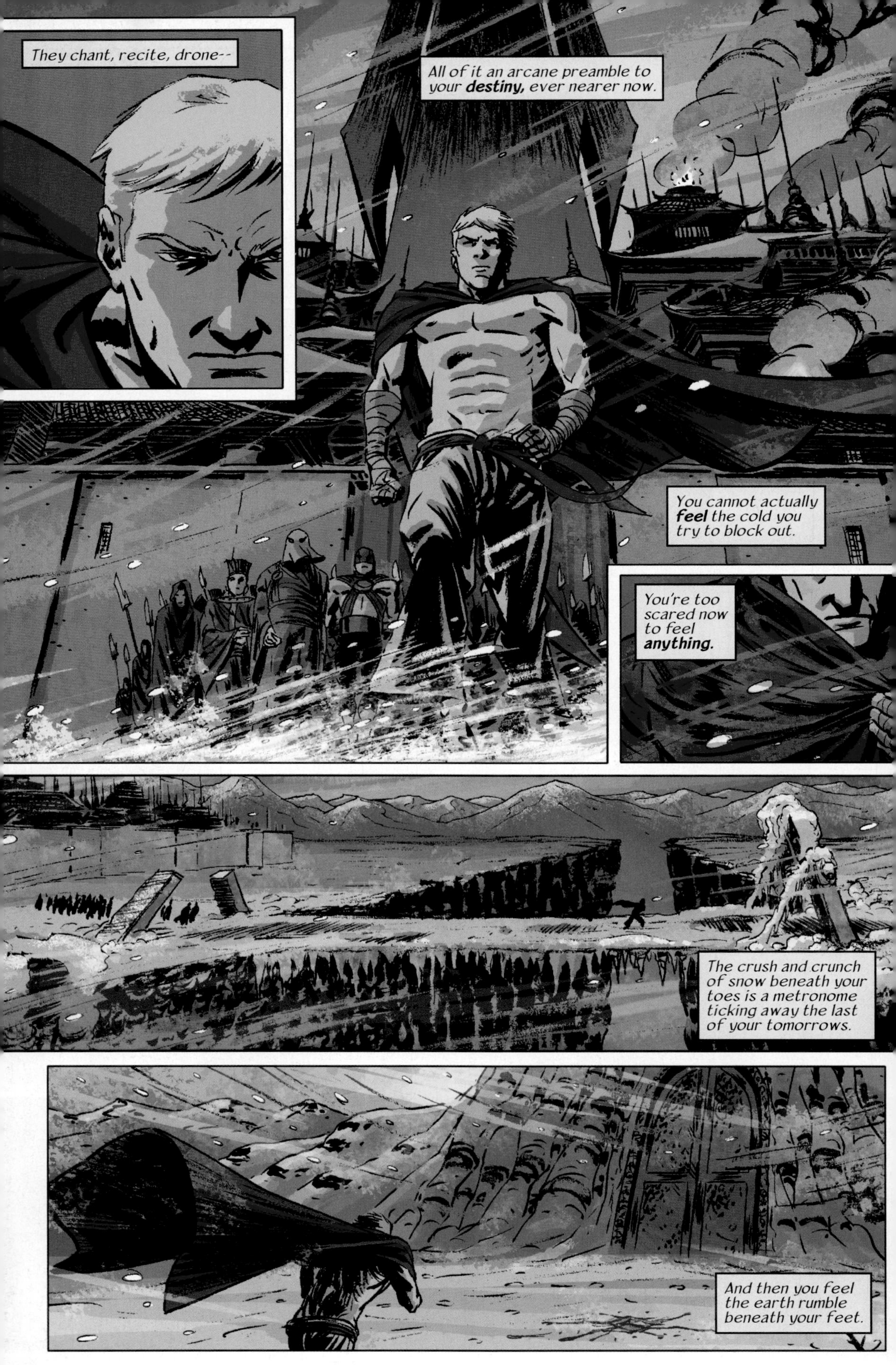
They chant, recite, drone--
All of it an arcane preamble to your **destiny,** ever nearer now.
You cannot actually **feel** the cold you try to block out.
You're too scared now to feel **anything.**
The crush and crunch of snow beneath your toes is a metronome ticking away the last of your tomorrows.
And then you feel the earth rumble beneath your feet.

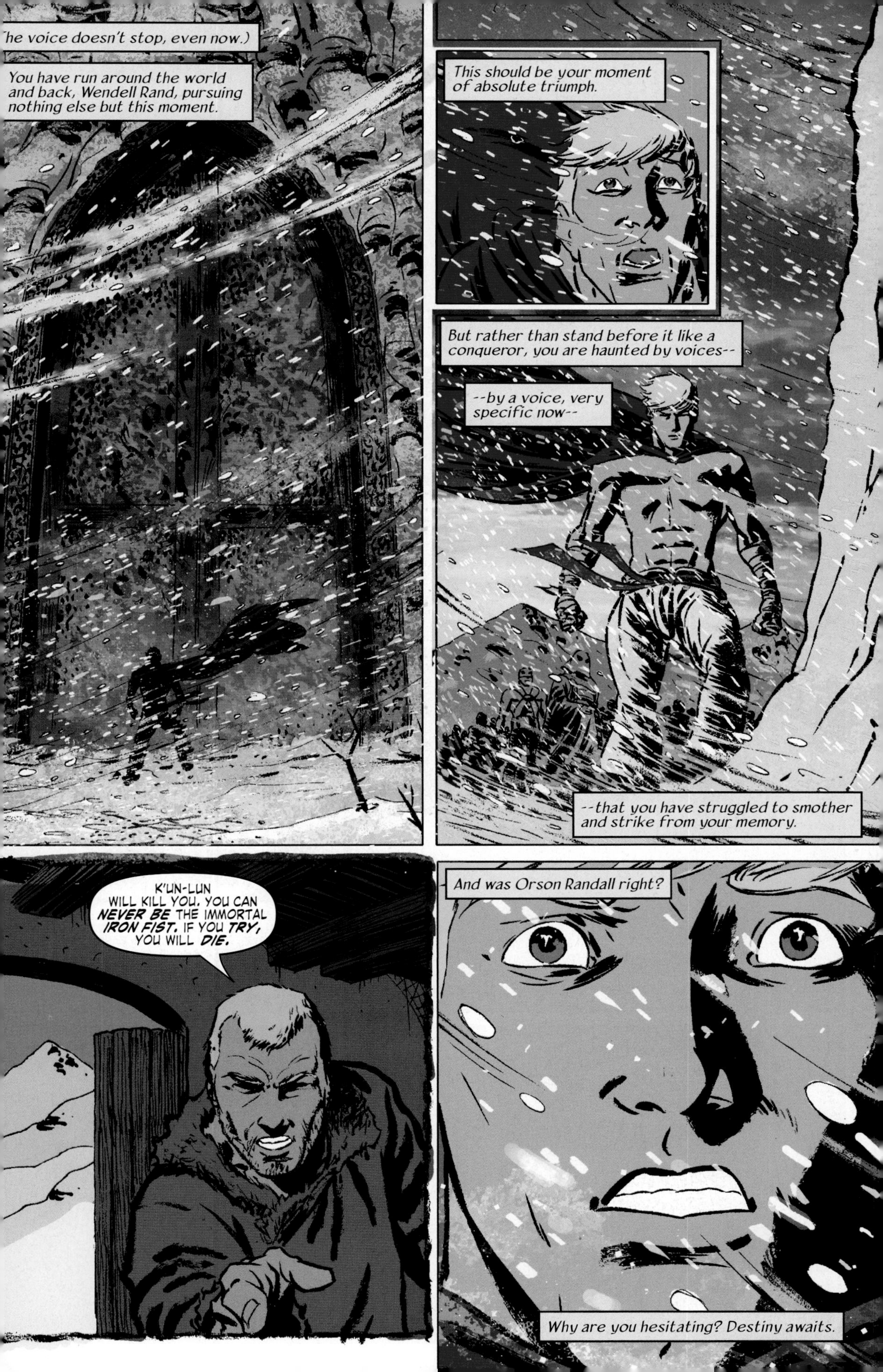

(The voice doesn't stop, even now.)
You have run around the world and back, Wendell Rand, pursuing nothing else but this moment.
This should be your moment of absolute triumph.
But rather than stand before it like a conqueror, you are haunted by voices--
--by a voice, very specific now--
--that you have struggled to smother and strike from your memory.
K'UN-LUN WILL KILL YOU. YOU CAN NEVER BE THE IMMORTAL IRON FIST. IF YOU TRY, YOU WILL DIE.
And was Orson Randall right?
Why are you hesitating? Destiny awaits.

NU-AN WAS *ALWAYS* CORRUPT. THE PLEASURES OF THE WORLD OF MEN HAVE LONG INTOXICATED HIM, EVEN BEFORE HIS FATHER DIED.

EVEN BEFORE *PHINEAS RANDALL* SHATTERED THE DIMENSIONAL BARRIER THAT SEPARATES EARTH FROM K'UN-LUN.

THUS AS NU-AN BECAME THE NEW YU-TI, OUR MONARCH BECAME A TYRANT.

OF COURSE, THE PREVIOUS YU-TI THOUGHT "THE MACHINE" AN ABOMINATION. BUT HIS SON...

...WANTED IT MADE AND OPERATED IN *SECRET* AND HE PAID RANDALL TO DO IT.

THE ROOT OF MY FAMILY'S FORTUNE WAS THE *RANDALL FORTUNE*. AND THAT CAME FROM K'UN-LUN.

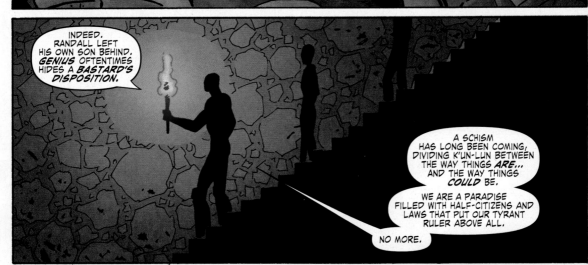

INDEED. RANDALL LEFT HIS OWN SON BEHIND. *GENIUS* OFTENTIMES HIDES A *BASTARD'S* DISPOSITION.

A SCHISM HAS LONG BEEN COMING, DIVIDING K'UN-LUN BETWEEN THE WAY THINGS *ARE*... AND THE WAY THINGS *COULD* BE.

WE ARE A PARADISE FILLED WITH HALF-CITIZENS AND LAWS THAT PUT OUR TYRANT RULER ABOVE ALL.

NO MORE.

YOU'RE TALKING ABOUT *REVOLUTION*, MASTER. YOU'D NEED *AN ARMY*.

HNN, QUITE.

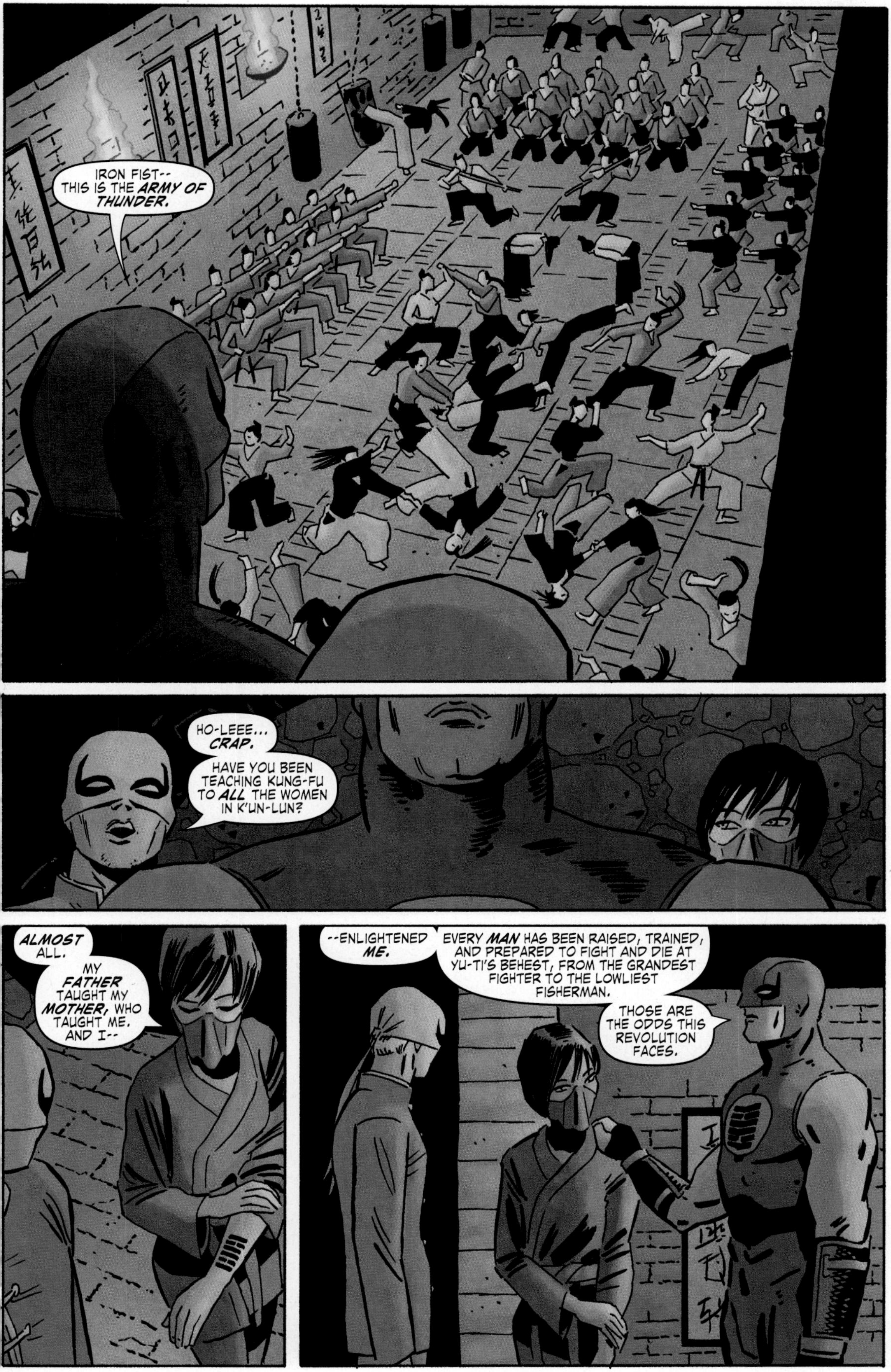
IRON FIST--
THIS IS THE ARMY OF THUNDER.
HO-LEEE... CRAP.
HAVE YOU BEEN TEACHING KUNG-FU TO ALL THE WOMEN IN K'UN-LUN?
ALMOST ALL.
MY FATHER TAUGHT MY MOTHER, WHO TAUGHT ME. AND I--
--ENLIGHTENED ME.
EVERY MAN HAS BEEN RAISED, TRAINED, AND PREPARED TO FIGHT AND DIE AT YU-TI'S BEHEST, FROM THE GRANDEST FIGHTER TO THE LOWLIEST FISHERMAN.
THOSE ARE THE ODDS THIS REVOLUTION FACES.

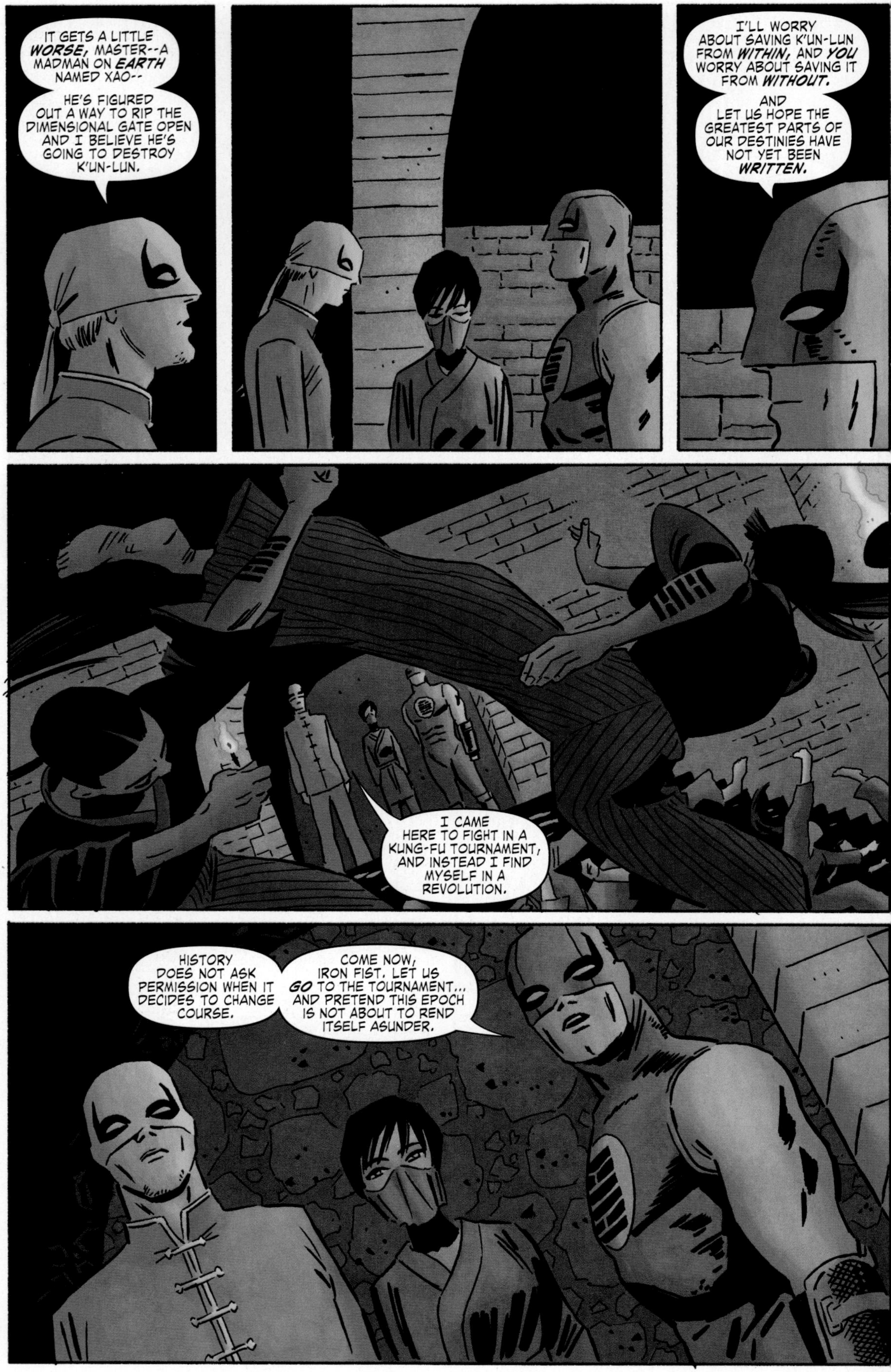
IT GETS A LITTLE WORSE, MASTER--A MADMAN ON EARTH NAMED XAO--
HE'S FIGURED OUT A WAY TO RIP THE DIMENSIONAL GATE OPEN AND I BELIEVE HE'S GOING TO DESTROY K'UN-LUN.
I'LL WORRY ABOUT SAVING K'UN-LUN FROM WITHIN, AND YOU WORRY ABOUT SAVING IT FROM WITHOUT.
AND LET US HOPE THE GREATEST PARTS OF OUR DESTINIES HAVE NOT YET BEEN WRITTEN.
I CAME HERE TO FIGHT IN A KUNG-FU TOURNAMENT, AND INSTEAD I FIND MYSELF IN A REVOLUTION.
HISTORY DOES NOT ASK PERMISSION WHEN IT DECIDES TO CHANGE COURSE.
COME NOW, IRON FIST. LET US GO TO THE TOURNAMENT... AND PRETEND THIS EPOCH IS NOT ABOUT TO REND ITSELF ASUNDER.

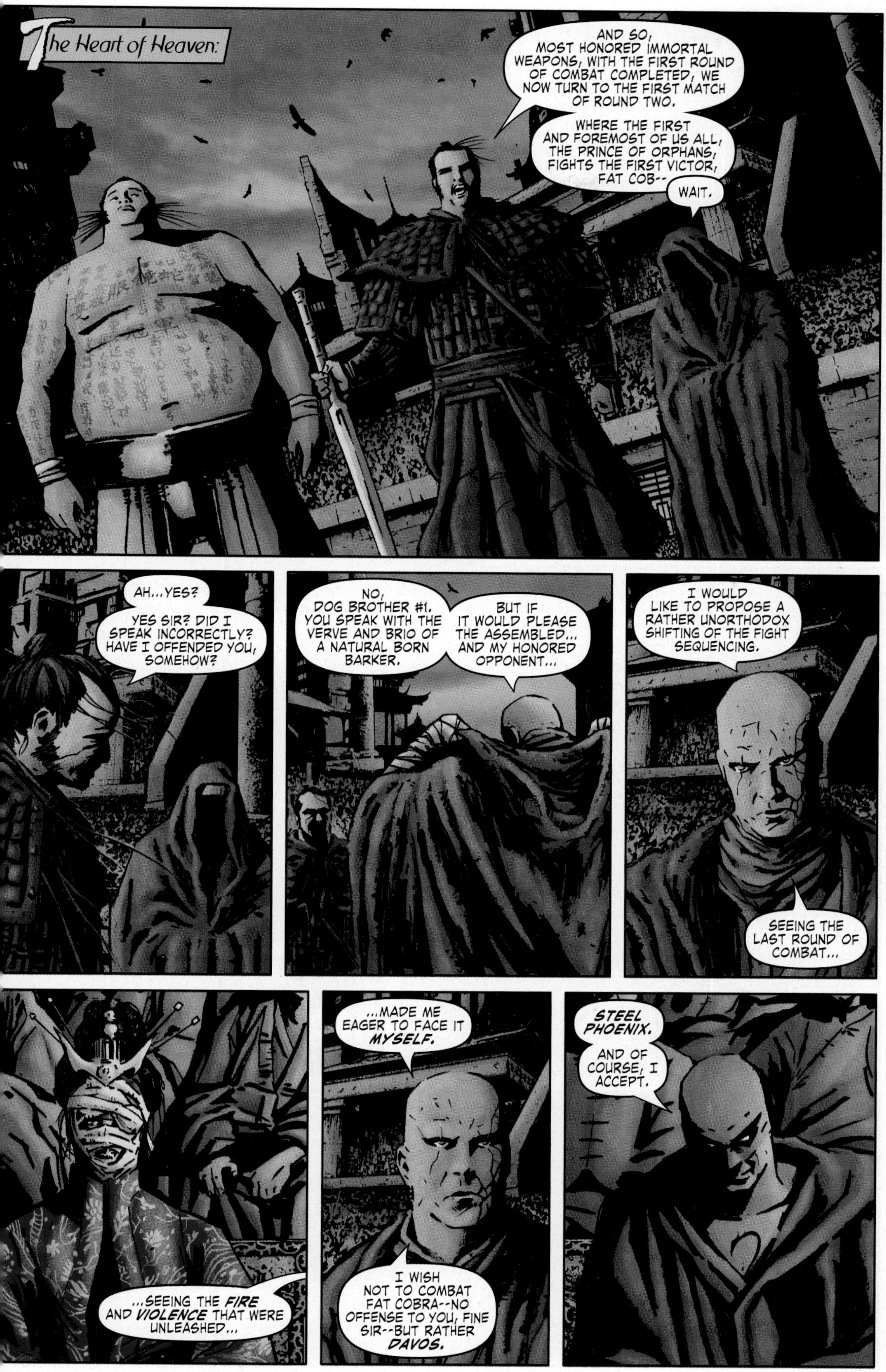
The Heart of Heaven:
AND SO, MOST HONORED IMMORTAL WEAPONS, WITH THE FIRST ROUND OF COMBAT COMPLETED, WE NOW TURN TO THE FIRST MATCH OF ROUND TWO.
WHERE THE FIRST AND FOREMOST OF US ALL, THE PRINCE OF ORPHANS, FIGHTS THE FIRST VICTOR, FAT COB--
WAIT.
AH...YES?
YES SIR? DID I SPEAK INCORRECTLY? HAVE I OFFENDED YOU, SOMEHOW?
NO, DOG BROTHER #1. YOU SPEAK WITH THE VERVE AND BRIO OF A NATURAL BORN BARKER.
BUT IF IT WOULD PLEASE THE ASSEMBLED... AND MY HONORED OPPONENT...
I WOULD LIKE TO PROPOSE A RATHER UNORTHODOX SHIFTING OF THE FIGHT SEQUENCING.
SEEING THE LAST ROUND OF COMBAT...
...SEEING THE FIRE AND VIOLENCE THAT WERE UNLEASHED...
...MADE ME EAGER TO FACE IT MYSELF.
I WISH NOT TO COMBAT FAT COBRA--NO OFFENSE TO YOU, FINE SIR--BUT RATHER DAVOS.
STEEL PHOENIX.
AND OF COURSE, I ACCEPT.

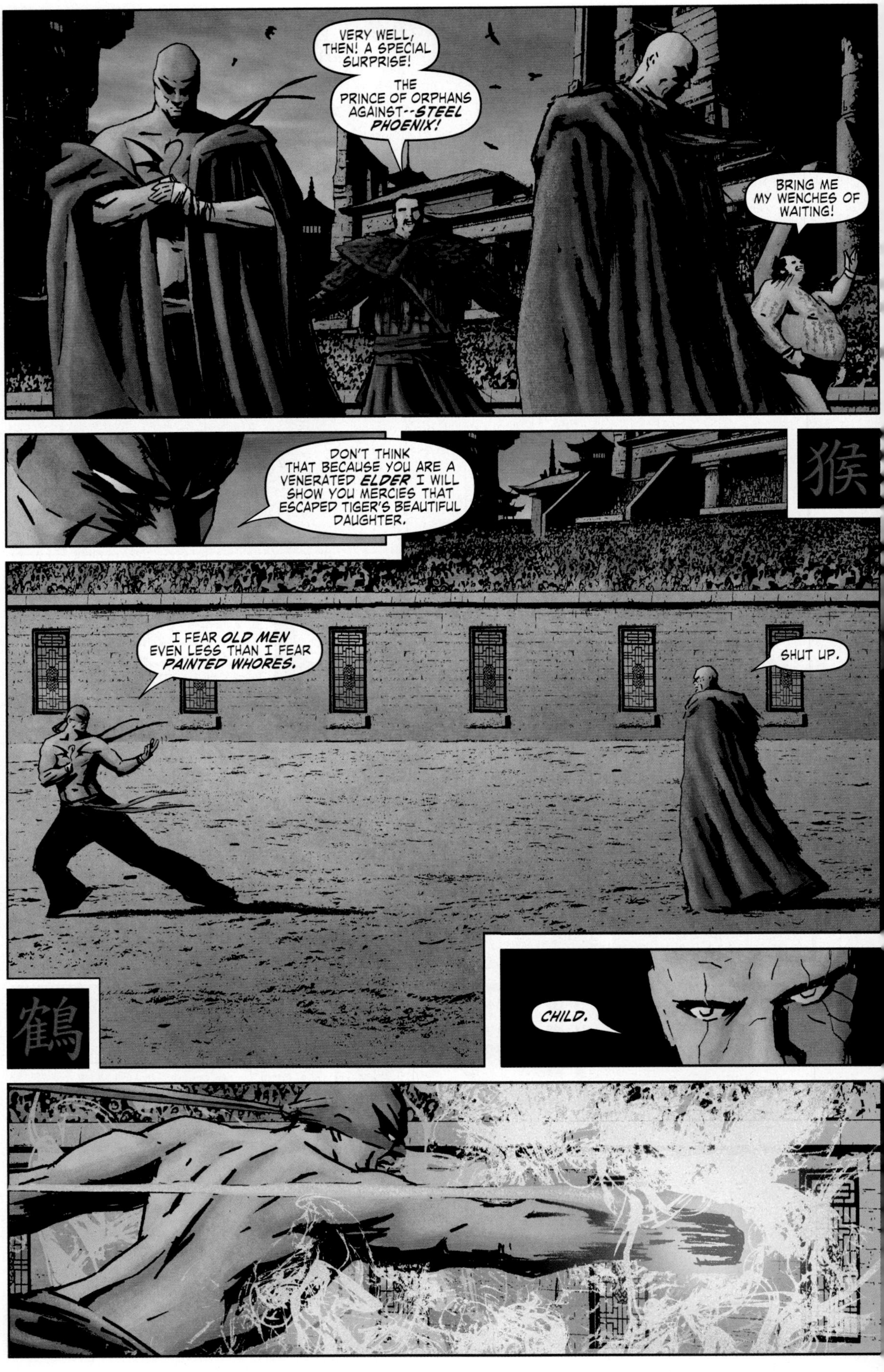

VERY WELL, THEN! A SPECIAL SURPRISE!
THE PRINCE OF ORPHANS AGAINST--STEEL PHOENIX!
BRING ME MY WENCHES OF WAITING!
DON'T THINK THAT BECAUSE YOU ARE A VENERATED ELDER I WILL SHOW YOU MERCIES THAT ESCAPED TIGER'S BEAUTIFUL DAUGHTER.
猴
I FEAR OLD MEN EVEN LESS THAN I FEAR PAINTED WHORES.
SHUT UP.
鶴
CHILD.

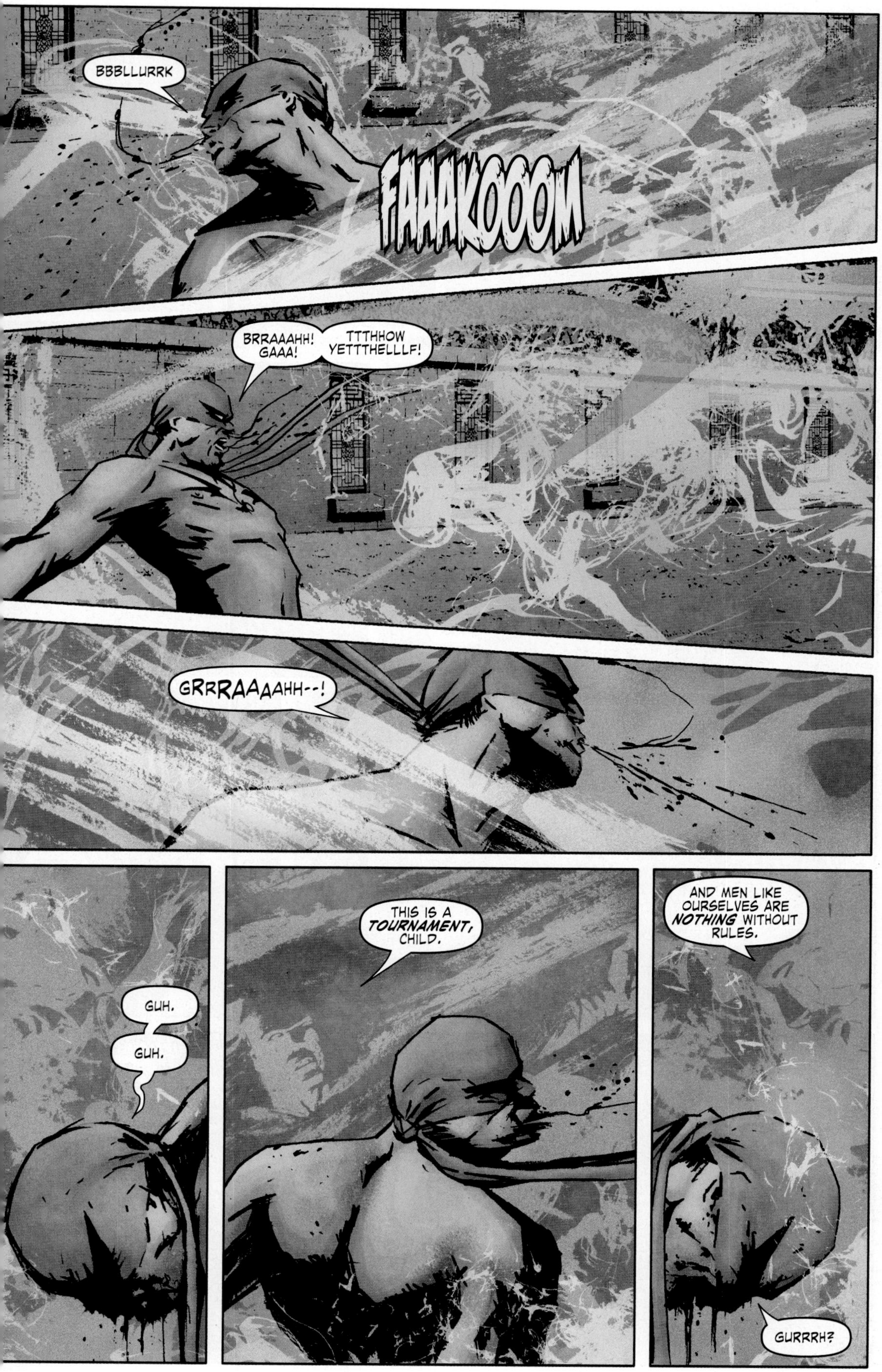
BBBLLURRK
FAAAKOOOM
BRRAAAHH! GAAA!
TTTHHOW YETTTHELLLF!
GRRRAAAAHH--!
GUH.
GUH.
THIS IS A *TOURNAMENT,* CHILD.
AND MEN LIKE OURSELVES ARE *NOTHING* WITHOUT RULES.
GURRRH?

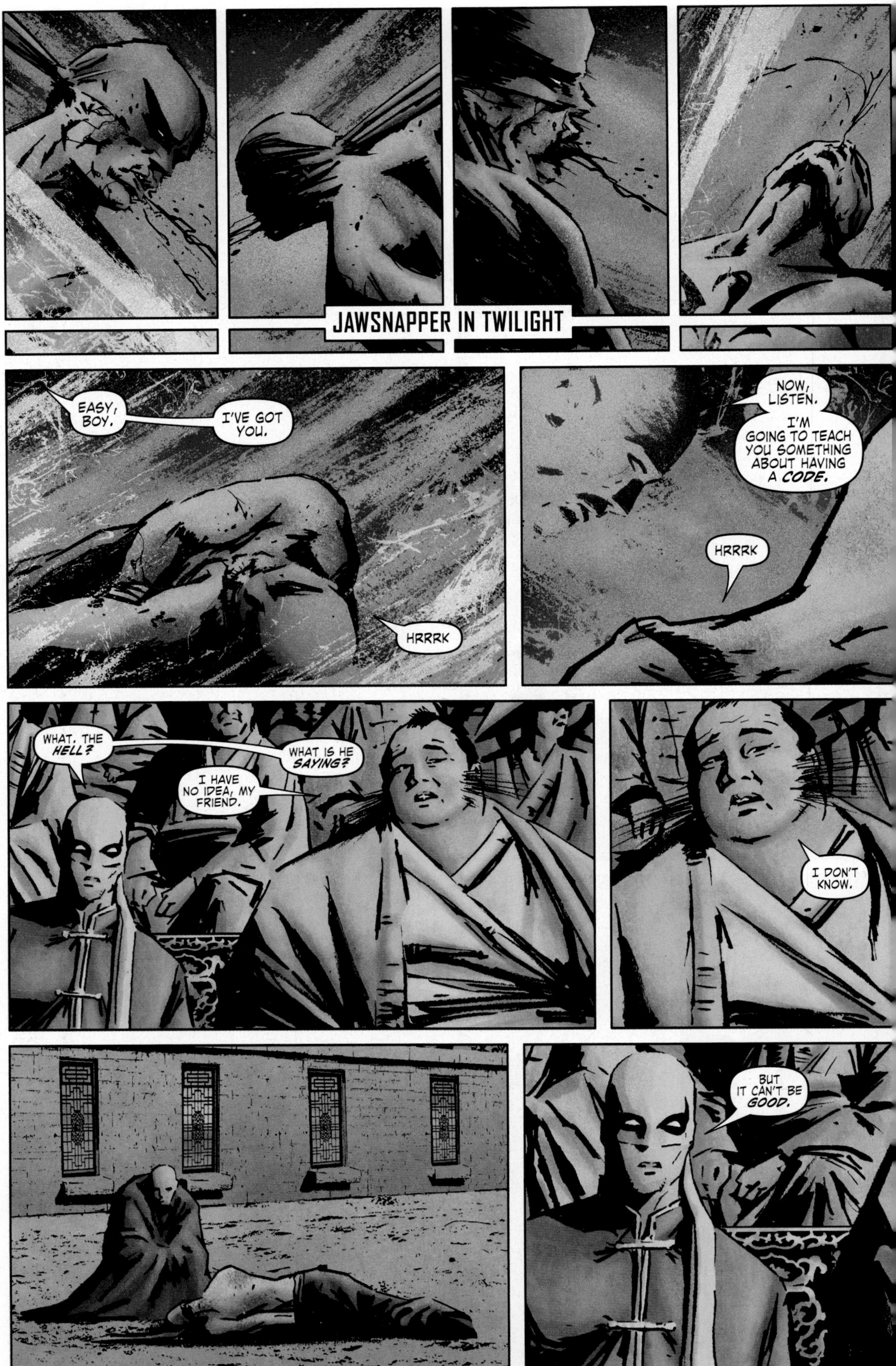
JAWSNAPPER IN TWILIGHT
EASY, BOY.
I'VE GOT YOU.
HRRRK
NOW, LISTEN.
I'M GOING TO TEACH YOU SOMETHING ABOUT HAVING A *CODE.*
HRRRK
WHAT. THE *HELL?*
WHAT IS HE *SAYING?*
I HAVE NO IDEA, MY FRIEND.
I DON'T KNOW.
BUT IT CAN'T BE *GOOD.*

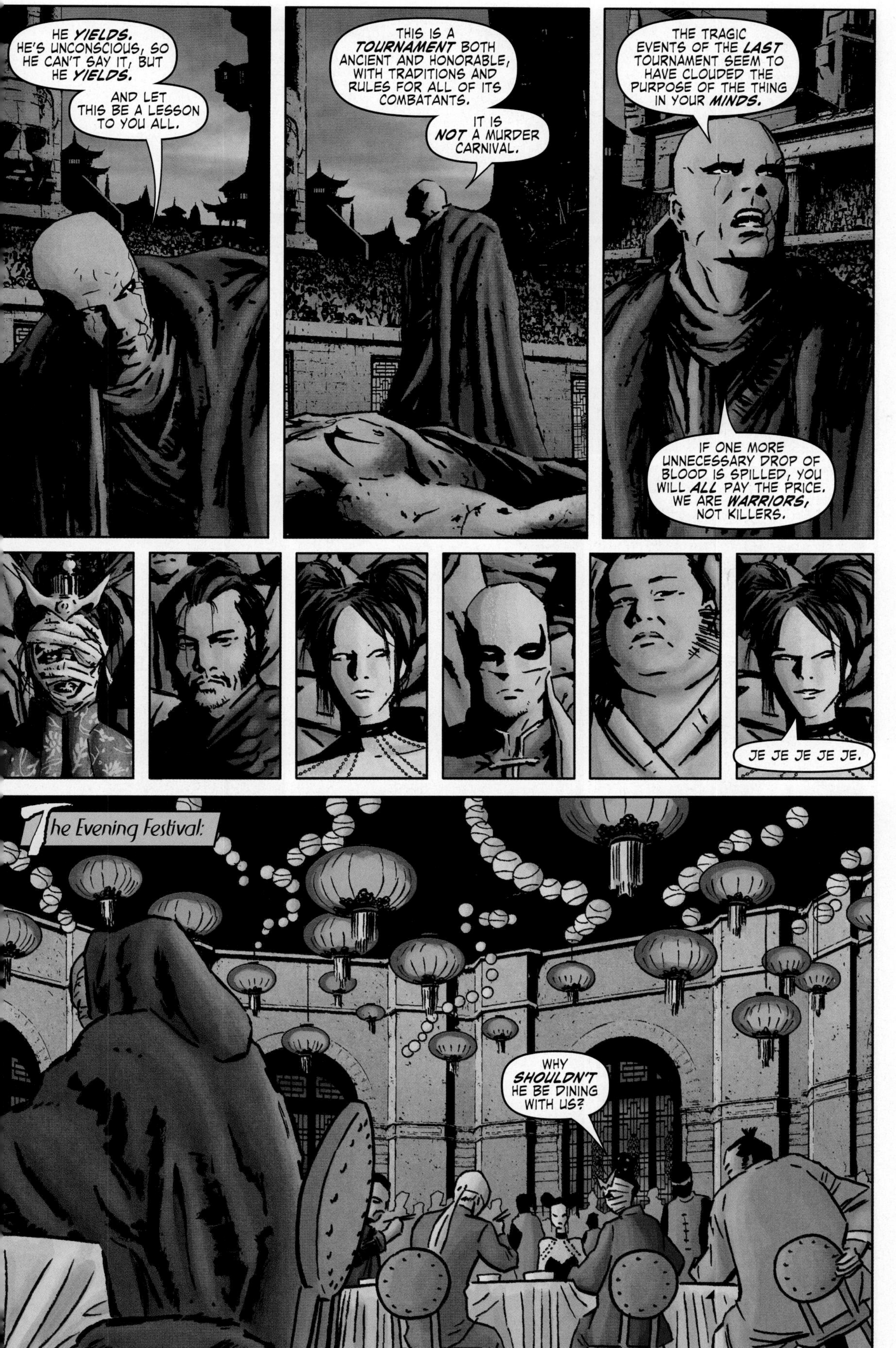
HE YIELDS. HE'S UNCONSCIOUS, SO HE CAN'T SAY IT, BUT HE YIELDS.
AND LET THIS BE A LESSON TO YOU ALL.
THIS IS A TOURNAMENT BOTH ANCIENT AND HONORABLE, WITH TRADITIONS AND RULES FOR ALL OF ITS COMBATANTS.
IT IS NOT A MURDER CARNIVAL.
THE TRAGIC EVENTS OF THE LAST TOURNAMENT SEEM TO HAVE CLOUDED THE PURPOSE OF THE THING IN YOUR MINDS.
IF ONE MORE UNNECESSARY DROP OF BLOOD IS SPILLED, YOU WILL ALL PAY THE PRICE. WE ARE WARRIORS, NOT KILLERS.
JE JE JE JE JE.
The Evening Festival:
WHY SHOULDN'T HE BE DINING WITH US?

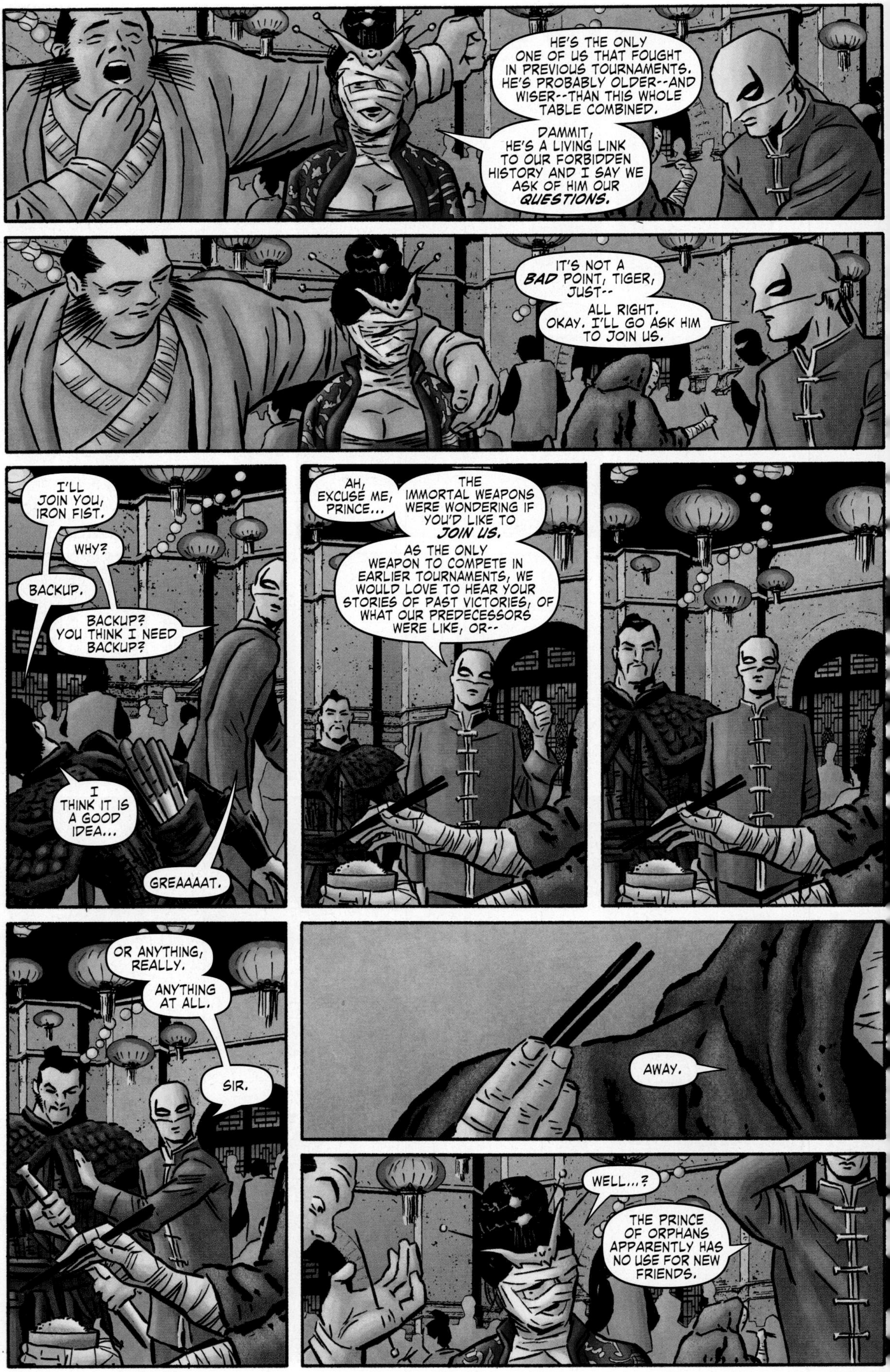
HE'S THE ONLY ONE OF US THAT FOUGHT IN PREVIOUS TOURNAMENTS. HE'S PROBABLY OLDER--AND WISER--THAN THIS WHOLE TABLE COMBINED.
DAMMIT, HE'S A LIVING LINK TO OUR FORBIDDEN HISTORY AND I SAY WE ASK OF HIM OUR QUESTIONS.
IT'S NOT A BAD POINT, TIGER, JUST--
ALL RIGHT. OKAY. I'LL GO ASK HIM TO JOIN US.
I'LL JOIN YOU, IRON FIST.
WHY?
BACKUP.
BACKUP? YOU THINK I NEED BACKUP?
I THINK IT IS A GOOD IDEA...
GREAAAAT.
AH, EXCUSE ME, PRINCE...
THE IMMORTAL WEAPONS WERE WONDERING IF YOU'D LIKE TO JOIN US.
AS THE ONLY WEAPON TO COMPETE IN EARLIER TOURNAMENTS, WE WOULD LOVE TO HEAR YOUR STORIES OF PAST VICTORIES, OF WHAT OUR PREDECESSORS WERE LIKE, OR--
OR ANYTHING, REALLY.
ANYTHING AT ALL.
SIR.
AWAY.
WELL...?
THE PRINCE OF ORPHANS APPARENTLY HAS NO USE FOR NEW FRIENDS.

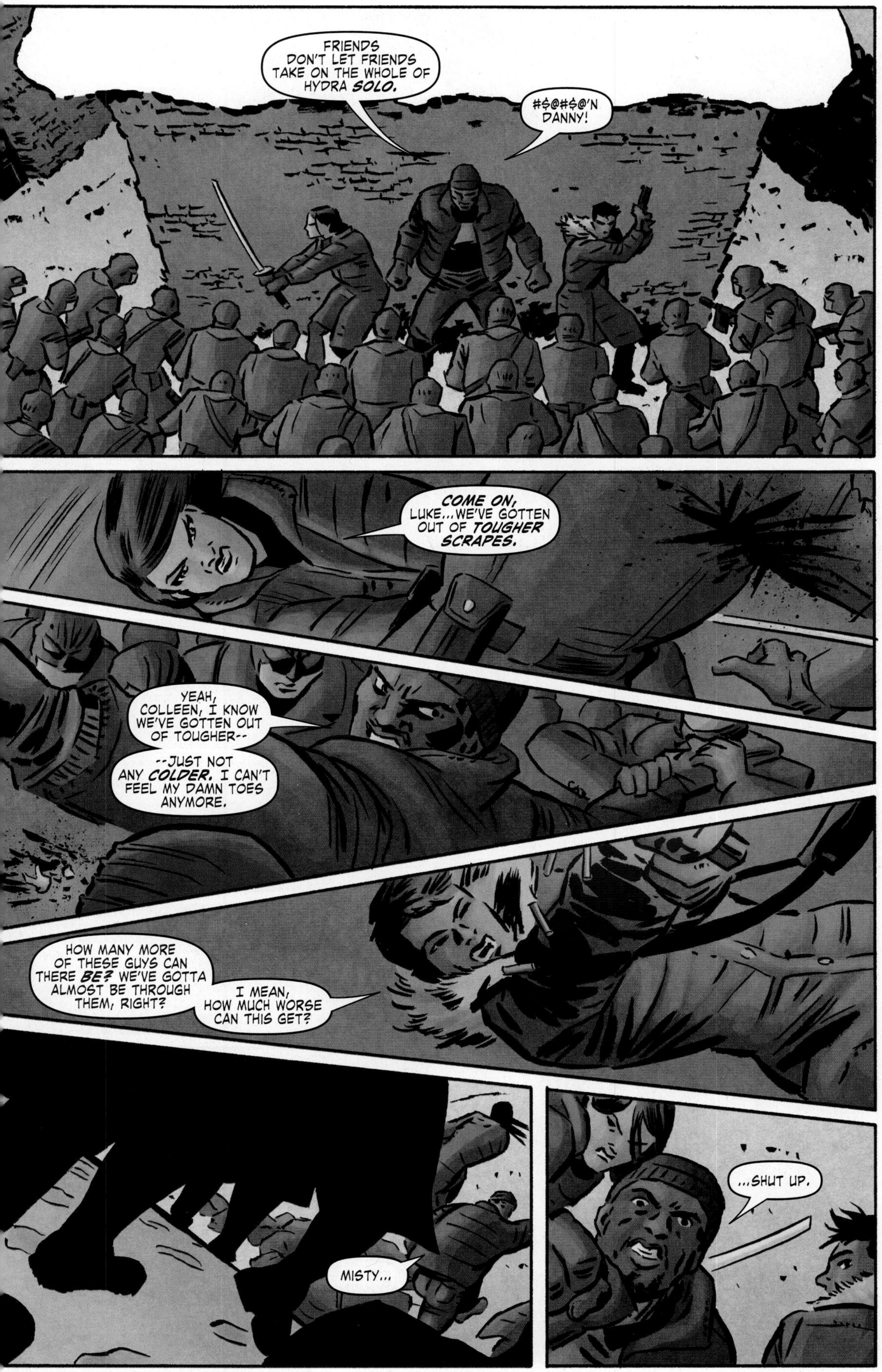
FRIENDS DON'T LET FRIENDS TAKE ON THE WHOLE OF HYDRA *SOLO.*
#$@#$@'N DANNY!
COME ON, LUKE...WE'VE GOTTEN OUT OF *TOUGHER SCRAPES.*
YEAH, COLLEEN, I KNOW WE'VE GOTTEN OUT OF TOUGHER--
--JUST NOT ANY *COLDER.* I CAN'T FEEL MY DAMN TOES ANYMORE.
HOW MANY MORE OF THESE GUYS CAN THERE *BE?* WE'VE GOTTA ALMOST BE THROUGH THEM, RIGHT?
I MEAN, HOW MUCH WORSE CAN THIS GET?
MISTY...
...SHUT UP.

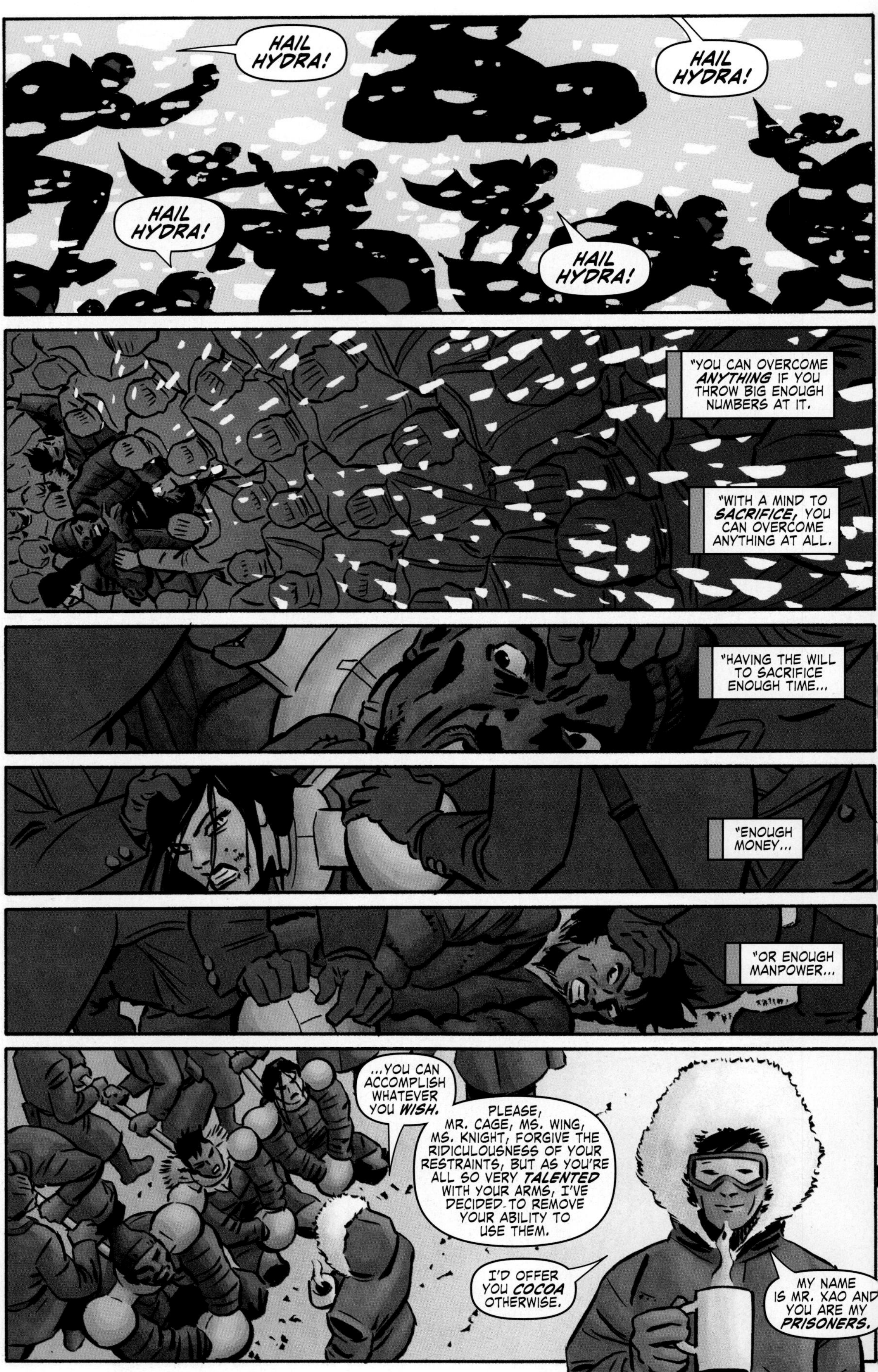
HAIL HYDRA!
HAIL HYDRA!
HAIL HYDRA!
HAIL HYDRA!
"YOU CAN OVERCOME ANYTHING IF YOU THROW BIG ENOUGH NUMBERS AT IT.
"WITH A MIND TO SACRIFICE, YOU CAN OVERCOME ANYTHING AT ALL.
"HAVING THE WILL TO SACRIFICE ENOUGH TIME...
"ENOUGH MONEY...
"OR ENOUGH MANPOWER...
...YOU CAN ACCOMPLISH WHATEVER YOU WISH.
PLEASE, MR. CAGE, MS. WING, MS. KNIGHT, FORGIVE THE RIDICULOUSNESS OF YOUR RESTRAINTS, BUT AS YOU'RE ALL SO VERY TALENTED WITH YOUR ARMS, I'VE DECIDED TO REMOVE YOUR ABILITY TO USE THEM.
I'D OFFER YOU COCOA OTHERWISE.
MY NAME IS MR. XAO AND YOU ARE MY PRISONERS.

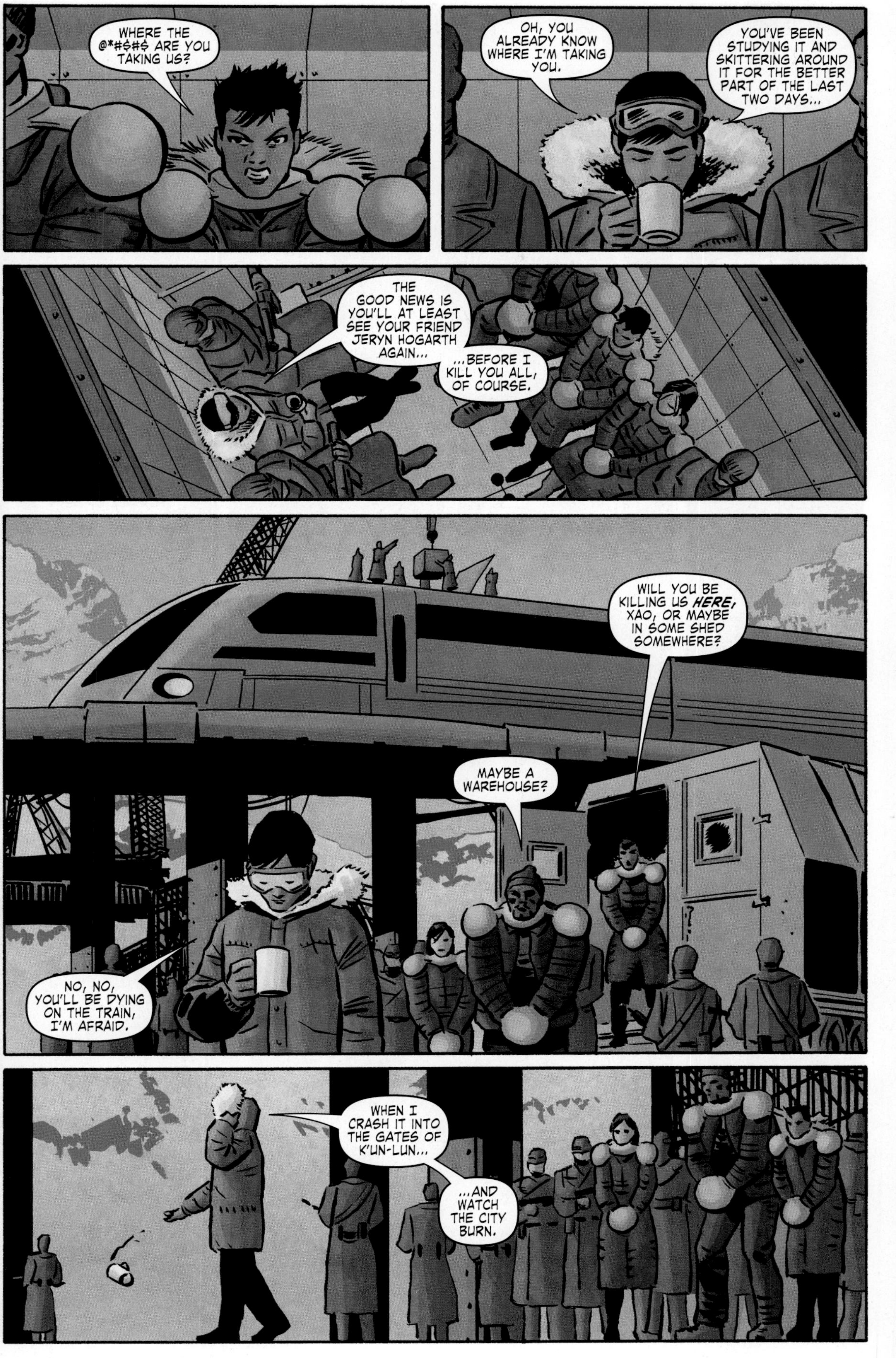
WHERE THE @*#$#$ ARE YOU TAKING US?
OH, YOU ALREADY KNOW WHERE I'M TAKING YOU.
YOU'VE BEEN STUDYING IT AND SKITTERING AROUND IT FOR THE BETTER PART OF THE LAST TWO DAYS...
THE GOOD NEWS IS YOU'LL AT LEAST SEE YOUR FRIEND JERYN HOGARTH AGAIN...
...BEFORE I KILL YOU ALL, OF COURSE.
WILL YOU BE KILLING US *HERE*, XAO, OR MAYBE IN SOME SHED SOMEWHERE?
MAYBE A WAREHOUSE?
NO, NO, YOU'LL BE DYING ON THE TRAIN, I'M AFRAID.
WHEN I CRASH IT INTO THE GATES OF K'UN-LUN...
...AND WATCH THE CITY BURN.

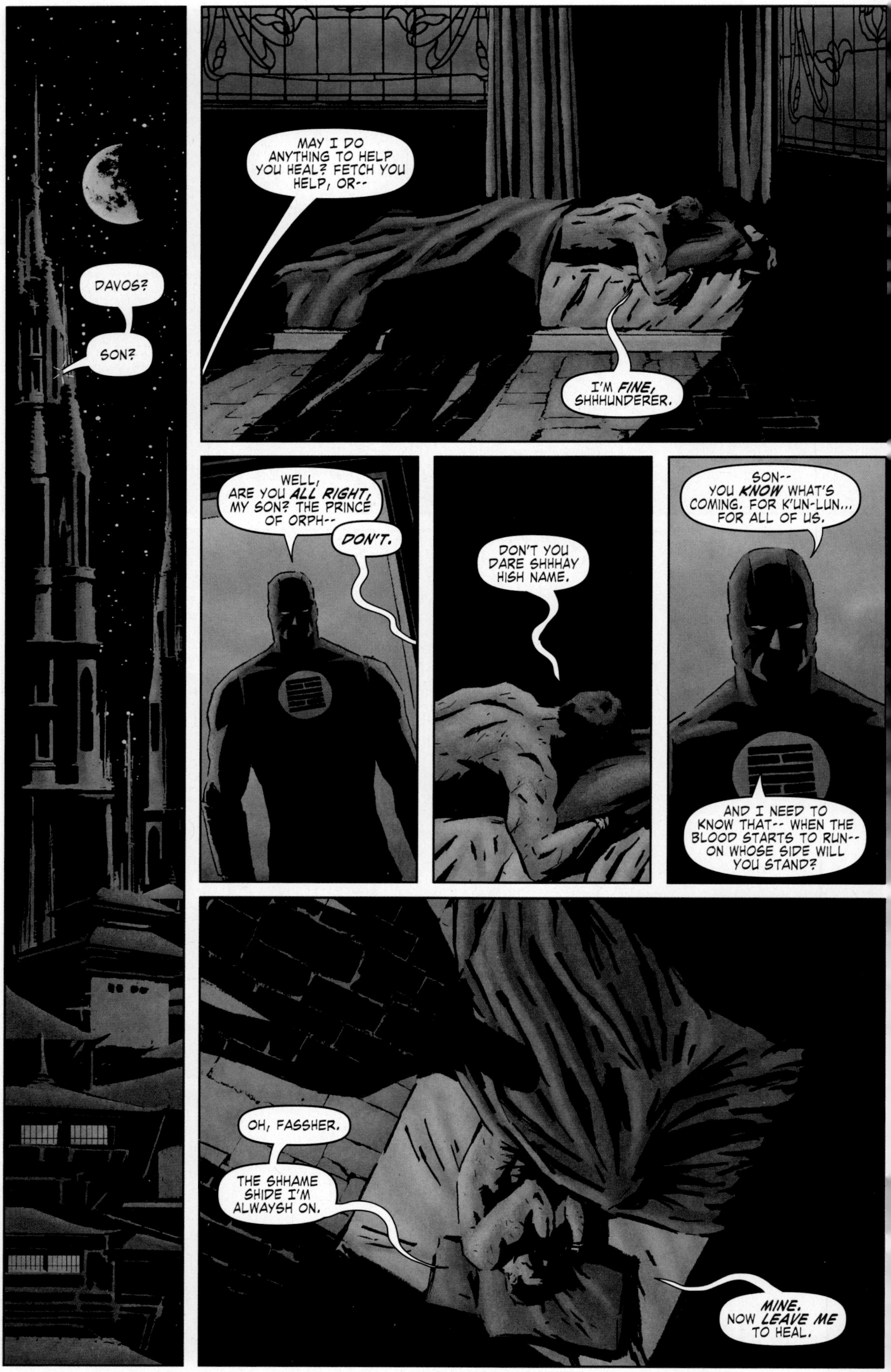

DAVOS?
SON?
MAY I DO ANYTHING TO HELP YOU HEAL? FETCH YOU HELP, OR--
I'M *FINE,* SHHHUNDERER.
WELL, ARE YOU *ALL RIGHT,* MY SON? THE PRINCE OF ORPH--
DON'T.
DON'T YOU DARE SHHHAY HISH NAME.
SON-- YOU *KNOW* WHAT'S COMING. FOR K'UN-LUN... FOR ALL OF US.
AND I NEED TO KNOW THAT-- WHEN THE BLOOD STARTS TO RUN-- ON WHOSE SIDE WILL YOU STAND?
OH, FASSHER.
THE SHHAME SHIDE I'M ALWAYSH ON.
MINE. NOW *LEAVE ME* TO HEAL.

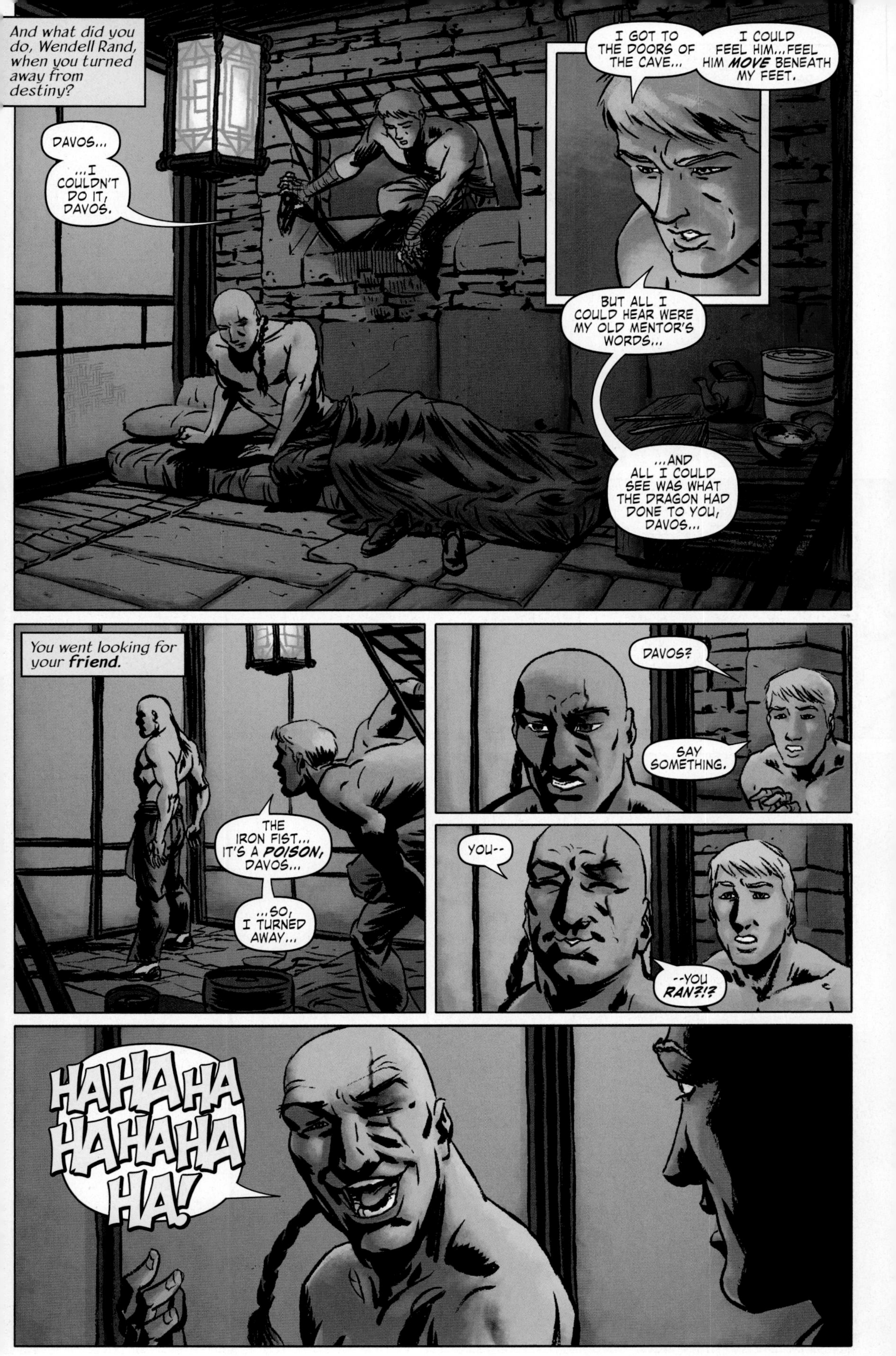
And what did you do, Wendell Rand, when you turned away from destiny?
DAVOS...
...I COULDN'T DO IT, DAVOS.
I GOT TO THE DOORS OF THE CAVE...
I COULD FEEL HIM...FEEL HIM MOVE BENEATH MY FEET.
BUT ALL I COULD HEAR WERE MY OLD MENTOR'S WORDS...
...AND ALL I COULD SEE WAS WHAT THE DRAGON HAD DONE TO YOU, DAVOS...
You went looking for your friend.
THE IRON FIST... IT'S A POISON, DAVOS...
...SO, I TURNED AWAY...
DAVOS?
SAY SOMETHING.
YOU--
--YOU RAN?!?
HAHAHA HAHAHA HA!

DAVOS-- C'MON--

STOP LAUGHING...

HO HO HO HO-- I'M SORRY, I JUST--

STOP IT!

I NEVER THOUGHT YOU WERE A--A COWARD!

With that word-- with one single, tiny word--

DAMN YOU, DAVOS--

--you snap.

And all the bad blood between you boils up to the surface.

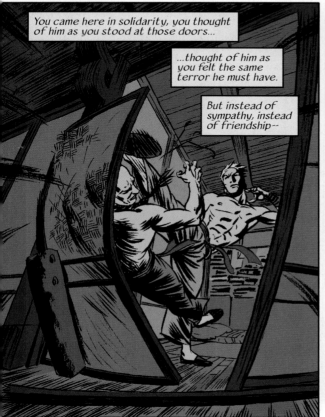

You came here in solidarity, you thought of him as you stood at those doors...

...thought of him as you felt the same terror he must have.

But instead of sympathy, instead of friendship--

--there is nothing but hate.

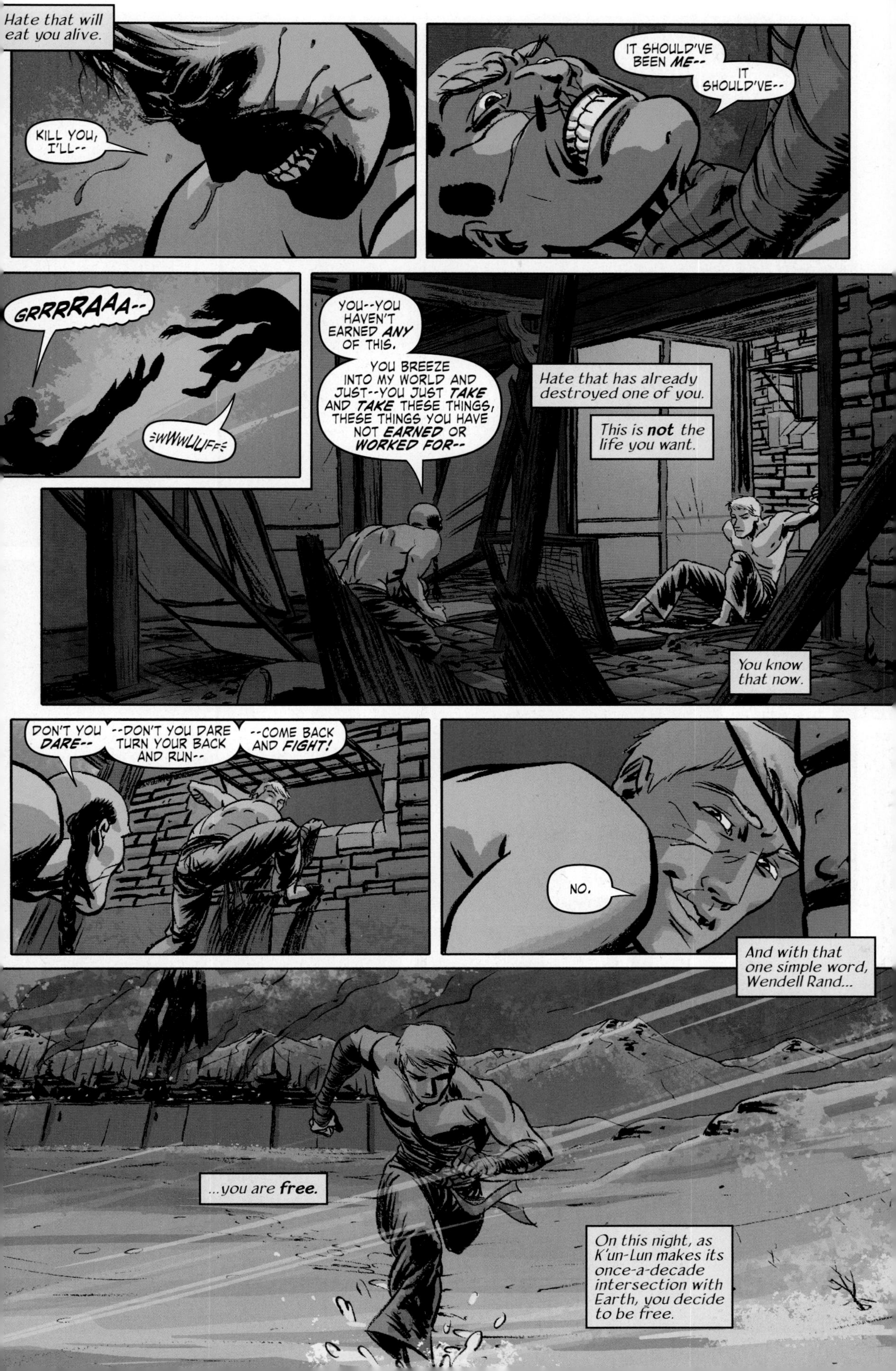
Hate that will eat you alive.
KILL YOU, I'LL--
IT SHOULD'VE BEEN ME--
IT SHOULD'VE--
GRRRRAAA--
WWWUUFF
YOU--YOU HAVEN'T EARNED ANY OF THIS.
YOU BREEZE INTO MY WORLD AND JUST--YOU JUST TAKE AND TAKE THESE THINGS, THESE THINGS YOU HAVE NOT EARNED OR WORKED FOR--
Hate that has already destroyed one of you.
This is not the life you want.
You know that now.
DON'T YOU DARE--
--DON'T YOU DARE TURN YOUR BACK AND RUN--
--COME BACK AND FIGHT!
NO.
And with that one simple word, Wendell Rand...
...you are free.
On this night, as K'un-Lun makes its once-a-decade intersection with Earth, you decide to be free.

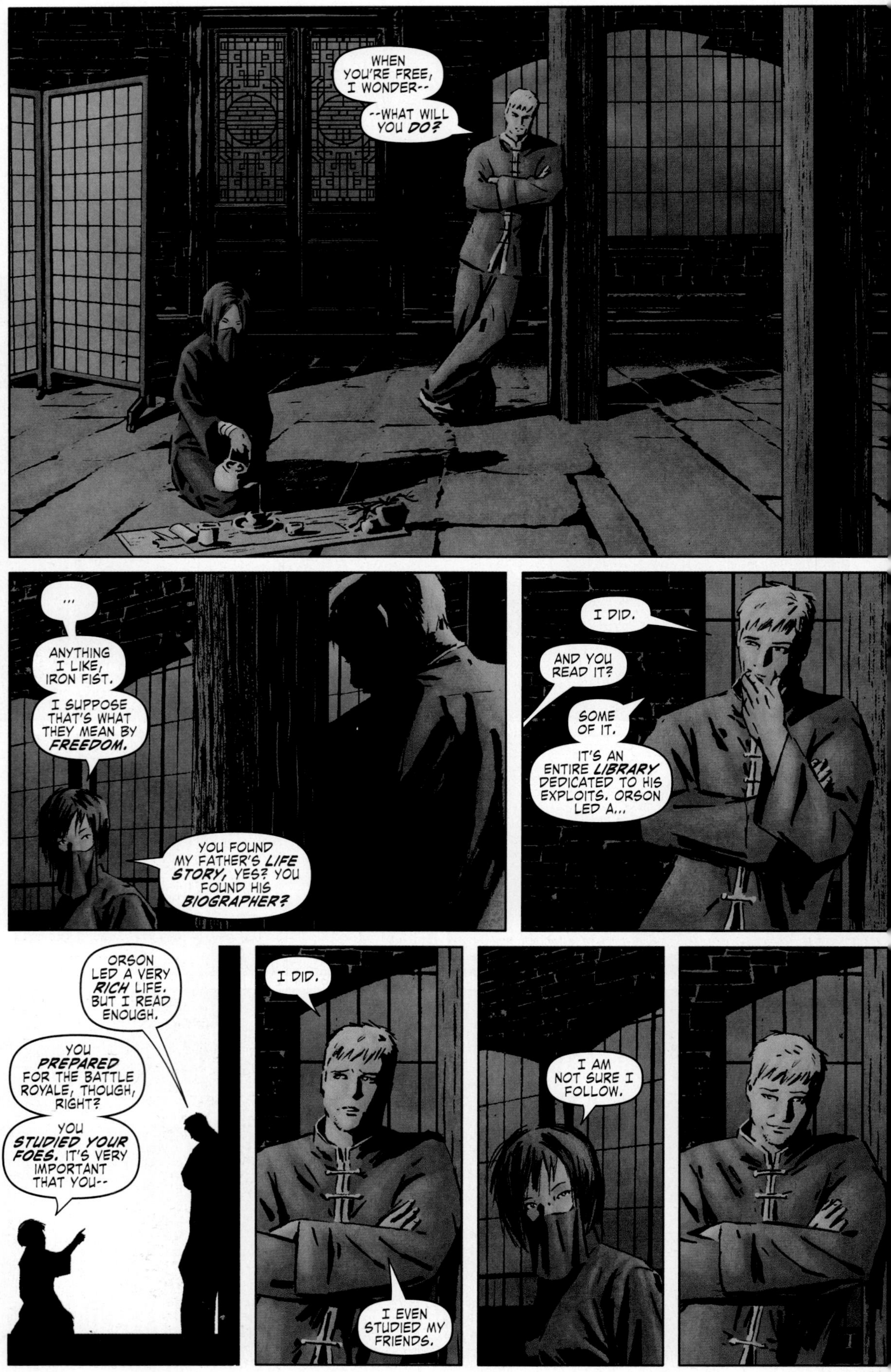
WHEN YOU'RE FREE, I WONDER--
--WHAT WILL YOU DO?
...
ANYTHING I LIKE, IRON FIST.
I SUPPOSE THAT'S WHAT THEY MEAN BY FREEDOM.
YOU FOUND MY FATHER'S LIFE STORY, YES? YOU FOUND HIS BIOGRAPHER?
I DID.
AND YOU READ IT?
SOME OF IT.
IT'S AN ENTIRE LIBRARY DEDICATED TO HIS EXPLOITS. ORSON LED A...
ORSON LED A VERY RICH LIFE. BUT I READ ENOUGH.
YOU PREPARED FOR THE BATTLE ROYALE, THOUGH, RIGHT?
YOU STUDIED YOUR FOES. IT'S VERY IMPORTANT THAT YOU--
I DID.
I EVEN STUDIED MY FRIENDS.
I AM NOT SURE I FOLLOW.

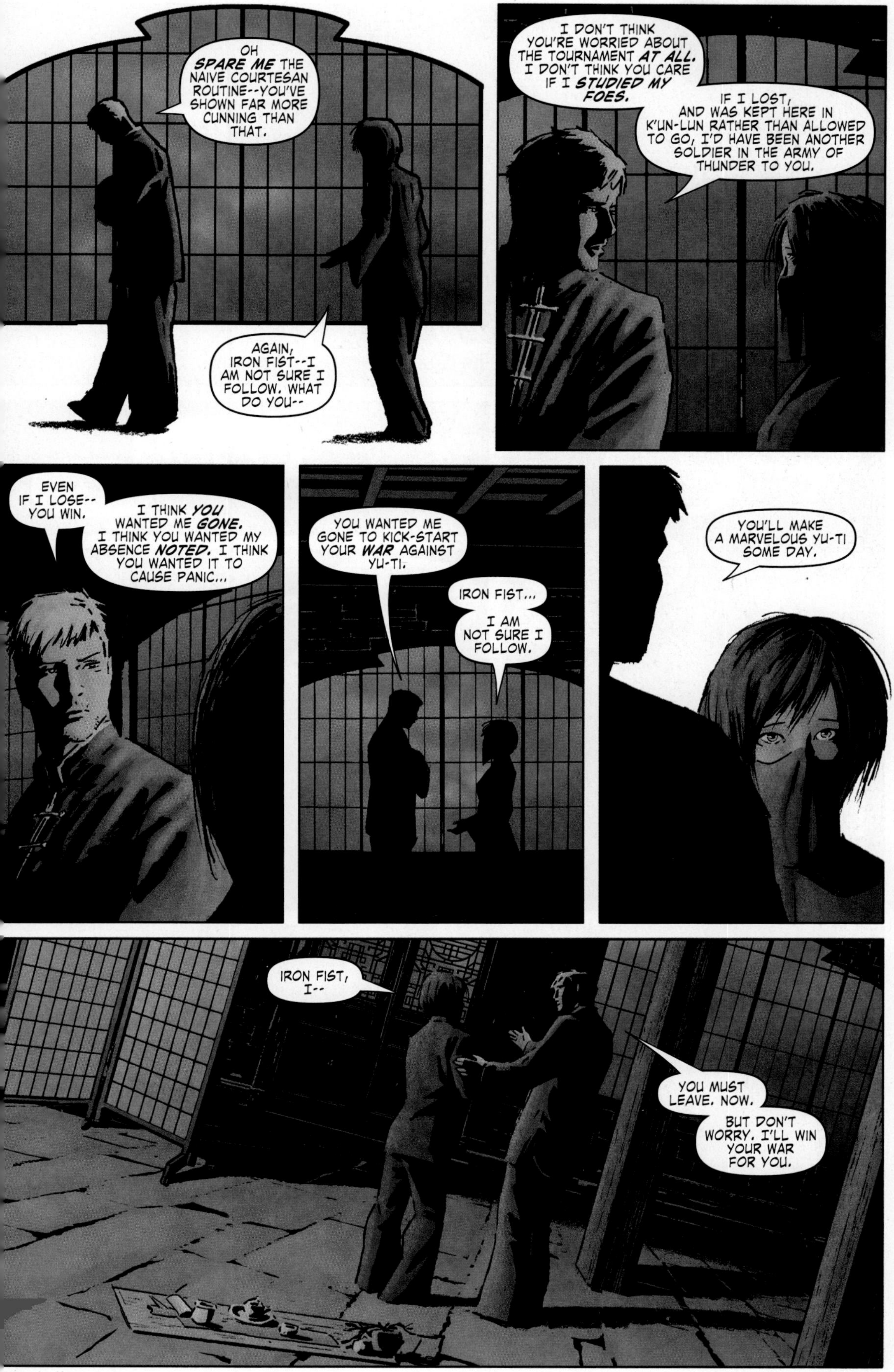
OH SPARE ME THE NAIVE COURTESAN ROUTINE--YOU'VE SHOWN FAR MORE CUNNING THAN THAT.
AGAIN, IRON FIST--I AM NOT SURE I FOLLOW. WHAT DO YOU--
I DON'T THINK YOU'RE WORRIED ABOUT THE TOURNAMENT AT ALL. I DON'T THINK YOU CARE IF I STUDIED MY FOES.
IF I LOST, AND WAS KEPT HERE IN K'UN-LUN RATHER THAN ALLOWED TO GO, I'D HAVE BEEN ANOTHER SOLDIER IN THE ARMY OF THUNDER TO YOU.
EVEN IF I LOSE--YOU WIN.
I THINK YOU WANTED ME GONE. I THINK YOU WANTED MY ABSENCE NOTED. I THINK YOU WANTED IT TO CAUSE PANIC...
YOU WANTED ME GONE TO KICK-START YOUR WAR AGAINST YU-TI.
IRON FIST...
I AM NOT SURE I FOLLOW.
YOU'LL MAKE A MARVELOUS YU-TI SOME DAY.
IRON FIST, I--
YOU MUST LEAVE. NOW.
BUT DON'T WORRY. I'LL WIN YOUR WAR FOR YOU.

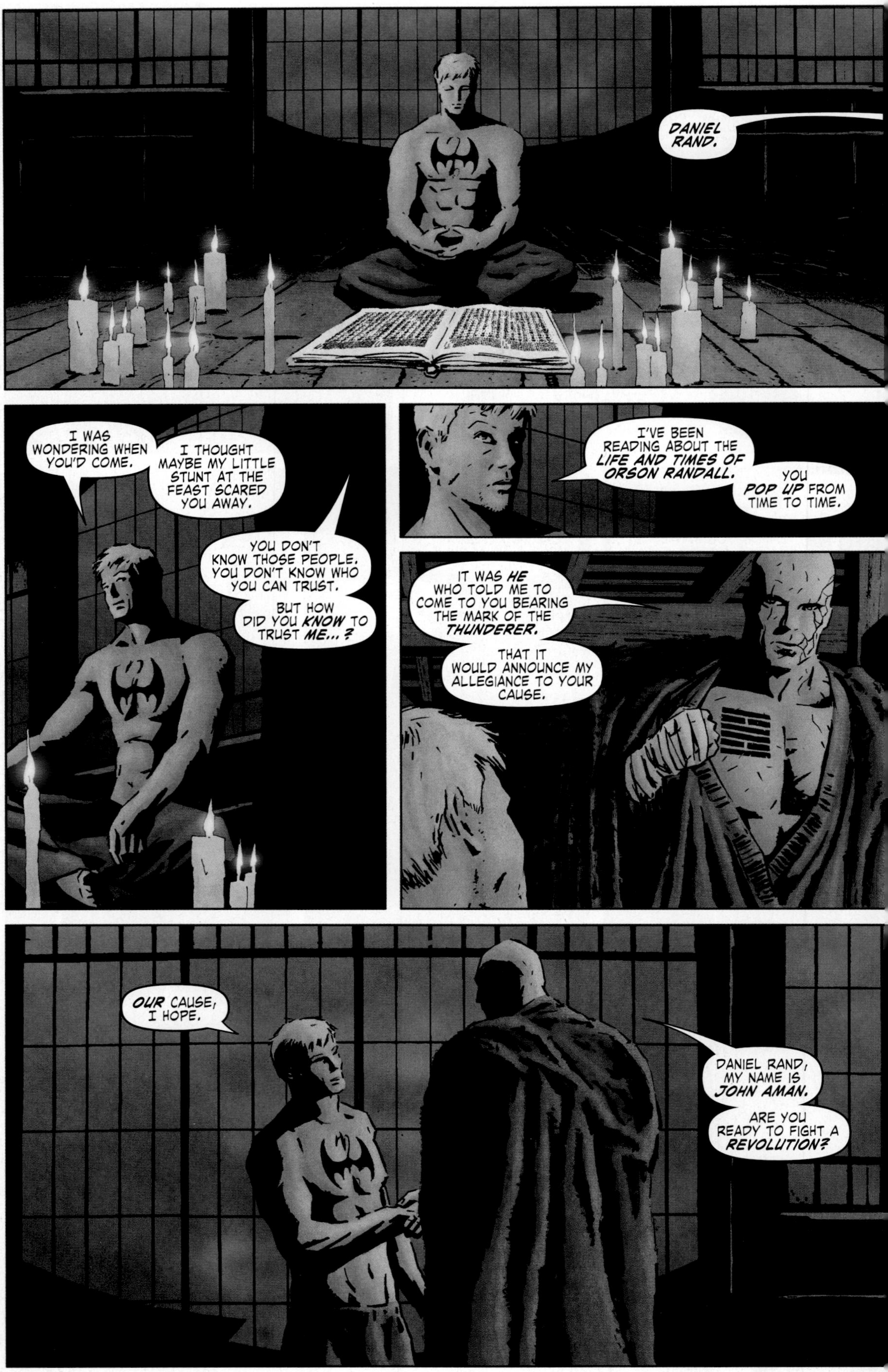
DANIEL RAND.
I WAS WONDERING WHEN YOU'D COME.
I THOUGHT MAYBE MY LITTLE STUNT AT THE FEAST SCARED YOU AWAY.
YOU DON'T KNOW THOSE PEOPLE. YOU DON'T KNOW WHO YOU CAN TRUST.
BUT HOW DID YOU KNOW TO TRUST ME...?
I'VE BEEN READING ABOUT THE LIFE AND TIMES OF ORSON RANDALL.
YOU POP UP FROM TIME TO TIME.
IT WAS HE WHO TOLD ME TO COME TO YOU BEARING THE MARK OF THE THUNDERER.
THAT IT WOULD ANNOUNCE MY ALLEGIANCE TO YOUR CAUSE.
OUR CAUSE, I HOPE.
DANIEL RAND, MY NAME IS JOHN AMAN.
ARE YOU READY TO FIGHT A REVOLUTION?

鐵拳 13

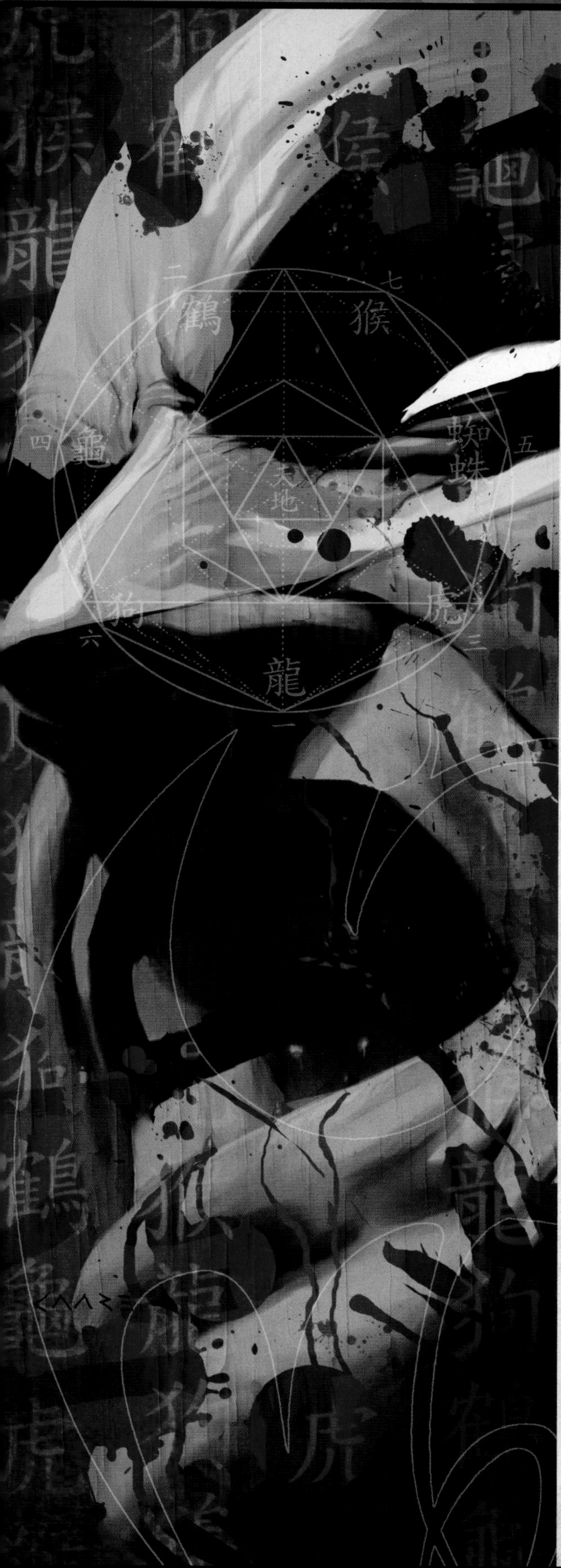
鶴
猴
龜
蜘蛛
天地
狗
虎
龍

The 7 Capital Cities of Heaven

六

Round 6

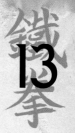

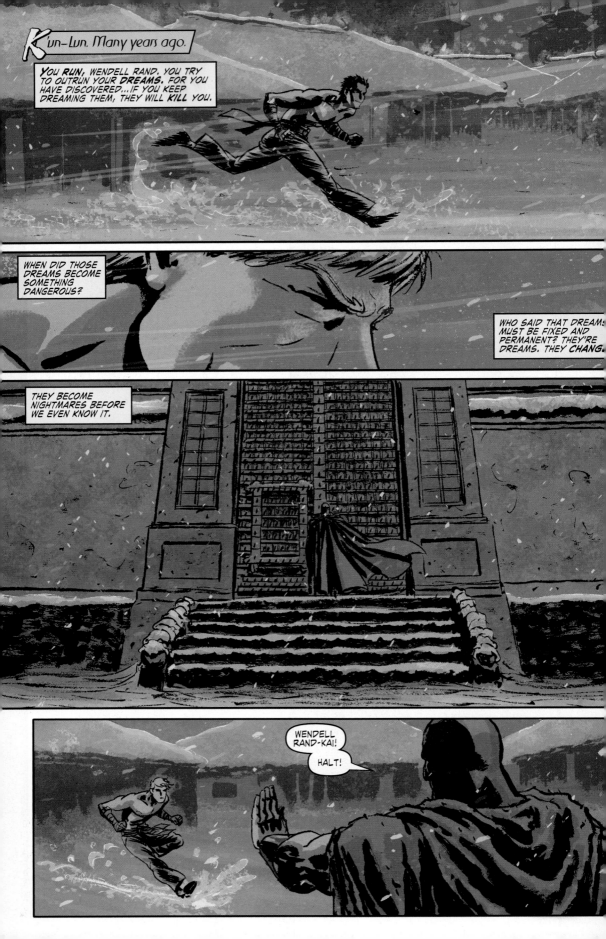

Kun-Lun. Many years ago.

YOU **RUN**, WENDELL RAND. YOU TRY TO OUTRUN YOUR **DREAMS**. FOR YOU HAVE DISCOVERED...IF YOU KEEP DREAMING THEM, THEY WILL **KILL** YOU.

WHEN DID THOSE DREAMS BECOME SOMETHING DANGEROUS?

WHO SAID THAT DREAMS MUST BE FIXED AND PERMANENT? THEY'RE DREAMS. THEY **CHANG...**

THEY BECOME NIGHTMARES BEFORE WE EVEN KNOW IT.

WENDELL RAND-KAI!

HALT!

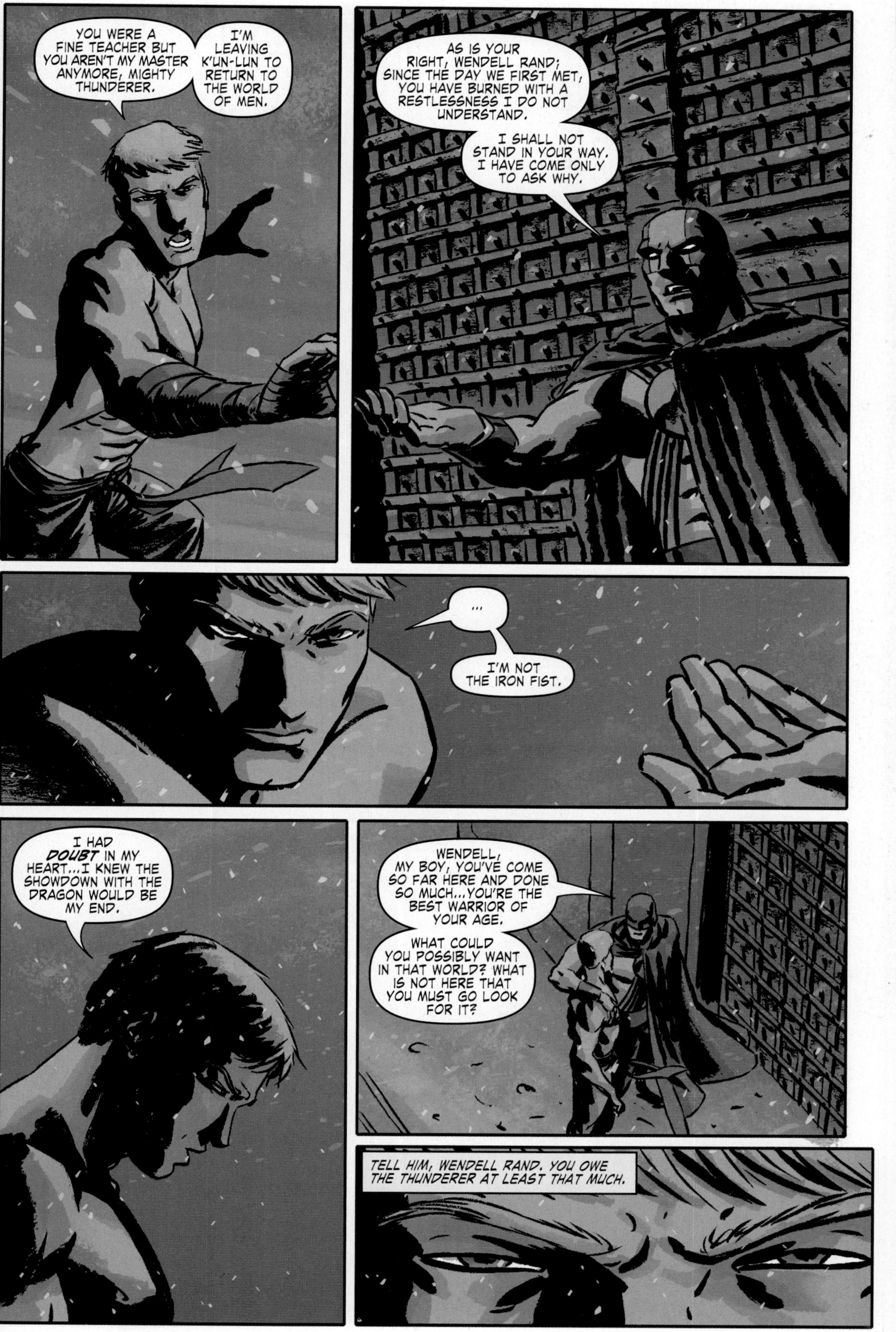
YOU WERE A FINE TEACHER BUT YOU AREN'T MY MASTER ANYMORE, MIGHTY THUNDERER.
I'M LEAVING K'UN-LUN TO RETURN TO THE WORLD OF MEN.
AS IS YOUR RIGHT, WENDELL RAND; SINCE THE DAY WE FIRST MET, YOU HAVE BURNED WITH A RESTLESSNESS I DO NOT UNDERSTAND.
I SHALL NOT STAND IN YOUR WAY. I HAVE COME ONLY TO ASK WHY.
...
I'M NOT THE IRON FIST.
I HAD DOUBT IN MY HEART...I KNEW THE SHOWDOWN WITH THE DRAGON WOULD BE MY END.
WENDELL, MY BOY, YOU'VE COME SO FAR HERE AND DONE SO MUCH...YOU'RE THE BEST WARRIOR OF YOUR AGE.
WHAT COULD YOU POSSIBLY WANT IN THAT WORLD? WHAT IS NOT HERE THAT YOU MUST GO LOOK FOR IT?
TELL HIM, WENDELL RAND. YOU OWE THE THUNDERER AT LEAST THAT MUCH.

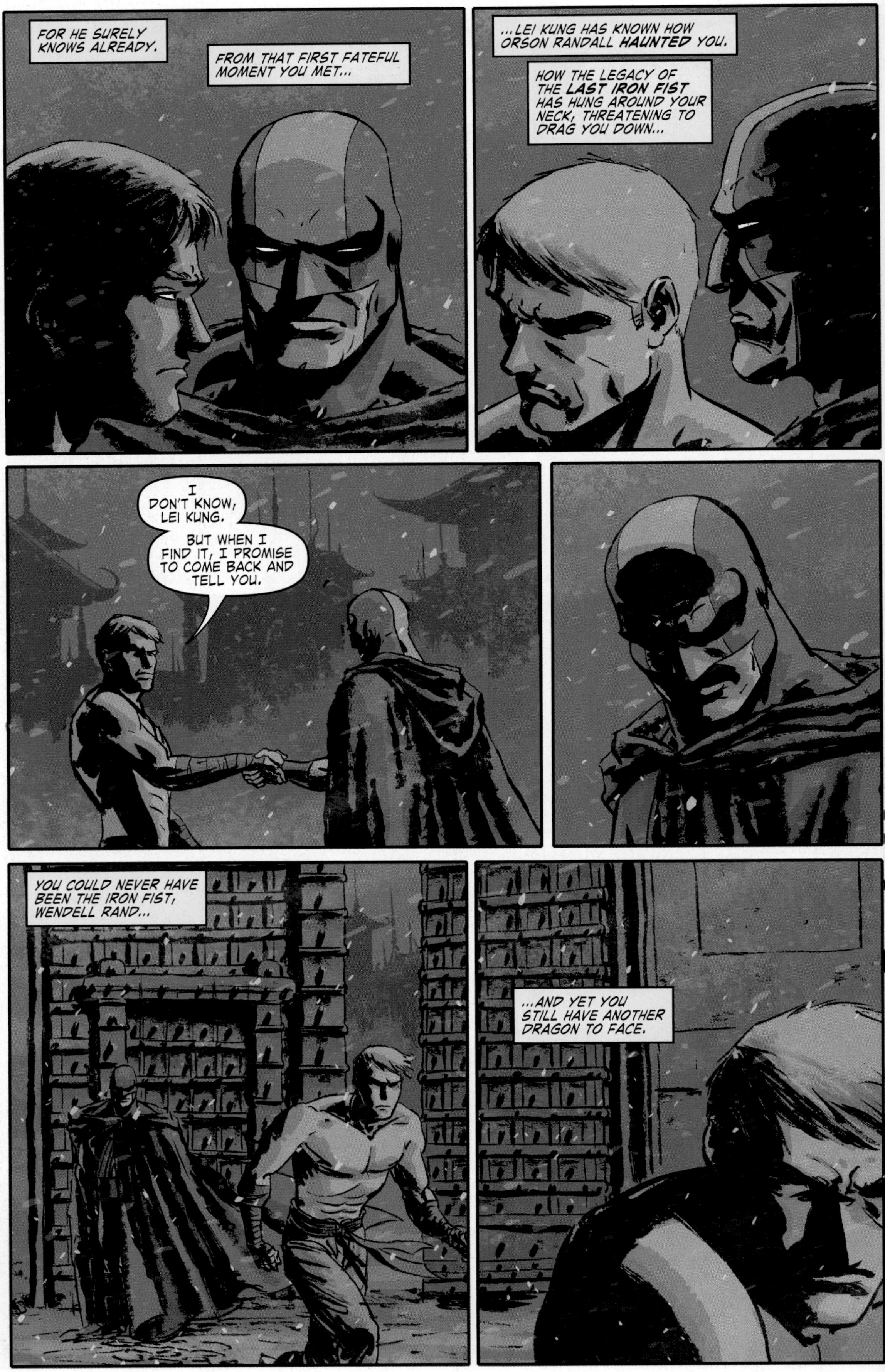
FOR HE SURELY KNOWS ALREADY.
FROM THAT FIRST FATEFUL MOMENT YOU MET...
...LEI KUNG HAS KNOWN HOW ORSON RANDALL HAUNTED YOU.
HOW THE LEGACY OF THE LAST IRON FIST HAS HUNG AROUND YOUR NECK, THREATENING TO DRAG YOU DOWN...
I DON'T KNOW, LEI KUNG.
BUT WHEN I FIND IT, I PROMISE TO COME BACK AND TELL YOU.
YOU COULD NEVER HAVE BEEN THE IRON FIST, WENDELL RAND...
...AND YET YOU STILL HAVE ANOTHER DRAGON TO FACE.

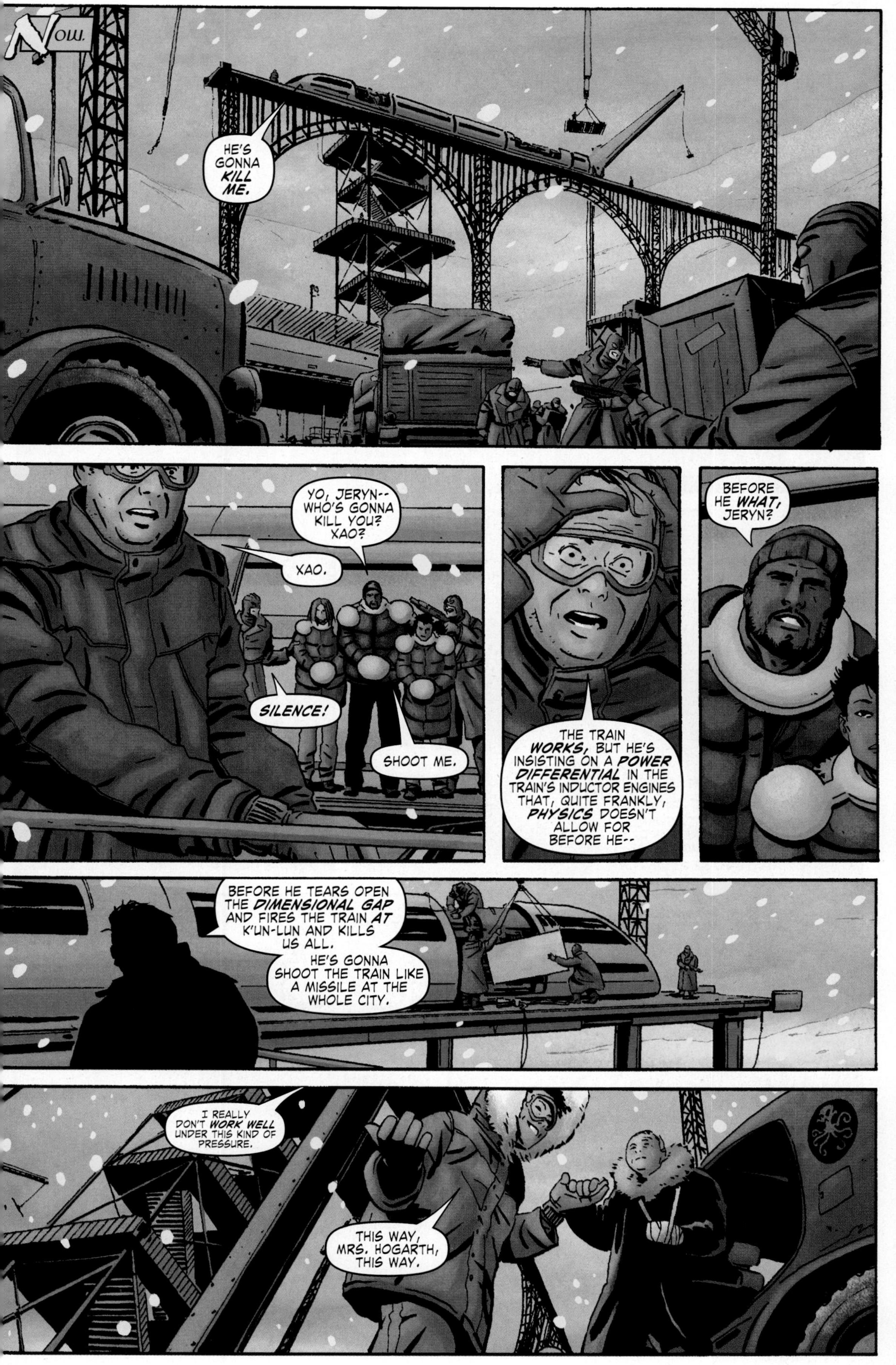
Now.
HE'S GONNA KILL ME.
YO, JERYN--WHO'S GONNA KILL YOU? XAO?
XAO.
SILENCE!
SHOOT ME.
THE TRAIN WORKS, BUT HE'S INSISTING ON A POWER DIFFERENTIAL IN THE TRAIN'S INDUCTOR ENGINES THAT, QUITE FRANKLY, PHYSICS DOESN'T ALLOW FOR BEFORE HE--
BEFORE HE WHAT, JERYN?
BEFORE HE TEARS OPEN THE DIMENSIONAL GAP AND FIRES THE TRAIN AT K'UN-LUN AND KILLS US ALL.
HE'S GONNA SHOOT THE TRAIN LIKE A MISSILE AT THE WHOLE CITY.
I REALLY DON'T WORK WELL UNDER THIS KIND OF PRESSURE.
THIS WAY, MRS. HOGARTH, THIS WAY.

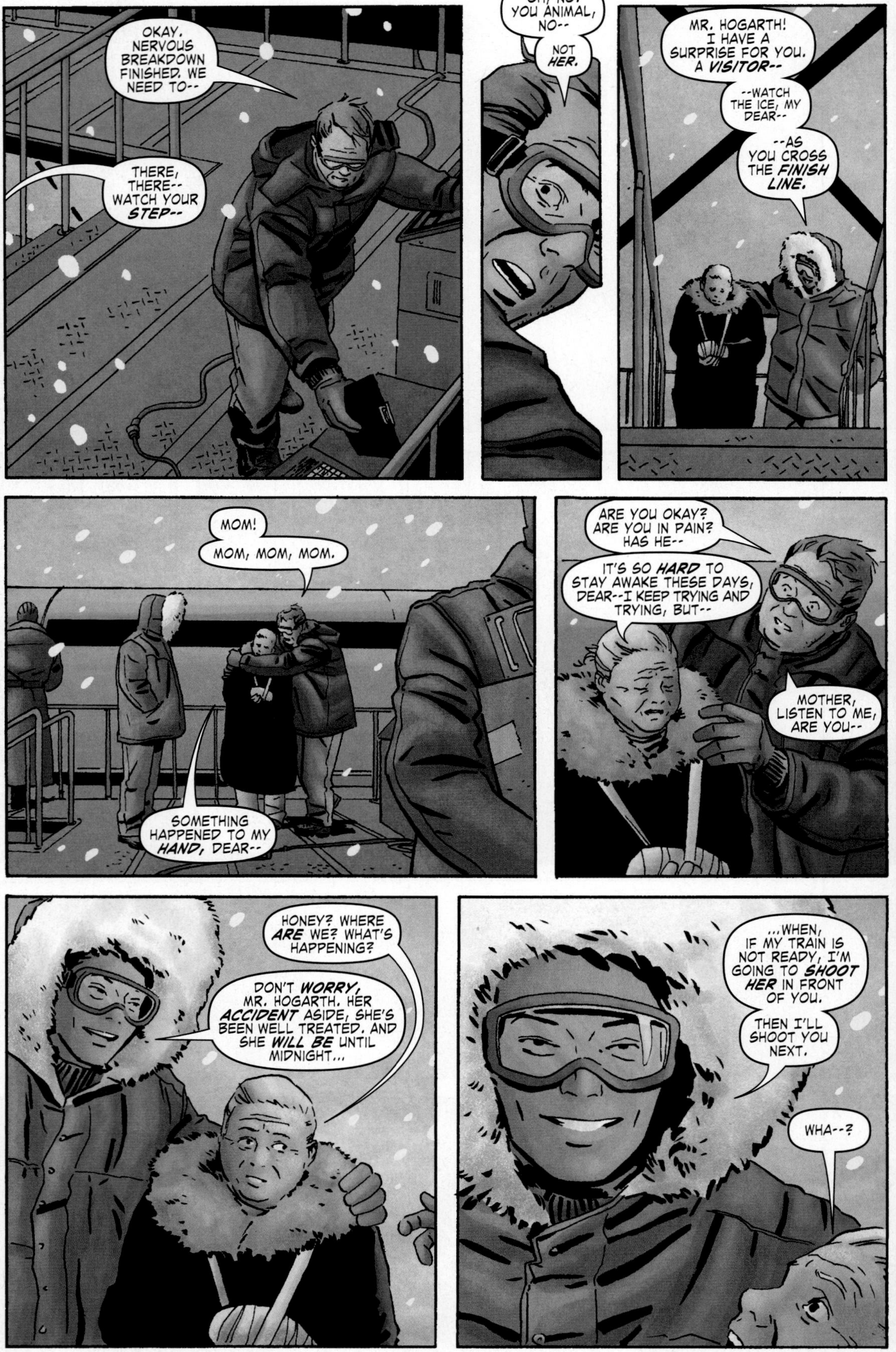
OKAY. NERVOUS BREAKDOWN FINISHED. WE NEED TO--
THERE, THERE-- WATCH YOUR STEP--
OH, NO. YOU ANIMAL, NO--
NOT HER.
MR. HOGARTH! I HAVE A SURPRISE FOR YOU. A VISITOR--
--WATCH THE ICE, MY DEAR--
--AS YOU CROSS THE FINISH LINE.
MOM!
MOM, MOM, MOM.
SOMETHING HAPPENED TO MY HAND, DEAR--
ARE YOU OKAY? ARE YOU IN PAIN? HAS HE--
IT'S SO HARD TO STAY AWAKE THESE DAYS, DEAR--I KEEP TRYING AND TRYING, BUT--
MOTHER, LISTEN TO ME, ARE YOU--
HONEY? WHERE ARE WE? WHAT'S HAPPENING?
DON'T WORRY, MR. HOGARTH. HER ACCIDENT ASIDE, SHE'S BEEN WELL TREATED. AND SHE WILL BE UNTIL MIDNIGHT...
...WHEN, IF MY TRAIN IS NOT READY, I'M GOING TO SHOOT HER IN FRONT OF YOU.
THEN I'LL SHOOT YOU NEXT.
WHA--?

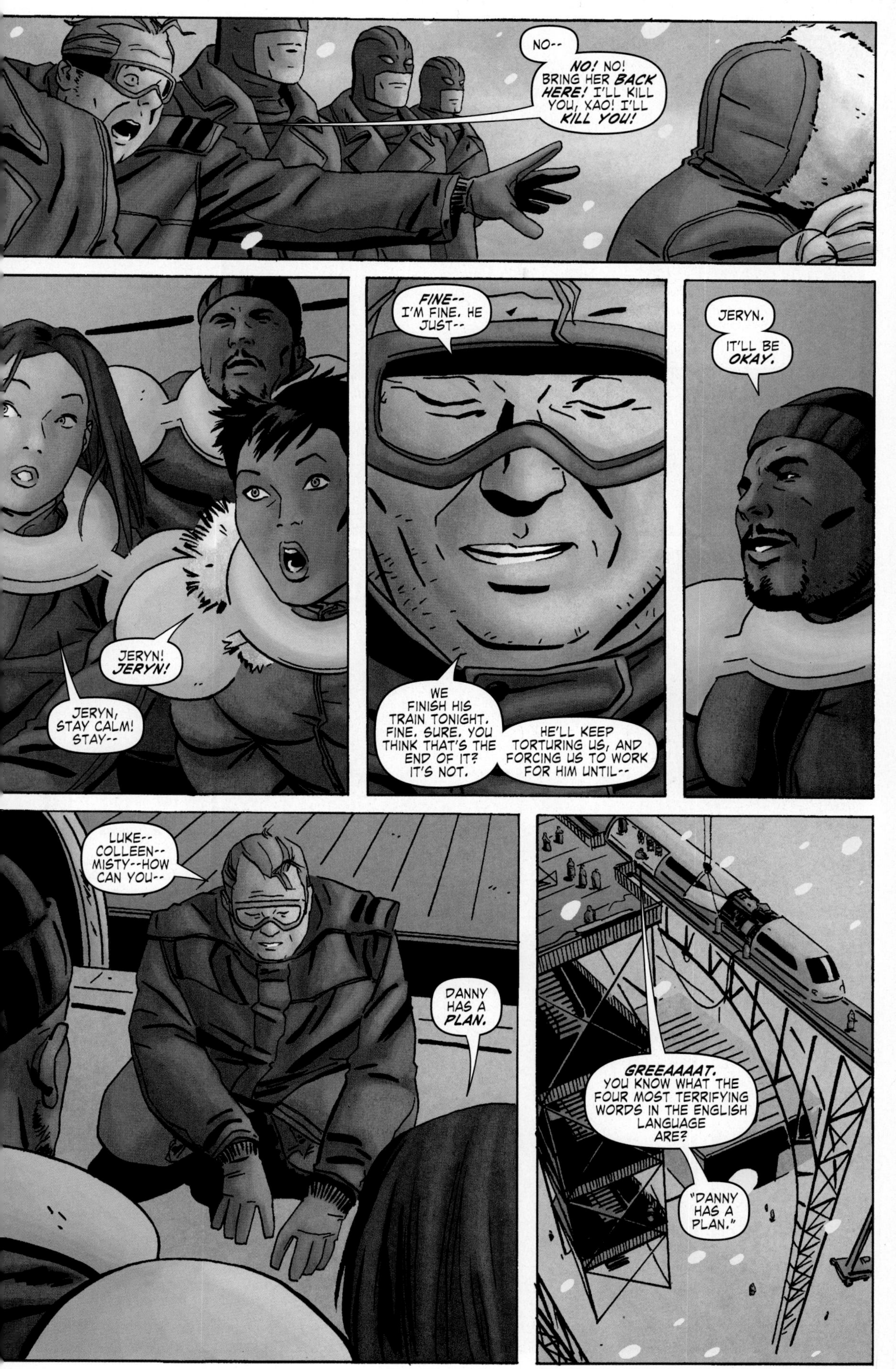
NO--
NO! NO! BRING HER BACK HERE! I'LL KILL YOU, XAO! I'LL KILL YOU!
FINE-- I'M FINE. HE JUST--
JERYN.
IT'LL BE OKAY.
JERYN! JERYN!
JERYN, STAY CALM! STAY--
WE FINISH HIS TRAIN TONIGHT. FINE, SURE. YOU THINK THAT'S THE END OF IT? IT'S NOT.
HE'LL KEEP TORTURING US, AND FORCING US TO WORK FOR HIM UNTIL--
LUKE-- COLLEEN-- MISTY--HOW CAN YOU--
DANNY HAS A PLAN.
GREEAAAAT. YOU KNOW WHAT THE FOUR MOST TERRIFYING WORDS IN THE ENGLISH LANGUAGE ARE?
"DANNY HAS A PLAN."

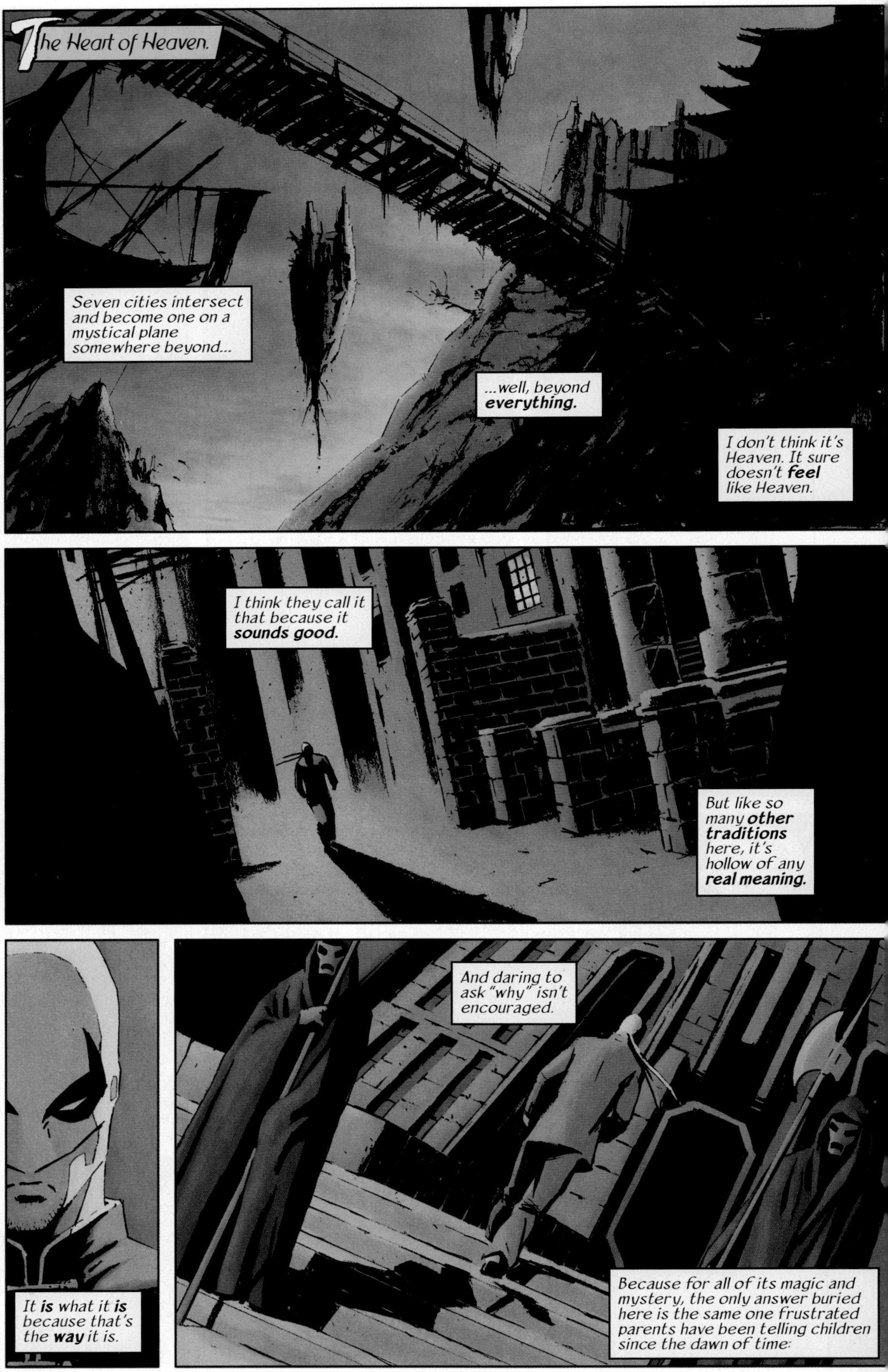
The Heart of Heaven.
Seven cities intersect and become one on a mystical plane somewhere beyond...
...well, beyond **everything.**
I don't think it's Heaven. It sure doesn't **feel** like Heaven.
I think they call it that because it **sounds good.**
But like so many **other traditions** here, it's hollow of any **real meaning.**
It **is** what it **is** because that's the **way** it is.
And daring to ask "why" isn't encouraged.
Because for all of its magic and mystery, the only answer buried here is the same one frustrated parents have been telling children since the dawn of time:

MASTER. I KNOW ABOUT THE RANDALL GATE.

I KNOW THAT YOU'VE BEEN VISITING THE WORLD OF MEN AS YOU LIKE, AND I KNOW YOU'VE PAID HANDSOMELY FOR THE PRIVILEGE.

YOUR FORTUNE WAS THE ROOT OF *MY FATHER'S FORTUNE.*

I KNOW ABOUT IT, NU-AN. I KNOW ABOUT IT *ALL.*

YOU. *IMPUDENT.* WHELP.

"...Because I said so."

AND YOU. *TYRANT.*

YOU LIAR. YOU PIG.

YOU SPOILED *BRAT.*

WHEN YOUR FATHER WAS THE YU-TI OF K'UN-LUN, HE RULED WITH COMPASSION AND KINDNESS.

YOUR REGIME HAS ALL BEEN IN SERVICE OF--WHAT? YOUR OWN *HEDONISM?*

THIS IS YOUR ONE CHANCE IN THIS LIFE TO DO RIGHT BY YOUR PEOPLE.

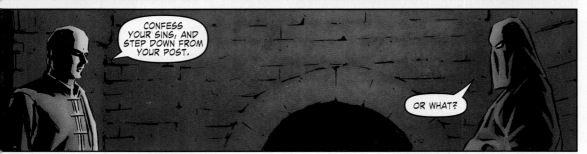

CONFESS YOUR SINS, AND STEP DOWN FROM YOUR POST.

OR WHAT?

OR I *TELL* ALL WHO POPULATE K'UN-LUN OF YOUR CRIMES AGAINST THEM.

AND LET *THEM* DECIDE WHAT TO DO.

I'LL TAKE MY CHANCES IN THE COURT OF PUBLIC OPINION, IRON FIST.

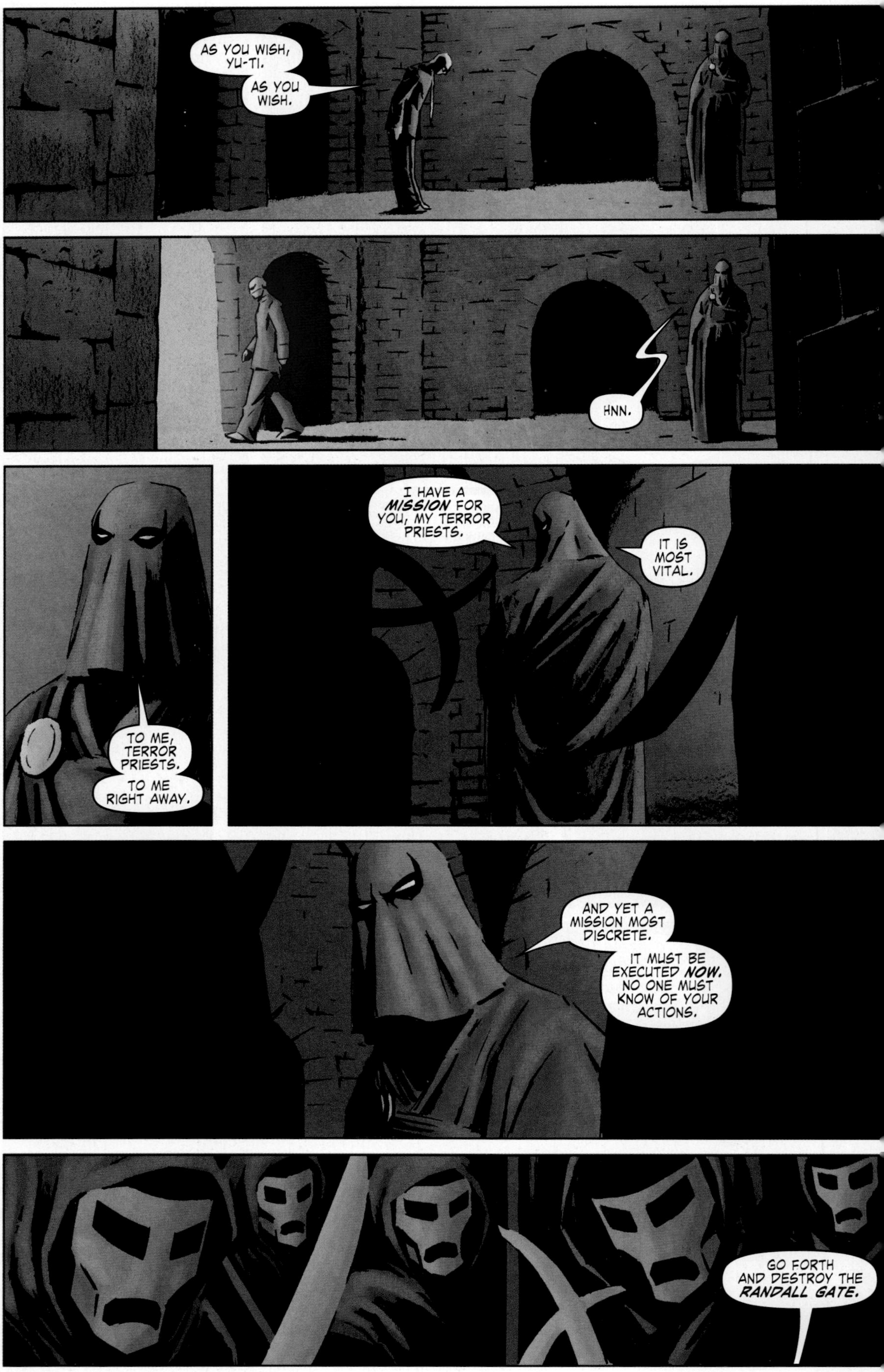
AS YOU WISH, YU-TI.
AS YOU WISH.
HNN.
TO ME, TERROR PRIESTS.
TO ME RIGHT AWAY.
I HAVE A *MISSION* FOR YOU, MY TERROR PRIESTS.
IT IS MOST VITAL.
AND YET A MISSION MOST DISCRETE.
IT MUST BE EXECUTED *NOW.* NO ONE MUST KNOW OF YOUR ACTIONS.
GO FORTH AND DESTROY THE *RANDALL GATE.*

AND THERE THEY GO.

MY GOD, DANNY--

--IF THEY DESTROY THE GATE--

LET THEM *TRY,* THUNDERER. THEY'LL FAIL.

YOUR *SECRET ARMY* WILL SEE TO THAT.

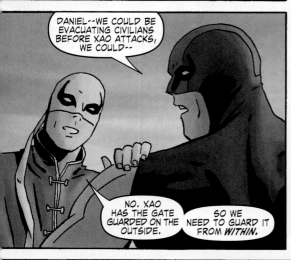

DANIEL--WE COULD BE EVACUATING CIVILIANS BEFORE XAO ATTACKS, WE COULD--

NO, XAO HAS THE GATE GUARDED ON THE OUTSIDE.

SO WE NEED TO GUARD IT FROM *WITHIN.*

TRUST ME, I HAVE A PLAN.

THOSE WORDS DO NOT EXACTLY FILL ME WITH *CONFIDENCE.*

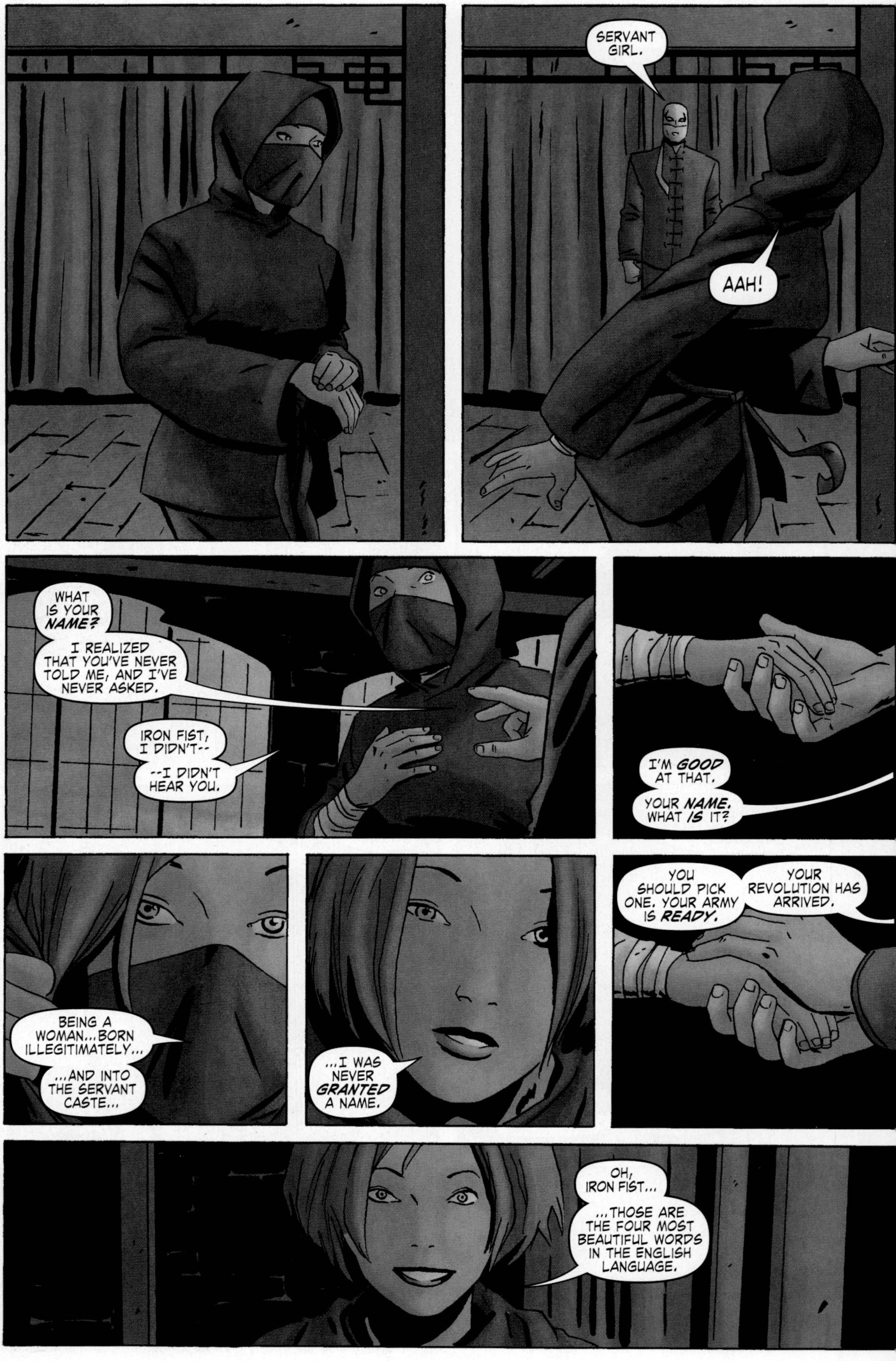
SERVANT GIRL.
AAH!
WHAT IS YOUR NAME?
I REALIZED THAT YOU'VE NEVER TOLD ME, AND I'VE NEVER ASKED.
IRON FIST, I DIDN'T--
--I DIDN'T HEAR YOU.
I'M GOOD AT THAT.
YOUR NAME. WHAT IS IT?
BEING A WOMAN...BORN ILLEGITIMATELY...
...AND INTO THE SERVANT CASTE...
...I WAS NEVER GRANTED A NAME.
YOU SHOULD PICK ONE. YOUR ARMY IS READY.
YOUR REVOLUTION HAS ARRIVED.
OH, IRON FIST...
...THOSE ARE THE FOUR MOST BEAUTIFUL WORDS IN THE ENGLISH LANGUAGE.

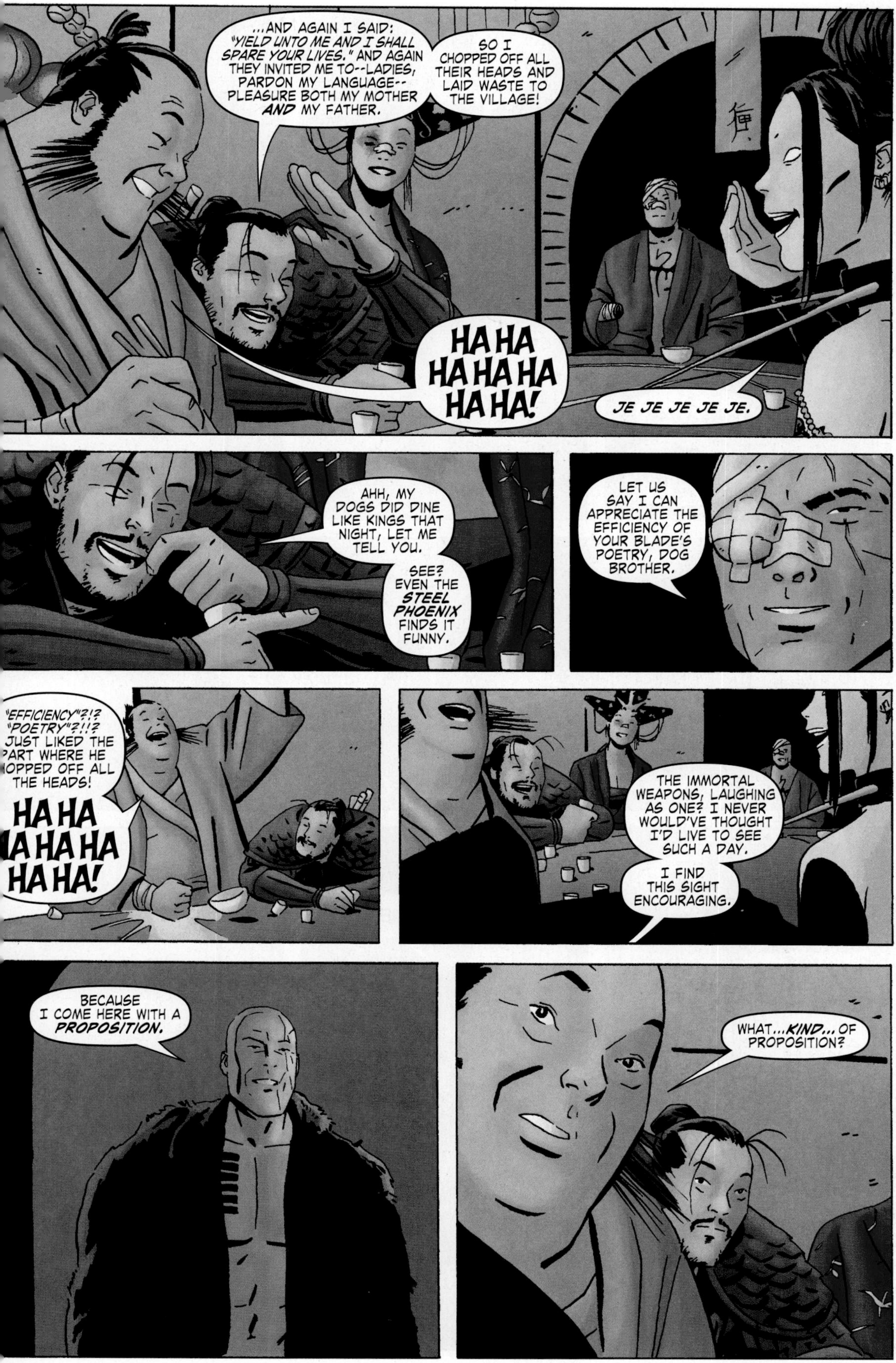
...AND AGAIN I SAID: "YIELD UNTO ME AND I SHALL SPARE YOUR LIVES." AND AGAIN THEY INVITED ME TO--LADIES, PARDON MY LANGUAGE-- PLEASURE BOTH MY MOTHER AND MY FATHER.
SO I CHOPPED OFF ALL THEIR HEADS AND LAID WASTE TO THE VILLAGE!
HA HA HA HA HA HA HA!
JE JE JE JE JE.
AHH, MY DOGS DID DINE LIKE KINGS THAT NIGHT, LET ME TELL YOU.
SEE? EVEN THE STEEL PHOENIX FINDS IT FUNNY.
LET US SAY I CAN APPRECIATE THE EFFICIENCY OF YOUR BLADE'S POETRY, DOG BROTHER.
"EFFICIENCY"?!? "POETRY"?!!? JUST LIKED THE PART WHERE HE HOPPED OFF ALL THE HEADS!
HA HA HA HA HA HA HA!
THE IMMORTAL WEAPONS, LAUGHING AS ONE? I NEVER WOULD'VE THOUGHT I'D LIVE TO SEE SUCH A DAY.
I FIND THIS SIGHT ENCOURAGING.
BECAUSE I COME HERE WITH A PROPOSITION.
WHAT...KIND... OF PROPOSITION?

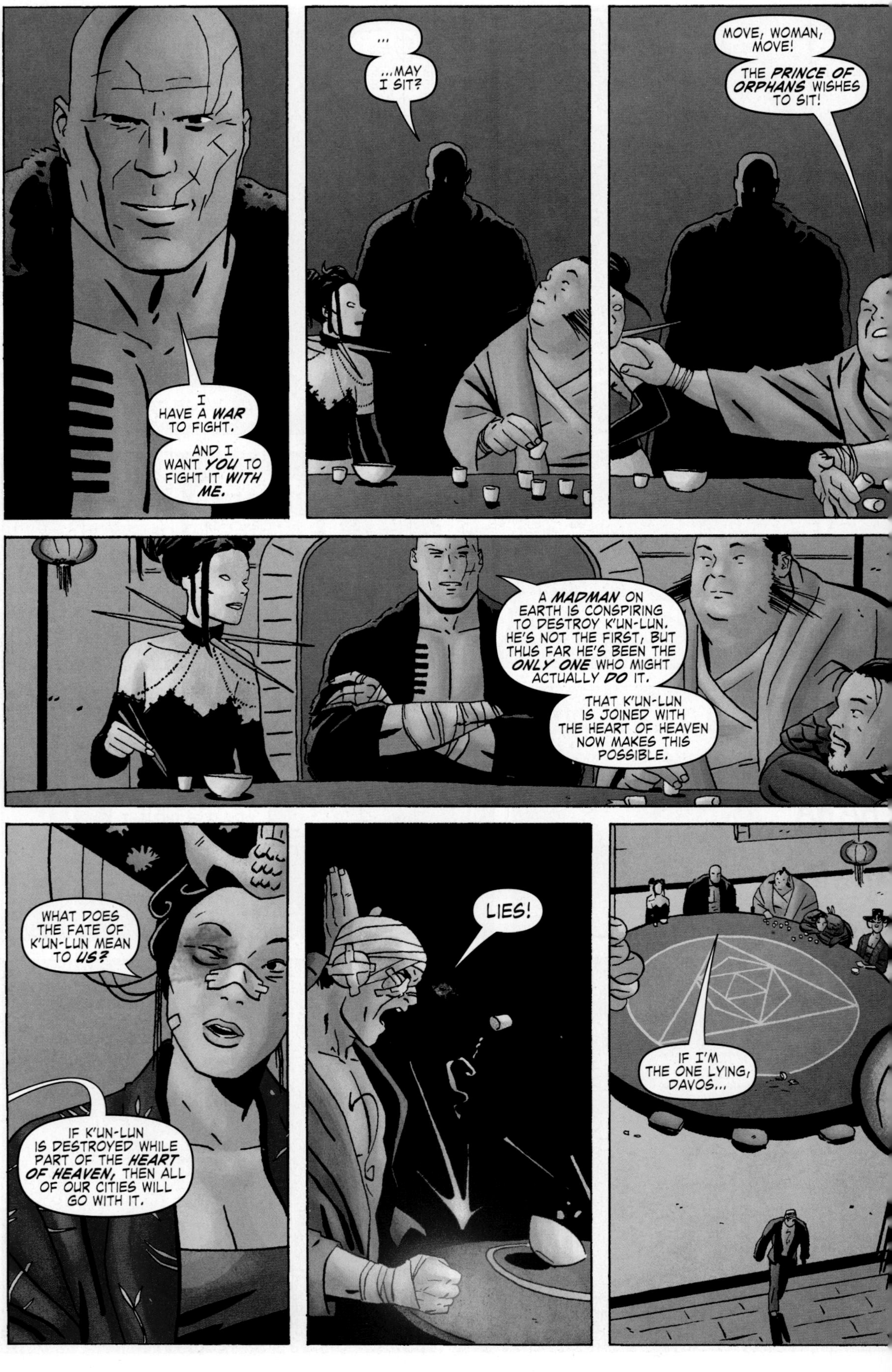

I HAVE A WAR TO FIGHT.
AND I WANT YOU TO FIGHT IT WITH ME.
...
...MAY I SIT?
MOVE, WOMAN, MOVE!
THE PRINCE OF ORPHANS WISHES TO SIT!
A MADMAN ON EARTH IS CONSPIRING TO DESTROY K'UN-LUN. HE'S NOT THE FIRST, BUT THUS FAR HE'S BEEN THE ONLY ONE WHO MIGHT ACTUALLY DO IT.
THAT K'UN-LUN IS JOINED WITH THE HEART OF HEAVEN NOW MAKES THIS POSSIBLE.
WHAT DOES THE FATE OF K'UN-LUN MEAN TO US?
IF K'UN-LUN IS DESTROYED WHILE PART OF THE HEART OF HEAVEN, THEN ALL OF OUR CITIES WILL GO WITH IT.
LIES!
IF I'M THE ONE LYING, DAVOS...

"...THEN WHO IS IT THAT YOU'RE RUSHING TO CONFRONT?"

FATHER.

DON'T TELL ME YOU BELIEVE THIS RIDICULOUS CONSPIRACY. THAT XAO WISHES TO DESTROY K'UN-LUN. THAT THE HEART OF HEAVEN IS AT RISK.

XAO'S GRUDGE IS MY GRUDGE; CRANE MOTHER'S, TOO--FOR THE CRIMES AGAINST K'UN-ZI.

HERE WE ARE IN YOUR ARMORY, AND YET...

...WHERE ARE YOUR ARMS? TELL ME YOU'VE NOT BEEN SO EASILY DUPED BY THE IRON FIST AND HIS...STOOGE, JOHN AMAN.

ka-klank

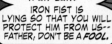

CRANE MOTHER ONLY WANTED TO DESTROY THE IRON FIST. XAO IS MERELY HER PUPPET.

SHE HAS SAID NOTHING OF DESTROYING K'UN-LUN.

IRON FIST IS LYING SO THAT YOU WILL PROTECT HIM FROM US-- FATHER, DON'T BE A FOOL.

DAVOS... THEY ARE MANIACS INTENT ON DESTROYING US ALL.

JOIN US, BOY. THERE ARE INNOCENT LIVES AT RISK THAT HAVE NOTHING TO DO WITH EVERYTHING THAT'S WRONG BETWEEN YOU AND I.

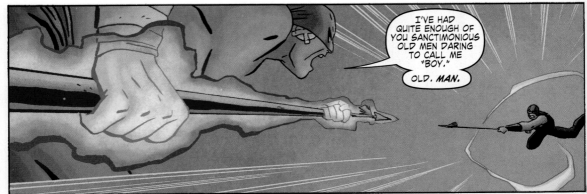

I'VE HAD QUITE ENOUGH OF YOU SANCTIMONIOUS OLD MEN DARING TO CALL ME "BOY."

OLD. *MAN.*

KSSHH
KSSHH

HII-YAH!!

YAAH-HAA!!

THERE IS NO ULTERIOR MOTIVE HERE.

NO ONE IS TRYING TO TRICK YOU OR MANIPULATE YOU AS YOU HAVE TRICKED AND MANIPULATED SO MANY, MY SON--

XAO WILL DESTROY US ALL!

XAO IS A MOPPET IN A MAN SUIT. HE COULDN'T PLAN HIS WAY OUT OF A PAPER BAG!

THUNK

CRANE MOTHER-- XAO--THEY'VE BOTH *BETRAYED* YOU! USED YOU!

THAT'S WHAT THIS IS *REALLY* ABOUT, ISN'T IT?

YOU'VE FINALLY MET YOUR TREACHEROUS MATCH AND CAN'T BELIEVE YOU'VE BEEN BESTED.

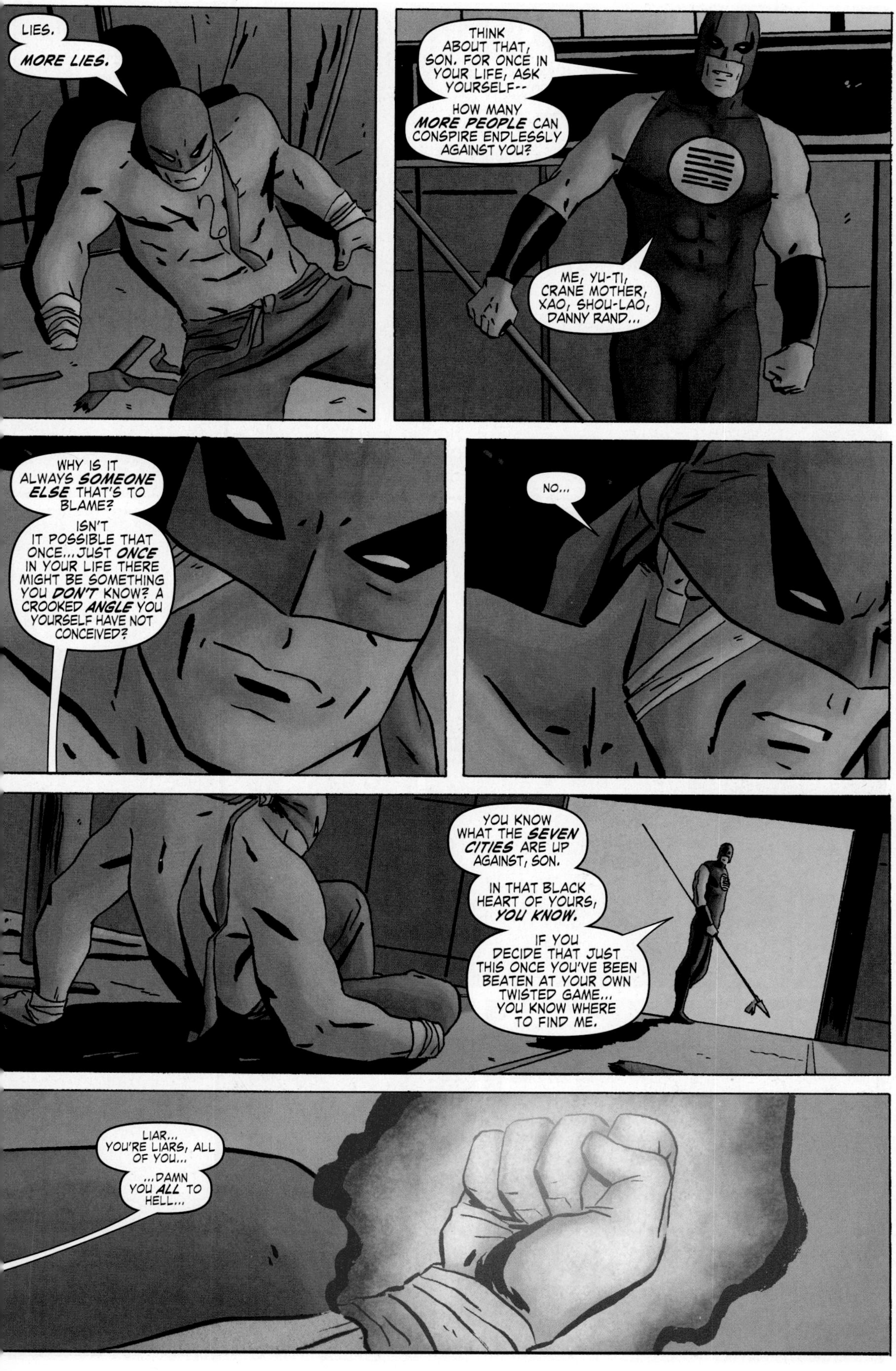
LIES.
MORE LIES.
THINK ABOUT THAT, SON. FOR ONCE IN YOUR LIFE, ASK YOURSELF--
HOW MANY MORE PEOPLE CAN CONSPIRE ENDLESSLY AGAINST YOU?
ME, YU-TI, CRANE MOTHER, XAO, SHOU-LAO, DANNY RAND...
WHY IS IT ALWAYS SOMEONE ELSE THAT'S TO BLAME?
ISN'T IT POSSIBLE THAT ONCE...JUST ONCE IN YOUR LIFE THERE MIGHT BE SOMETHING YOU DON'T KNOW? A CROOKED ANGLE YOU YOURSELF HAVE NOT CONCEIVED?
NO...
YOU KNOW WHAT THE SEVEN CITIES ARE UP AGAINST, SON.
IN THAT BLACK HEART OF YOURS, YOU KNOW.
IF YOU DECIDE THAT JUST THIS ONCE YOU'VE BEEN BEATEN AT YOUR OWN TWISTED GAME... YOU KNOW WHERE TO FIND ME.
LIAR... YOU'RE LIARS, ALL OF YOU...
...DAMN YOU ALL TO HELL...

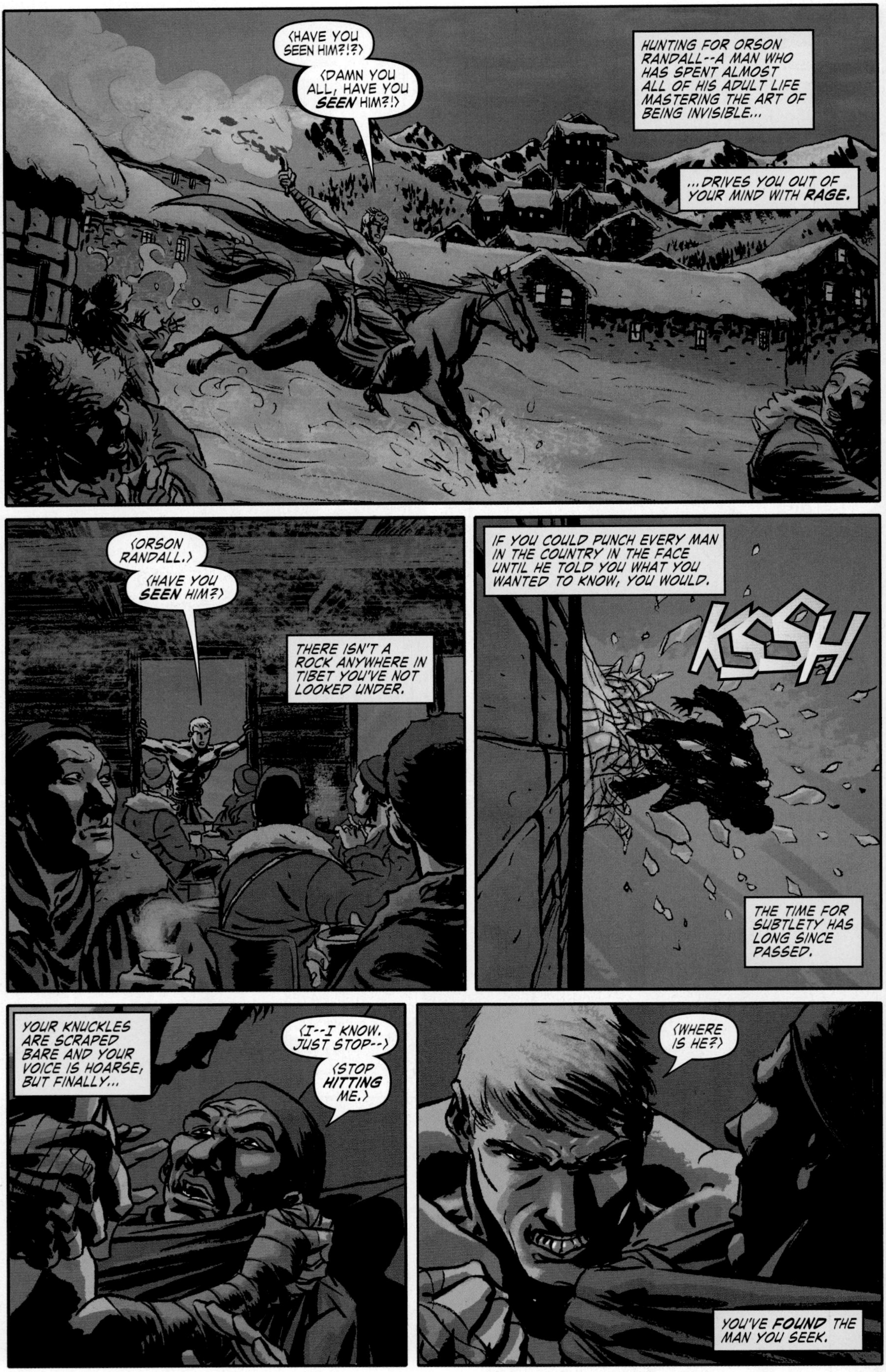

‹HAVE YOU SEEN HIM?!?›
‹DAMN YOU ALL, HAVE YOU **SEEN** HIM?!›
HUNTING FOR ORSON RANDALL--A MAN WHO HAS SPENT ALMOST ALL OF HIS ADULT LIFE MASTERING THE ART OF BEING INVISIBLE...
...DRIVES YOU OUT OF YOUR MIND WITH **RAGE.**
‹ORSON RANDALL.›
‹HAVE YOU **SEEN** HIM?›
THERE ISN'T A ROCK ANYWHERE IN TIBET YOU'VE NOT LOOKED UNDER.
IF YOU COULD PUNCH EVERY MAN IN THE COUNTRY IN THE FACE UNTIL HE TOLD YOU WHAT YOU WANTED TO KNOW, YOU WOULD.
KSSH
THE TIME FOR SUBTLETY HAS LONG SINCE PASSED.
YOUR KNUCKLES ARE SCRAPED BARE AND YOUR VOICE IS HOARSE, BUT FINALLY...
‹I--I KNOW. JUST STOP--›
‹STOP **HITTING** ME.›
‹WHERE IS HE?›
YOU'VE **FOUND** THE MAN YOU SEEK.

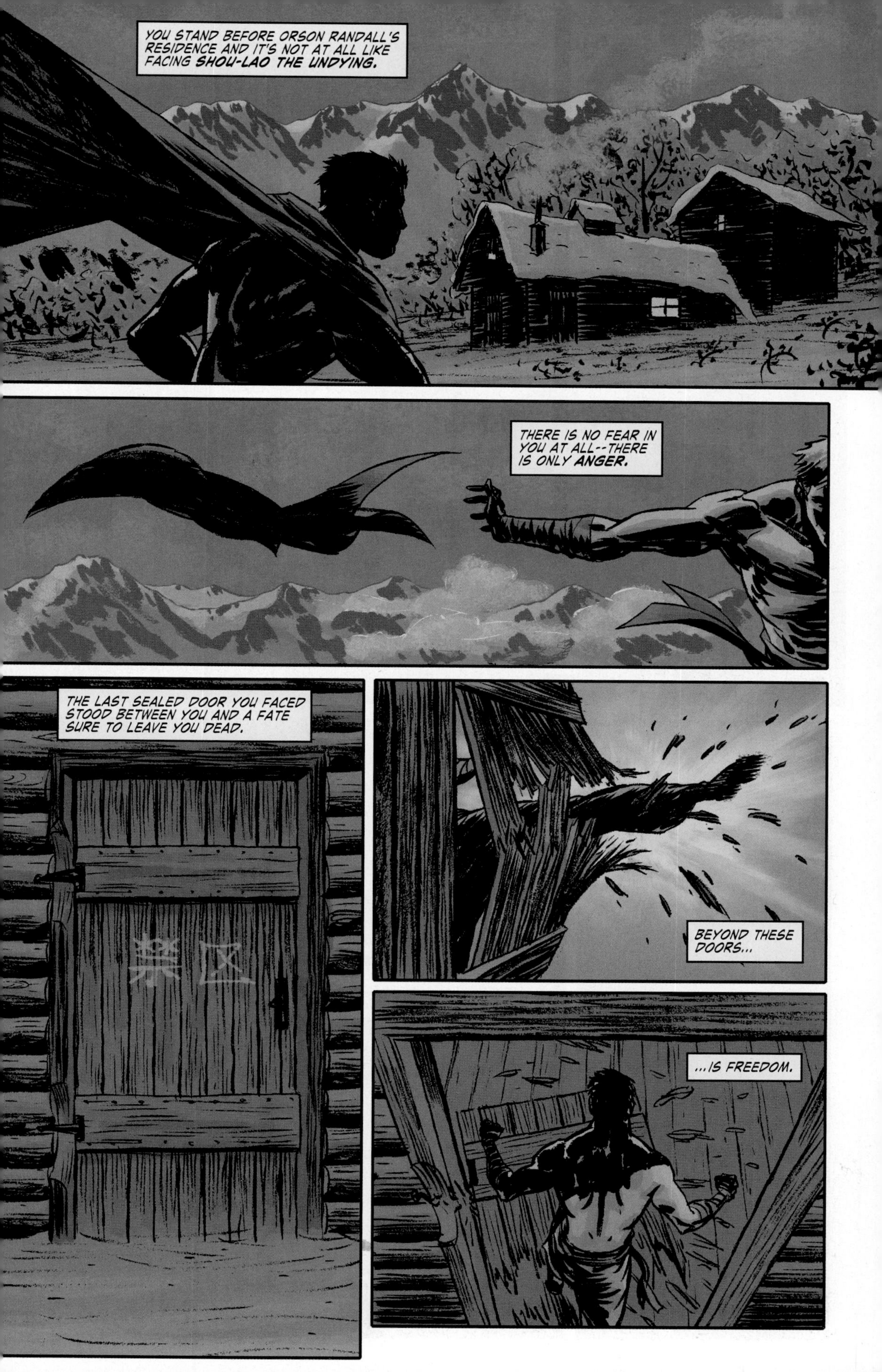
YOU STAND BEFORE ORSON RANDALL'S RESIDENCE AND IT'S NOT AT ALL LIKE FACING SHOU-LAO THE UNDYING.
THERE IS NO FEAR IN YOU AT ALL--THERE IS ONLY ANGER.
THE LAST SEALED DOOR YOU FACED STOOD BETWEEN YOU AND A FATE SURE TO LEAVE YOU DEAD.
禁区
BEYOND THESE DOORS...
...IS FREEDOM.

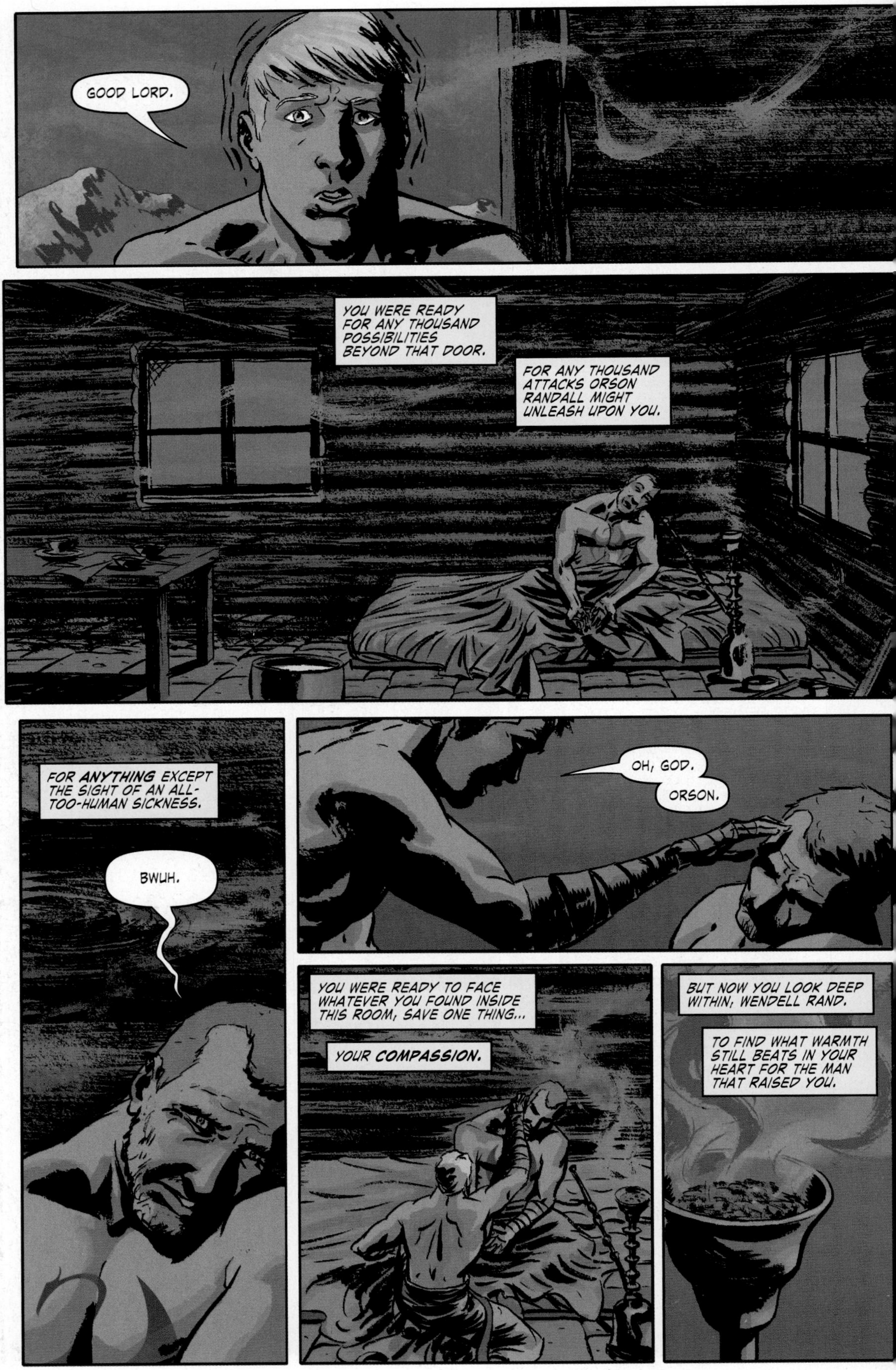
GOOD LORD.
YOU WERE READY FOR ANY THOUSAND POSSIBILITIES BEYOND THAT DOOR.
FOR ANY THOUSAND ATTACKS ORSON RANDALL MIGHT UNLEASH UPON YOU.
FOR ANYTHING EXCEPT THE SIGHT OF AN ALL-TOO-HUMAN SICKNESS.
BWUH.
OH, GOD.
ORSON.
YOU WERE READY TO FACE WHATEVER YOU FOUND INSIDE THIS ROOM, SAVE ONE THING...
YOUR COMPASSION.
BUT NOW YOU LOOK DEEP WITHIN, WENDELL RAND.
TO FIND WHAT WARMTH STILL BEATS IN YOUR HEART FOR THE MAN THAT RAISED YOU.

HE'S GONNA *FREEZE US* TO DEATH. *THAT'S* HOW XAO IS GONNA KILL US.

SHUT *UP*, LUKE.

YOUR TRAIN IS MIRACULOUS ENOUGH-- BUT WERE YOU ABLE TO MAKE IT PERFORM *MY* MIRACLE?

MOMENT OF *TRUTH*, MR. HOGARTH. YOUR *MOTHER* IS WAITING.

I HATE BULLIES, XAO, MORE THAN *ANYTHING* I HATE BULLIES.

I MADE THE DAMN TRAIN WORK, BUT I CURSED YOUR NAME EVERY STEP OF THE WAY.

VRRRRKKKKKKKKK

YES. *YES!*

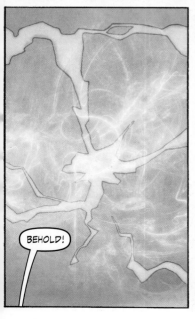

BEHOLD!

THE BARRIER OF SPACE-TIME WEAKENS!

K'UN-LUN IS MINE!

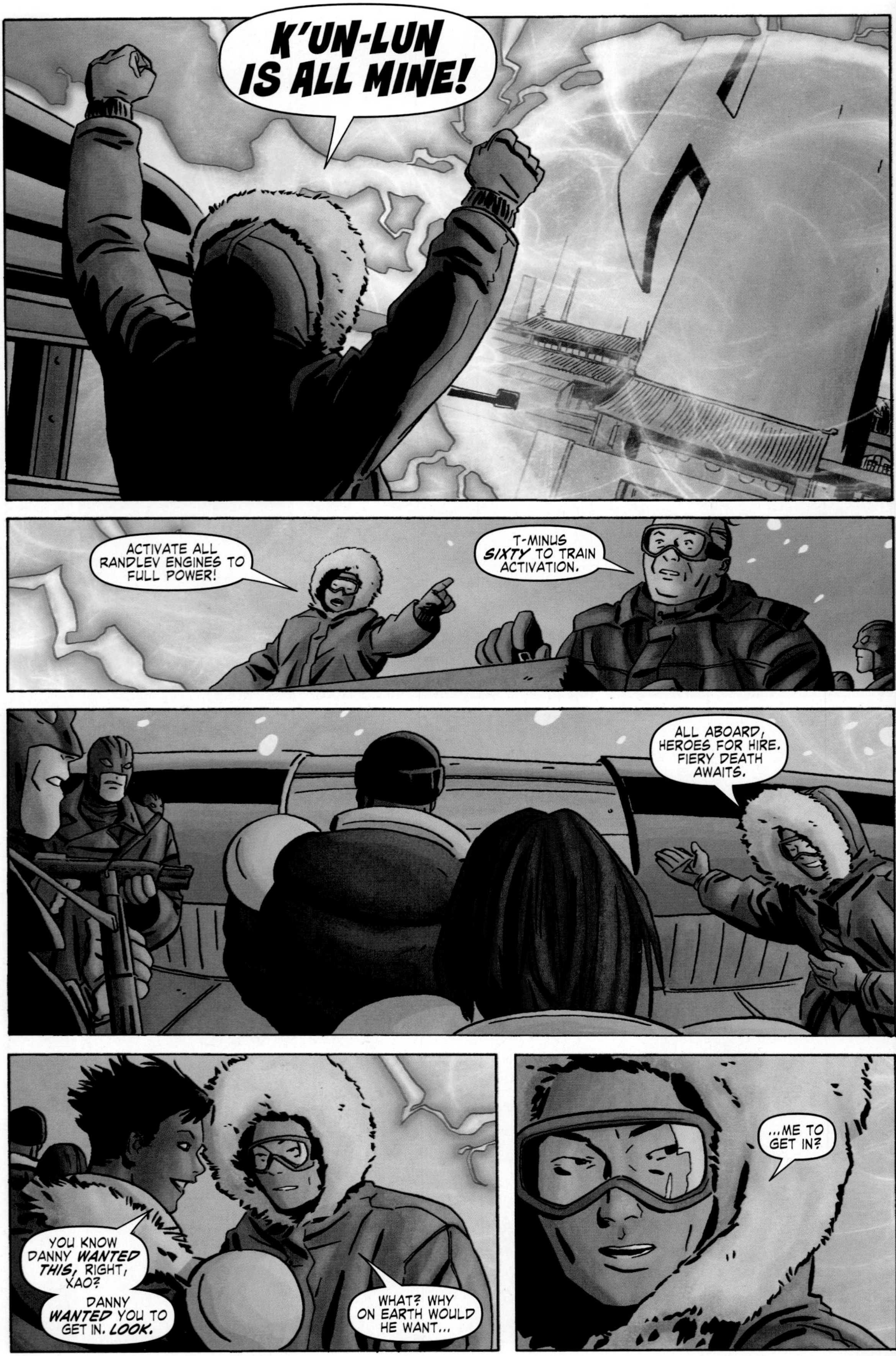
K'UN-LUN IS ALL MINE!
ACTIVATE ALL RANDLEV ENGINES TO FULL POWER!
T-MINUS SIXTY TO TRAIN ACTIVATION.
ALL ABOARD, HEROES FOR HIRE. FIERY DEATH AWAITS.
YOU KNOW DANNY WANTED THIS, RIGHT, XAO?
DANNY WANTED YOU TO GET IN. LOOK.
WHAT? WHY ON EARTH WOULD HE WANT...
...ME TO GET IN?

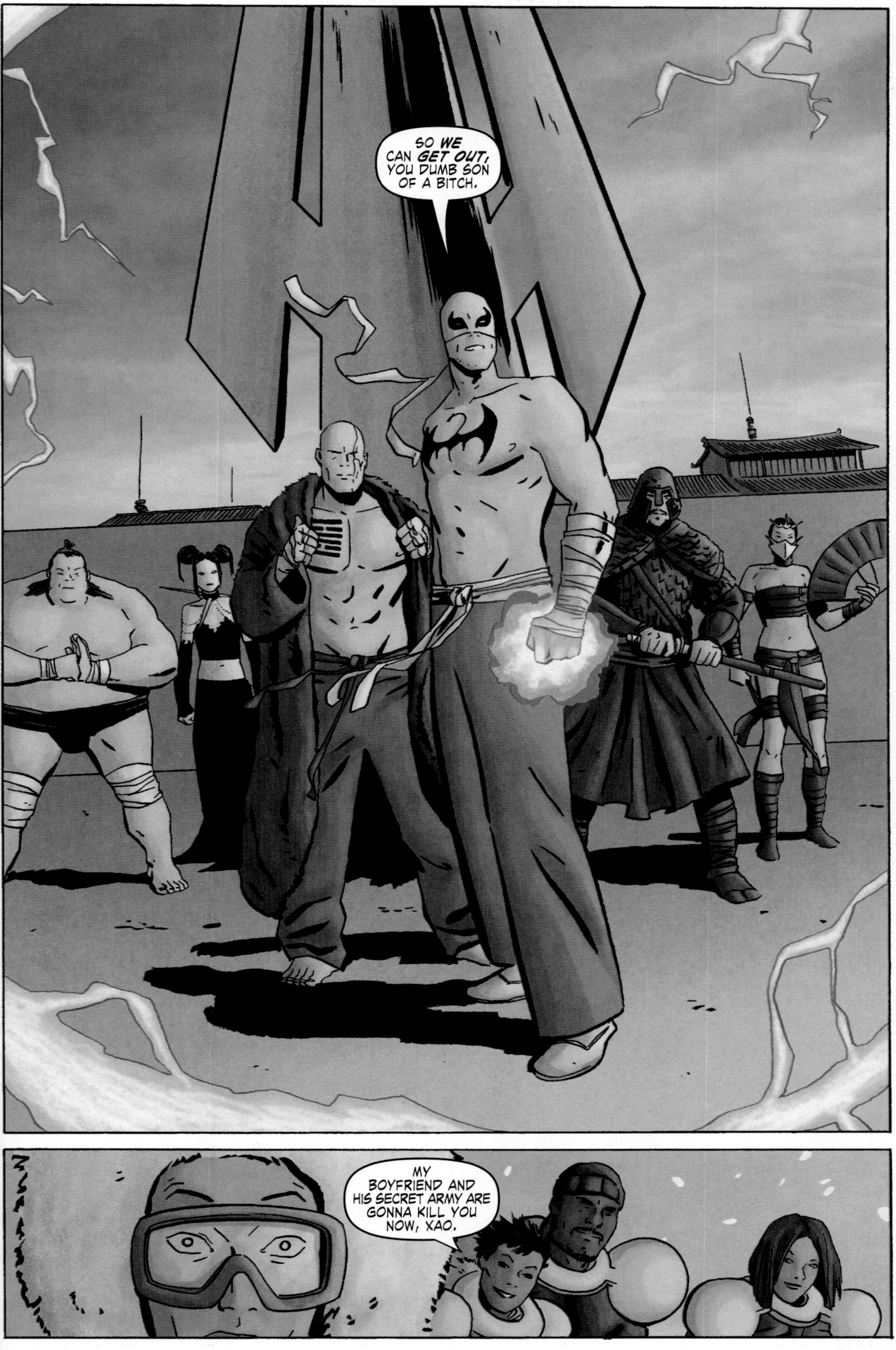
SO **WE** CAN **GET OUT**, YOU DUMB SON OF A BITCH.
MY BOYFRIEND AND HIS SECRET ARMY ARE GONNA KILL YOU NOW, XAO.

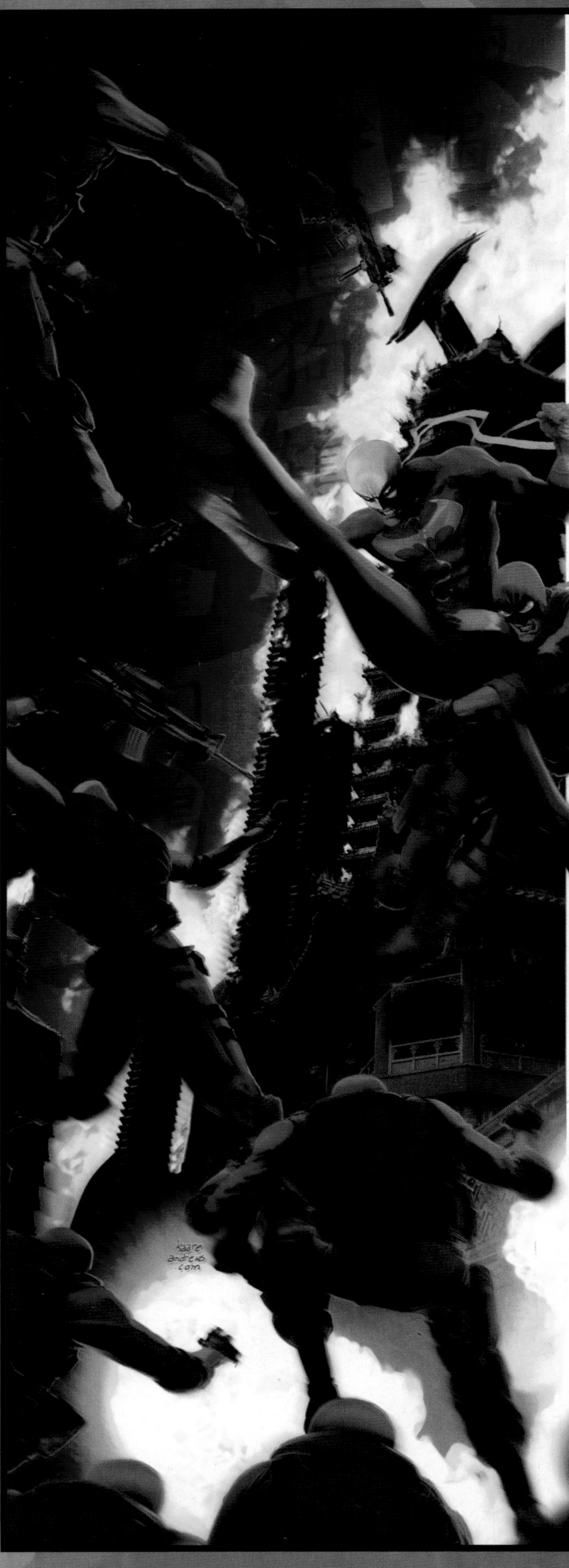
kaare
andrews
.com

鐵拳

14

The 七 Capital Cities of Heaven

七

Round 7

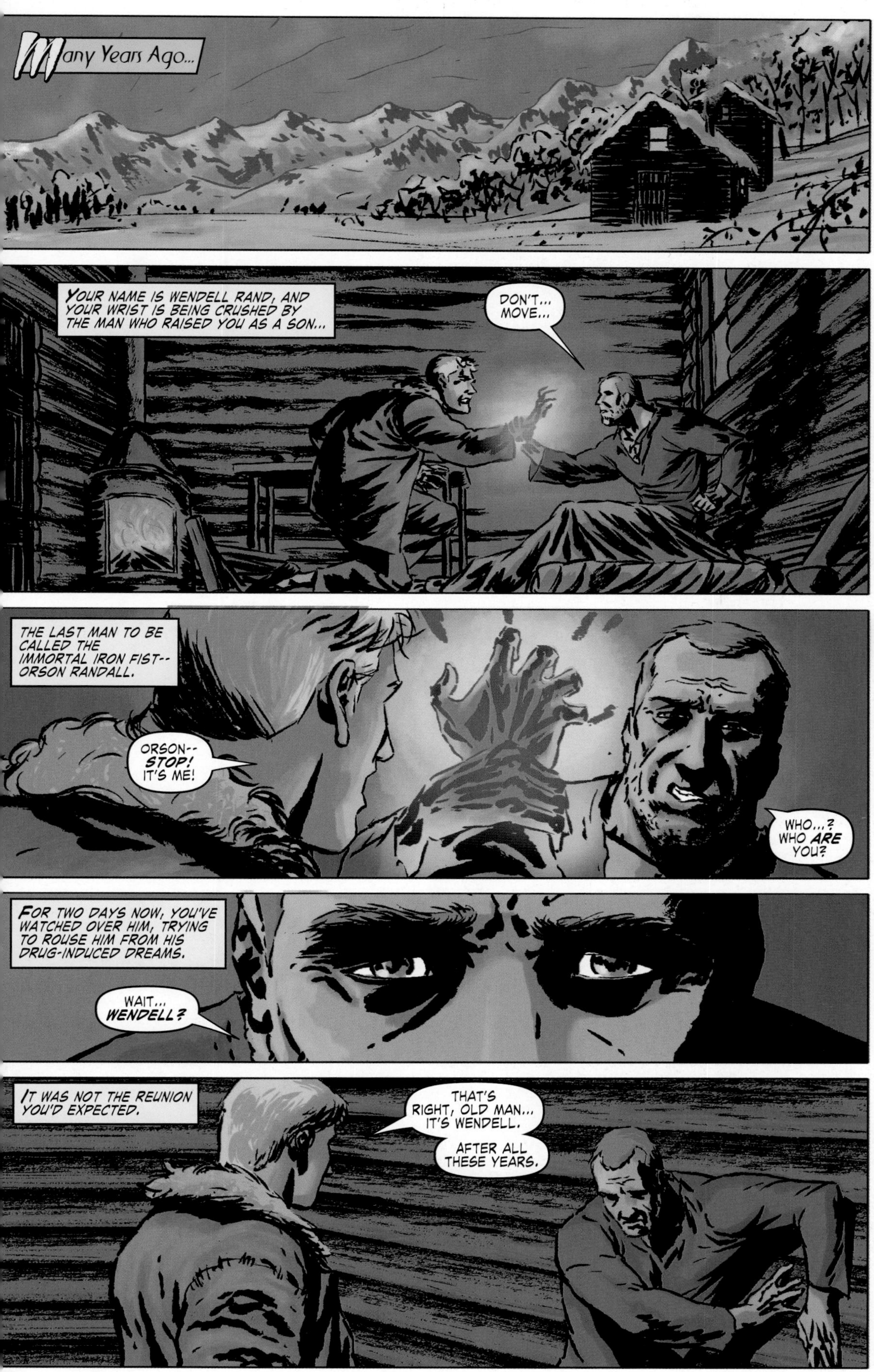
Many Years Ago...
YOUR NAME IS WENDELL RAND, AND YOUR WRIST IS BEING CRUSHED BY THE MAN WHO RAISED YOU AS A SON...
DON'T... MOVE...
THE LAST MAN TO BE CALLED THE IMMORTAL IRON FIST-- ORSON RANDALL.
ORSON-- STOP! IT'S ME!
WHO...? WHO ARE YOU?
FOR TWO DAYS NOW, YOU'VE WATCHED OVER HIM, TRYING TO ROUSE HIM FROM HIS DRUG-INDUCED DREAMS.
WAIT... WENDELL?
IT WAS NOT THE REUNION YOU'D EXPECTED.
THAT'S RIGHT, OLD MAN... IT'S WENDELL.
AFTER ALL THESE YEARS.

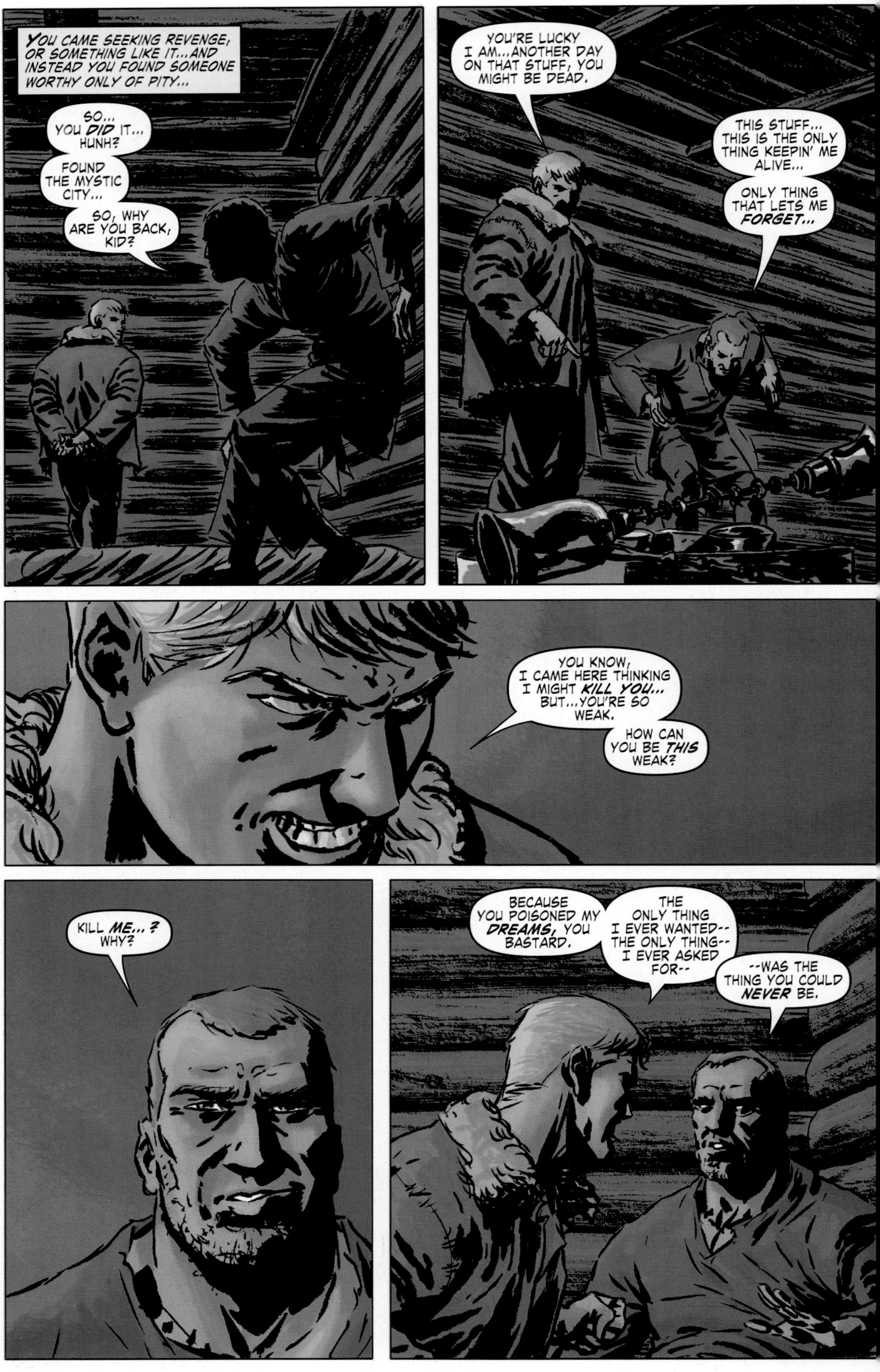
YOU CAME SEEKING REVENGE, OR SOMETHING LIKE IT...AND INSTEAD YOU FOUND SOMEONE WORTHY ONLY OF PITY...
SO... YOU DID IT... HUNH?
FOUND THE MYSTIC CITY...
SO, WHY ARE YOU BACK, KID?
YOU'RE LUCKY I AM...ANOTHER DAY ON THAT STUFF, YOU MIGHT BE DEAD.
THIS STUFF... THIS IS THE ONLY THING KEEPIN' ME ALIVE...
ONLY THING THAT LETS ME FORGET...
YOU KNOW, I CAME HERE THINKING I MIGHT KILL YOU... BUT...YOU'RE SO WEAK.
HOW CAN YOU BE THIS WEAK?
KILL ME...? WHY?
BECAUSE YOU POISONED MY DREAMS, YOU BASTARD.
THE ONLY THING I EVER WANTED-- THE ONLY THING-- I EVER ASKED FOR--
--WAS THE THING YOU COULD NEVER BE.

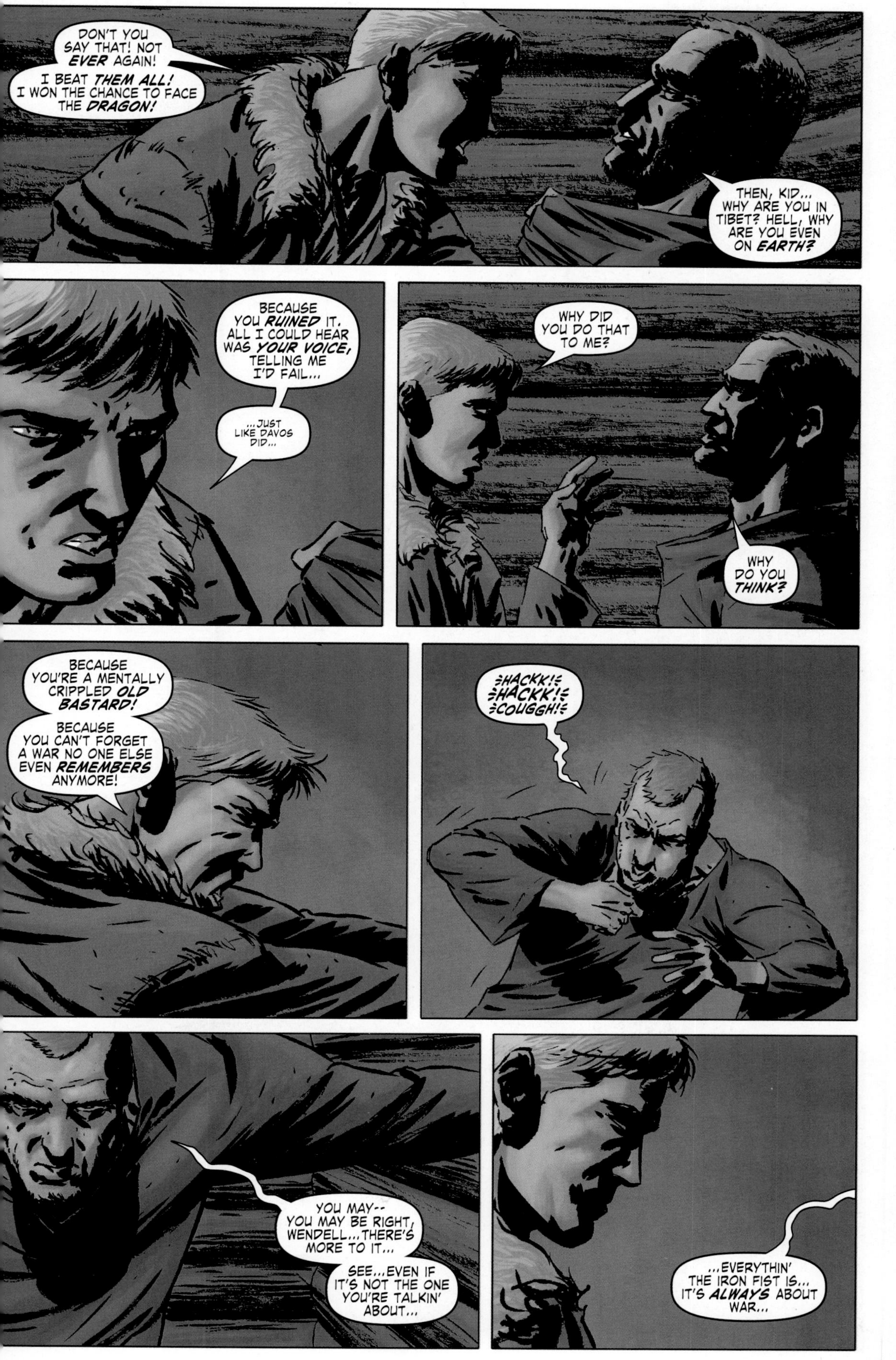
DON'T YOU SAY THAT! NOT EVER AGAIN!
I BEAT THEM ALL! I WON THE CHANCE TO FACE THE DRAGON!
THEN, KID... WHY ARE YOU IN TIBET? HELL, WHY ARE YOU EVEN ON EARTH?
BECAUSE YOU RUINED IT. ALL I COULD HEAR WAS YOUR VOICE, TELLING ME I'D FAIL...
...JUST LIKE DAVOS DID...
WHY DID YOU DO THAT TO ME?
WHY DO YOU THINK?
BECAUSE YOU'RE A MENTALLY CRIPPLED OLD BASTARD!
BECAUSE YOU CAN'T FORGET A WAR NO ONE ELSE EVEN REMEMBERS ANYMORE!
HACKK! HACKK! COUGGH!
YOU MAY-- YOU MAY BE RIGHT, WENDELL... THERE'S MORE TO IT...
SEE... EVEN IF IT'S NOT THE ONE YOU'RE TALKIN' ABOUT...
...EVERYTHIN' THE IRON FIST IS... IT'S ALWAYS ABOUT WAR...

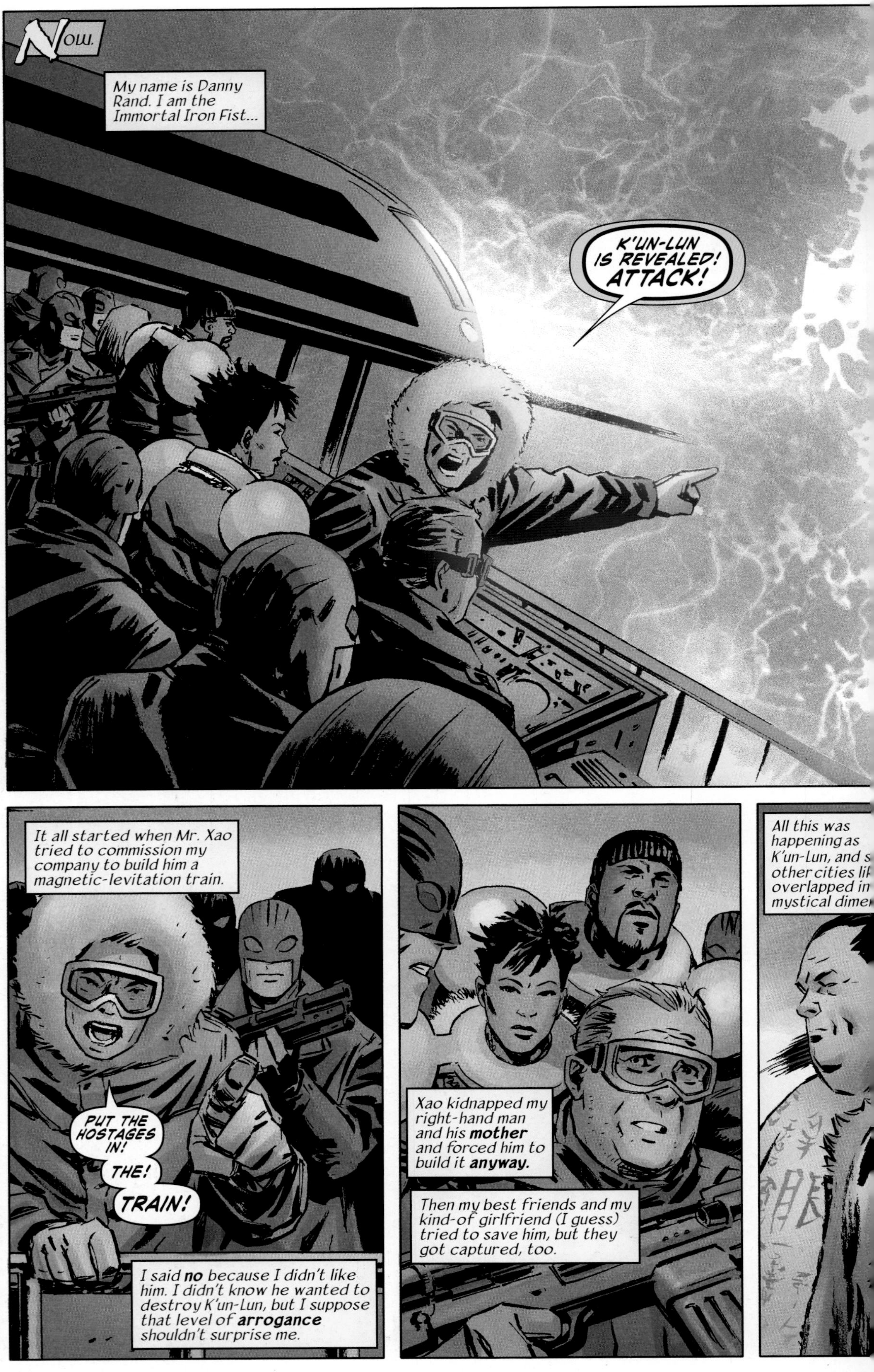
Now.
My name is Danny Rand. I am the Immortal Iron Fist...
K'UN-LUN IS REVEALED! ATTACK!
It all started when Mr. Xao tried to commission my company to build him a magnetic-levitation train.
PUT THE HOSTAGES IN!
THE!
TRAIN!
I said **no** because I didn't like him. I didn't know he wanted to destroy K'un-Lun, but I suppose that level of **arrogance** shouldn't surprise me.
Xao kidnapped my right-hand man and his **mother** and forced him to build it **anyway.**
Then my best friends and my kind-of girlfriend (I guess) tried to save him, but they got captured, too.
All this was happening as K'un-Lun, and s other cities lik overlapped in mystical dime

...and this is the front line of a war that threatens to rend Heaven itself asunder.

It's a war I'm not sure we can win.

...ere I met six fighters, ...powered like myself, ...I fought most of them ...tournament.

If K'un-Lun falls, all of their cities will fall.

Maybe it's for the best-- K'un-Lun, I discovered, has been teetering on the brink of total revolution anyway, led by a corrupt tyrant.

A secret army of the oppressed is ready to rise up and **change** K'un-Lun.

Which is pretty lucky for me, because I absolutely have **use** for an army right now...

AMAN. LEI KUNG.

YOU STOP THE LEGION. I'LL STOP *THE TRAIN.*

...considering I'm not sure I'm going to be alive after I pull this next stunt.

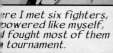

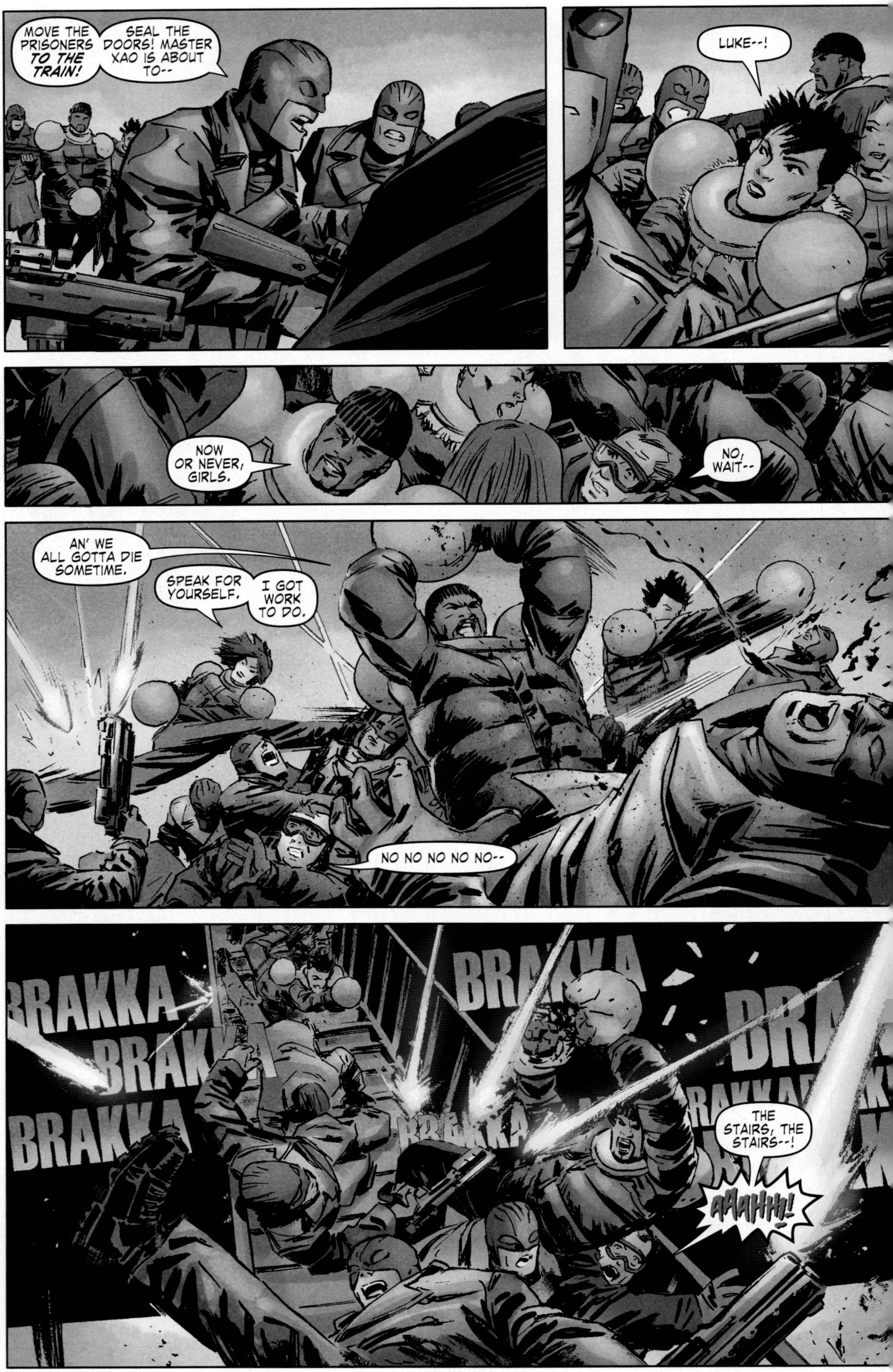
MOVE THE PRISONERS TO THE TRAIN!
SEAL THE DOORS! MASTER XAO IS ABOUT TO--
LUKE--!
NOW OR NEVER, GIRLS.
NO, WAIT--
AN' WE ALL GOTTA DIE SOMETIME.
SPEAK FOR YOURSELF.
I GOT WORK TO DO.
NO NO NO NO NO--
BRAKKA
BRAKKA
BRAKKA
BRAKKA
THE STAIRS, THE STAIRS--!
AAAHHH!

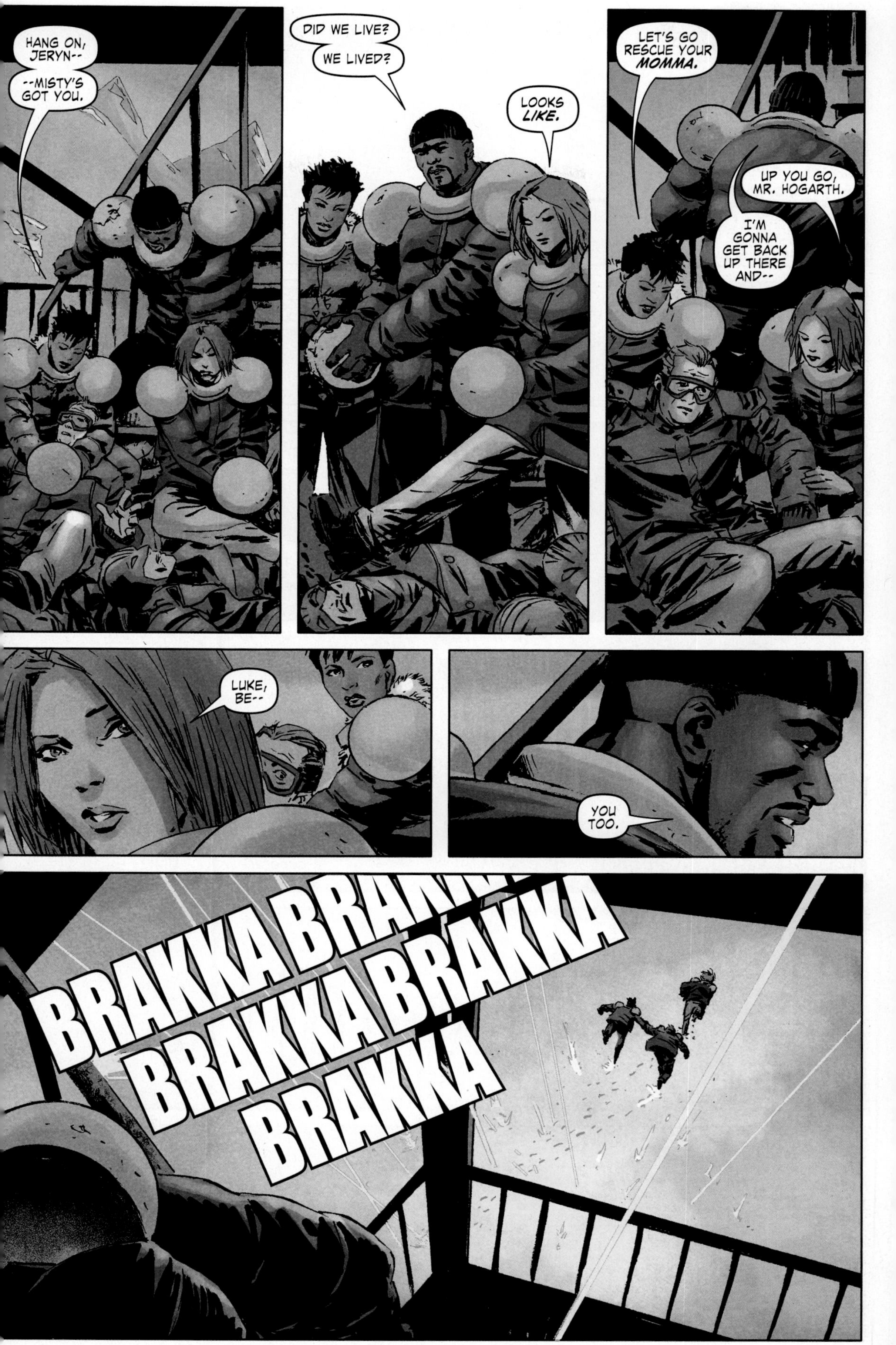

HANG ON, JERYN--
--MISTY'S GOT YOU.
DID WE LIVE?
WE LIVED?
LOOKS LIKE.
LET'S GO RESCUE YOUR MOMMA.
UP YOU GO, MR. HOGARTH.
I'M GONNA GET BACK UP THERE AND--
LUKE, BE--
YOU TOO.
BRAKKA BRAKKA BRAKKA BRAKKA BRAKKA

I'M NOT SURE THIS IS GOING TO WORK.

IT SHOULD BE *FAIRLY APPARENT* WHEN IT EITHER DOES OR DOESN'T, AND EITHER WAY SHOULD TAKE THE TRAIN OFF THE BOARD.

The train is experimental. Magnetic levitation.

THEN IT'S ON YOU TO FOLLOW WITH *ALL HELL* BEHIND ME.

LADIES AND GENTLEMEN, IT'S BEEN AN HONOR TO FIGHT YOU...

...AND TO FIGHT ALONG*SIDE* YOU.

Frictionless...efficient... made possible by electromagnetic suspension.

WHAT'S HE DOING? *WHAT IS THE IRON FIST DOING?!?*

BUT, MASTER--THE PRISONERS ARE ESCAPING!!

TO *HELL* WITH THE PRISONERS! ENGAGE TRAIN! DESTROY K'UN-LUN! GO! *GO!*

I extend the chi of Shou-Lao out from my fist...

VIIIIIIII

...and I find the electromagnetic fields the train generates.

VIIIIIIIIIIII

It takes a moment--

--to learn how to use it--

--to give myself over to it...to allow myself--

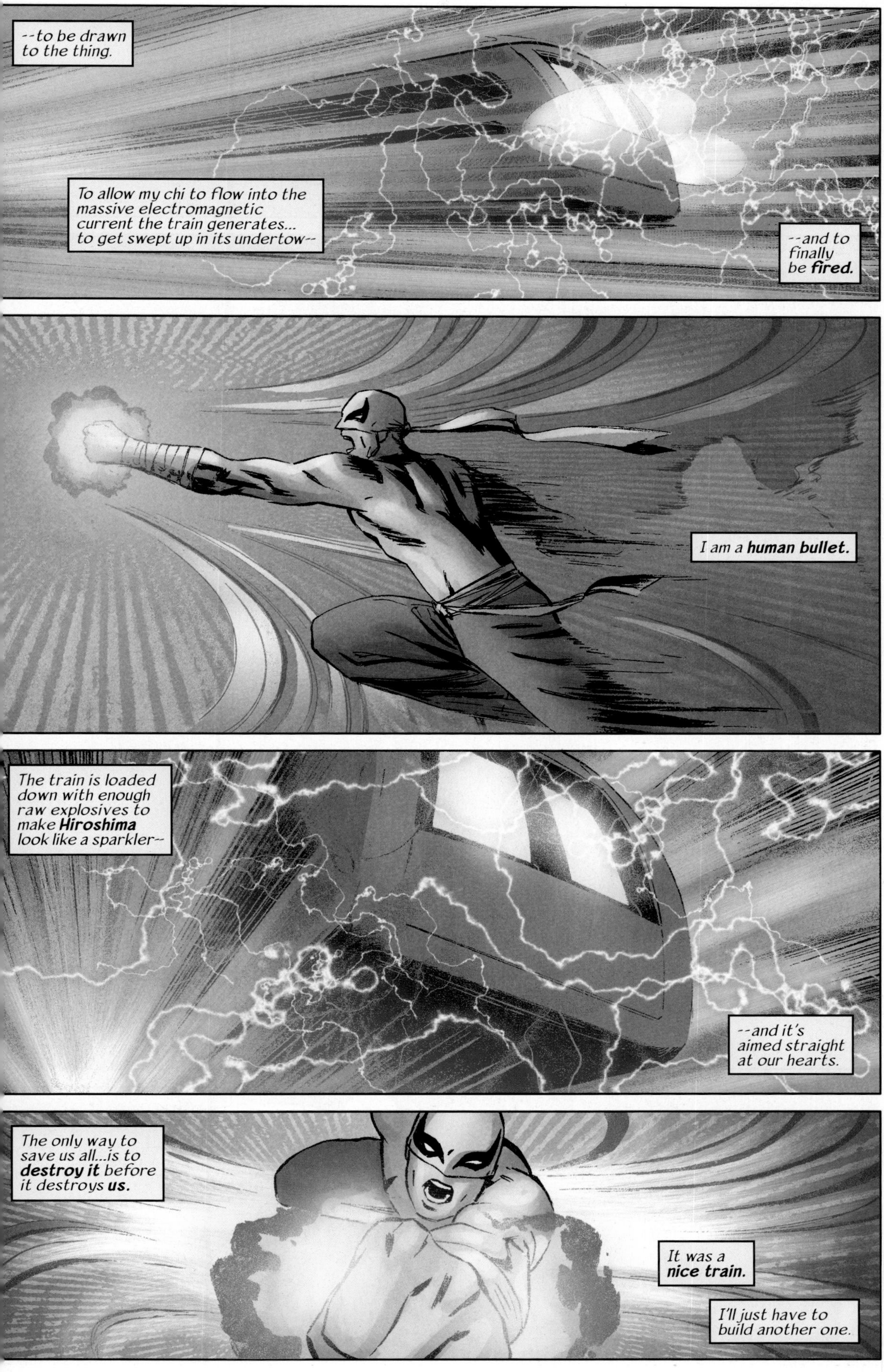
--to be drawn to the thing.
To allow my chi to flow into the massive electromagnetic current the train generates... to get swept up in its undertow--
--and to finally be **fired.**
I am a **human bullet.**
The train is loaded down with enough raw explosives to make **Hiroshima** look like a sparkler--
--and it's aimed straight at our hearts.
The only way to save us all...is to **destroy it** before it destroys **us.**
It was a **nice train.**
I'll just have to build another one.

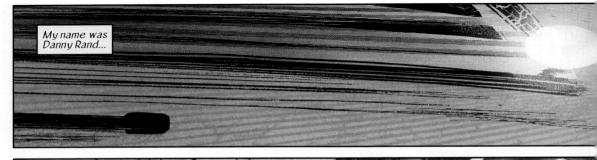

My name was
Danny Rand...

NO.

NO NO NO NO.

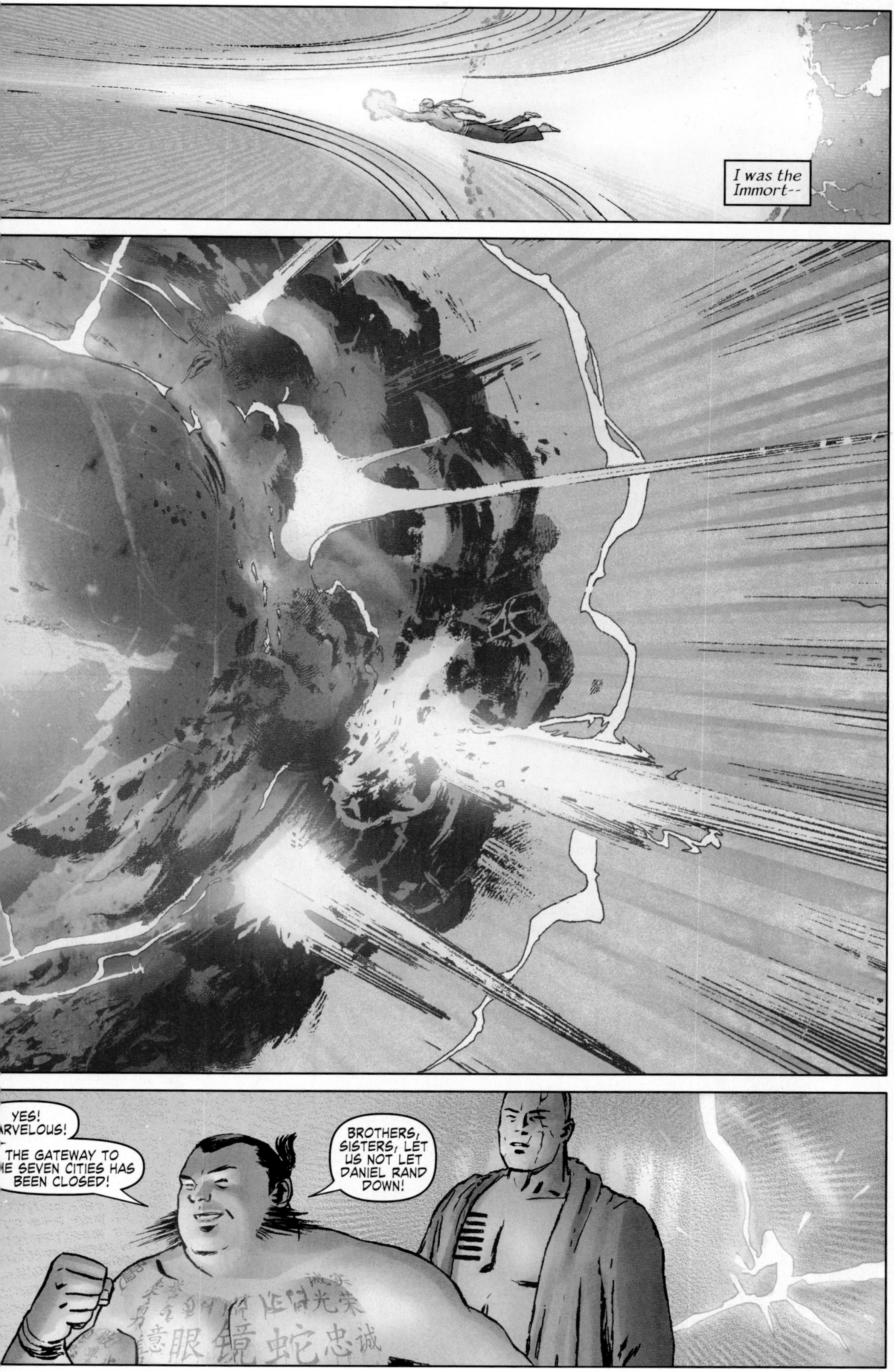
I was the Immort--
YES! ARVELOUS!
THE GATEWAY TO HE SEVEN CITIES HAS BEEN CLOSED!
BROTHERS, SISTERS, LET US NOT LET DANIEL RAND DOWN!

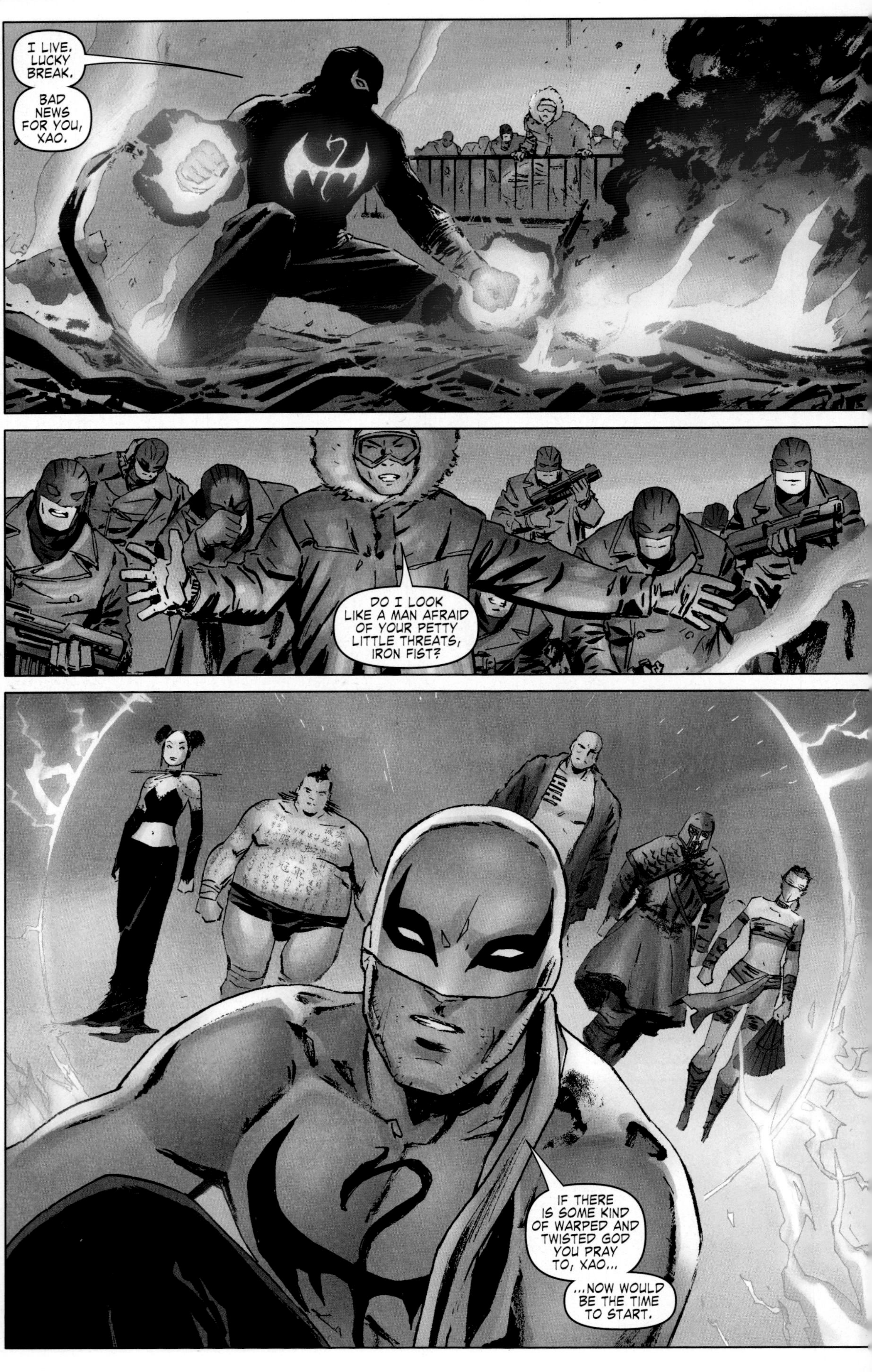
I LIVE. LUCKY BREAK.
BAD NEWS FOR YOU, XAO.
DO I LOOK LIKE A MAN AFRAID OF YOUR PETTY LITTLE THREATS, IRON FIST?
IF THERE IS SOME KIND OF WARPED AND TWISTED GOD YOU PRAY TO, XAO...
...NOW WOULD BE THE TIME TO START.

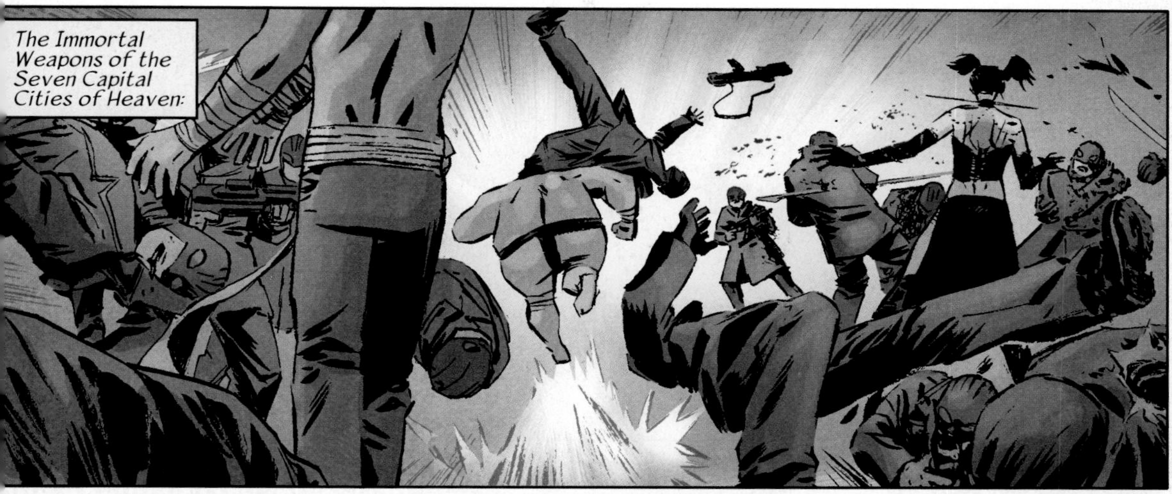
The Immortal Weapons of the Seven Capital Cities of Heaven:

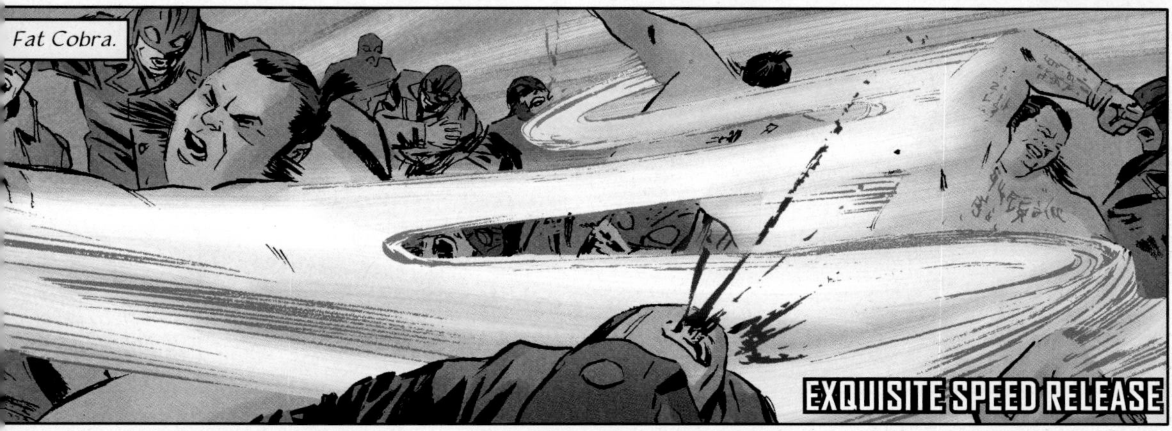
Fat Cobra.
EXQUISITE SPEED RELEASE

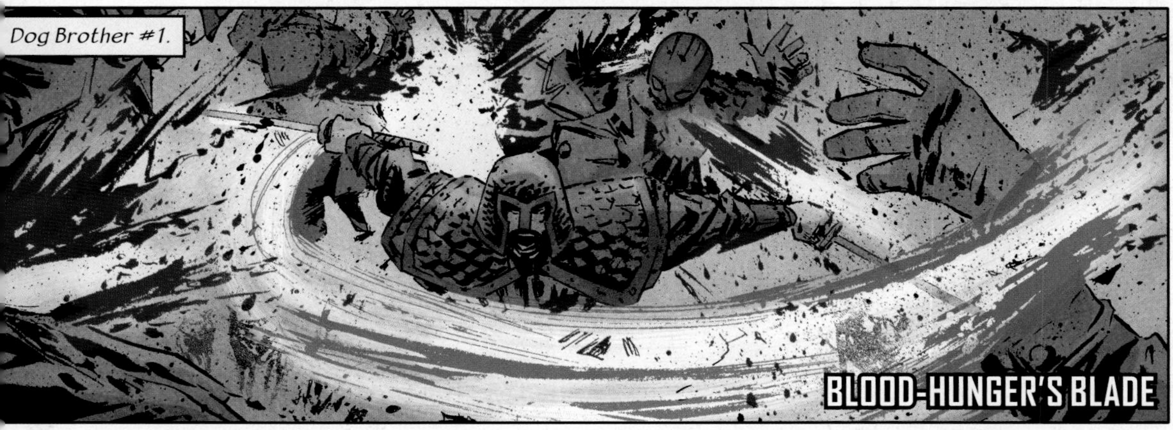
Dog Brother #1.
BLOOD-HUNGER'S BLADE

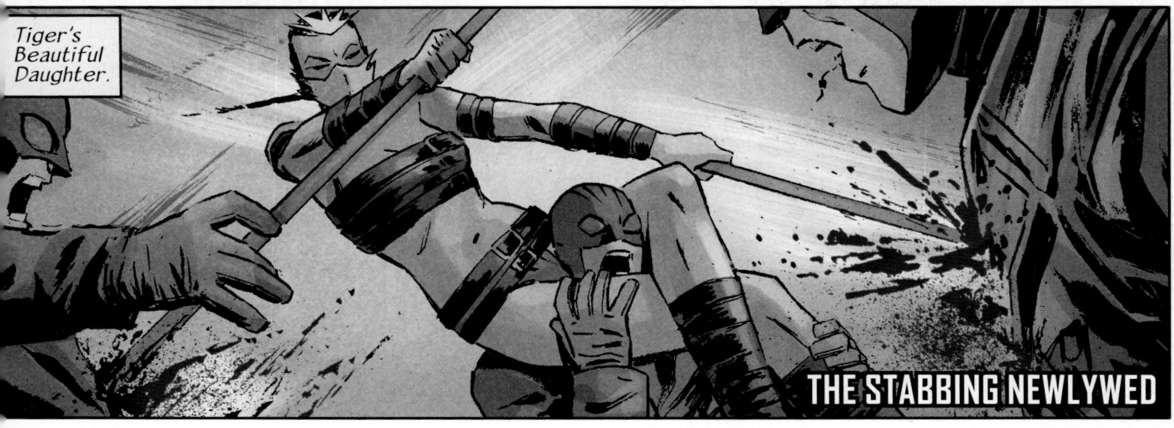
Tiger's Beautiful Daughter.
THE STABBING NEWLYWED

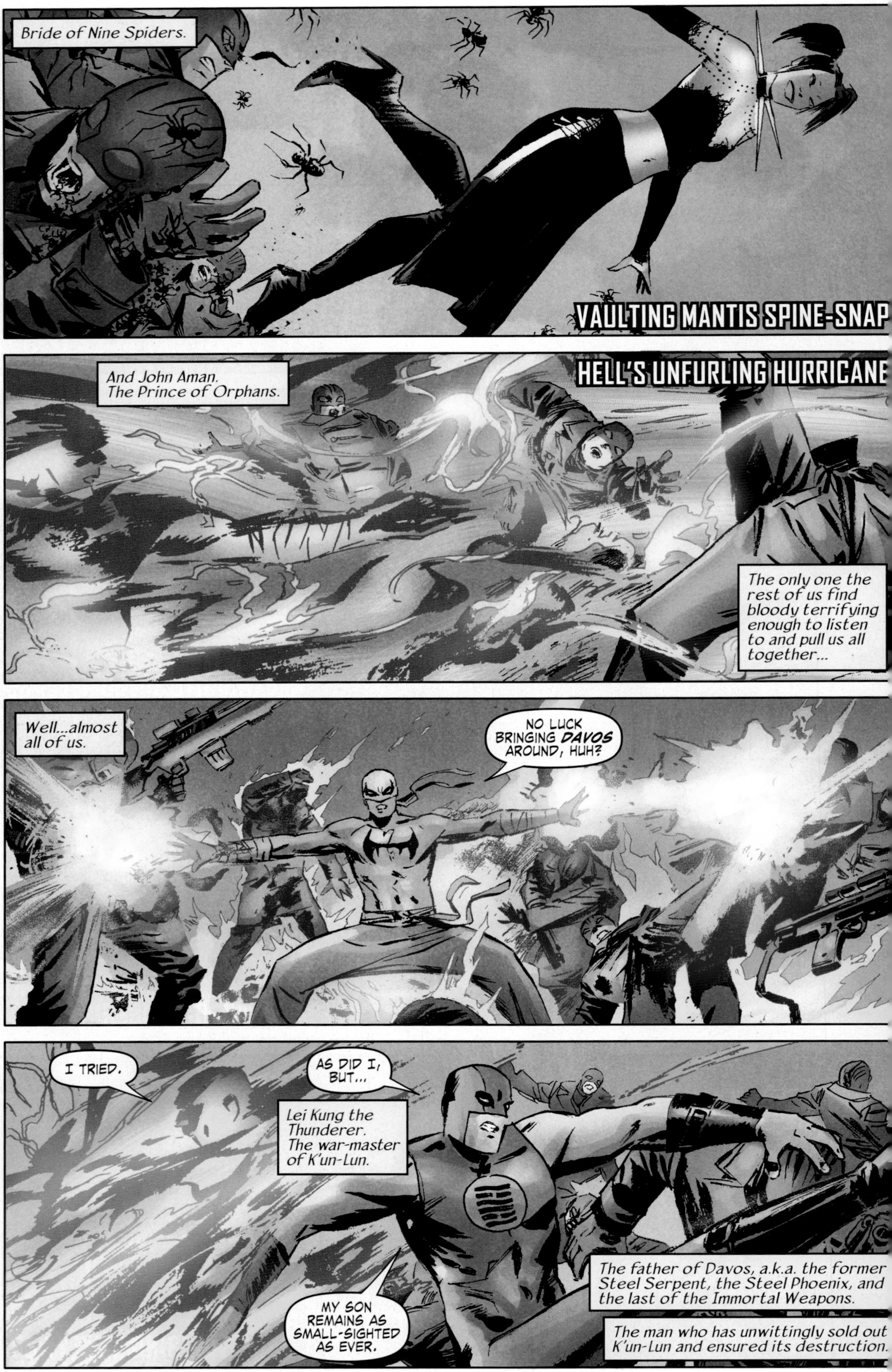
Bride of Nine Spiders.
VAULTING MANTIS SPINE-SNAP
And John Aman. The Prince of Orphans.
HELL'S UNFURLING HURRICANE
The only one the rest of us find bloody terrifying enough to listen to and pull us all together...
Well...almost all of us.
NO LUCK BRINGING DAVOS AROUND, HUH?
I TRIED.
AS DID I, BUT...
Lei Kung the Thunderer. The war-master of K'un-Lun.
MY SON REMAINS AS SMALL-SIGHTED AS EVER.
The father of Davos, a.k.a. the former Steel Serpent, the Steel Phoenix, and the last of the Immortal Weapons.
The man who has unwittingly sold out K'un-Lun and ensured its destruction.

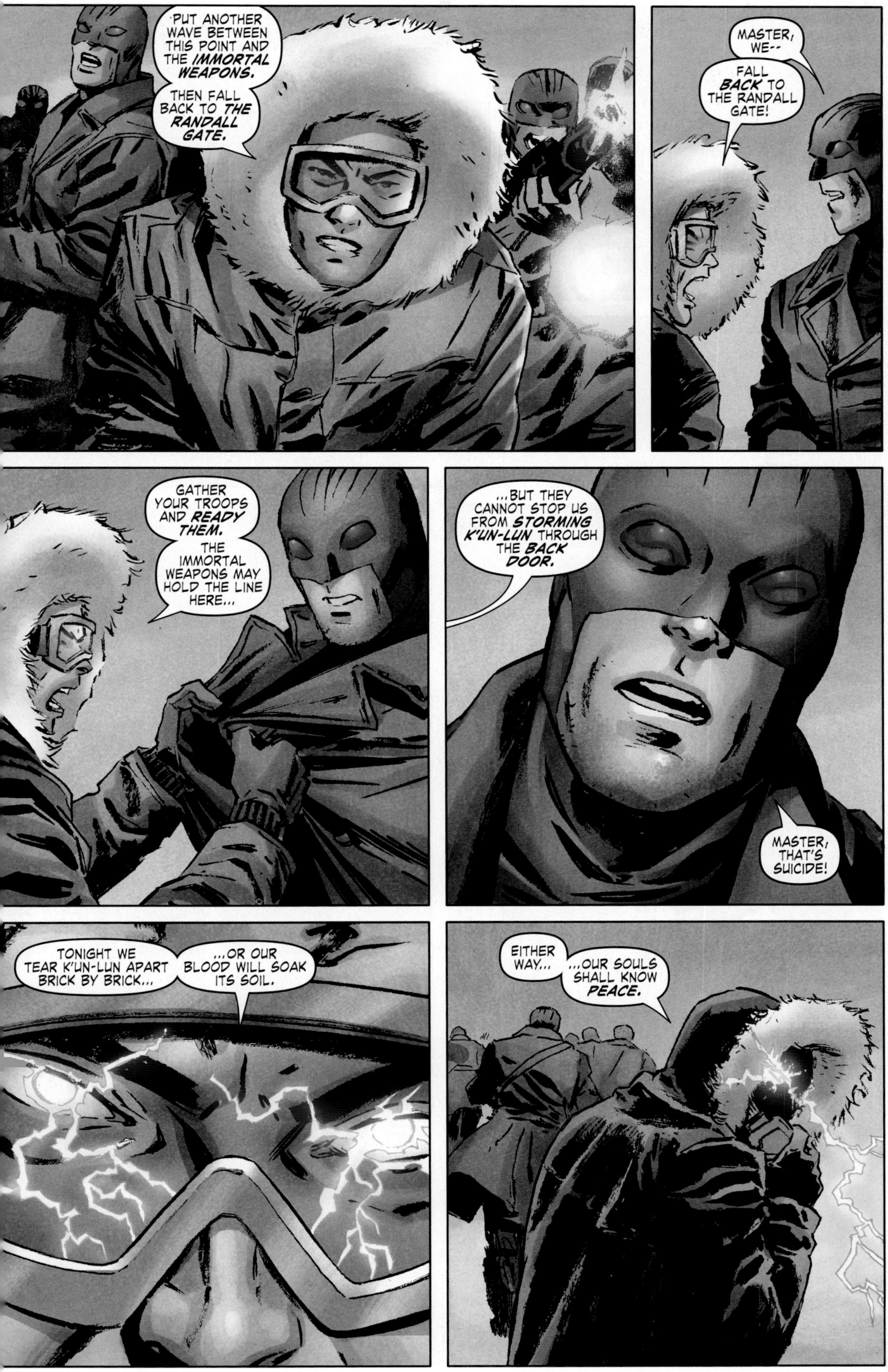
PUT ANOTHER WAVE BETWEEN THIS POINT AND THE IMMORTAL WEAPONS.
THEN FALL BACK TO THE RANDALL GATE.
MASTER, WE--
FALL BACK TO THE RANDALL GATE!
GATHER YOUR TROOPS AND READY THEM.
THE IMMORTAL WEAPONS MAY HOLD THE LINE HERE...
...BUT THEY CANNOT STOP US FROM STORMING K'UN-LUN THROUGH THE BACK DOOR.
MASTER, THAT'S SUICIDE!
TONIGHT WE TEAR K'UN-LUN APART BRICK BY BRICK...
...OR OUR BLOOD WILL SOAK ITS SOIL.
EITHER WAY...
...OUR SOULS SHALL KNOW PEACE.

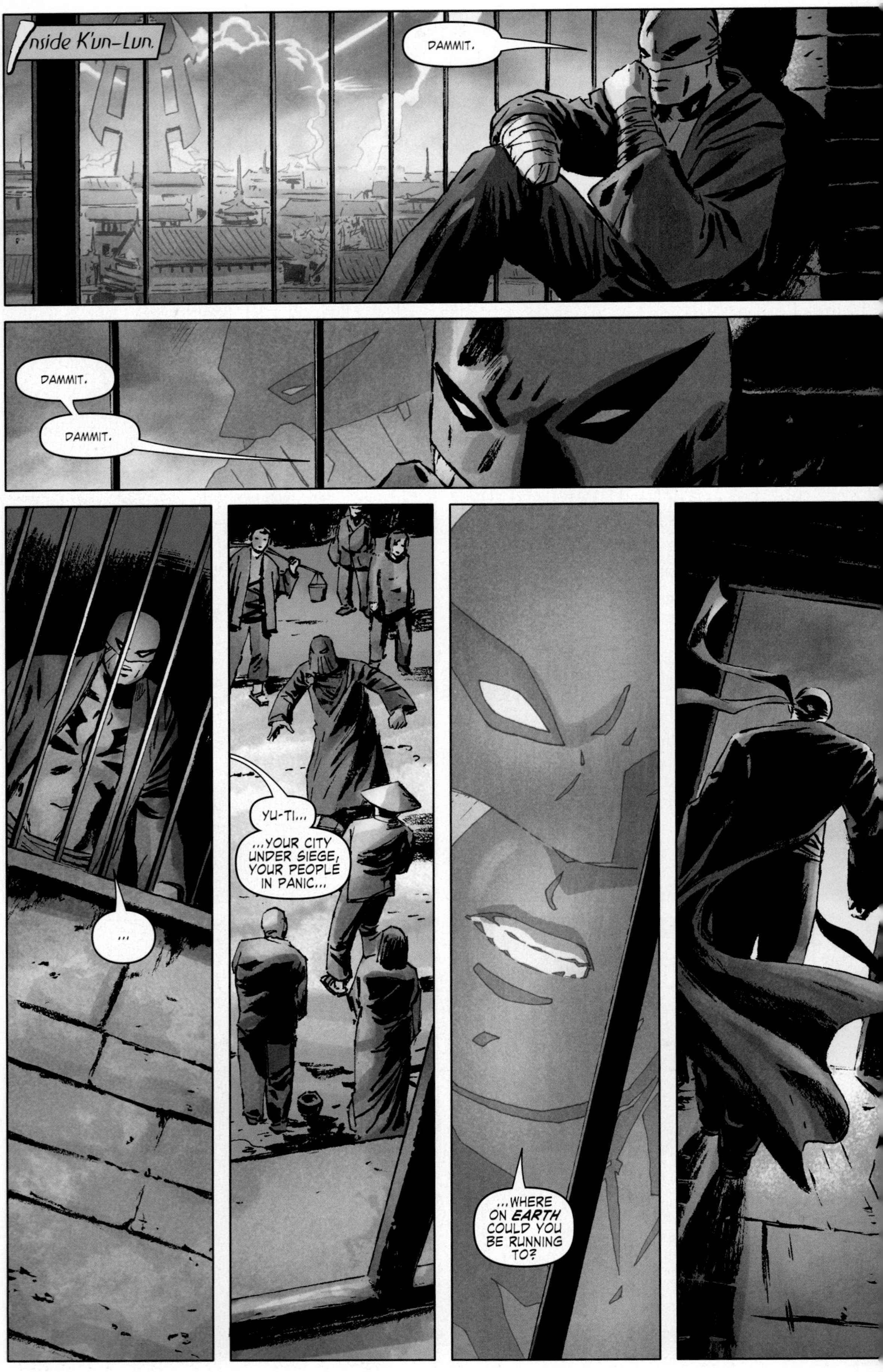
Inside K'un-Lun.
DAMMIT.
DAMMIT.
DAMMIT.
...
YU-TI...
...YOUR CITY UNDER SIEGE, YOUR PEOPLE IN PANIC...
...WHERE ON EARTH COULD YOU BE RUNNING TO?

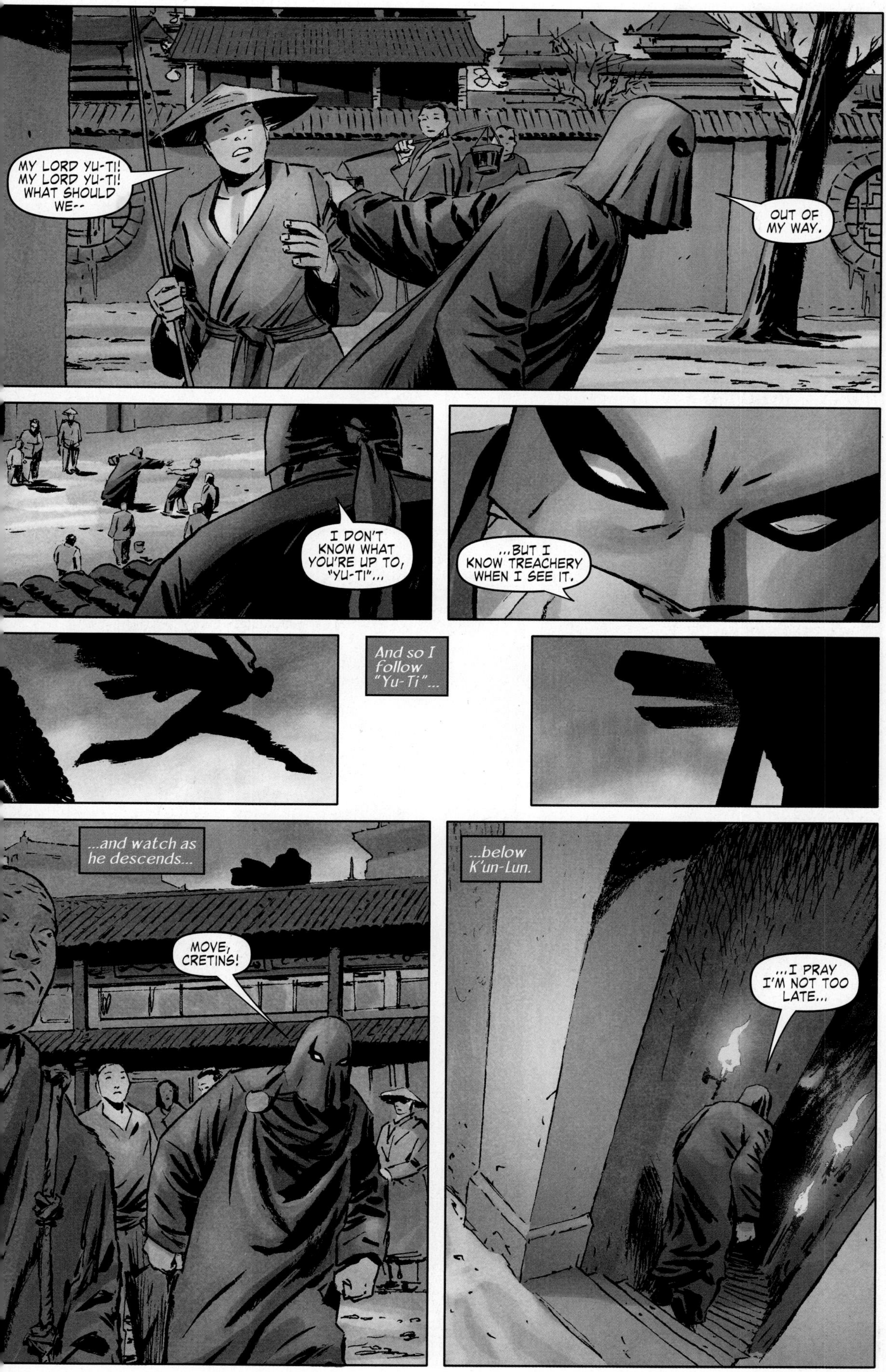

MY LORD YU-TI! MY LORD YU-TI! WHAT SHOULD WE--
OUT OF MY WAY.
I DON'T KNOW WHAT YOU'RE UP TO, "YU-TI"...
...BUT I KNOW TREACHERY WHEN I SEE IT.
And so I follow "Yu-Ti"...
...and watch as he descends...
MOVE, CRETINS!
...below K'un-Lun.
...I PRAY I'M NOT TOO LATE...

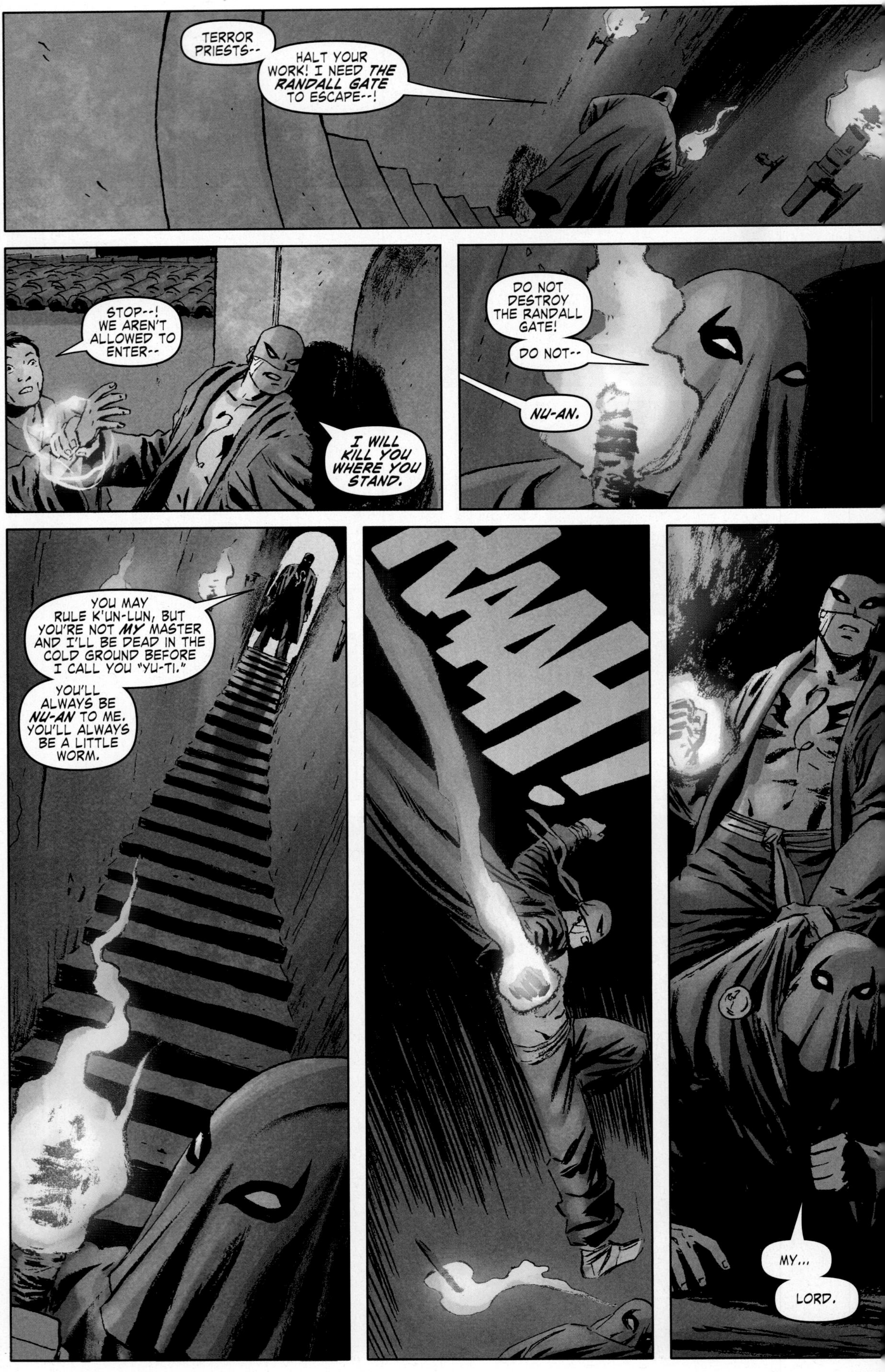
TERROR PRIESTS--
HALT YOUR WORK! I NEED THE RANDALL GATE TO ESCAPE--!
STOP--! WE AREN'T ALLOWED TO ENTER--
I WILL KILL YOU WHERE YOU STAND.
DO NOT DESTROY THE RANDALL GATE!
DO NOT--
NU-AN.
YOU MAY RULE K'UN-LUN, BUT YOU'RE NOT MY MASTER AND I'LL BE DEAD IN THE COLD GROUND BEFORE I CALL YOU "YU-TI."
YOU'LL ALWAYS BE NU-AN TO ME. YOU'LL ALWAYS BE A LITTLE WORM.
MY...
LORD.

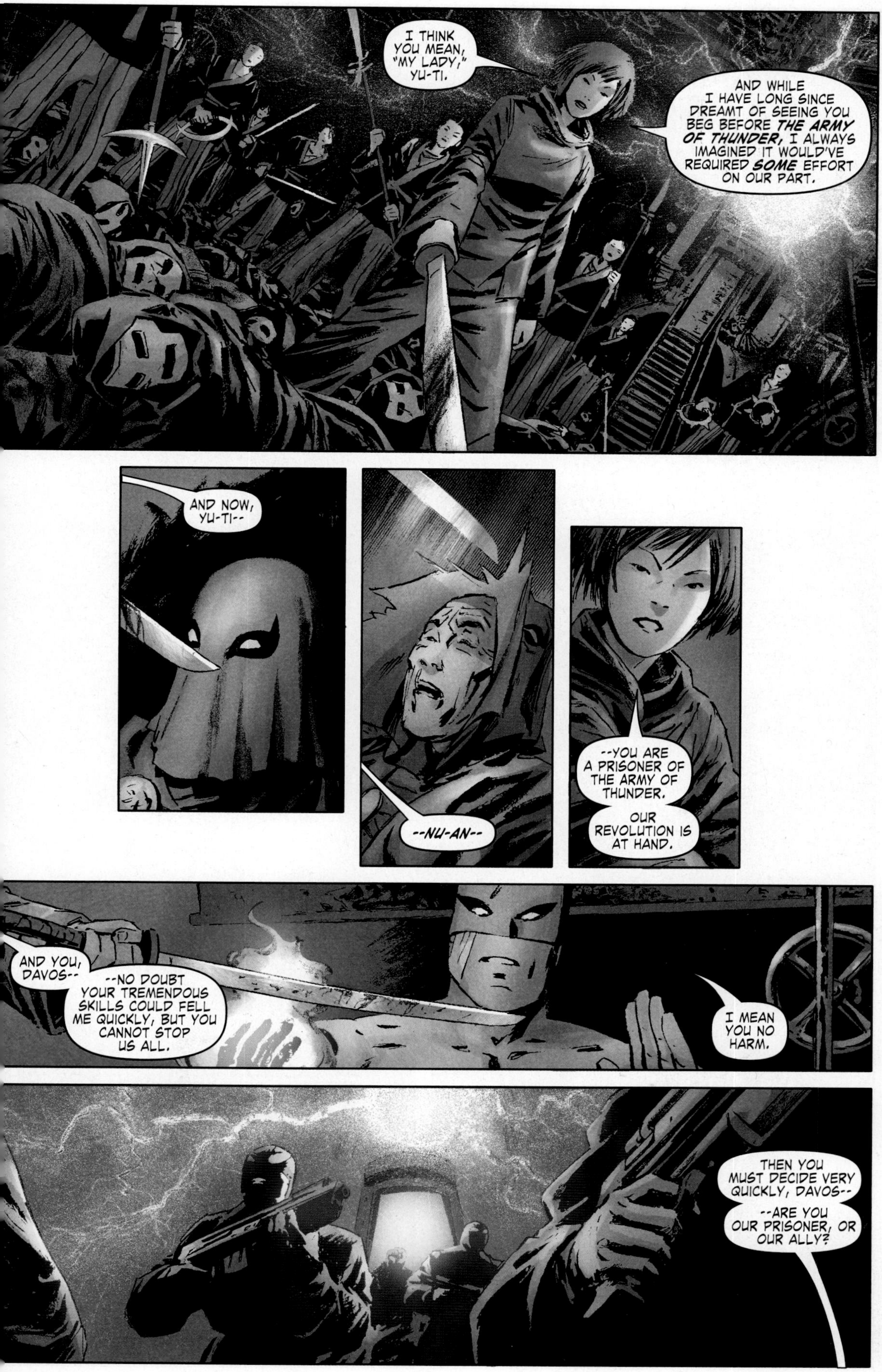
I THINK YOU MEAN, "MY LADY," YU-TI.
AND WHILE I HAVE LONG SINCE DREAMT OF SEEING YOU BEG BEFORE THE ARMY OF THUNDER, I ALWAYS IMAGINED IT WOULD'VE REQUIRED SOME EFFORT ON OUR PART.
AND NOW, YU-TI--
--NU-AN--
--YOU ARE A PRISONER OF THE ARMY OF THUNDER.
OUR REVOLUTION IS AT HAND.
AND YOU, DAVOS--
--NO DOUBT YOUR TREMENDOUS SKILLS COULD FELL ME QUICKLY, BUT YOU CANNOT STOP US ALL.
I MEAN YOU NO HARM.
THEN YOU MUST DECIDE VERY QUICKLY, DAVOS--
--ARE YOU OUR PRISONER, OR OUR ALLY?

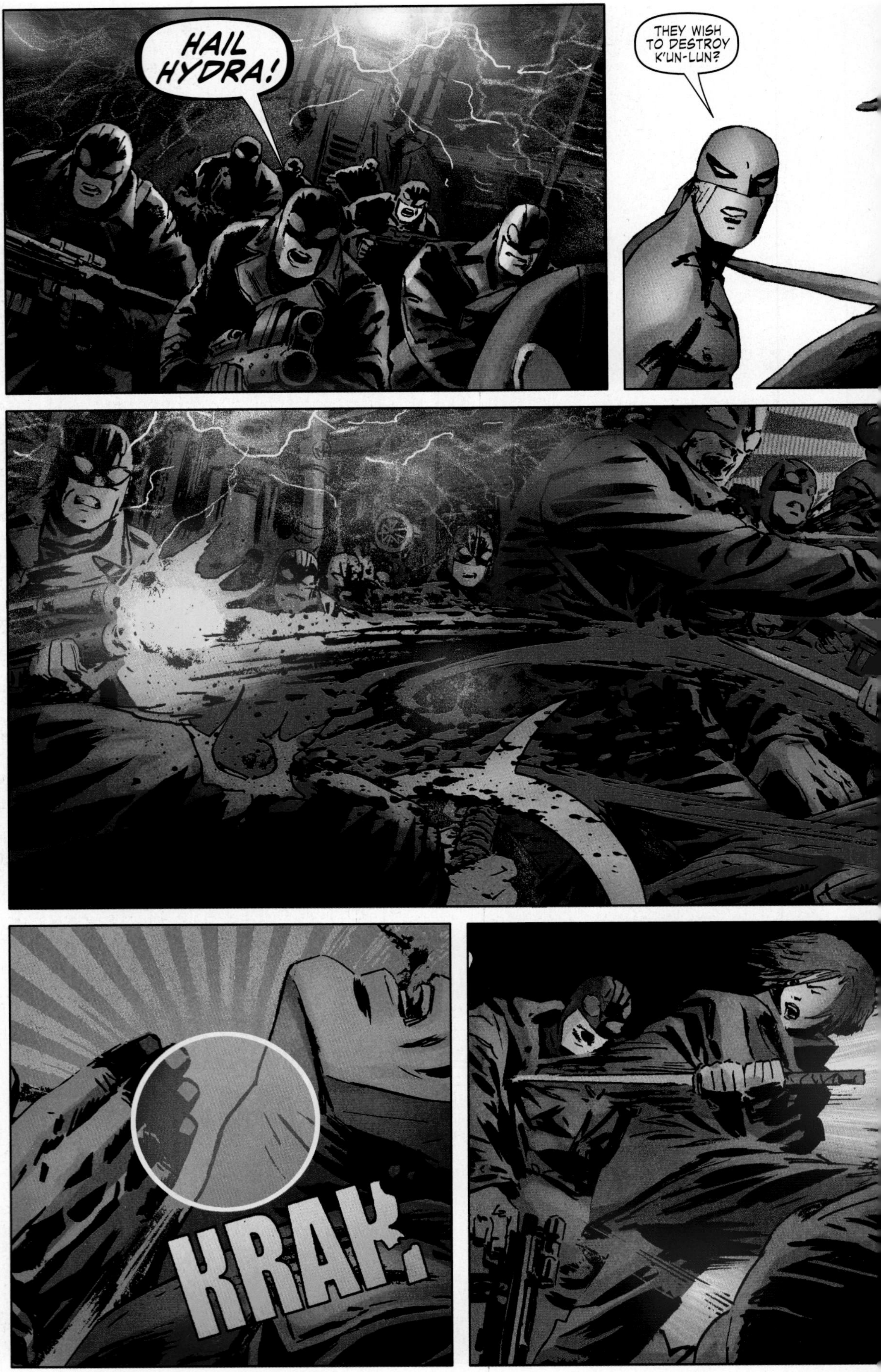
HAIL HYDRA!
THEY WISH TO DESTROY K'UN-LUN?
KRAK!

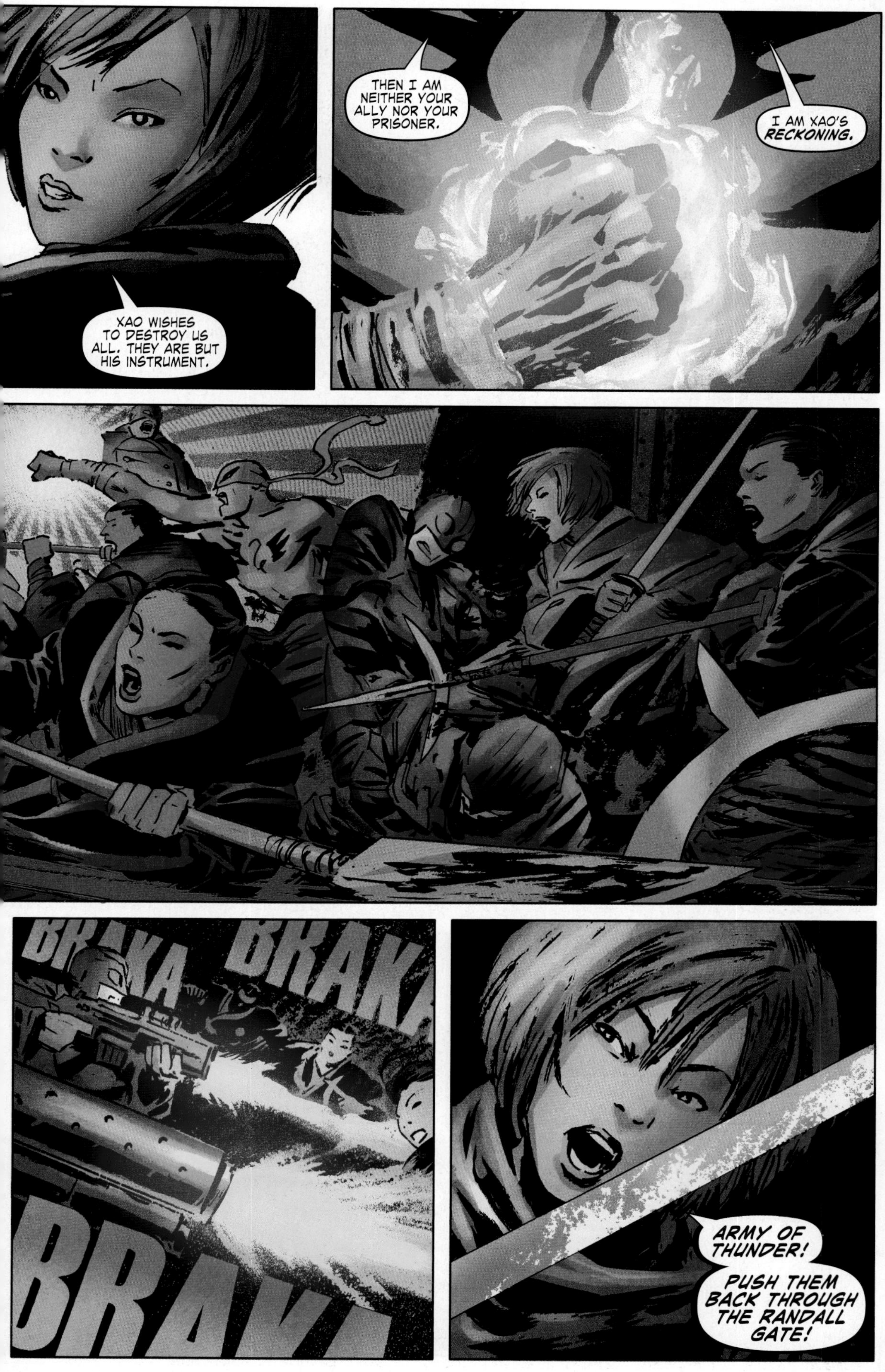
XAO WISHES TO DESTROY US ALL. THEY ARE BUT HIS INSTRUMENT.
THEN I AM NEITHER YOUR ALLY NOR YOUR PRISONER.
I AM XAO'S *RECKONING.*
BRAKA
BRAKA
BRAKA
ARMY OF THUNDER!
PUSH THEM BACK THROUGH THE RANDALL GATE!

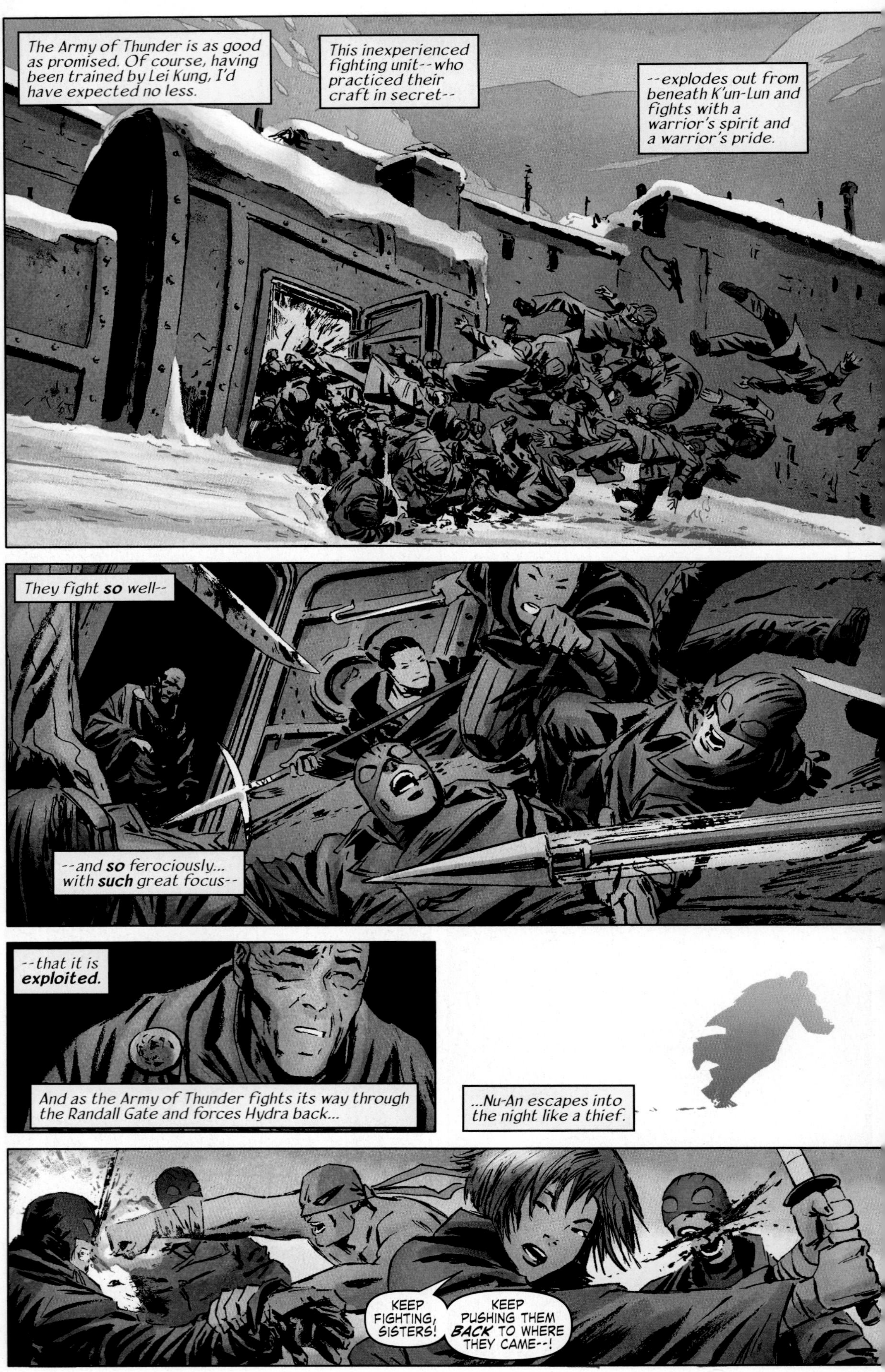
The Army of Thunder is as good as promised. Of course, having been trained by Lei Kung, I'd have expected no less.
This inexperienced fighting unit--who practiced their craft in secret--
--explodes out from beneath K'un-Lun and fights with a warrior's spirit and a warrior's pride.
They fight so well--
--and so ferociously... with such great focus--
--that it is exploited.
And as the Army of Thunder fights its way through the Randall Gate and forces Hydra back...
...Nu-An escapes into the night like a thief.
KEEP FIGHTING, SISTERS!
KEEP PUSHING THEM BACK TO WHERE THEY CAME--!

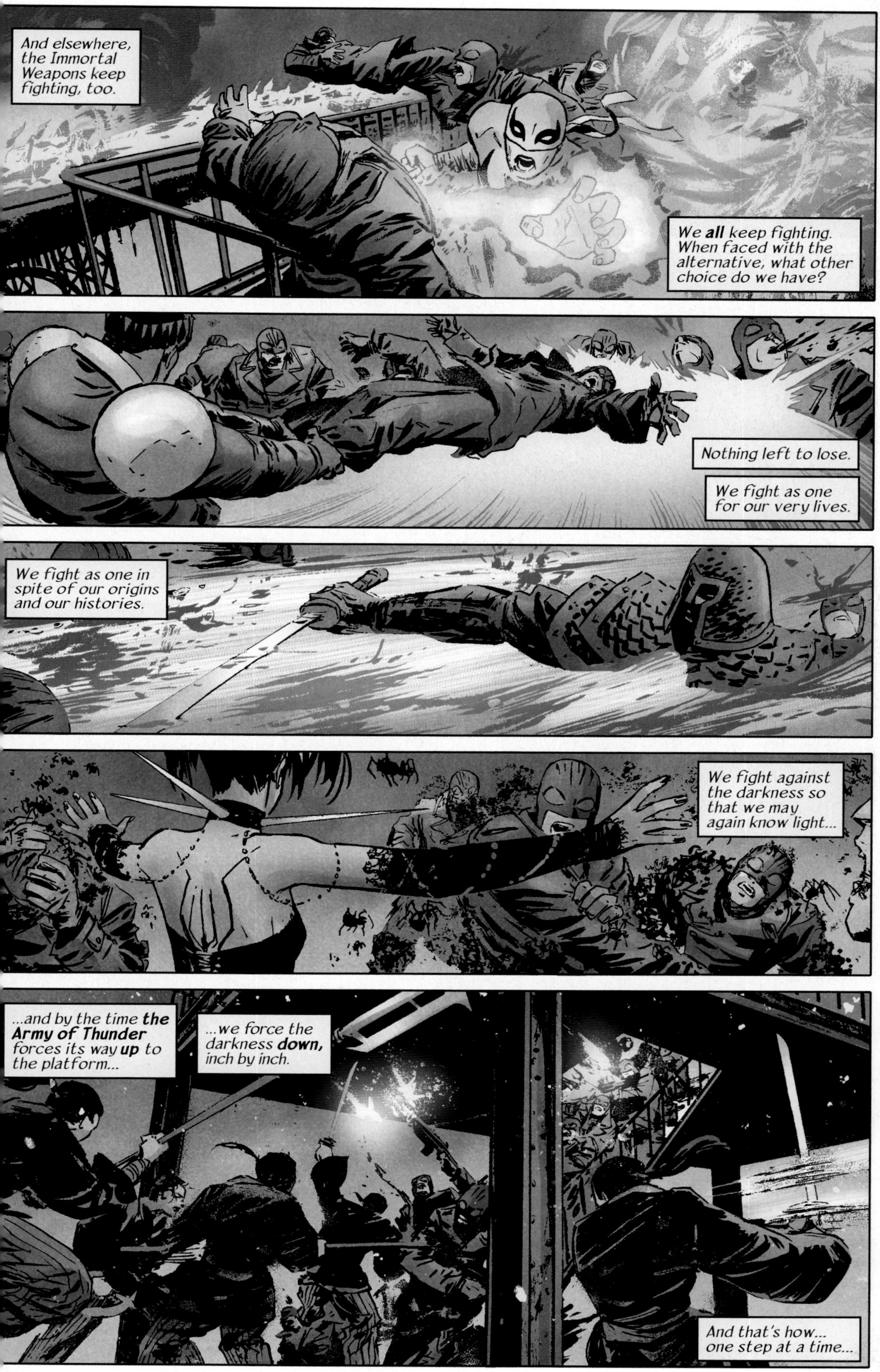
And elsewhere, the Immortal Weapons keep fighting, too.
We **all** keep fighting. When faced with the alternative, what other choice do we have?
Nothing left to lose.
We fight as one for our very lives.
We fight as one in spite of our origins and our histories.
We fight against the darkness so that we may again know light...
...and by the time **the Army of Thunder** forces its way **up** to the platform...
...we force the darkness **down,** inch by inch.
And that's how... one step at a time...

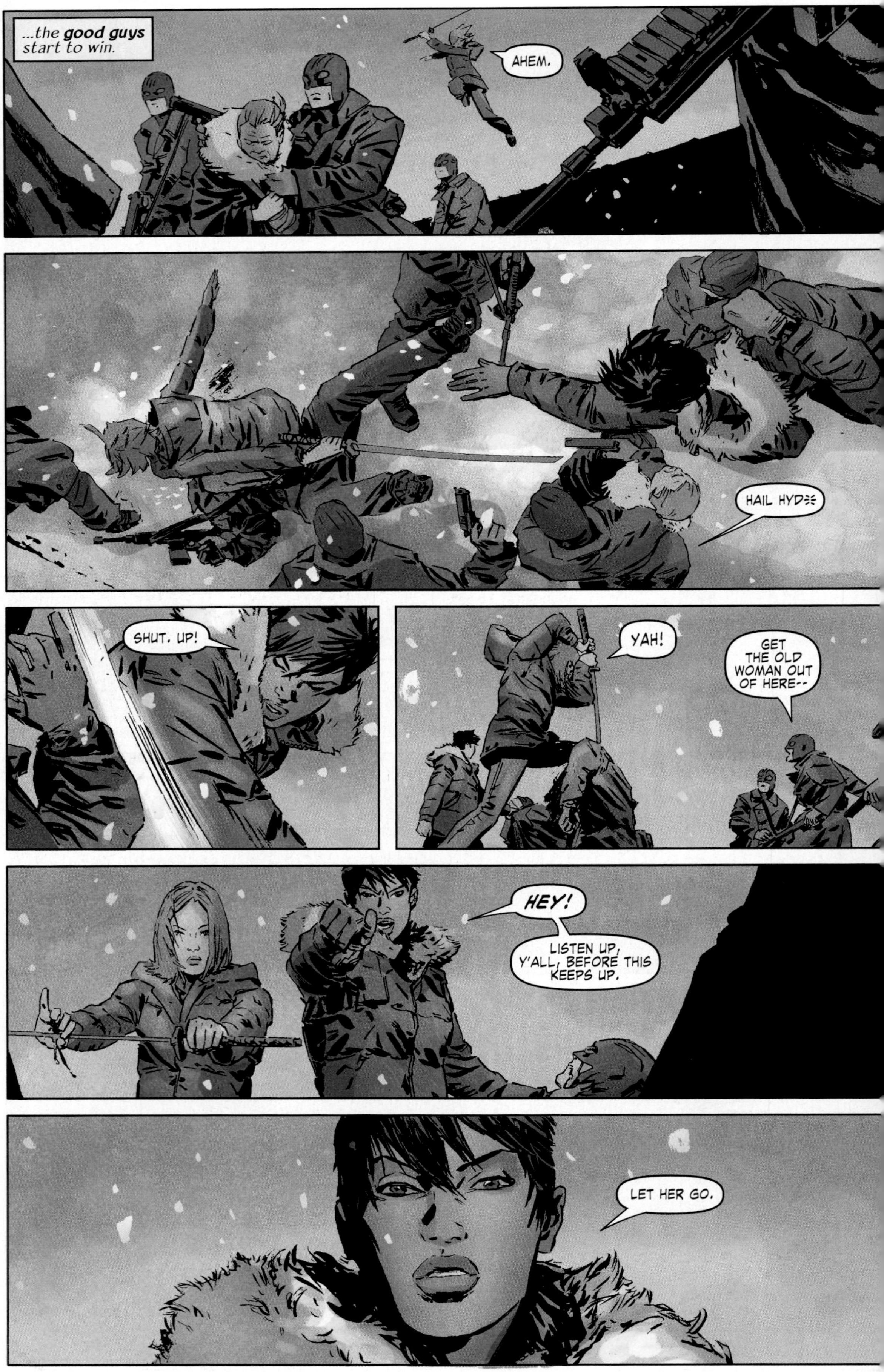
...the good guys start to win.
AHEM.
HAIL HYD≡
SHUT. UP!
YAH!
GET THE OLD WOMAN OUT OF HERE--
HEY!
LISTEN UP, Y'ALL, BEFORE THIS KEEPS UP.
LET HER GO.

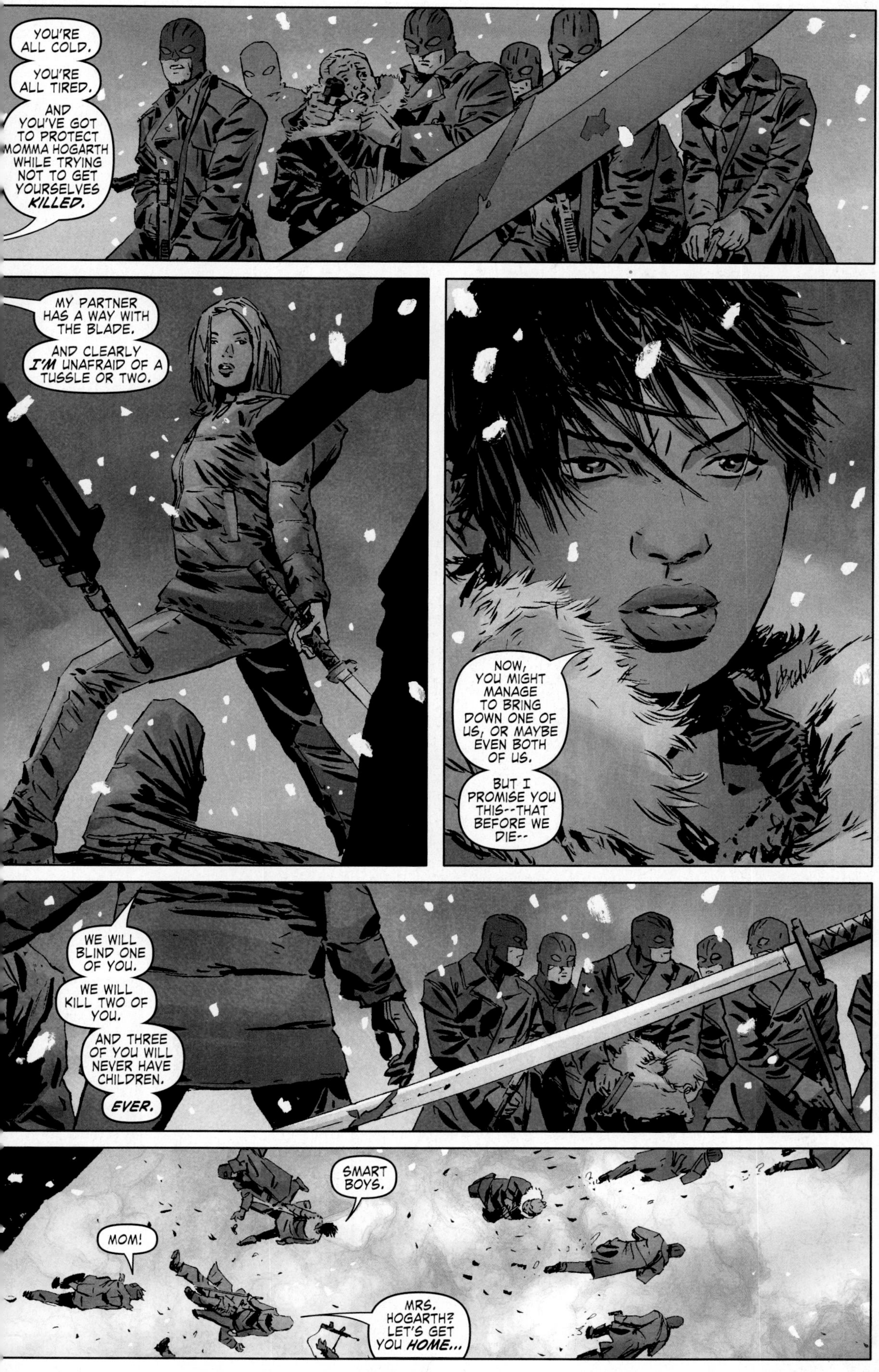
YOU'RE ALL COLD.
YOU'RE ALL TIRED.
AND YOU'VE GOT TO PROTECT MOMMA HOGARTH WHILE TRYING NOT TO GET YOURSELVES KILLED.
MY PARTNER HAS A WAY WITH THE BLADE.
AND CLEARLY I'M UNAFRAID OF A TUSSLE OR TWO.
NOW, YOU MIGHT MANAGE TO BRING DOWN ONE OF US, OR MAYBE EVEN BOTH OF US.
BUT I PROMISE YOU THIS--THAT BEFORE WE DIE--
WE WILL BLIND ONE OF YOU.
WE WILL KILL TWO OF YOU.
AND THREE OF YOU WILL NEVER HAVE CHILDREN.
EVER.
SMART BOYS.
MOM!
MRS. HOGARTH? LET'S GET YOU HOME...

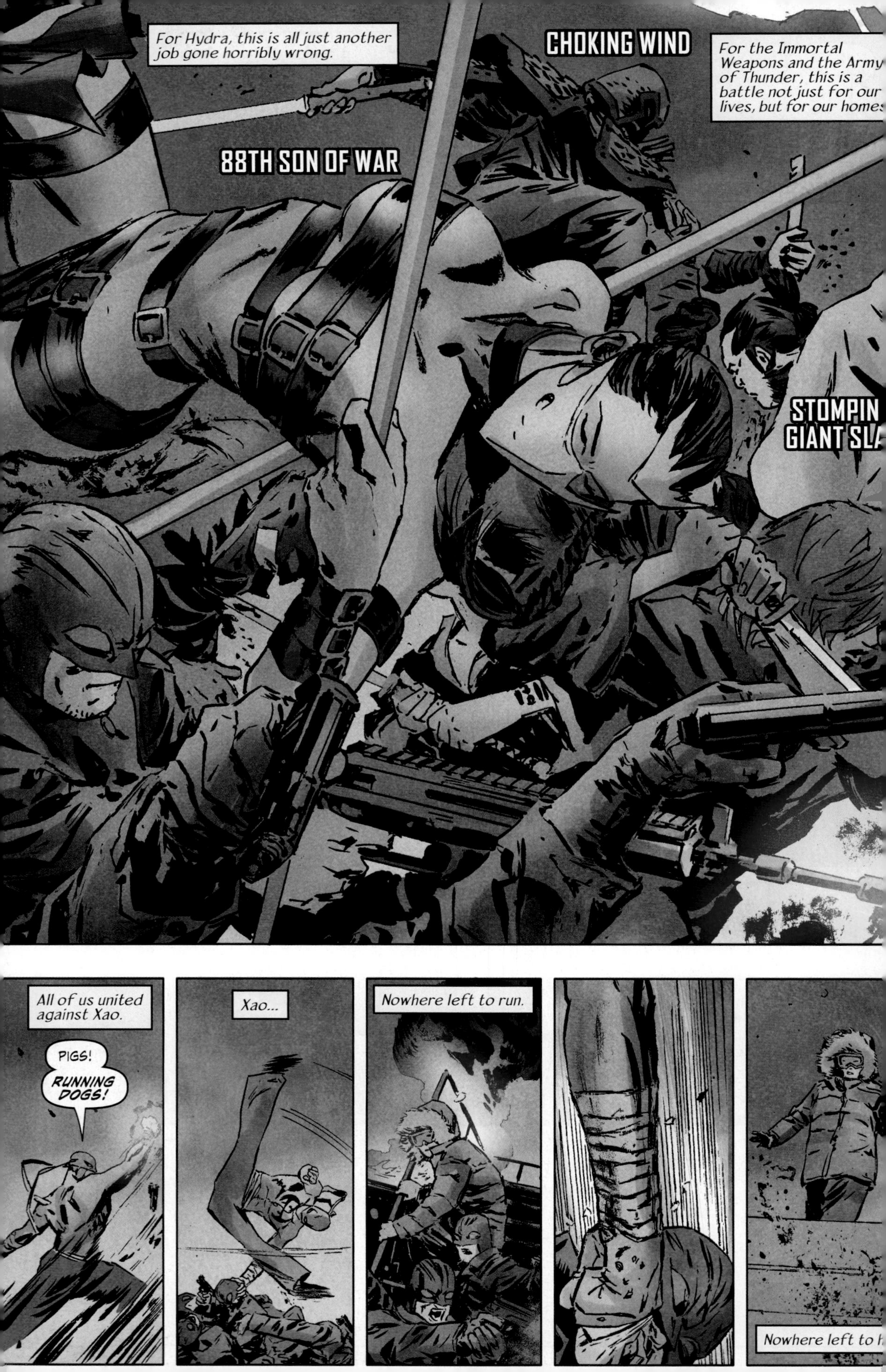
For Hydra, this is all just another job gone horribly wrong.
CHOKING WIND
For the Immortal Weapons and the Army of Thunder, this is a battle not just for our lives, but for our homes
88TH SON OF WAR
STOMPIN
GIANT SLA
All of us united against Xao.
PIGS!
RUNNING DOGS!
Xao...
Nowhere left to run.
Nowhere left to

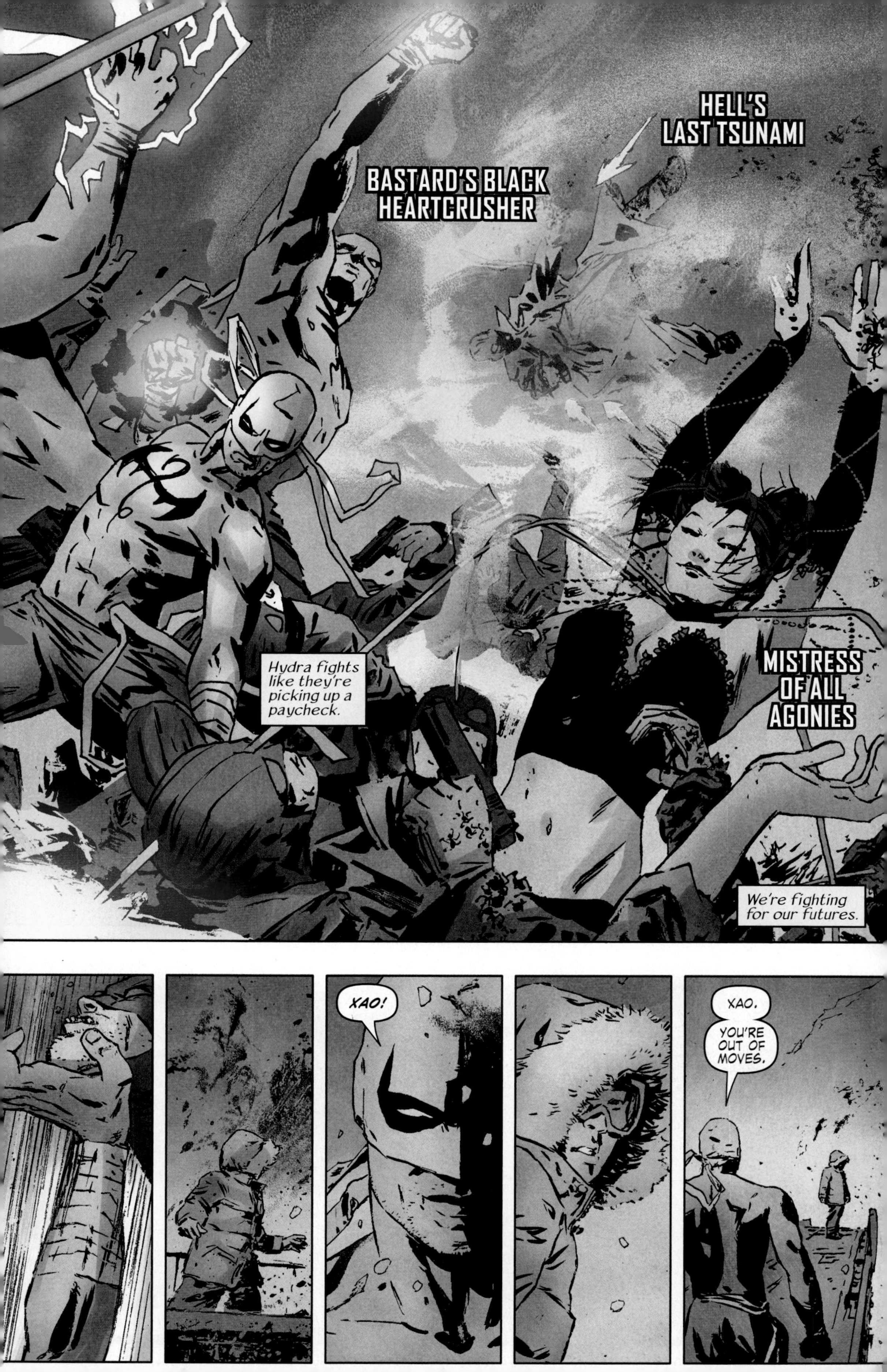
HELL'S LAST TSUNAMI
BASTARD'S BLACK HEARTCRUSHER
Hydra fights like they're picking up a paycheck.
MISTRESS OF ALL AGONIES
We're fighting for our futures.
XAO!
XAO.
YOU'RE OUT OF MOVES.

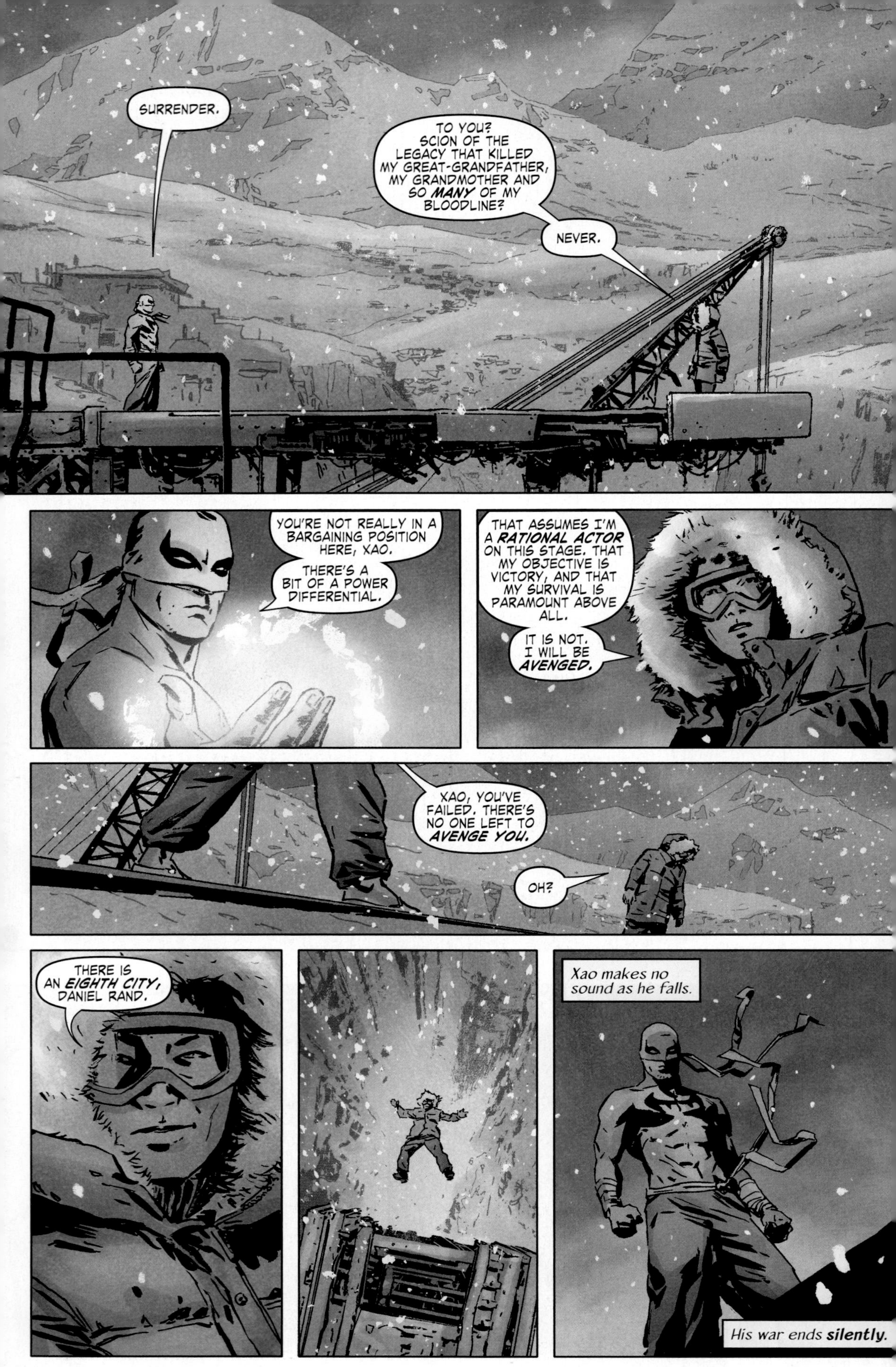
SURRENDER.
TO YOU? SCION OF THE LEGACY THAT KILLED MY GREAT-GRANDFATHER, MY GRANDMOTHER AND SO MANY OF MY BLOODLINE?
NEVER.
YOU'RE NOT REALLY IN A BARGAINING POSITION HERE, XAO.
THERE'S A BIT OF A POWER DIFFERENTIAL.
THAT ASSUMES I'M A RATIONAL ACTOR ON THIS STAGE. THAT MY OBJECTIVE IS VICTORY, AND THAT MY SURVIVAL IS PARAMOUNT ABOVE ALL.
IT IS NOT. I WILL BE AVENGED.
XAO, YOU'VE FAILED. THERE'S NO ONE LEFT TO AVENGE YOU.
OH?
THERE IS AN EIGHTH CITY, DANIEL RAND.
Xao makes no sound as he falls.
His war ends silently.

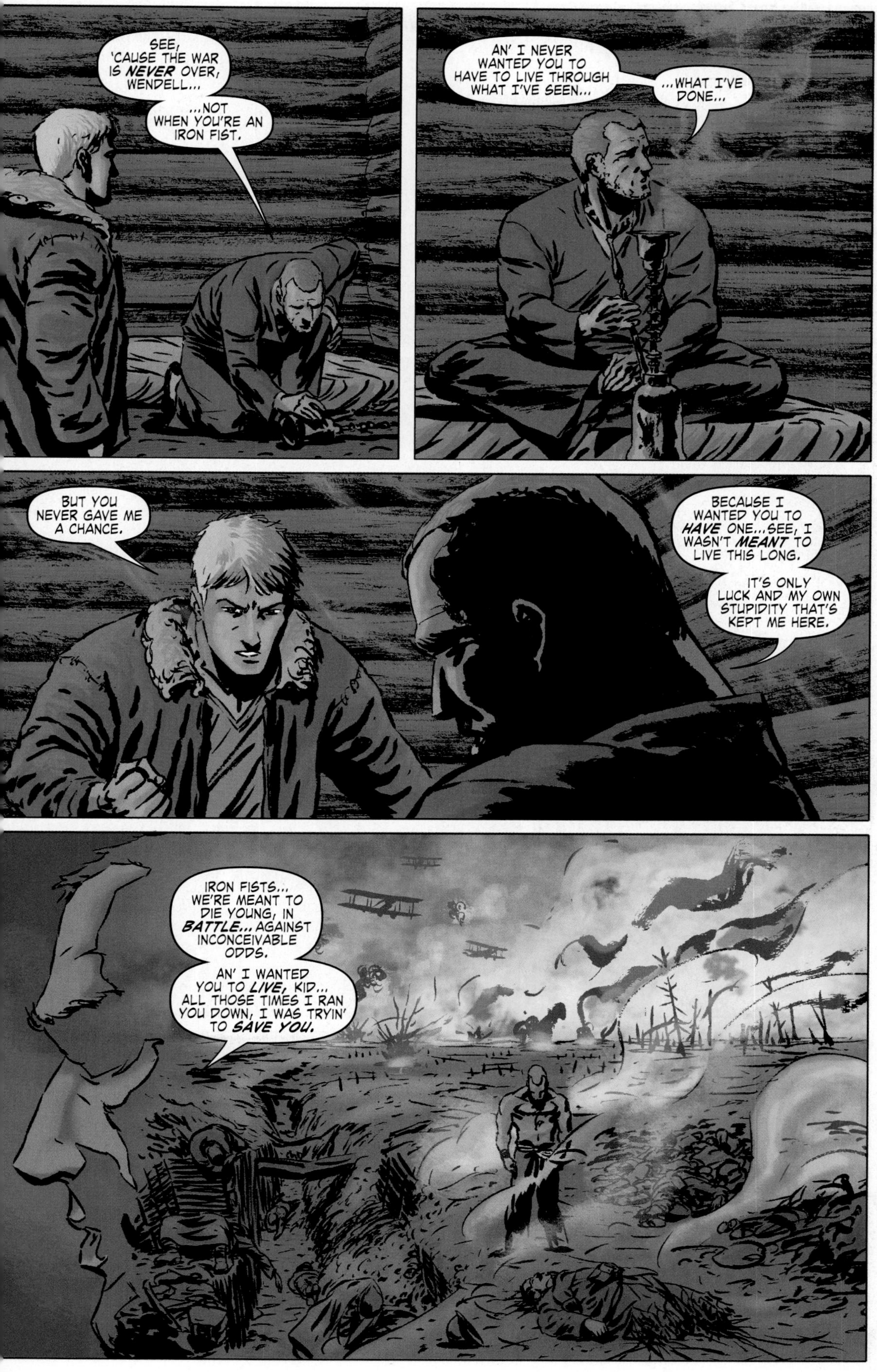
SEE, 'CAUSE THE WAR IS NEVER OVER, WENDELL...
...NOT WHEN YOU'RE AN IRON FIST.
AN' I NEVER WANTED YOU TO HAVE TO LIVE THROUGH WHAT I'VE SEEN...
...WHAT I'VE DONE...
BUT YOU NEVER GAVE ME A CHANCE.
BECAUSE I WANTED YOU TO HAVE ONE...SEE, I WASN'T MEANT TO LIVE THIS LONG.
IT'S ONLY LUCK AND MY OWN STUPIDITY THAT'S KEPT ME HERE.
IRON FISTS... WE'RE MEANT TO DIE YOUNG, IN BATTLE... AGAINST INCONCEIVABLE ODDS.
AN' I WANTED YOU TO LIVE, KID... ALL THOSE TIMES I RAN YOU DOWN, I WAS TRYIN' TO SAVE YOU.

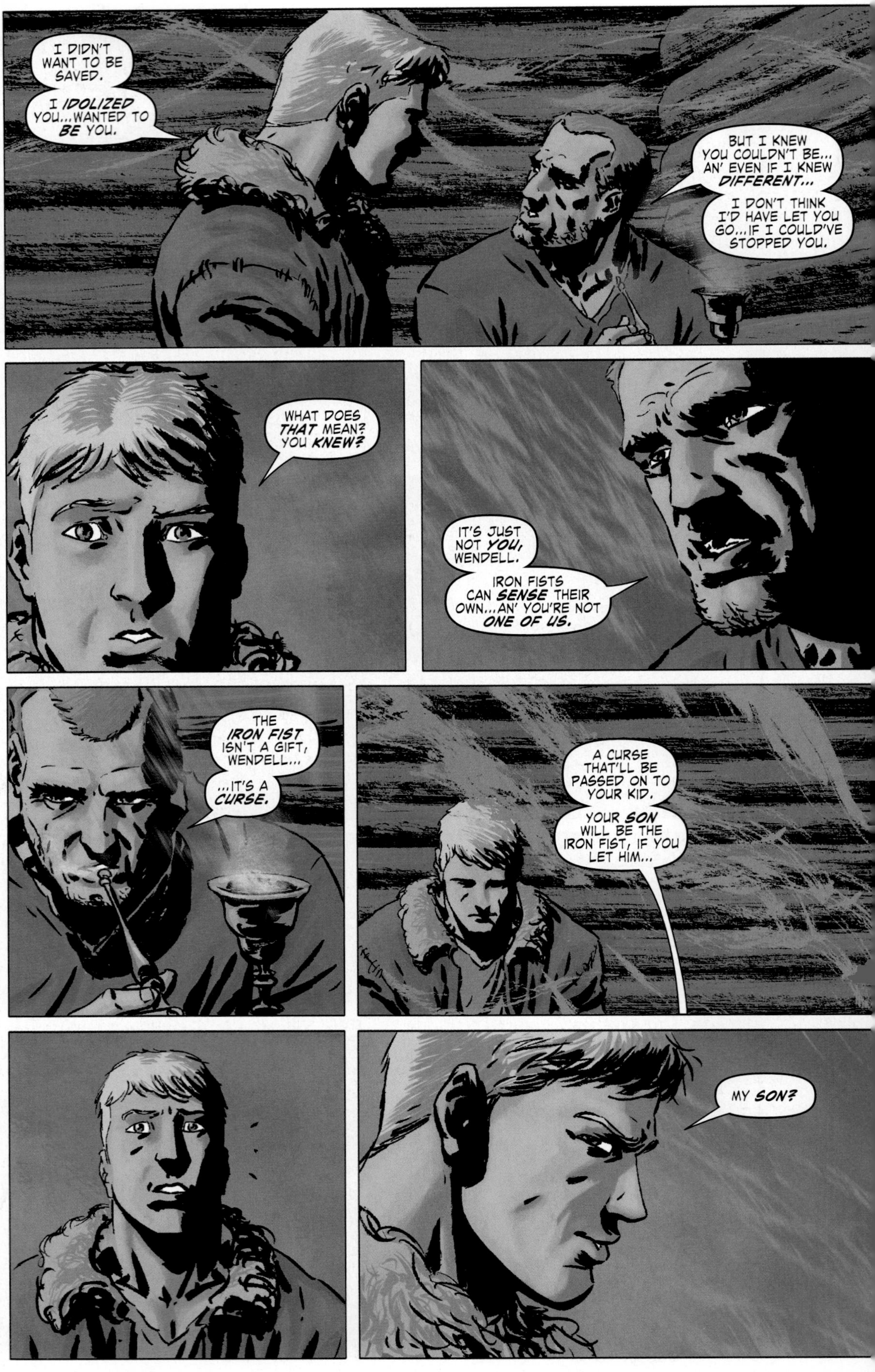
I DIDN'T WANT TO BE SAVED.
I *IDOLIZED* YOU...WANTED TO *BE* YOU.
BUT I KNEW YOU COULDN'T BE... AN' EVEN IF I KNEW *DIFFERENT...*
I DON'T THINK I'D HAVE LET YOU GO...IF I COULD'VE STOPPED YOU.
WHAT DOES *THAT* MEAN? YOU *KNEW?*
IT'S JUST NOT *YOU,* WENDELL.
IRON FISTS CAN *SENSE* THEIR OWN...AN' YOU'RE NOT *ONE OF US.*
THE *IRON FIST* ISN'T A GIFT, WENDELL...
...IT'S A *CURSE.*
A CURSE THAT'LL BE PASSED ON TO YOUR KID.
YOUR *SON* WILL BE THE IRON FIST, IF YOU LET HIM...
MY *SON?*

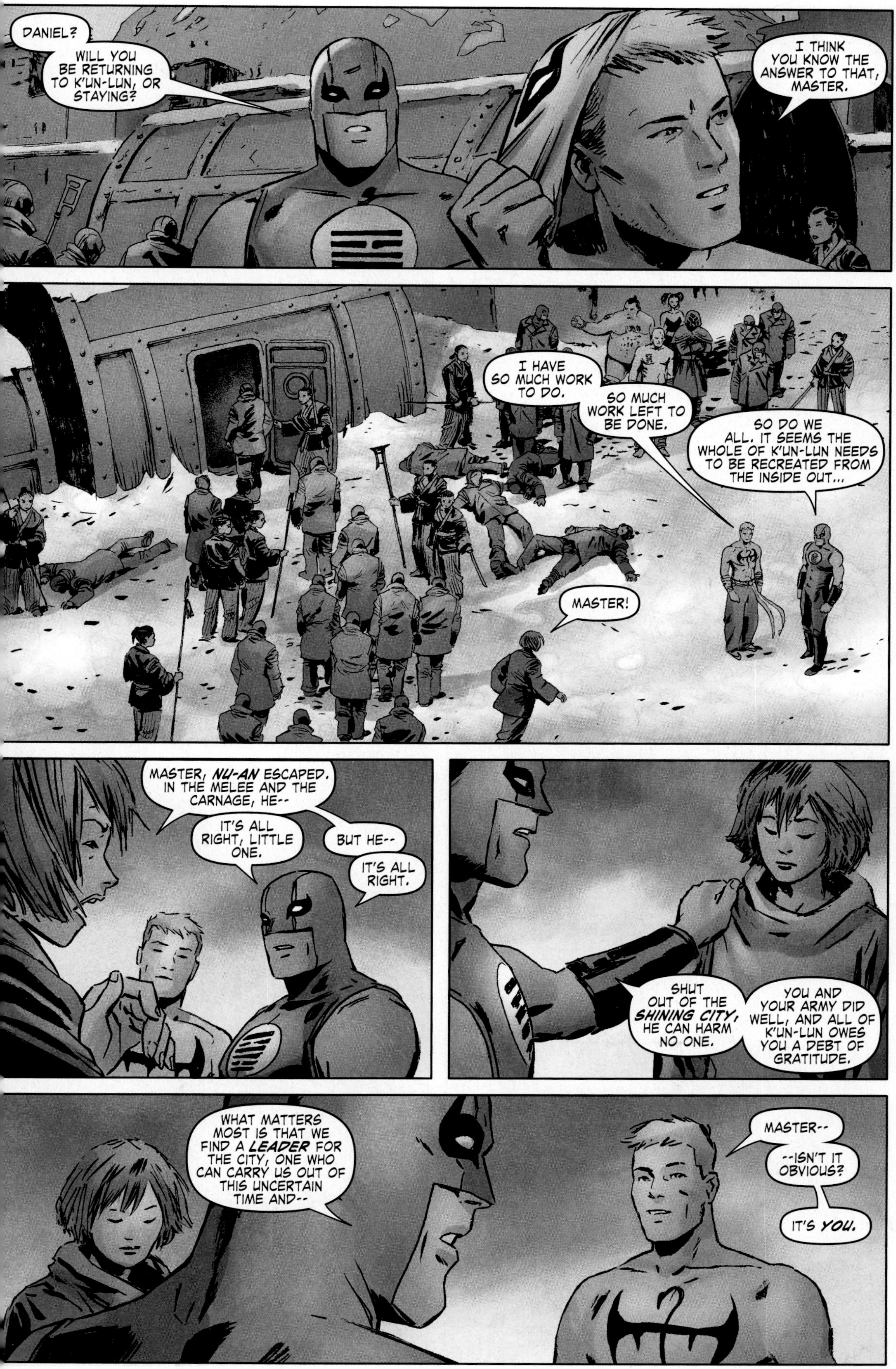
DANIEL?
WILL YOU BE RETURNING TO K'UN-LUN, OR STAYING?
I THINK YOU KNOW THE ANSWER TO THAT, MASTER.
I HAVE SO MUCH WORK TO DO.
SO MUCH WORK LEFT TO BE DONE.
SO DO WE ALL. IT SEEMS THE WHOLE OF K'UN-LUN NEEDS TO BE RECREATED FROM THE INSIDE OUT...
MASTER!
MASTER, NU-AN ESCAPED. IN THE MELEE AND THE CARNAGE, HE--
IT'S ALL RIGHT, LITTLE ONE.
BUT HE--
IT'S ALL RIGHT.
SHUT OUT OF THE SHINING CITY, HE CAN HARM NO ONE.
YOU AND YOUR ARMY DID WELL, AND ALL OF K'UN-LUN OWES YOU A DEBT OF GRATITUDE.
WHAT MATTERS MOST IS THAT WE FIND A LEADER FOR THE CITY, ONE WHO CAN CARRY US OUT OF THIS UNCERTAIN TIME AND--
MASTER--
--ISN'T IT OBVIOUS?
IT'S YOU.

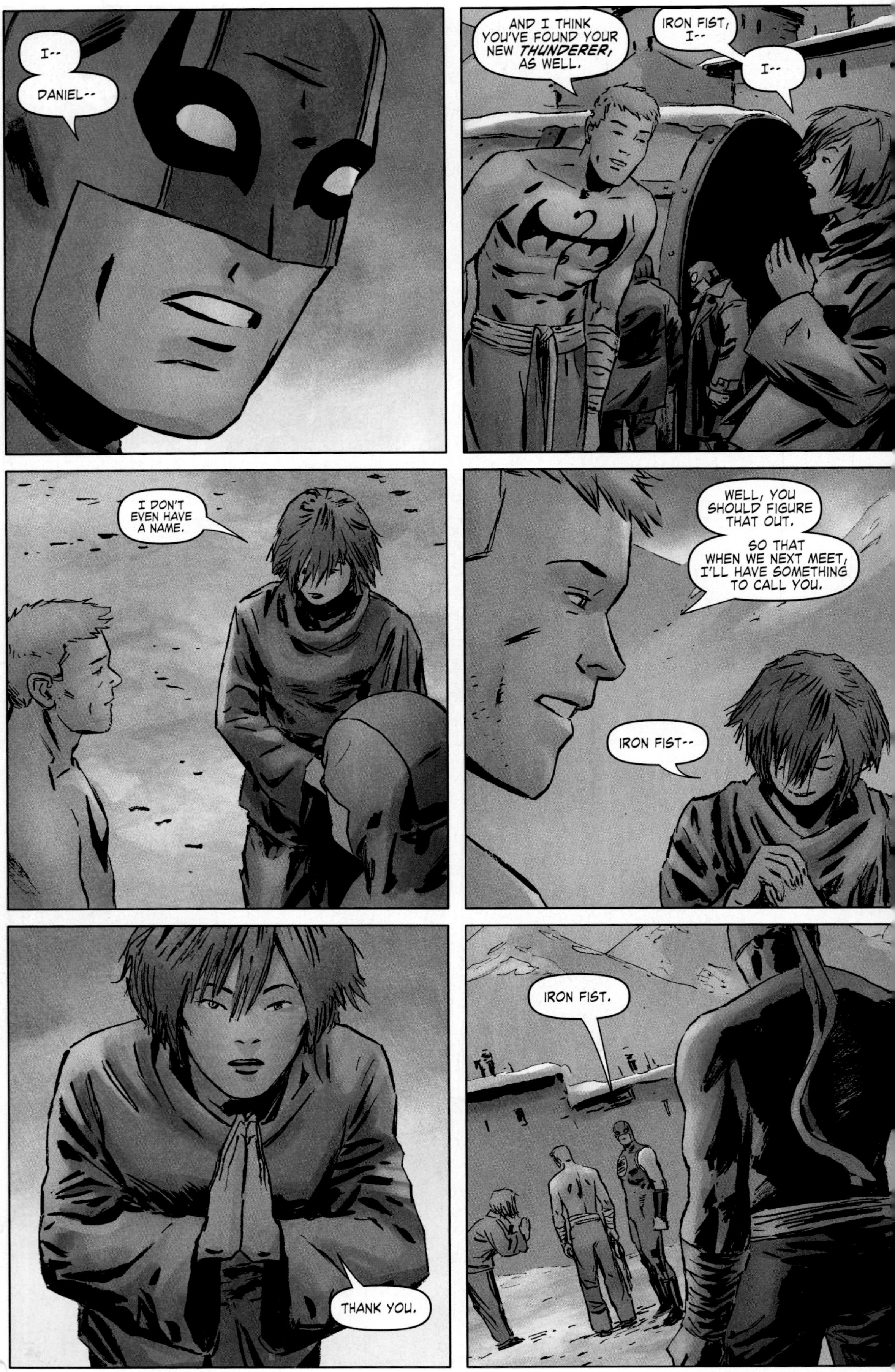
I--
DANIEL--
AND I THINK YOU'VE FOUND YOUR NEW THUNDERER, AS WELL.
IRON FIST, I--
I--
I DON'T EVEN HAVE A NAME.
WELL, YOU SHOULD FIGURE THAT OUT.
SO THAT WHEN WE NEXT MEET, I'LL HAVE SOMETHING TO CALL YOU.
IRON FIST--
THANK YOU.
IRON FIST.

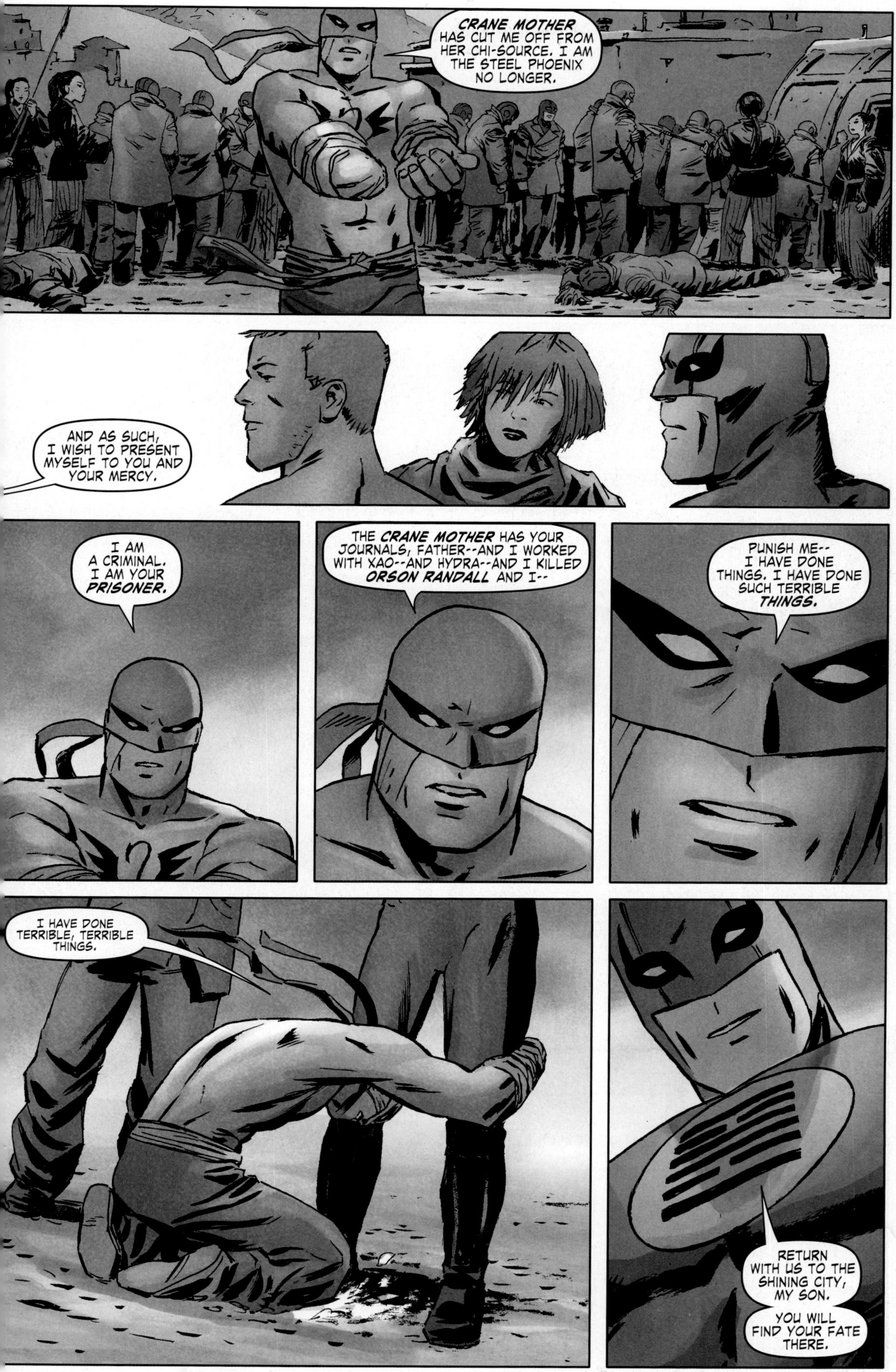
CRANE MOTHER HAS CUT ME OFF FROM HER CHI-SOURCE. I AM THE STEEL PHOENIX NO LONGER.
AND AS SUCH, I WISH TO PRESENT MYSELF TO YOU AND YOUR MERCY.
I AM A CRIMINAL. I AM YOUR PRISONER.
THE CRANE MOTHER HAS YOUR JOURNALS, FATHER--AND I WORKED WITH XAO--AND HYDRA--AND I KILLED ORSON RANDALL AND I--
PUNISH ME-- I HAVE DONE THINGS. I HAVE DONE SUCH TERRIBLE THINGS.
I HAVE DONE TERRIBLE, TERRIBLE THINGS.
RETURN WITH US TO THE SHINING CITY, MY SON.
YOU WILL FIND YOUR FATE THERE.

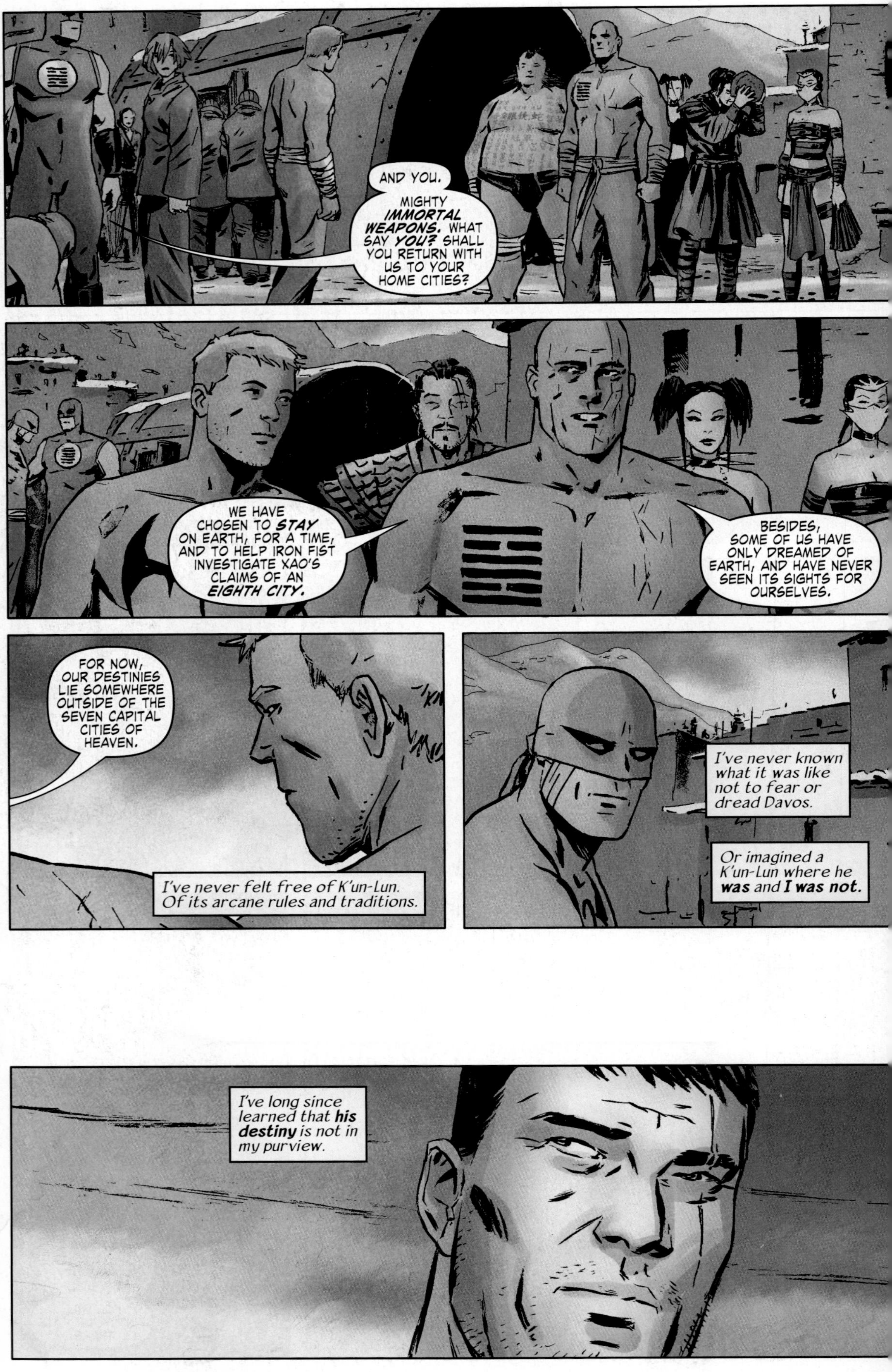
AND YOU.
MIGHTY IMMORTAL WEAPONS. WHAT SAY YOU? SHALL YOU RETURN WITH US TO YOUR HOME CITIES?
WE HAVE CHOSEN TO STAY ON EARTH, FOR A TIME, AND TO HELP IRON FIST INVESTIGATE XAO'S CLAIMS OF AN EIGHTH CITY.
BESIDES, SOME OF US HAVE ONLY DREAMED OF EARTH, AND HAVE NEVER SEEN ITS SIGHTS FOR OURSELVES.
FOR NOW, OUR DESTINIES LIE SOMEWHERE OUTSIDE OF THE SEVEN CAPITAL CITIES OF HEAVEN.
I've never felt free of K'un-Lun. Of its arcane rules and traditions.
I've never known what it was like not to fear or dread Davos.
Or imagined a K'un-Lun where he was and I was not.
I've long since learned that his destiny is not in my purview.

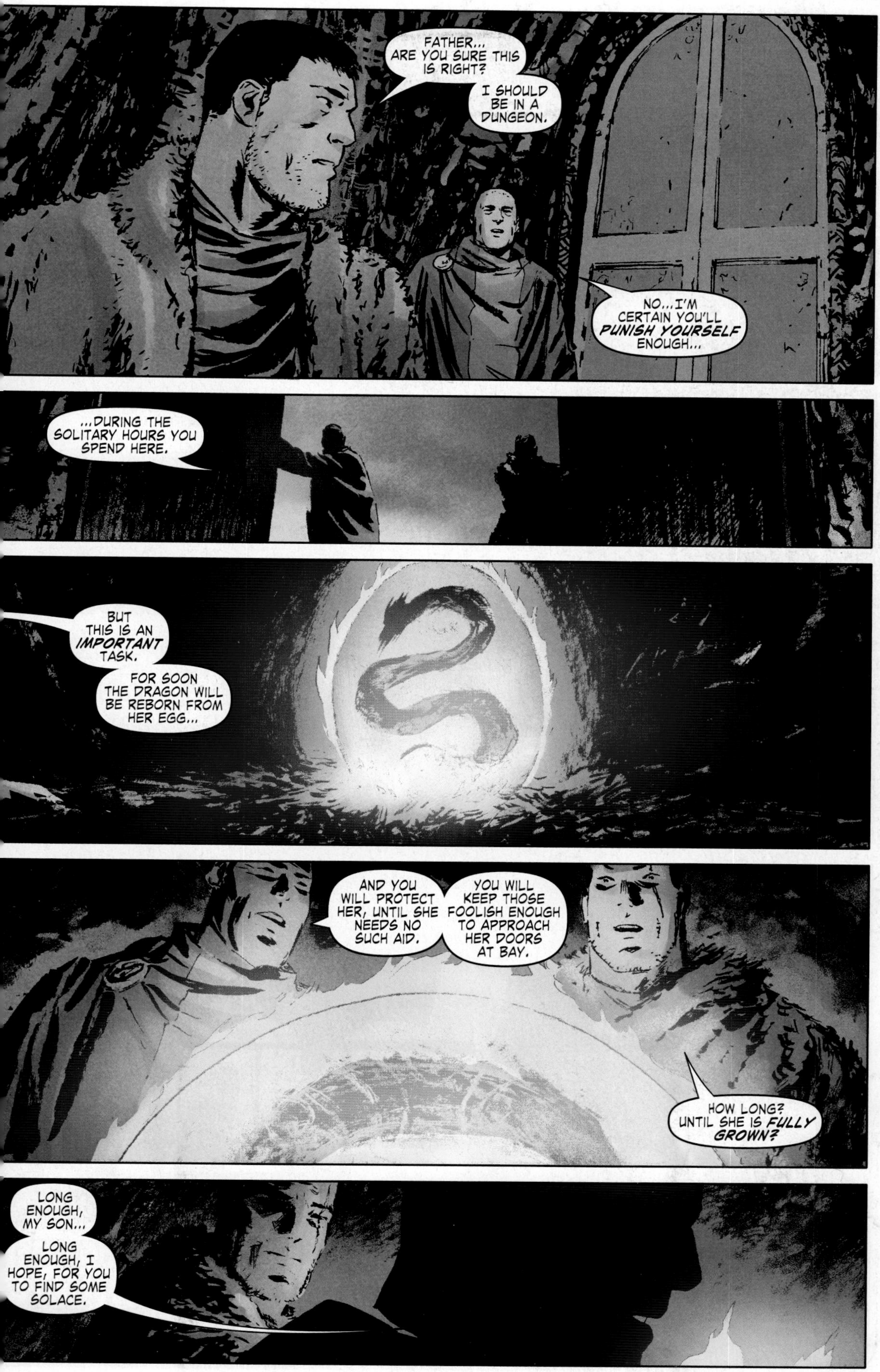
FATHER... ARE YOU SURE THIS IS RIGHT?
I SHOULD BE IN A DUNGEON.
NO...I'M CERTAIN YOU'LL PUNISH YOURSELF ENOUGH...
...DURING THE SOLITARY HOURS YOU SPEND HERE.
BUT THIS IS AN IMPORTANT TASK.
FOR SOON THE DRAGON WILL BE REBORN FROM HER EGG...
AND YOU WILL PROTECT HER, UNTIL SHE NEEDS NO SUCH AID.
YOU WILL KEEP THOSE FOOLISH ENOUGH TO APPROACH HER DOORS AT BAY.
HOW LONG? UNTIL SHE IS FULLY GROWN?
LONG ENOUGH, MY SON...
LONG ENOUGH, I HOPE, FOR YOU TO FIND SOME SOLACE.

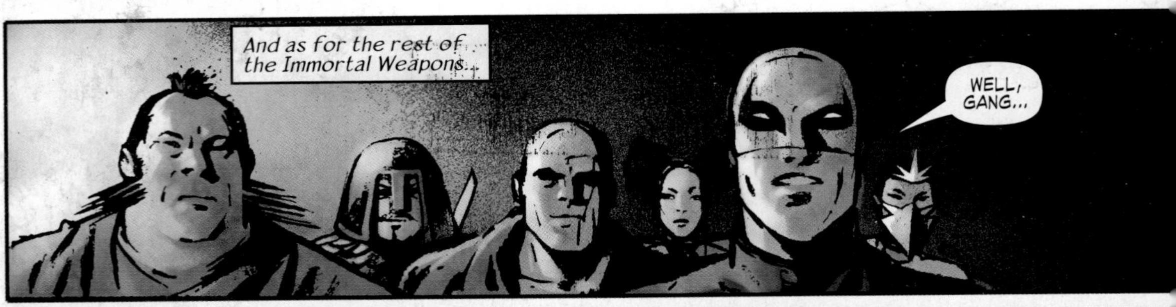
And as for the rest of the Immortal Weapons...
WELL, GANG...

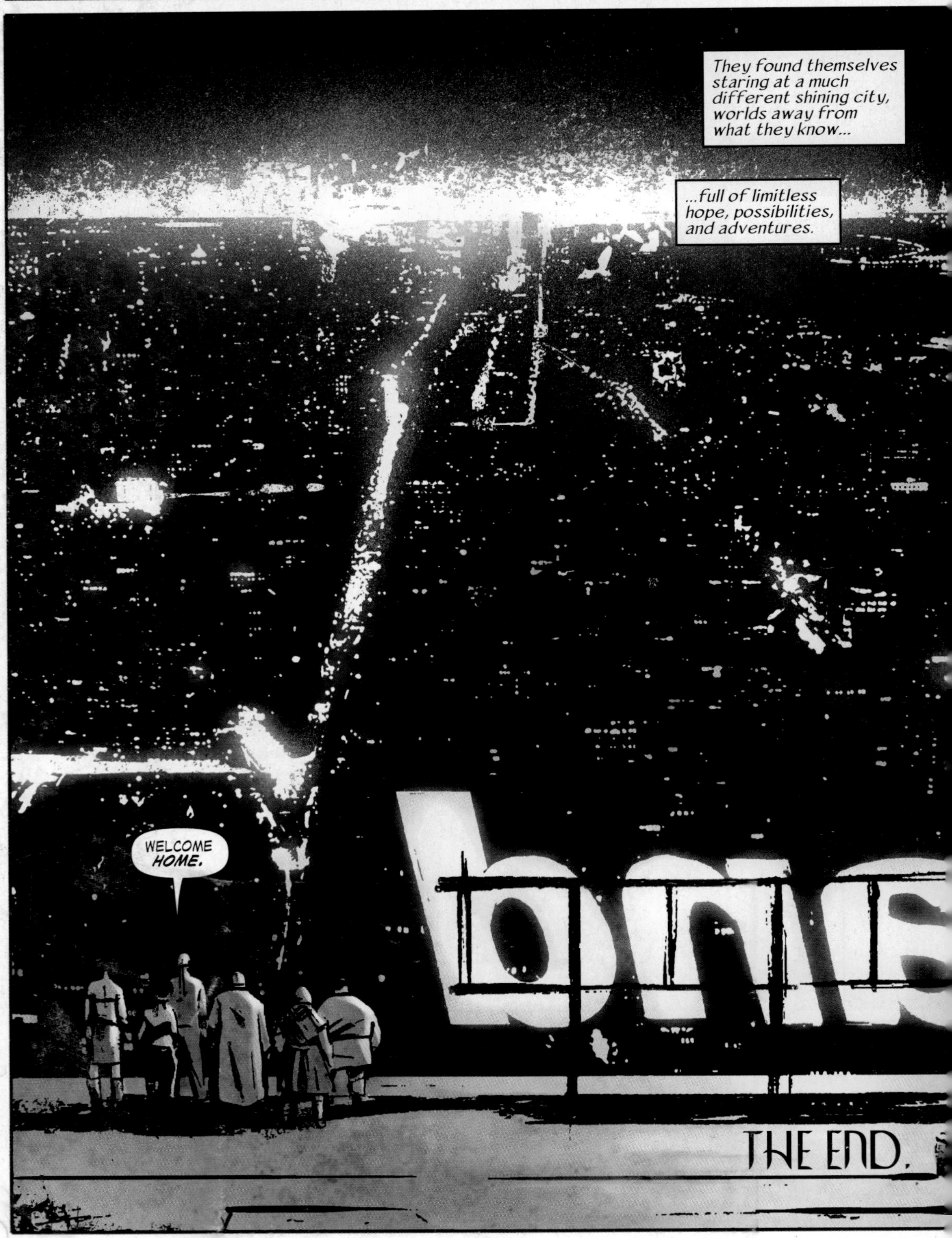
They found themselves staring at a much different shining city, worlds away from what they know...
...full of limitless hope, possibilities, and adventures.
WELCOME HOME.
THE END.